Foundations
of Christian Faith

Foundations
of Christian Faith

AN INTRODUCTION
TO THE IDEA
OF CHRISTIANITY

KARL RAHNER

TRANSLATED BY WILLIAM V. DYCH

DARTON LONGMAN & TODD
LONDON

Published in Great Britain by
Darton Longman & Todd Ltd
89 Lillie Road London SW6 1UD

1st Edition 1978

ISBN 0 232 51406 2

Originally published as *Grundkurs des Glaubens:
Einführung in den Begriff des Christentums*
© Verlag Herder KG Freiburg im Breisgau 1976

English translation by William V. Dych
Copyright © 1978 by The Seabury Press, Inc.

Printed in the United States of America

Contents

Abbreviations

D.S.: H. Denzinger and A. Schönmetzer, *Enchiridion Symbolorum, Definitionum et Declarationum De Rebus Fidei Et Morum.* Freiburg: Herder, 1976.

The Documents of Vatican II, ed. Walter Abbott, S.J. (New York: America Press, 1966), are cited by the following titles:

Dei Verbum: Dogmatic Constitution on Divine Revelation

Gaudium et spes: Pastoral Constitution on the Church in the Modern World

Lumen gentium: Dogmatic Constitution on the Church

Nostra aetate: Declaration on the Relationship of the Church to Non-Christian Religions

Optatam totius: Decree on Priestly Formation

Unitatis redintegratio: Decree on Ecumenism

Preface

For whom has this book been written? That is not an easy question to answer even for the author. When one considers the depths and the incomprehensibility of the mystery that Christianity is all about, and considers the immense variety of people whom Christianity tries to reach, it is naturally impossible to say something about the idea of Christianity to everyone at the same time. To some people an "Introduction to the Idea of Christianity" will appear too "high," too complicated and too abstract, while to others it will appear too primitive. The author would like to address himself to readers who are educated to some extent and who are not afraid to "wrestle with an idea," and he simply has to hope that he will find readers for whom the book is neither too advanced nor too primitive.

The following reflections, then, are intended to proceed on a "first level of reflection." In this Preface I do not intend to offer any subtle epistemological reflections or explanations of what that means. The presupposition of this undertaking is simply this: I do not intend, on the *one* hand, simply to repeat what Christianity proclaims after the manner of a catechism and in the traditional formulations, but rather, to the extent that it is possible in such a short essay, I shall try to reach a renewed understanding of this message and to arrive at an "idea" of Christianity. Without prejudice to its uniqueness and its incomparability, I shall try as far as possible to situate Christianity within the intellectual horizon of people today. In doing so we shall not proceed as though Christians did not already know what Christianity is *before* reflections of this kind. Neither, however, will this book begin with a faith in which everything is completely settled and simply repeat what is said in every traditional catechism. To accomplish what we have in mind is going to require some rather strenuous thinking and some hard intellectual work.

On the *other* hand, however, such a first introduction cannot set out to work through all of the investigations and questions and problems which per se are pertinent in the philosophy of knowledge and the philosophy of language, in the sociology, history, phenomenology and philosophy of religion, in fundamental theology, exegesis and biblical theology, and finally in systematic theology. That is impossible for a book like this, and even impossible for an individual theologian today, and finally and especially it is impossible for the reader for whom this book is intended. To require this would be to make it impossible to give an "account of our hope," that is, an intellectually honest justification of Christian faith for those Christians for whom this book has been written. Such readers could only be referred to the church's catechism and told that they should simply believe what is taught there and in this way save their souls.

This book, therefore, proceeds from the conviction, and it will try to confirm this in the process, that between the simple faith of the catechism on the one hand, and on the other the process of working through all of the disciplines we mentioned and many more besides, there is a way of giving an intellectually honest justification of Christian faith, and this precisely on the level that we called the "first level of reflection." This *has* to be possible because even the scientific expert in theology can be competent in only one or the other of these disciplines at most. But he cannot be competent in all of the disciplines which per se would be necessary on a higher and second or further level of reflection if he had to confront his theology in an explicit and scientifically adequate way with all the questions and tasks of these disciplines.

In other areas of life too, of course, a person does not live the totality of his existence and the broad individual dimensions of it from out of a reflexive study of all of the contemporary sciences, and yet he can and must be responsible before his intellectual conscience in an indirect and summary way for the totality of this existence. From these insights comes the intention of this book: to express the whole of Christianity and to give an honest account of it on a "first level of reflection." The reader himself must decide whether this goal is reached. But he also has to be critical of himself, of course, and ask himself whether perhaps the real cause of a failure in this undertaking does not lie in himself. This to be sure is not inconceivable a priori.

Such an attempt to proceed on a first level of reflection and in this way to make the whole of Christianity thematic to some extent and to show its legitimacy can be labelled "pre-scientific." But anyone who does this must be asked whether anybody today can reflect upon the totality of his existence in any way other than this "pre-scientific" way. We would have to ask him whether it is very sensible to take a "scientific" attitude in an undertaking of this kind in view of the fact that no single individual can any longer master all of today's sciences. We would also have to ask him whether such "pre-scientific" reflection does not demand so much precision and so much strenuous thinking that it may take its place confidently alongside of the many individual scientific disciplines. These disciplines are indeed relevant per se in such reflection. But they can no longer be made use of directly by the individual theologian and Christian if he is trying to address himself to the single whole of Christianity at a time when all of these individual disciplines must be further and intensively developed. But because of their complexity and because of the difficulty and the pluralism of their methods, they have moved beyond the realm within which an individual Christian and also an individual theologian must give an account of his faith. There is an "ivory tower" kind of specialization in the individual theological disciplines and in itself it is completely justified. But that is not what we are about here.

The topic, "The Foundations of Christian Faith," has occupied the author for many years. While he was professor in Munich and in Münster he gave such a course twice under the title, "An Introduction to the Idea of Christianity." Since this book had its origins in these courses, it has several characteristics which the reworking of it for publication did not intend to remove. For example, the individual sections, measured against the greater or lesser importance of their topic and in comparison with one another, might not always have the length which they deserve, since this "ideal" is very difficult to reach in class lectures. Secondly, if one begins with the general and abstract question, what all can and should be treated in such an "Introduction to the Idea of Christianity," the actual selection might appear somewhat arbitrary to some. Such selectivity, however, is unavoidable.

In this respect, first of all, some might miss an extended treatment of the possibility of religious and theological statements in general from the viewpoint of a theory of knowledge and a theory of science. Some might have the impression that important dogmatic themes are treated too briefly, perhaps the theology of the Trinity, the theology of the cross, the doctrine of the Christian life, and eschatology. Some might discover that the social and political aspects of Christianity's self-understanding in the area of social criticism are not developed. Some might think that especially the eighth and ninth chapters give at most a sketch of the topics treated there. With regard to these and similar assessments of the limits of this book, the author can say in its justification only this: every author has the right to be selective. He can also pose the counter-question: How can this or a similar selection be avoided if a book of 470 pages, which is not all that long considering the topic, is to attempt to give a first introduction to the whole of the idea of Christianity? Such an attempt would have to be declared impossible or illegitimate from the outset if allowance cannot be made for such inevitable limits. To be sure more justice could be done to the topic than is done here. But even a more adequate performance of the task would presumably run up against the same limits which the reader of this book as well as its author will certainly notice.

In view of the origins of this book and its introductory character, the author considered it superfluous to add subsequently explanatory footnotes and references to literature. In the framework of this book that would seem to him to be a learned pretense to which he is not inclined. The author also decided to forego giving references to pertinent writings of his own, although not infrequently he had the impression that he has written more precisely and more extensively elsewhere on this or that particular topic. Hence texts which have already been published elsewhere have been incorporated into this book, extensively reworked in varying degrees and integrated into the larger whole. This includes the first section of Chapter Two (cf. the author's *Grace in Freedom*), and especially larger parts of Chapter Six on Christology, which are taken partly from my *Theological Investigations,* and partly from the Christology which I published along with Wilhelm Thüsing. Likewise an essay which appeared earlier in my *Theological Investigations* has been reworked in the final section of the book.

Perhaps one thing that will strike many readers most at first glance is that there are practically no references to individual texts of scripture in support of what has been said. This fact has several reasons which have to be seen together. First of all, the author wants to avoid at all costs giving the impression that he is an exegete and that he works as an exegete in the sense of a scientific expert. He hopes, however, that on the whole he has taken sufficient account of the problems and the results of contemporary exegesis and biblical theology. These have to be presupposed here given the nature and the purpose of this book. Besides, the reader has access to the exegetical material in both scholarly and popular literature that is readily available. This material can and must be presupposed here if this book is not to go beyond its limits or lose its character as an introduction to the idea of Christianity.

Christianity, to be sure, is a religion that is based upon very definite historical events. The length of the sixth chapter, which makes up almost a third of the book, gives witness in its own way to the fact that the author is aware of the historical nature of Christianity. Moreover, these historical events have to be gathered from the "sources." But this original and critical investigation of the sources can and must be presupposed in a first introduction to the idea of Christianity. We can and must limit ourselves to reporting briefly and as conscientiously as possible what this original work on the sources has produced as material for systematic reflection. If more were attempted here, the result would not be a solid work of exegesis, but only a pseudoscientific sham which benefits no one. Finally, a theology which works systematically and conceptually is not merely a problematical appendix to exegesis and biblical theology. If both of these cannot be done in a single book, then it is better and more honest to avoid even the appearance that one intends to do both at once.

If what is being offered here is an introduction, then neither should the reader expect that this book is a final summary of the previous theological work of the author. It is not that and does not intend to be. In view of its topic, however, this book on the foundations of the faith has a somewhat more comprehensive and more systematic character than one might be accustomed to in the other theological writings of the author.

At the end of the book a detailed table of contents has been added to the shorter one at the beginning. The short table of contents enables the reader to get a quick overview of the whole book. The long one clarifies in detail the course of the reflections and so is a kind of topical index.

In the long history of this work since 1964 the author has received abundant help. He cannot mention by name here all those who helped him during those many years in Munich and Münster. But in addition to my two fellow Jesuits, Karl H. Neufeld and Harald Schöndorf, there are two other names I must mention. Elisabeth von der Lieth in Hamburg and Albert Raffelt in Freiburg in Breisgau took care of a large part of the final editing of the text by organizing the original class lectures and shortening them. To both my sincere and cordial thanks.

Munich, June 1976   Karl Rahner, S.J.

Foundations
of Christian Faith

Introduction

1. General Preliminary Reflections

This book will try to give an "introduction to the idea of Christianity." It is meant, first of all, to be merely an *introduction* and no more. It is self-evident that an undertaking of this kind has more to do with a personal decision to believe than do other scientific or theological publications or academic presentations. Nevertheless, it is meant to be an introduction within the framework of intellectual reflection, and is not intended directly and immediately for religious edification, although it is clear that the relationship of a theology of the spirit and of the intellect to a theology of the heart, of decision, and of religious life poses a very difficult problem. Secondly, it is intended to be an introduction to the idea of *Christianity*. We are presupposing here the existence of our own personal Christian faith in its normal ecclesial form, and we are trying, thirdly, to reach an *idea* of this. This word "idea" is added in order to make it clear that we are dealing here with an idea and all that this demands in the sense of Hegel's *"Anstrengung des Begriffs."* Anyone who is just looking for religious inspiration and shies away from the demands of patient, laborious, and at times tedious reflection should not enter into this investigation.

By the very nature of the case this introduction is an experiment. One does not know in advance whether the experiment will succeed even to a limited extent, or whether it can succeed. For this also depends on the reader of these pages. In the subject matter of this book we are not dealing with this or that particular theological question, but for one who is a Christian and wants to be a Christian, we are dealing with the totality of his own existence. Of course we shall have to show, and this motif is present throughout, that a person can be a Christian without having examined the totality of his Christian existence in a scientifically adequate way. Since, moreover, this cannot and therefore need not be done, he does not thereby become intellectually dishonest.

For a Christian, his Christian existence is ultimately the totality of his existence. This totality opens out into the dark abysses of the wilderness which we call God. When one undertakes something like this, he stands before the great thinkers, the saints, and finally Jesus Christ. The abyss of existence opens up in front of him. He knows that he has not thought enough, has not loved enough, and has not suffered enough.

There have always been attempts like this to express the structure of Christianity, of Christian faith and of Christian life, as a single whole, even if only in theoretical reflection. Every profession of faith, beginning with the Apostles' Creed and continuing down to Paul VI's Creed of the People of God, is such an attempt at a summary expression of Christian faith and of Christian self-understanding, and hence, although very brief, is an introduction to Christianity or to the idea of Christianity. St. Augustine's *Enchiridion on Faith, Hope and Charity,* St. Bonaventure's *Breviloquium* or St. Thomas Aquinas' *Compendium of Theology to Brother Reginald* are also basically such attempts to give a relatively brief overview of the whole and of the essentials of Christianity.

But there must always be new attempts at such reflection upon the single whole of Christianity. They are always conditioned, since it is obvious that reflection in general, and all the more so scientific theological reflection, does not capture and cannot capture the whole of this reality which we realize in faith, hope, love, and prayer. It is precisely this permanent and insurmountable difference between the original Christian actualization of existence and reflection upon it which will occupy us throughout. The insight into this difference is a key insight which represents a necessary presupposition for an introduction to the idea of Christianity.

Ultimately what we want to do is merely reflect upon the simple question: "What is a Christian, and why can one live this Christian existence today with intellectual honesty?" The question begins with the fact of Christian existence, although this existence looks very different today in individual Christians. This difference is conditioned by personal levels of maturity, by very different kinds of social situations and hence also of religious situations, by psychological differences, and so on. But we also want to reflect here upon this fact of our Christian existence, and we want to justify it before the demands of conscience and of truth by giving an "account of our hope" (1 Pet. 3:15).

2. Preliminary Remarks on Methodology

THE CALL OF VATICAN II FOR AN INTRODUCTORY COURSE

The external stimulus for our asking what is the nature and the meaning of an "introduction to the idea of Christianity" as a foundational course within theology is Vatican II's Decree on Priestly Formation. We read there:

> In the reform of ecclesiastical studies, the first object must be a better integration of philosophy and theology. These subjects should work together harmoniously to unfold ever more deeply the mystery of Christ, that mystery which affects the whole history of the human race, is constantly at work in the Church, and becomes effective in a special way in the priestly ministry.
>
> That this understanding may be communicated to the students from the very start of their training, ecclesiastical studies should begin with an introductory course of suitable duration. In this introduction the mystery of salvation should be presented in such a way that the students will see clearly the meaning of ecclesiastical studies, their interrelationship, and their pastoral intent. Then they will be helped thereby to root their whole personal lives in faith and to permeate them with it. They will be strengthened to embrace their vocation with personal commitment and a joyful heart. (*Optatam totius*, art. 14)

The decree calls for an intrinsic integration of philosophy and theology. The overriding thematic task of such a theology is to concentrate the whole of theology on the mystery of Christ. This whole of theology should be presented to the students in an introductory course of sufficient duration, a course in which the mystery of Christ will be presented in such a way that the meaning, the interrelationship, and the pastoral intent of theological studies will become clear to the student right at the beginning of his studies in theology. The course should help him to deepen the roots of his personal and priestly life as a life of faith, and to permeate it with this faith. Therein lies the meaning of this introduction for his Christian as well as for his theological and priestly existence.

This raises the question whether there is a theoretical foundation for such an introductory course as a special, independent and responsible theological discipline, and hence not just as a pious and general introduction to theology. If there is such a foundation and if there are reasons for it, then the specific direction and the concrete shape of such a fundamental course must follow from them, and this would have significance not just for the education of priests.

THE "THEOLOGICAL ENCYCLOPEDIA" IN THE NINETEENTH CENTURY

The encyclopedia as it was originally conceived in the nineteenth century is still of interest in this context. It was not only meant to be a collection of the contents of all the theological knowledge that was then known, but was also to be a reconstruction of this knowledge from its origin and in its unity. We can recall here the Tübingen theologian Franz Anton Staudenmaier. According to his "encyclopedia" of 1834 this discipline offers the "systematic outline of the whole of theology," the "compact sketch of its concrete idea according to all its essential determinations." He writes: "For just as the human spirit is organic and is a system of living powers, so also in scientific knowledge it wants to see an organism, a system, and it does not rest until it has produced by its organizing activity a systematic interrelationship among the essential parts which form the content. This systematic interrelationship among the different parts of a science in accordance with its essential and basic concepts is presented in the encyclopedia." According to him, the encyclopedia develops the necessary and organic interrelationship of all the parts of theology, and thus it presents the parts as a real science by grasping them in the unity and the totality of their interrelationships. It is a real organism and bears its life principle within itself.

Hence the encyclopedists wanted to understand the different disciplines in the light of the original unity of theology, and they wanted to make the difference between theology and philosophy and between reason and revelation intelligible in the light of their equally original interrelationship. In fact, therefore, a philosophy of revelation is antecedent to all of this. Proceeding in this way the encyclopedists wanted to reach the real subject matter of theology itself and to offer thereby an introduction that did justice to this subject matter.

Something similar could be found in Johann Sebastian Drey, for example, or also in Schelling's "Lectures on the Method of Academic Study" of 1802.

Admittedly the execution of this encyclopedic introduction to theology betrayed this basic grand conception. For the subject matter of theology was explained objectively and the content of revelation was assigned accordingly to the material disciplines of theology. But there remained to be treated in the formal foundations of theology only the manner and way the material is acquired, is structured into a science, and is subjectively interpreted. To the extent that the encyclopedia did this, it led to absurdity, for it had now lost any real contact with its content. Basically it was given only as a kind of introduction to all that was actually going on in theology, as an overview and an introduction for beginners. But such an encyclopedia is basically superfluous, for it speaks to some too much in inconsequential generalities, and it offers to others nothing which did not have to be said again by way of introduction at the beginning of the individual disciplines.

Hence to explain and justify an introductory course one can indeed legitimately appeal to the original intention of the theological encyclopedia of the nineteenth century. Its actual execution, however, offers no points of contact. Moreover, the question of its theoretical foundation will have to be approached differently in view of the contemporary situation of theology and its addressee.

THE ADDRESSEE OF CONTEMPORARY THEOLOGY

The average person who comes to theology today, and this includes not only those who are preparing for the priesthood, does not feel secure in a faith which is taken for granted and is supported by a homogeneous religious milieu common to everyone. Even the young theology student possesses a faith which is under challenge and is by no means to be taken for granted, a faith which today must ever be won anew and is still in the process of being formed, and he need not be ashamed of this. He can readily acknowledge this situation in which he finds himself because he is living in an intellectual and spiritual situation today, or is even coming from such a situation himself, which does not allow Christianity to appear as something indisputable and to be taken for granted.

Just thirty or forty years ago, when I studied theology myself, the theology student was a person for whom Christianity, the faith, his religious existence, prayer, and firm intention to serve in a quite normal priestly activity were all things to be taken for granted. In those days he perhaps had certain theological problems during his studies. In theology he reflected perhaps very basically and in a precise and penetrating way upon all the individual questions of theology. But still this took place on the foundation of a Christianity which was taken for granted, and which existed by means of a religious education which was taken for granted and in a Christian milieu which was taken for granted. Our faith was partially and essentially conditioned by a quite definite sociological situation which at that time supported us and which today does not exist.

Now this means for the study of theology that academic instruction must take this situation into account, that it is ridiculous for theology professors to set up as their highest ideal the attempt to demonstrate before the young theologians right at the beginning their scholarliness in the problematic of their learned discipline. If theology students today live in a situation of crisis for their faith, then the beginning of their theological studies must help them, so far as this is possible, to overcome this crisis in the situation of their faith honestly. If we consider the two aspects just mentioned of the personal situation of today's young theologian, and if we are convinced that theology itself must respond to this situation right at the beginning, then we have to admit that in the concrete theological disciplines as they are offered today do not accomplish this by themselves. They are too much scholarship for its own sake, they are too splintered and fragmented to be really able to respond in an adequate way to the personal situation of theology students today.

In addition to this reason for a "foundational course" prompted by the external situation, there is a still more basic reason for undertaking on a first level of reflection what a "foundational course" is supposed to accomplish. Such a first level of reflection, and we shall clarify what this means, is necessary because of the pluralism of theological sciences which can no longer be completely unified and integrated. But here we run into a dilemma. This first level of reflection has the task, in a kind of legitimate flanking maneuver, of avoiding having to conduct a scientifically exact and complete investigation of all the theological disciplines, an undertaking that is not practically feasible, and of arriving nevertheless at an intellectually honest affirmation of Christian faith. But the intellectual and scientific rigor which such a first level of reflection demands is no less than that which an individual theological discipline requires of its students. The scientific and theoretical demands of a foundational course are not easily reconciled with the fact that on the practical level it must be structured according to the actual situation of a theological beginner. The title "foundational course" very easily gives the false impression that we are dealing with an introduction which cheaply absolves the beginning theologian of any rigorous thinking. On the other hand, however, it should and must recognize that it is trying to help the *beginner* to get his start in theology as a whole. It is naturally very difficult to satisfy both of these demands at the same time. But in any case, it is the scientific and theoretical grounds for the foundational course and not the pedagogical and the didactic that are decisive.

PLURALISM IN CONTEMPORARY THEOLOGY AND PHILOSOPHY

Theology has in fact become fragmented into an immense number of individual disciplines, with each individual discipline offering an enormous amount of material, employing its own very differentiated and difficult methodology, and having very little contact with other related or neighboring theological disciplines. We must acknowledge this situation of contemporary theology soberly, and we may not build up our hopes that it could be changed by the theological disciplines themselves. There is indeed an effort being made in theology to bring dogma and exegesis closer together, for example, or to do more theology in canon law than was the case twenty years ago. Such efforts to establish contacts are obviously useful but they can no longer overcome the pluralism in theology today.

Nor can this pluralism be overcome by the much-celebrated practice of teamwork. There is, of course, too little of the kind of cooperation that is necessary and sensible. But in the human sciences all cooperation has very clear limits. In the natural sciences exactly proven results can be taken over from one specialty to another and from one researcher to another. They can be understood to some extent, and in any case they can be made use of without having to evaluate the method and how it was acquired and the certainty of its results. But in the human sciences the real understanding of an assertion and the evaluation of its validity depend upon one's personal participation in the discovery of what is asserted. And it is precisely this which is no longer possible in theology for the representative of another discipline.

A second aspect of this whole situation follows from a similar pluralism in contemporary philosophy. The neo-scholastic school philosophy which we older theologians learned after a fashion forty years ago does not exist any more. Philosophy today has become fragmented into a pluralism of philosophies. This irreducible and insurmountable pluralism of philosophies is a fact today which we cannot evade. Every theology, of course, is always a theology which arises out of the secular anthropologies and self-interpretations of man. These latter as such are never entirely absorbed into these explicit philosophies, but they are to some extent. Hence this situation too necessarily produces an immense pluralism of theologies.

Further, we must be clear about the fact that today philosophy, or the philosophies, no longer represent by themselves the only and obvious and adequate juncture where theology comes into contact with man's secular knowledge and self-understanding. Theology is a theology that can be genuinely preached only to the extent that it succeeds in establishing contact with the total secular self-understanding which man has in a particular epoch, succeeds in engaging in conversation with it, in catching onto it, and in allowing itself to be enriched by it in its language and even more so in the very matter of theology itself. Hence today we have not only an interdisciplinary fragmentation in theology, we have not only a pluralism of philosophies which can no longer be integrated by a single individual, but in addition to this we have the fact that the philosophies no longer furnish the only self-interpretation of man that is significant for theology. Instead, as theologians today we must necessarily enter into dialogue with a pluralism of historical, sociological, and natural sciences, a dialogue no longer mediated by philosophy. These sciences no longer bow before philosophy's claim that they are to be mediated by philosophy or clarified by philosophy, or even that they are able to be clarified by philosophy.

This makes the difficulty of a scientific theology very evident. Theology itself has become a vast number of individual sciences. It must be in contact with so many different philosophies in order to be able to be scientific in this immediate sense. But it must also have contact with the sciences which no longer admit of philosophical interpretation. Finally, there must be added all the various non-scientific manifestations of the life of the spirit in art, in poetry, and in society, a variety which is so great that not everything which appears there is mediated either by the philosophies or by the pluralistic sciences themselves, and yet it represents a form of the spirit and of human self-understanding with which theology must have something to do.

THE JUSTIFICATION OF FAITH ON A "FIRST LEVEL OF REFLECTION"

In dogmatic theology there is in the dogmatic treatise "De fide" (on faith as such) a so-called *analysis fidei.* This analysis of faith considers the inner structure of fundamental theology's arguments for the credibility of faith, and considers the significance which these have for faith and for making an act of faith. It says there that in the Catholic understanding these arguments or proofs of credibility do not intrinsically establish faith in its properly theological character as *assensus super omnia firmus propter auctoritatem ipsius Dei revelantis* (as a firm and indubitable assent because of the authority of the revealing God Himself), but that they belong to faith nevertheless, and that such arguments of credibility have their function in faith as a whole. But it is assumed in this context that under certain circumstances and for theologically uneducated people or the *rudes,* an entire reflexive fundamental theology, or even an abreviated form of it, is not necessary as a presupposition of faith. Faith is not thereby made impossible for them, for it is possible in other ways. The old theology of faith always knew that for the *rudes* or the uneducated, coming to faith through an adequate reflection upon all of the intellectual grounds of credibility is not possible and is not necessary.

So I would like to formulate the thesis that in today's situation all of us with all of our theological study are and remain unavoidably *rudes* in a certain sense, and that we ought to admit that to ourselves and also to the world frankly and courageously.

Such a statement is not a permit for laziness, intellectual sloth, or intellectual indifference with regard to reflection upon propositions of the faith nor upon their foundation in fundamental theology. It is not a permit for laziness and indifference with regard to that responsibility for our hope and for our faith which in the concrete is necessary and possible for each particular person in his own particular situation, and is available to him there. But with regard to many theological reflections I can say: "I *cannot* accomplish it and therefore I *need not* be able to." Obviously I can still be a Christian who lives his faith with that intellectual honesty which is required of every person. There follows from this statement the theoretical possibility of giving a justification of the faith which is antecedent to the task and the method of contemporary scientific enquiry, both theological and secular. Thus this justification of the faith includes fundamental theology and dogmatic theology together. It takes place on a first level of reflection where faith gives an account of itself. This level must be distinguished from faith's second level of reflection, where the pluralistic theological sciences, each in its own area and each with its own specific method, give an account of themselves in a way which for the whole of the faith is inaccessible to all of us today, and all the more so to beginners in theology.

This scientifically first level both of reflection on the faith and of giving an account of it in an intellectually honest way constitutes a first science in its own right. As the individual theological disciplines are understood today, they are so constituted in their content, in the length and the breadth of their problematic, and in the differentiation of their methods and the difficulty in learning them, that they can no longer offer to a concrete person a basic understanding of the faith and a foundation for it. On the one hand he needs this understanding and this foundation and as an intellectual person he requires them, but on the other hand he cannot acquire them through these sciences as such. It must be theoretically possible to ground faith in a way which is antecedent to the legitimate tasks and methods of these contemporary disciplines.

This other way of grounding faith, which does not take upon itself all the tasks of the theological disciplines, nor examine all of the metaphysical presuppositions upon which faith is based, nor go into the introductory sciences, exegesis, the theology of the New Testament, and so on, cannot be for this reason unscientific. The unscientific nature of this different kind of discipline which we are striving for lies in the object, not in the subject and his method. I recognize that I cannot work through the whole of theology today because it has become fragmented many times over and is contained within a pluralism of philosophies and other sciences. But I also know as a Christian that I do not have to take that path in order to reflect intellectually on the justification of my Christian situation. So I reflect now with all exactness and rigor, and hence in a scientific way, upon that mode of justifying the faith, and of course also upon the content of the faith, which saves me from having to take the other path through all of the theological and secular sciences in order to give the first intellectual justification of my faith. I am spared this at least provisionally at the beginning of studies, and for most theological problems I am spared it permanently.

There is an "illative sense," as Cardinal Newman puts it, precisely in those areas which imply a decision affecting the whole person. There is a convergence of probabilities, a certainty, an honest and responsible decision which is knowledge and a free act together. It makes possible, to put it paradoxically, the scientific nature of being legitimately unscientific in such vital questions. There is a first level of reflection which has to be distinguished from the level of reflection of science in the contemporary sense because life and existence require such a level. It is this first level of reflection that is intended in a foundational course that is the first step in theological studies.

THE CONTENT OF THE INTRODUCTION

In a first reflection upon one's own Christian existence and its foundation such as the introductory course intends to offer, we are to be sure still on the level where there is a *unity of philosophy and theology,* for we are reflecting upon the concrete whole of the human self-realization of a Christian. That is really "philosophy." We are reflecting upon a Christian existence and upon the intellectual foundation of a Christian self-realization, and that is basically "theology." We are theoretically, practically, and didactically justified in philosophizing here within theology itself, and this "philosophy" need not have any scruple about the fact that it is constantly stepping over into areas that are properly theological.

This original unity of course is already present in the concrete life of the Christian. He is a believing Christian, and he is at the same time, indeed as a requirement of his own faith, a reflective person who reflects upon the whole of his existence. Here there exist both philosophical and theological objectivity, and in his own life both realities enter from the outset into a unity at least in principle. It is characteristic of this unity that in the appropriate place explicit reference is made to theological data which possibly cannot be reached by a secular philosophy as such.

If we wanted to formulate the unity between philosophy and theology in this foundational course somewhat differently, we could say that in the foundational course we must reflect *first of all* upon man as the universal question which he is for himself, and hence we must philosophize in the most proper sense. This question, which man *is* and not only *has*, must be regarded as the condition which makes hearing the Christian answer possible. *Secondly,* the transcendental and the historical conditions which make revelation possible must be reflected upon in the manner and within the limits which are possible on the first level of reflection, so that the point of mediation between question and answer, between philosophy and theology, will be seen. *Thirdly* and finally, we must reflect upon the fundamental assertion of Christianity as the answer to the question which man is, and hence we must do theology. These three moments mutually condition one another and therefore form a unity, a unity that is of course differentiated. The question creates the condition for really hearing, and only the answer brings the question to its reflexive self-presence. This circle is essential and is not supposed to be resolved in the foundational course, but to be reflected upon as such.

By its very nature the foundational course must necessarily be a quite specific *unity of fundamental theology and dogmatic theology.* The usual fundamental theology, which really misunderstands itself in its normal self-understanding, has a particular characteristic which cannot characterize this foundational course as foundational course. This particular characteristic of the traditional fundamental theology from the nineteenth century until our own day consists in this, that the facticity of divine revelation is to be reflected upon in a purely formal way, as it were, and, in a certain sense at least, is to be proven. As fundamental theology is in fact usually understood, it does not consider any particular theological data or any individual dogmas, except when it becomes dogmatic ecclesiology. But that brings it into a noteworthy difficulty, at least from the viewpoint of the purpose of this foundational course. The point of our foundational course in theology is precisely this, to give people confidence from the very *content* of Christian dogma itself that they can believe with intellectual honesty. In practice it is the case that a fundamental theology of the traditional kind, despite its formal clarity, precision, and cogency, very often remains unfruitful for the life of faith because the concrete person, and indeed with a certain theoretical justification, has the impression that the formal event of revelation is not really all that absolutely clear and certain.

In other words, if this introductory course does what it is supposed to do, then we must strive for a closer unity between fundamental theology and dogmatic theology, between the fundamental foundation of faith and reflection upon the content of faith than was the case in our previous theological disciplines and their divisions.

Nor can it be objected against this that the central truths of the faith are mysteries in the strict sense. They are that of course. But mystery is not to be identified with a statement which is senseless and unintelligible for us. If, moreover, the horizon of human existence which grounds and encompasses all human knowledge is a mystery, and it is, then man has a positive affinity, given at least with grace, to those Christian mysteries which constitute the basic content of faith. Besides, these mysteries do not consist in a rather large number of individual propositions which are unfortunately unintelligible. The only really absolute mysteries are the self-communication of God in the depths of existence, called grace, and in history, called Jesus Christ, and this already includes the mystery of the Trinity in the economy of salvation and of the immanent Trinity. And this one mystery can be brought close to man if he understands himself as oriented towards the mystery which we call God.

Hence there is really only one question, whether this God wanted to be merely the eternally distant one, or whether beyond that he wanted to be the innermost center of our existence in free grace and in self-communication. But our whole existence, borne by this question, calls for the affirmation of this second possibility as actually realized. It calls out to this mystery, which remains a mystery. But it is not so distant from this mystery that this mystery is nothing but a *sacrificium intellectus.*

In view of the subject matter, then, an intrinsic unity between fundamental theology and dogmatic theology is altogether possible. This is especially true if we begin with the good Thomistic presupposition that fundamental theology is done under the "light of faith," and is a justification of faith by faith. It is in faith's behalf and in faith's presence. But how is this to be done unless one reflects upon the very reality that is believed in, and not merely upon the formal event of revelation as such?

The third thing which seems to be important in connection with the content of a foundational course is to mention a few rather concrete cautions and requirements with regard to what does *not* belong in such a foundational course. First of all, great caution seems to be called for against taking a *too narrowly Christological approach*. The decree of the Second Vatican Council that we have already mentioned does say of course that the theologians should be introduced to the mystery of Christ right at the beginning. But if it says at the same time that this mystery of Christ affects the whole history of the human race, and indeed in all times and places, then a too narrow concentration of the foundational course on Jesus Christ as the key and the solution to all existential problems and as the total foundation of faith would be too simple a conception. It is not true that one has only to preach Jesus Christ and then he has solved all problems. Today Jesus Christ is himself a problem, and to realize this we only have to look at the demythologizing theology of a post-Bultmann age. The question is this: Why and in what sense may one risk his life in faith in this concrete Jesus of Nazareth as the crucified and risen God-Man? This is what has to be justified. Hence we cannot begin with Jesus Christ as the absolute and final datum, but we must begin further back than that. We have several sources of experience and knowledge, all of which have to be explored and mediated. There is a knowledge of God which is not mediated completely by an encounter with Jesus Christ. It is neither necessary nor objectively justified to begin in this foundational course simply with the doctrine of Jesus Christ, even though this foundational course is called in the conciliar decree *Optatam totius* an introduction to the mystery of Christ.

The same thing is also true about *formal hermeneutics:* to do this exclusively is *too narrow an approach*. There is certainly something like a formal theology of fundamentals, as distinguished from fundamental theology, and it belongs in this foundational course if used in the right way and from the right point of view. But it would certainly be false to think that we are dealing here only with a formal hermeneutic of theological language after the manner of post-Bultmann theology, or only with proving the legitimacy of any theology at all from the viewpoint of a theory of knowledge or a philosophy of language. This is so simply because, given the structure of man as seen in divine revelation, the concrete, a posteriori experience of salvation and of the historical facts of salvation cannot be turned into a purely transcendental, formal structure without Christianity ceasing to be Christianity.

We must also include a *caution against a mere biblicism.* Because of the way theological studies were done, Evangelical theology structured the whole of theology to a large extent from exegesis and biblical theology, including the introductory sciences and so on. Philosophy and systematic theology were frequently a very secondary matter, a subsequent superstructure, a summary of biblical theology. If we were to imitate something like this, which is basically obsolete, we would rob the foundational course of its real essence. The foundational course is not an introduction to sacred scripture. In the appropriate places and in the proper way, of course, we shall also have to do some exegesis or biblical theology in this foundational course. But in reflecting, for example, upon the historical credibility of the resurrection and upon the self-understanding of Jesus that is ascribed to him by dogmatic theology, we can make use of only as much scriptural data here as is sufficiently certain today from an honest exegesis. By the very nature of the foundational course, as distinguished from *later and necessary* biblical theology, fundamental theology, ecclesiology and dogmatic theology, we may include only as much exegesis and biblical theology in the foundational course as is absolutely necessary. Then later exegesis and biblical theology can gather, organize and incorporate the rest of the positive, biblical material which must also be included in the church's theology.

3. Some Basic Epistemological Problems

THE RELATION BETWEEN REALITY AND CONCEPT, BETWEEN ORIGINAL
SELF-POSSESSION AND REFLECTION

We are calling this essay an introduction to the *idea* of Christianity in order to indicate that our concern here cannot be a mystagogical initiation into Christianity, but is an inquiry on the level of conceptual thought in theology and in the philosophy of religion on the first level of reflection. We are dealing with the idea, not with the reality immediately; here as nowhere else idea and reality are incommensurate with each other, although, on the other hand, nowhere does the idea require turning to the reality itself in order to be understood as much as it does here. Even if *our* attempt should founder, it must be possible in principle according to the claim of Christianity. For, on the one hand, Christianity exists in the individual person in his concrete, historically conditioned finiteness only if this person accepts it with at least a minimum of knowledge that he has personally acquired and that is encompassed by faith, and, on the other hand, this knowledge is what is understood of Christianity as something that is in principle accessible to everyone and can be grasped by everyone.

Not everyone can be an expert in theology in the strict sense. But if, nevertheless, Christianity is to be able to be something which can be grasped personally by everyone, then in principle there must be an introduction to Christianity on a first level of reflection. In other sciences it might be the case that the more specialized something becomes, the more inaccessible it is for the non-specialist, and the more it becomes important and becomes precisely the real truth of this science. This cannot be the case in theology, because in its scientific pursuits theology does not just turn its attention subsequently to a knowledge which is salvific for all, but it intends to be this salvific knowledge which is for everybody. For reflection upon one's prior understanding of existence belongs in some form and to some degree to this very understanding of existence, and is not merely a supplementary luxury for specialists.

There is in man an inescapable *unity in difference between one's original self-possession and reflection.* This is disputed in different ways by theological rationalism on the one hand, and on the other by the philosophy of religion of so-called classical "modernism." For basically every rationalism is based upon the conviction that a reality is present for man in spiritual and free self-possession only through the objectifying concept, and this becomes genuinely and fully real in scientific knowledge. Conversely, what is called "modernism" in the classical understanding lives by the conviction that the concept or reflection is something *absolutely* secondary in relation to the original self-possession of existence in self-consciousness and freedom, so that reflection could also be dispensed with.

But there is not just the purely objective "in itself" of a reality on the one hand, and the "clear and distinct idea" of it on the other, but there is also a more original unity, not indeed for everything and anything, but certainly for the actualization of human existence, and this is a unity of reality and its "self-presence" which is more, and is more original, than the unity of this reality and the concept which objectifies it. When I love, when I am tormented by questions, when I am sad, when I am faithful, when

I feel longing, this human and existentiell* reality is a unity, an original unity of reality and its own self-presence which is not *totally* mediated by the concept which objectifies it in scientific knowledge. This unity of reality and the original self-presence of this reality in the person is already present in man's free self-realization. That is one side of the question.

Nevertheless it must be added that a moment of reflection, and consequently of universality and spiritual communicability, belongs even to this original knowledge itself, although this moment of reflection does not capture this unity and transpose it integrally into objectifying concepts. This original unity which we are driving at between reality and its knowledge of itself always exists in man only with and in and through what we can call language, and thus also reflection and communicability. At that moment when this element of reflection would no longer be present, this original self-possession would also cease to exist.

The tension between original knowledge and its concept, which moments belong together and yet are not one, is not something static. It has a history in two directions. The original self-presence of the subject in the actual realization of his existence strives to translate itself more and more into the conceptual, into the objectified, into language, into communication with another. Everyone strives to tell another, especially someone he loves, what he is suffering. Consequently in this tension between original knowledge and the concept which always accompanies it there is a tendency towards greater conceptualization, towards language, towards communication, and also towards theoretical knowledge of itself.

But there is also movement in the opposite direction within this tension. One who has been formed by a common language, and educated and indoctrinated from without, experiences clearly perhaps only very slowly what he has been talking about for a long time. It is precisely we theologians who are always in danger of talking about heaven and earth, about God and man with an arsenal of religious and theological concepts which is almost limitless in its size and proportions. We can acquire in theology a very great skill in talking and perhaps not have really understood from the depths of our existence what we are really talking about. To that extent reflection,

---

*The two spellings, "existential" and "existentiell," follow the German usage. "Existential," as in Rahner's phrase "supernatural existential," refers to an element in man's ontological constitution precisely as human being, an element which is constitutive of his existence as man prior to his exercise of freedom. It is an aspect of concrete human nature precisely as human. "Existentiell," as in Rahner's phrase "existentiell Christology," refers to the free, personal and subjective appropriation and actualization of something which can also be spoken of in abstract theory or objective concepts without such a subjective and personal realization. —Trans.

conceptualization and language have a necessary orientation to that original knowledge, to that original experience in which what is meant and the experience of what is meant are still one.

Insofar as religious knowledge also manifests this tension between an original self-knowledge acquired through what we do and what we suffer, and its conceptualization, there is also within theology this dual movement in its irreducible unity and difference. This tension is a fluid relationship and not simply something static. Although this movement reaches its goal only asymptotically, we should be coming to know better and better in a conceptual way what we have already experienced and lived through prior to such conceptualization, although not entirely without it. Conversely, we should show again and again that all these theological concepts do not make the reality itself present to man from outside of him, but they are rather the expression of what has already been experienced and lived through more originally in the depths of existence. We can to some extent become present to ourselves on a conceptual level, and we can try again and again to relate our theological concepts back to their original experience. Hence what we are trying to do here is both justified and necessary. Should we fail, this failure could only be understood by Christians as the mandate and the task to try again and harder.

THE SELF-PRESENCE OF THE SUBJECT IN KNOWLEDGE

We often imagine the essential nature of knowledge after the model of a tablet on which an object is inscribed, whereby the object comes from outside, as it were, and appears on the tablet. We imagine knowledge in the likeness of a mirror in which some object or other is reflected. It is only such paradigms of knowledge that make intelligible the famous problem how the "in itself" *(An-sich)* of something can enter into knowledge, how an object can get into knowledge as it were. These paradigms are always present in epistemology as an a priori, especially in the defense of so-called realism, the "image" or "copy" theory of knowledge or the doctrine of truth as the correspondence between a statement and an object. They are presupposed there as something to be taken for granted. In all of these models of knowledge the known is something which comes from outside, is the other which presents itself from outside according to its own law, and informs the receptive faculty of knowledge.

But in reality knowledge has a much more complex structure. At least the spiritual knowledge of a personal subject is not of such a nature that the object presents itself from outside and is "possessed" as known in this way. It is rather a knowledge in which the knowing subject possesses in knowledge both itself and its knowledge. This occurs not only when in a second and subsequent act the subject reflects upon its own self-presence in its knowledge, that is to say, when it reflects upon the fact that it knew something in the first act and now makes this earlier knowledge itself the object of its knowledge. The knowing possession of knowledge as such, as distinguished from its objectified object, and the knowing possession of self are characteristics of all knowledge. In knowledge not only is something known, but the subject's knowing is always co-known.

In the simple and original act of knowledge, whose attention is focused upon some object which encounters it, the knowing that is co-known and the knowing subject that is co-known are not the *objects* of the knowledge. Rather the consciousness of the act of knowing something and the subject's consciousness of itself, that is, the subject's presence to itself, are situated so to speak at the other pole of the single relationship between the knowing subject and the known object. This latter pole refers to the luminous realm, as it were, within which the individual object upon which attention is focused in a particular primary act of knowledge can become manifest. This subjective consciousness of the knower always remains unthematic in the primary knowledge of an object presenting itself from without. It is something which goes on, so to speak, behind the back of the knower, who is looking away from himself and at the object. Moreover, even if this knower in an act of reflection explicitly makes the co-known self-presence of the subject and his knowing the object of a new act of knowledge, the same thing happens again. This new act itself, which makes the subjective co-consciousness the object of the subsequent act in a conceptual way, also includes once again such an original self-presence of the subject and his knowledge of this second, reflexive act as the condition of its possibility, as its subjective pole.

This reflexive act does not make the original self-presence of the knower and his knowing superfluous. In fact its object is basically only this original, luminous self-presence of the subject. But this conceptualized and thematized self-presence of the subject and its knowing is never identical with the original self-presence and never recaptures its content completely. Just as in the case of the relationship between immediately experienced joy, anxiety, love, or suffering and the content of a reflexive concept of joy, anxiety, love, or suffering, so too exactly, but in a much more original way, is the relationship between the necessary self-presence of the subject and his knowledge of what is objectively known, a self-presence at the subjective pole of the knowledge relationship, and the reflexive objectification of this self-presence. The reflexive self-presence always refers back to this original self-presence of the subject, even in an act whose attention is upon something quite different, and it never recaptures this original, subjective self-presence completely. Nor can the tension and polarity between the two poles of "subject" and "object" be resolved when the subject makes himself his own object. For then the object is the conceptually objectified subject, and the knowledge of this concept includes once again on the subjective pole of this tension and polarity the original, unthematic self-knowledge of the subject as its original condition.

APRIORITY AND ESSENTIAL OPENNESS

But it is not the case that this co-known, unthematic self-presence of the subject and its self-knowledge is merely an accompanying phenomenon in every act of knowledge which grasps an object, so that the knowledge of this object in its structure and content would be completely independent of the structure of the subjective self-presence. Rather the structure of the subject itself is an a priori, that is, it forms an antecedent law governing what and how something can become manifest to the knowing subject. The ears, for example, constitute an a priori law, a screen, as it were, which determines that only sounds can register in the ears. The same is true of the eyes and all the other organs of sense knowledge. They select according to their own law from the fullness of the possibilities of the world impinging upon them, and according to their own law they give these realities the possibility of approaching and presenting themselves, or they exclude them.

This in no way implies that the realities which present themselves cannot manifest themselves as they actually are. A keyhole forms an a priori law governing what key fits in, but it thereby discloses something about the key itself. The a priori structure of a faculty of knowledge is disclosed most simply by the fact that it is constant in every individual act of knowledge of an object that is given to it, and indeed even when the object of this act is, or rather would be, the denial or the impugning of these a priori structures. For the sake of brevity we cannot illustrate this point in our sense knowledge of the manifold of immediate events in time and space. Instead we shall turn immediately to the totality of man's spiritual knowledge in which this knowing, subjective self-possession, the *reditio completa*, the complete return of the subject to itself, as Thomas Aquinas calls it, really takes place.

If we ask what the a priori structures of this self-possession are, then we must say that, without prejudice to the mediation of this self-possession by the experience of sense objects in time and space, this subject is fundamentally and by its very nature pure openness for absolutely everything, for being as such. This is shown by the fact that the denial of such an unlimited openness of the spirit to absolutely everything implicitly posits and affirms such an openness. For a subject which knows itself to be finite, and in its knowledge is not just unknowing with regard to the limited nature of the possibility of its objects, has already transcended its finiteness. It has differentiated itself as finite from a subjectively and unthematically given horizon of possible objects that is of infinite breadth. Anyone who says objectively and thematically that there is no truth affirms this statement as true, otherwise the statement would make no sense. By the fact that in such an act and on its subjective pole the subject necessarily affirms the existence of truth, although he does this in unthematic knowledge, he already experiences himself in possession of such a knowledge. The same is also true in the experience of the subjective, unlimited openness of the subject. Insofar as he experiences himself as conditioned and limited by sense experience, and all too much conditioned and limited, he has nevertheless already transcended this sense experience. He has posited himself as the subject of a pre-apprehension *(Vorgriff)* which has no intrinsic limit, because even the suspicion of such an intrinsic limitation of the subject posits this pre-apprehension itself as going beyond the suspicion.

TRANSCENDENTAL EXPERIENCE

We shall call *transcendental experience* the subjective, unthematic, necessary and unfailing consciousness of the knowing subject that is co-present in every spiritual act of knowledge, and the subject's openness to the unlimited expanse of all possible reality. It is an *experience* because this knowledge, unthematic but ever-present, is a moment within and a condition of possibility for every concrete experience of any and every object. This experience is called *transcendental* experience because it belongs to the necessary and inalienable structures of the knowing subject itself, and because it consists precisely in the transcendence beyond any particular group of possible objects or of categories. Transcendental experience is the experience of *transcendence,* in which experience the structure of the subject and therefore also the ultimate structure of every conceivable object of knowledge are present together and in identity. This transcendental experience, of course, is not merely an experience of pure knowledge, but also of the will and of freedom. The same character of transcendentality belongs to them, so that basically one can ask about the source and the destiny of the subject as a knowing being and as a free being together.

If the specific nature of this transcendental experience is clear, an experience which as such can never be objectively represented in its own self, but only by an abstract concept of it; if it is clear that this transcendental experience is not constituted by the fact that one speaks of it; if it is clear that one must speak of it because it is always there, but for this reason it can also be constantly overlooked; if it is clear that by its very nature it can never have the novel attraction of an object that is unexpectedly encountered, if all of this is clear then one understands the difficulty of the task we are undertaking: we can also speak of the term of this transcendental experience only indirectly.

UNTHEMATIC KNOWLEDGE OF GOD

We shall be concerned later with showing that there is present in this transcendental experience an unthematic and anonymous, as it were, knowledge of God. Hence the original knowledge of God is not the kind of knowledge in which one grasps an object which happens to present itself directly or indirectly from outside. It has rather the character of a transcendental experience. Insofar as this subjective, non-objective luminosity of the subject in its transcendence is always orientated towards the holy mystery, the knowledge of God is always present unthematically and without name, and not just when we begin to speak of it. All talk about it, which necessarily goes on, always only points to this transcendental experience as such, an experience in which he whom we call "God" encounters man in silence, encounters him as the absolute and the incomprehensible, as the term of his transcendence which cannot really be incorporated into any system of coordinates. When this transcendence is the transcendence of *love*, it also experiences this term as the *holy* mystery.

We shall be going into this in detail later, but one thing which should be mentioned here in order to clarify what transcendence means is that if man is a being of transcendence towards the holy and absolutely real mystery, and if the term and source of the transcendence in and through which man as such exists, and which constitutes his original essence as subject and as person, is this absolute and holy mystery, then strangely enough we can and must say: mystery in its incomprehensibility is what is *self-evident* in human life. If transcendence is not something which we practice on the side as a metaphysical luxury of our intellectual existence, but if this transcendence is rather the plainest, most obvious and most necessary condition of possibility for *all* spiritual understanding and comprehension, then the holy mystery really is the one thing that is self-evident, the one thing which is grounded in itself even from our point of view. For all other understanding, however clear it might appear, is grounded in this transcendence. All clear understanding is grounded in the darkness of God.

Hence upon close examination the mysteriousness of this term of transcendence is not simply the contrary of the notion of the self-evident. In our knowledge only that is self-evident for us which is self-evident in itself. But everything we understand becomes intelligible, but not really self-evident, only by the fact that it is derived from something else and thus resolved: into axioms on the one hand, and on the other into the elementary data of sense experience. But it is thereby derived and made intelligible either in the mute opaqueness of sense data, or in the half-light of ontology, and hence in the absolute and holy mystery.

What is made intelligible is grounded ultimately in the one thing that is self-evident, in mystery. Mystery is something with which we are always familiar, something which we love, even when we are terrified by it or perhaps even annoyed and angered, and want to be done with it. For the person who has touched his own spiritual depths, what is more familiar, thematically or unthematically, and what is more self-evident than the silent question which goes beyond everything which has already been mastered and controlled, than the unanswered question accepted in humble love, which alone brings wisdom? In the ultimate depths of his being man knows nothing more surely than that his knowledge, that is, what is called knowledge in everyday parlance, is only a small island in a vast sea that has not been traveled. It is a floating island, and it might be more familiar to us than the sea, but ultimately it is borne by the sea and only because it is can we be borne by it. Hence the existentiell question for the knower is this: Which does he love more, the small island of his so-called knowledge or the sea of infinite mystery? Is the little light with which he illuminates this island—we call it science and scholarship—to be an eternal light which will shine forever for him? That would surely be hell.

If a person wants, of course, in the concrete decisions of his life he can always choose to accept this infinite question only as a thorn in the side of his knowledge and his mastery and control. He can refuse to have anything to do with the absolute question except insofar as this question drives him to more and more individual questions and individual answers. But only when one begins to ask about asking itself, and to think about thinking itself, only when one turns his attention to the scope of knowledge and not only to the objects of knowledge, to transcendence and not only to what is understood categorically in time and space within this transcendence, only then is one just on the threshold of becoming a religious person. From this perspective it is easier to understand that not many are, that maybe they are not capable of being, that they feel that it demands too much. But anyone who has once raised the question about his transcendence and about its term can no longer let it go unanswered. For even if he were to say that it is a question which cannot be answered, which should not be answered, and which, because it demands too much, should be left alone, even then he would have already given an answer to this question, whether the right one or the wrong one is here beside the point.

The Hearer of the Message

1. The Interlocking of Philosophy and Theology

What kind of a hearer does Christianity anticipate so that its real and ultimate message can even be heard? This is the first question we have to ask. It is meant not in a moral sense, but in the sense of existential ontology.

If we must first of all speak about the person who is to be the hearer of the Christian message, if in this sense we are speaking about presuppositions, what we want to examine is the specific way in which these presuppositions and the Christian message are interwoven. This does not mean that Christianity simply presumes these presuppositions as given ready-made and as having already been actualized by everyone reflexively and especially in freedom, so that wherever these presuppositions are not present there is no potential hearer of the Christian message.

When the reality of man is understood correctly, there exists an inescapable circle between his horizons of understanding and what is said, heard and understood. Ultimately the two mutually presuppose each other. Consequently, intertwined in this specific way, Christianity assumes that these presuppositions which it makes are inescapably and necessarily present in the ultimate depths of human existence, even when this existence is interpreted differently in its reflexive self-interpretation, and that at the same time the Christian message itself creates these presuppositions by its call. It summons man before the real truth of his being. It summons him before the truth in which he remains inescapably caught, although this prison is ultimately the infinite expanse of the incomprehensible mystery of God.

This implies at this point in our investigation a specific kind of interlocking between philosophy and theology. The presuppositions which are to be considered here refer to man's essential being. They refer to his essential being as something which is always historically constituted, and thus as existing in confrontation with Christianity as grace and as historical message. Hence they refer to something which is accessible to every theoretical reflection upon and self-interpretation of human existence, and this we call philosophy. And these very presuppositions themselves belong to the content of a revealed theology which announces Christianity to man so that this essential being of his, which is inescapable and is always historically oriented, does not remain hidden from him.

If, then, we are going to discuss such an anthropology as the presupposition for hearing and understanding the real message of Christianity, we do not have to be concerned about separating philosophy and theology methodologically in the sharpest possible way. Even the most basic, self-grounded and most transcendental philosophy of human existence is always achieved only within historical experience. Indeed, it is itself a moment in human history, and hence we can never philosophize as though man has not had that experience which is the experience of Christianity. This is true at least with regard to the experience of what we call grace, although this does not have to be reflexive and understood and objectified as an experience of grace. A philosophy that is absolutely free of theology is not even possible in our historical situation. The fundamental autonomy of this philosophy can only consist in the fact that it reflects upon its historical origins and asks whether it sees itself as still bound to these origins in history and in grace as something valid, and whether this self-experience of man can still be experienced today as something valid and binding. Conversely, dogmatic theology also wants to tell man what he is, and what he still remains even if he rejects this message of Christianity in disbelief.

Hence theology itself implies a philosophical anthropology which enables this message of grace to be accepted in a really philosophical and reasonable way, and which gives an account of it in a humanly responsible way. We make assertions about man and about his situation, which now in any case is inescapable, assertions about what the Christian message encounters in man or what it itself creates as the presupposition and as the point of its own contact with man. And everyone is then asked whether he can recognize himself as that person who is here trying to express his self-understanding, or whether in responsibility to himself and to his existence he can affirm as the conviction which is to be the truth for him that he is not such a person as Christianity tells him he is.

2. Man as Person and Subject

PERSONHOOD AS PRESUPPOSITION OF THE CHRISTIAN MESSAGE

With regard to the presuppositions of the revealed message of Christianity, the first thing to be said about man is that he is person and subject.

There is no need to explain in any great detail that a notion of person and subject is of fundamental importance for the possibility of Christian revelation and the self-understanding of Christianity. A personal relationship to God, a genuinely dialogical history of salvation between God and man, the acceptance of one's own, unique, eternal salvation, the notion of responsibility before God and his judgment, all of these assertions of Christianity, however they are to be explained more precisely, imply that man is what we want to say here: person and subject. The same thing is true when we speak of a verbal revelation in Christianity, when we say that God has spoken to man, has called him into his presence, that in prayer man can and should speak with God. All of these assertions are terribly obscure and difficult, but they make up the concrete reality of Christianity. And none of this would be intelligible unless we include in our understanding of Christianity explicitly or implicitly what we mean here by "person" and "subject."

What exactly is understood by these terms can only follow from the whole of our anthropology, and hence only after we have treated man's transcendence, his responsibility and freedom, his orientation towards the incomprehensible mystery, his being in history and in the world, and his social nature. All of these determinations are part of that by which his true personhood is constituted. The point here, before we have treated these individual determinations, is to indicate at least in a provisional way what is meant when man is called person and subject.

THE HIDDENNESS AND RISK OF PERSONAL EXPERIENCE

Such language must always count on the "good will" of the hearer. For what he is supposed to hear is not what is contained immediately in the concept itself. By the very nature of the subject matter such concepts point to man's more original and basic experience of his subjectivity and personhood. They point to a basic experience which indeed does not simply take place in an absolutely wordless and unreflexive experience, but neither is it something which can be expressed in words and indoctrinated from without.

Both as an individual and in humanity as a whole man certainly experiences himself in a great variety of ways as the product of that which is not himself. We could even say that basically all the empirical sciences about man are aimed methodologically at explaining him and deriving him. They are aimed at seeing him as the result of and as the point of intersection between realities which on the one hand exist within the realm of empirical experience, but which on the other hand are not man himself, and yet establish and determine him in his reality and hence also explain him. All of the empirical anthropological sciences obviously have the right to unravel man, as it were, to analyze and to derive him in such a way that what they observe and establish in man is explained as the product and the result of data and of realities which are not this concrete person. Whether these sciences are called physics, chemistry, biochemistry, genetics, paleontology, sociology or whatever, they are all quite legitimately trying to derive and explain man, to dissolve him, as it were, into his empirical causes which can be specified and analyzed and isolated. These sciences are to a large extent correct in their methods and in their results, and everyone's own painful experience in his own existence shows how very right they are.

A person looks inside himself, looks back at his past and looks at the world around him, and he discovers either to his horror or to his relief that he can shift responsibility from himself for all the individual data that make up his reality, and he can place the burden for what he is on what is not him. He discovers that he has come to be through what is other than himself. And this other from which he has come is an implacable, impersonal nature, and this includes "history," which he can also interpret as "nature." From the Christian standpoint there is no reason to limit the claims of empirical anthropology within certain materially and regionally defined areas of human life, and to call what lies within the province of these empirical anthropologies "matter" or "body" or something similar, and then to differentiate from this another part which can be empirically and clearly separated, and call this "spirit" or "soul."

Naturally such a material separation is made with some justification in the usual Christian apologetics and theological anthropology in order to make oneself understood in more primitive and popular ways of thinking. But basically every *particular anthropology*, and we could also call them "regional" if the word is not understood geographically, for example, biochemistry, biology, genetics, sociology, and so on, approaches man from a definite standpoint, and does not claim to be the one and only anthropology. Sociology will develop its own anthropology in accordance with its methods. But if it has any sense it is not going to say that a biological anthropology or an anthropology of behavior patterns is meaningless. It might even make use of these anthropologies. But in doing so it is also recognizing that there are other anthropologies besides its own. And each of them has its own particular methods which are at least provisional, although there might be some final reservations about them.

But nevertheless each one intends to say something about man *as a whole*, and since it takes him as a single whole, it cannot forego wanting to assert something about this single whole. Hence each of these anthropologies tries to explain man from particular data, by reducing him to his elements and then reconstructing him back together again from this particular data. That is the right of every regional anthropology. Usually every such anthropology is also motivated by the secret desire not only to understand man, and not only to analyze and reconstruct him, but also really to control him thereby. The intention of every regional anthropology to explain man as a whole is legitimate. For man is a being whose origins lie within the world, that is, who has his roots in empirical realities. His being is such that these particular origins within the world always touch him as a single whole and in his entirety. That is why particular anthropologies, although they are particular, still remain anthropologies.

THE SPECIFIC CHARACTER OF PERSONAL EXPERIENCE

Philosophy and theology do not have a special preserve in man which belongs only to them, and which is closed to these other anthropologies like a holy land. But in the midst of these origins into which he seems to dissolve, which seem to make everything about him a product of the world, and from which nothing about him must be excepted a priori, nor may it be excepted—in the midst of this man experiences himself as person and as subject. When we say that man is subject and person, this is not an assertion about a particular part of him which could be isolated, so that all other particular anthropologies could be excluded from it, and the assertion itself would then belong to just such a particular anthropology. The specific character of this experience and therefore the specific character of the concrete way in which it is had must be constantly kept in mind. Man can indeed overlook something which he is, or better: he can overlook the totality of what he is, and especially is. What he experiences he can also suppress. This suppression is meant here not in the sense of depth psychology, but in a much more general and at the same time more ordinary sense. One can overlook something, show himself uninterested and leave it alone, although it is part of him. He does not allow the original experience to surface. On the one hand we can talk about it only in words and concepts, and yet what is meant is not just what is contained in language as such. And it can even be the case that a person simply does not want to express in word and on the level of conceptual objectification such hidden and total experiences which are, as it were, silent and unobtrusive, or perhaps he cannot bring them to expression.

At this point we do not yet have the opportunity to go into this peculiarity of man's self-interpretation, namely, that what is most basic and original and most self-evident can also be what is most able to be overlooked and is most able to be suppressed. Here we must only call attention to the possibility of existentielly not wanting something to be true, so that what is to be said about man's personhood and subjectivity does not confront an unwillingness to see from the outset.

Man experiences himself precisely as subject and person insofar as he becomes conscious of himself as the product of what is radically foreign to him. This element, namely, that man also *knows* about his radical origins in these causes, is not explained by these origins. When he analyzes and reconstructs himself, it is not yet explained by this process that he does this analysis and reconstruction *himself* and knows about it. Precisely in the fact that man experiences himself as something alien imposed upon himself and as produced; precisely insofar as he gives free rein to every conceivable possibility of analysis in the empirical anthropologies, analysis which reduces and dissolves man into what is not himself, and he does this even when this analysis in fact has not yet reached its conclusion; precisely in the fact that man gives his particular empirical anthropologies the right to explain him more and more, to reduce him and dismantle him, and, as spirit's retort to all of this as it were, perhaps in the future even actually to reconstruct him, in all of this he experiences himself as subject and as person. But he can overlook this fact because he loses sight of it in its apparent opposite.

In the fact that man raises analytical questions about himself and opens himself to the unlimited horizons of such questioning, he has already transcended himself and every conceivable element of such an analysis or of an empirical reconstruction of himself. In doing this he is affirming himself as more than the sum of such analyzable components of his reality. Precisely this consciousness of himself, this confrontation with the totality of all his conditions, and this very being-conditioned show him to be more than the sum of his factors. For a finite system of individual, distinguishable elements cannot have the kind of relationship to itself which man has to himself in the experience of his multiple conditioning and his reducibility. A finite system cannot confront itself in its totality. From its point of departure, which ultimately is imposed upon it, a finite system receives a relationship to a definite operation, although this might consist in maintaining the system itself, but it does not have a relationship to its own point of departure. It does not ask questions about itself. It is not a subject. The experience of radical questioning and man's ability to place himself in question are things which a finite system cannot accomplish.

It follows from our supposition, of course, that this standpoint outside of and above the system of empirical, individual and specifiable data may not be understood as an individual and separable element in the empirical reality of man. This is how the school theology likes to understand it when it speaks of spirit or of man's immortal soul as though what is meant by this were an element within the totality of man which can be encountered immediately and in itself, and distinguished empirically and in test-tube purity from the rest of him. This is understandable pedagogically, but ultimately it is a primitive conception. But if we do not go along with this primitive dualism, which comes ultimately from Greek anthropology and not from Christian anthropology, and instead realize that the one, single man as one has already confronted himself in a question which has already gone beyond every possible empirical and partial answer, has gone beyond it not in its positive content but in the radical nature of the question, then we experience man as subject. He is experienced as the subjectivity of these multiple objectivities with which the empirical human sciences are concerned. On the one hand, man's ability to be related to himself, his "having to do with himself," is not and cannot be one element in him alongside of other elements. But it is, nevertheless and for this reason, a reality which constitutes the subjectivity of man as distinguished from his objectivity, which is the other aspect of him.

Being a person, then, means the self-possession of a subject as such in a conscious and free relationship to the totality of itself. This relationship is the condition of possibility and the antecedent horizon for the fact that in his individual empirical experiences and in his individual sciences man has to do with himself as one and as a whole. Because man's having responsibility for the totality of himself is the condition of his empirical experience of self, it cannot be derived completely from this experience and its objectivities. Even when man would want to shift all responsibility for himself away from himself as someone totally determined from without, and thus would want to explain himself away, *he* is the one who does this and does it knowingly and willingly. *He* is the one who encompasses the sum of all the possible elements of such an explanation, and thus *he* is the one who shows himself to be something other than the subsequent product of such individual elements. We can indeed speak of finite systems which are self-directing and so in a certain sense have a relationship to themselves. But such a self-directing system has only a limited possibility of self-regulation. This is an element in this system, and hence it cannot explain how man confronts himself in his totality and places himself in question, and how he reflects upon the question of raising questions.

Man's actual presence to himself in which he confronts his own system with all its present and future possibilities, and hence confronts himself in his entirety, and places this in question and thus transcends it, this self-presence cannot be explained after the model of a self-regulating multiple system. Basically this is how all particular anthropologies by their very nature have to explain it. This subjectivity is itself an irreducible datum of existence, copresent in every individual experience as its a priori condition. The experience of it is a transcendental experience in a non-philosophical sense. Because of the transcendental nature of this experience, what we mean by personhood and subjectivity always eludes definition as an immediate, isolated, regional element in man. For the object of such a transcendental experience does not appear in its own reality when man is dealing with something individual and definable in an objective way, but when in such a process he is *being* subject and not dealing with a "subject" in an objective way. To say that man is person and subject, therefore, means first of all that man is someone who cannot be derived, who cannot be produced completely from other elements at our disposal. He is that being who is responsible for himself. When he explains himself, analyzes himself, reduces himself back to the plurality of his origins, he is affirming himself as the subject who is doing this, and in so doing he experiences himself as something necessarily prior to and more original than this plurality.

3. Man as Transcendent Being

What is meant more precisely by the subjectivity which man experiences becomes clearer when we say that man is a transcendent being.

THE TRANSCENDENT STRUCTURE OF KNOWLEDGE

In spite of the finiteness of his system man is always present to himself in his entirety. He can place everything in question. In his openness to everything and anything, whatever can come to expression can be at least a question for him. In the fact that he affirms the possibility of a merely *finite* horizon of questioning, this possibility is already surpassed, and man shows himself to be a being with an *infinite* horizon. In the fact that he experiences his finiteness radically, he reaches beyond this finiteness and experiences himself as a transcendent being, as spirit. The infinite horizon of human questioning is experienced as an horizon which recedes further and further the more answers man can discover.

Man can try to evade the mysterious infinity which opens up before him in his questions. Out of fear of the mysterious he can take flight to the familiar and the everyday. But the infinity which he experiences himself exposed to also permeates his everyday activities. Basically he is always still on the way. Every goal that he can point to in knowledge and in action is always relativized, is always a provisional step. Every answer is always just the beginning of a new question. Man experiences himself as infinite possibility because in practice and in theory he necessarily places every sought-after result in question. He always situates it in a broader horizon which looms before him in its vastness. He is the spirit who experiences himself as spirit in that he does not experience himself as *pure* spirit. Man is not the unquestioning and unquestioned infinity of reality. He is the question which rises up before him, empty, but really and inescapably, and which can never be settled and never adequately answered by him.

THE POSSIBILITY OF EVADING THE EXPERIENCE OF TRANSCENDENCE

A person can, of course, shrug his shoulders and ignore this experience of transcendence. He can devote himself to his concrete world, his work, his activity in the categorical realm of time and space, to the service of his system at certain points which are the focal points of reality for him. That is possible in three ways:

1. Most people will do this in a naive way. They live at a distance from themselves in that concrete part of their lives and of the world around them which can be manipulated and controlled. They have enough to do there, and it is very interesting and important. And if they ever reflect at all on anything which goes beyond all this, they can always say that it is more sensible not to break one's head over it.

2. Such an evasion of this question and of accepting human transcendence can also take place along with the resolve to accept categorical existence and its tasks, recognizing and accepting the fact that everything is encompassed by an ultimate question. This question is perhaps left as a

question. One believes that it can be postponed in silence and in a perhaps sensible scepticism. But when one explains that it cannot be answered, he is admitting that in the final analysis such a question cannot be evaded.

3. There is also a perhaps despairing involvement in the categorical realm of human existence. One goes about his business, he reads, he gets angry, he does his work, he does research, he achieves something, he earns money. And in a final, perhaps unadmitted despair he says to himself that the whole as a whole makes no sense, and that one does well to suppress the question about the meaning of it all and to reject it as an unanswerable and hence meaningless question.

We can never know unambiguously which of these three possibilities is the case in any given person.

THE PRE-APPREHENSION OF BEING

Man is a transcendent being insofar as all of his knowledge and all of his conscious activity is grounded in a pre-apprehension *(Vorgriff)* of "being" as such, in an unthematic but ever-present knowledge of the infinity of reality (as we can put it provisionally and somewhat boldly). We are presupposing that this infinite pre-apprehension is not grounded by the fact that it can apprehend nothingness as such. We must make this presupposition because nothingness grounds nothing. Nothingness cannot be the term of this pre-apprehension, cannot be what draws and moves and sets in motion that reality which man experiences as his real life and not as nothingness. To be sure, a person also has the experience of emptiness, of inner fragility, and, if we want to call it so lest we make it innocuous, of the absurdity of what confronts him. But he also experiences hope, the movement towards liberating freedom, and the responsibility which imposes upon him real burdens and also blesses them.

But if a person experiences *both* things and nevertheless his experience is *one*, and in it all the individual movements and experiences are borne by an ultimate and primordial movement, and if he cannot be a gnostic who either recognizes two primordial realities or accepts a dualism in the ultimate and primordial ground of being, if he cannot accept this because it contradicts the unity of his experience, then only *one* possibility is left: a person can understand that absolute being establishes limits and boundaries outside of itself, and that it could will something that is limited. But logically and existentielly he cannot think that the movements of hope and the desire to reach out that he really experiences are only a charming and foolish illusion. He cannot think that the ultimate ground of everything is empty nothingness, provided he gives the term "nothingness" any meaning at all, and does not simply use it to signal that real and genuine existentiell anxiety that he actually experiences.

Hence what grounds man's openness and his reaching out in the unlimited expanse of his transcendence cannot be nothingness, an absolutely empty void. For to assert that of a void would make absolutely no sense. But since on the other hand this pre-apprehension as merely a question is not self-explanatory, it must be understood as due to the working of that to which man is open, namely, being in an absolute sense. But the movement of transcendence is not the subject creating its own unlimited space as though it had absolute power over being, but it is the infinite horizon of being making itself manifest. Whenever man in his transcendence experiences himself as questioning, as disquieted by the appearance of being, as open to something ineffable, he cannot understand himself as subject in the sense of an *absolute* subject, but only in the sense of one who receives being, ultimately only in the sense of grace. In this context "grace" means the freedom of the ground of being which gives being to man, a freedom which man experiences in his finiteness and contingency, and means as well what we call "grace" in a more strictly theological sense.

THE PRE-APPREHENSION AS CONSTITUTIVE OF PERSON

Insofar as man is a transcendent being, he is confronted by himself, is responsible for himself, and hence is person and subject. For it is only in the presence of the infinity of being, as both revealed and concealed, that an existent is in a position and has a standpoint from out of which he can assume responsibility for himself. A finite system as such can experience itself as finite only if in its origins it has its own existence by the fact that, as this conscious subject, it comes from something else which is not itself and which is not just an individual system, but is the original unity which anticipates and is the fullness of every conceivable system and of every individual and distinct subject. We shall show later how it is from this that we can acquire an original, transcendental insight into what we call creatureliness.

It is self-evident that this transcendental experience of human transcendence is not the experience of some definite, particular objective thing which is experienced alongside of other objects. It is rather a basic mode of being which is prior to and permeates every objective experience. We must emphasize again and again that the transcendence meant here is not the thematically conceptualized "concept" of transcendence in which trancendence is reflected upon objectively. It is rather the a priori openness of the subject to being as such, which is present precisely when a person experiences himself as involved in the multiplicity of cares and concerns and fears and hopes of his everyday world. Real transcendence is always in the background, so to speak, in those origins of human life and human knowledge over which we have no control. This real transcendence is never captured by metaphysical reflection, and in its purity, that is, as not mediated objectively, it can be approached asymptotically at most, if at all, in mystical experience and perhaps in the experience of final loneliness in the face of death. Such an original experience of transcendence is something different from philosophical discussion about it, and precisely because it can usually be present only through the mediation of the categorical objectivity of man or of the world around him, this transcendental experience can easily be overlooked. It is present only as a secret ingredient, so to speak. But man is and remains a transcendent being, that is, he is that existent to whom the silent and uncontrollable infinity of reality is always present as mystery. This makes man totally open to this mystery and precisely in this way he becomes conscious of himself as person and as subject.

4. Man as Responsible and Free

FREEDOM AS NON-PARTICULAR DATUM

By the fact that man in his transcendence exists as open and indetermined, he is at the same time responsible for himself. He is left to himself and placed in his own hands not only in his knowledge, but also in his *actions*. It is in being consigned to himself that he experiences himself as responsible and free. What was said earlier about the relationship between man's personhood and his origins within and his determination by the world is especially true here. In the first and original instance, man's responsibility and freedom are not a particular, empirical datum of human reality alongside of others. If the more radical empirical psychology is, the less freedom it is able to find, that is perfectly consistent with its method. The traditional scholastic psychology of the schools wants to discover freedom directly as an individual, concrete datum within the realm of human transcendentality and personhood, and this is indeed a good intention, but it is doing something which basically contradicts the essence of freedom. It is not surprising if it meets with contradiction in empirical psychology. Empirical psychology must always relate one phenomenon to another and so obviously cannot discover any freedom. Even when we say in our everyday affairs that in this and that we were free, and in something else presumably not, we are not dealing with one regional phenomenon alongside of others that can be located unambiguously in time and space. Rather we are dealing at most with the application and concretization of a transcendental experience of freedom, which is something quite different from that experience with which the particular sciences are concerned.

In the first and primary instance, man's responsibility and freedom are not a particular, empirical datum in human reality alongside of other data. It is for this reason that the empirical anthropological sciences and also psychology can spare themselves the question of freedom. Of course the question of a person's freedom and responsibility is necessarily an issue in jurisprudence and in the philosophy of law. Nor do we deny that the notions of freedom, responsibility, accountability and unaccountability in the usual and everyday affairs of human life and also in the legal affairs of civil life have something to do with what we mean here. But certainly it is also clear that if there were not this transcendental experience of man's subjectivity and freedom, then neither could there be any freedom within the realm of his categorical experience, nor in civic life, nor in his personal life. But the real transcendental experience of freedom need not be explained in this primitive way as the experience of a datum that can be discovered directly within human consciousness, because in all these questions "I" always experience myself as the subject who is given over to himself. It is in this experience that something like real subjectivity and self-responsibility, and this not only in knowledge but also in action, is present as an a priori, transcendental experience of my freedom. It is only through this that I know that I am free and responsible for myself, even when I have doubts about it, raise questions about it, and cannot discover it as an individual datum of my categorical experience in time and space.

THE CONCRETE MEDIATION OF FREEDOM

Moreover, what we are calling transcendental freedom here, that is, a person's ultimate responsibility for himself, not only in knowledge, and hence not only as self-consciousness, but also as self-actualization, cannot ultimately remain hidden in an interior disposition, at least not for a genuine anthropology which sees man in the concrete and as a real unity. Freedom is always mediated by the concrete reality of time and space, of man's materiality and his history. A freedom which could not appear in the world would certainly not be a freedom of any special interest to us. Nor would it be freedom as Christianity understands it. But we shall always have to distinguish between freedom in its origin and freedom insofar as it enters into and is mediated to itself by the medium of the world and of concrete history. Reflexive freedom is always and necessarily hidden from itself because of this polarity between freedom in its origin and freedom in its categorical objectification, since it can always reflect directly only on its objectification. But this objectification always remains ambivalent. To that extent we can distinguish between freedom as originating and freedom as originated, between freedom in its origin and freedom in its concrete incarnation in the world. These are not, of course, two things which can be separated, but two moments which form the single unity of freedom.

If the empirical anthropologies establish individual elements of various kinds in man, and recognize and establish causal or functional relationships between these individual elements, and then cannot establish freedom as an individual datum within the realities they are investigating, man's real responsibility and freedom need not feel in the least threatened by this. The question whether a concrete, empirical, individual datum in the history of a person or of mankind can be interpreted as the product and incarnation of this original freedom, or whether in a particular case the opposite interpretation must be made, is a question which has not yet been decided by our considerations. And on the basis of theological data it is a question which cannot ultimately be decided about a person whose own history is still going on. For by its very nature this ultimate, transcendental freedom as concretely posited and in its origin eludes a completely unambiguous reflection. For this reason this is all the more so with regard to the presence or absence of freedom in the history of other people.

RESPONSIBILITY AND FREEDOM
AS REALITIES OF TRANSCENDENTAL EXPERIENCE

Like subjectivity and personhood, so too responsibility and freedom are realities of transcendental experience, that is, they are experienced when a subject as such experiences himself, and hence precisely not when he is objectified in a subsequent scientific reflection. When the subject experiences himself as subject, and hence as the existent which through its transcendence has an original and indissoluble unity and self-presence before being, and when this subject experiences his action as subjective action, although it cannot be made reflexive in the same way, then responsibility and freedom in an original sense are experienced in the depths of one's own existence. Corresponding to man's nature as a corporeal nature in the world, this freedom is always actualized in a multiplicity of concrete activities in time and space which are also multiple, in a multiplicity of involvements, in history and also in society. All of this is self-evident: this free action is not something which would take place only in the hidden depths of a person, outside of the world and outside of history. But man's real freedom, therefore, still continues to be one freedom because it is a transcendental characteristic of the one subject as such. We can only say, then, that because and insofar as I experience myself as person and as subject, I also experience myself as free, as free in a freedom which does not refer primarily to an individual, isolated psychic occurrence, but in a freedom which refers to the subject as one and as a whole in the unity of its entire actualization of existence.

How this is actualized in time and space, over the length and breadth of an historical existence and in the concrete multiplicity of human life, this is a question which we cannot decide unambiguously. This freedom, then, is not a neutral power which one has and possesses as something different from himself. It is rather a fundamental characteristic of a personal existent, who experiences himself in what he has already done and is still to do in time as self-possession, as one who is responsible and has to give an account, and this includes the moment when a subjective and personal response to the infinite and the incomprehensible confronts this existent in his transcendence, and is either accepted or rejected.

Just as with subjectivity, so too a person can evade his responsibility and freedom, and can interpret himself as the product of what is not himself. But this very act of self-interpretation which we perform—which we must not confuse with the content of this interpretation—is something done by the subject who denies his subjectivity or interprets his freedom as being condemned to the senseless arbitrariness of what is foreign to him. In doing this he is acting as a free subject, and in denying his subjectivity he is actually affirming it. In other words: freedom always concerns the person as such and as a whole. The object of freedom in its original sense is the subject himself, and all decisions about objects in his experience of the world around him are objects of freedom only insofar as they mediate this finite subject in time and space to himself. When freedom is really understood, it is not the power to be able to do this or that, but the power to decide about oneself and to actualize oneself.

This must not be understood, of course, as though the subject were outside of history, society and the world. It is rather the formality under which the essence of freedom has to be understood and discussed. The material content of what is being said here formally is something else again. If someone says that man always experiences himself as determined and controlled from without, as functional and dependent, as able to be analyzed and reduced into antecedents and consequences, the reply must be: the subject who knows this is always at the same time a responsible subject who is challenged to say something and to do something with man's absolute dependence and self-alienation and determination, challenged to take a position on it by either cursing it or accepting it, by being sceptical or by despairing, or whatever. So even when a person would abandon himself into the hands of the empirical anthropologies, he still remains in his own hands. He does not escape from his freedom, and the only question can be how he interprets himself, and freely interprets himself.

5. The Question of Personal Existence as a Question of Salvation

THE THEOLOGICAL AND ANTHROPOLOGICAL STARTING POINT FOR AN UNDERSTANDING OF "SALVATION"

Insofar as man as a free subject is responsible and accountable for himself, insofar as he is in his own hands as the object of an act of his real freedom, an act which is one in its origin and touches the whole of his human existence, we can now enter into a discussion of man's salvation and of the fact that the real question about personal existence is in truth a question about salvation. When one does not see the original starting point for an understanding of salvation in the subject and rooted in the very nature of freedom, salvation can only appear very strange and sound like mythology. But basically this is not the case. For the true theological notion of salvation does not mean a future situation which befalls a person unexpectedly like something coming from outside, and this happily or, if it is the opposite of salvation, unhappily. Nor does it mean something bestowed on him only on the basis of a moral judgment. It means rather the final and definitive validity of a person's true self-understanding and true self-realization in freedom before God by the fact that he accepts his own self as it is disclosed and offered to him in the choice of transcendence as interpreted in freedom. Man's eternity can only be understood as freedom existing beyond time in its real and definitive validity. Everything else can only be followed by more time, but not by eternity, eternity which is not the opposite of time, but is the fulfillment of time and of freedom actualized in time.

In view of this one of our most important and most difficult tasks is to make clear again and again that, in spite of what Christianity says about the *history* of salvation, what it says about man always refers to him in the deepest origins and roots of his being, in his transcendental essence. Consequently, we can speak about it ultimately only in such a way that the transcendental nature of the one question which man is in his transcendence towards the all-encompassing mystery is not made categorical in a *false* way.

SALVATION IN HISTORY

But man as a personal being of transcendence and of freedom is also and at the same time a being in the world, in time and in history. This assertion is fundamental in describing the presuppositions which the message of Christianity ascribes to man. For if the realm of transcendence and of salvation were not understood from the outset to include man's history and his being in the world and in time, then the question of salvation and the message of salvation could not take place in history nor refer to a historical reality.

On the other hand it is not necessary here to distinguish clearly between the notions of being in the world, being in time, and being in history, especially since the latter notion of historicity includes the other two as aspects of itself. But what these notions mean, and what is decisive for a correct interpretation of Christianity is this: being in the world, being in time and being in history are aspects of man which he does not merely *have* alongside of and in addition to his free personhood. They are rather aspects of the free subjectivity of a person as such. Man is not merely *also* a biological and social organism who exists in time with these characteristics. Rather his subjectivity and his free, personal self-interpretation take place precisely in and through his being in the world, in time, and in history, or better, in and through world, time and history. The question of salvation cannot be answered by bypassing man's historicity and his social nature. Transcendentality and freedom are realized in history. Even the profane study of history *(Historie)* is itself historical *(geschichtlich)*, and is a part of man's historical self-understanding taking place on a reflexive level. Man possesses his eternal essence, as something given to him and as something for which he is responsible in his freedom and reflection, in the fact that he experiences, suffers and acts out his history.

Historicity means that characteristic and fundamental determination of man by which he is placed in time precisely as a free subject, and through which a unique world is at his disposal, a world which he must create and suffer in freedom, and for which in both instances he must take responsibility. Man's being-in-the-world, his permanent dispersion in the other of a world which he finds and which is imposed upon him, a world of things and a world of persons, is an intrinsic element of the subject himself, an element which he must understand and live out in freedom, but which thereby becomes something of eternal validity for him. As subject man has not entered accidentally into this material and temporal world as into something which is ultimately foreign to him as subject and contradictory to his spiritual nature. Rather the subject's self-alienation in world is precisely the way in which the subject discovers himself and affirms himself in a definitive way. Time, world and history mediate the subject to himself and to that immediate and free self-possession towards which a personal subject is oriented and towards which he is always striving.

If man's historicity and therefore his concrete history is an intrinsic and constitutive element of a spiritual and free subject, then neither can the question of his salvation as the question addressed to the subject as a single whole and in his freedom leave out history. It is in history that the subject must work out his salvation by finding it there as offered to him and accepting it. If historicity is an existential of the subject himself, then there must be a history of salvation and its opposite, because the question of salvation is addressed to his freedom. Or conversely: what is meant by the question of salvation can be understood only in light of the essence of freedom. Hence salvation history and history as such must be ultimately coexistent, whereby of course a genuine differentiation is not excluded penultimately. If the subject involved in salvation is historical, then history itself is the history of salvation, although in a hidden way and always still in progress until the final and definitive interpretation. If the intercommunication of spiritual subjects in truth and in love and in society belongs to the realization of one's own existence because it is a historical existence, and belongs to it as an intrinsic and constitutive element and not as its extrinsic material, then the unity of the history of all mankind and the unity of a salvation history is from the outset a transcendental characteristic of the personal history of every individual, and vice versa, because we are dealing with the history of many subjects.

6. Man as Dependent

THE PRESENCE OF MYSTERY

In spite of his free subjectivity, man experiences himself as being at the disposal of other things, a disposal over which he has no control. First of all, being constituted as transcendental subject, he is in the presence of being as mystery, a mystery which constantly reveals itself and at the same time conceals itself. We mentioned earlier that his transcendentality cannot be understood as that of an absolute subject which experiences and possesses what opens before it as something subject to its own power. His transcendentality is rather a relationship which does not establish itself by its own power, but is experienced as something which was established by and is at the disposal of another, and which is grounded in the abyss of ineffable mystery.

MAN AS CONDITIONED BY WORLD AND BY HISTORY

Beyond that, man always experiences himself both in his activity in the world and also in his theoretical, objective reflection as one to whom an historical situation in a world of things and of persons has been given in advance, given without his having chosen it for himself, although it is in and through it that he discovers and is conscious of transcendence. Man is always conscious of his historical limitations, his historical origins, and the contingency of his origins. But this places him in the quite specific situation which characterizes man's nature: insofar as he experiences his historical conditioning, he is already beyond it in a certain sense, but nevertheless he cannot really leave it behind. Being situated in this way between the finite and the infinite is what constitutes man, and is shown by the fact that it is in his infinite transcendence and in his freedom that man experiences himself as dependent and historically conditioned.

Man never establishes his own freedom in some absolute sense, in the sense of a freedom which could make complete use of the material which is given to him in his freedom, or could cast it off in an absolute self-sufficiency. He never realizes completely his possibilities in the world and in history. Nor can he distance himself from them and withdraw into the pure essence of a pseudo-subjectivity or pseudo-interiority in such a way that he could honestly say that he had become independent of the world and the history that was given him. In an ultimate and inescapable way, man even as doer and maker is still receiving and being made. What he experiences in himself is always a synthesis: of possibilities presented to his freedom and his free disposition of self, of what is himself and what is the other, of acting and suffering, of knowing and doing, and these elements are synthesized in a unity which cannot be completely and objectively analyzed. Therefore insofar as reflection can never control or master or grasp the totality of the ground from out of which and towards which the subject is actualizing himself, man is the unknown not only in this or that area of his concrete reality, but he is the subject whose origin and end remain hidden from himself. He comes to the real truth about himself precisely by the fact that he patiently endures and accepts this knowledge that his own reality is not in his own hands.

All of the ideas which we have used here on that level of reflection which we have consciously chosen should be seen only as an attempt to evoke an understanding of existence in the light of which every individual, in the concrete experience of his own existence, must himself experience that this self-understanding is basically inescapable, whether one chooses to accept it or to protest against it. This is so however little the concepts, words and statements we have used can really and adequately recapture, or were intended to recapture, the real and original experience of personhood and freedom, of subjectivity, of history and historicity, and of dependence.

· II ·

Man in the Presence of Absolute Mystery

This second chapter is a conceptual reflection upon that transcendental experience in which a person comes into the presence of the absolute mystery which we call "God," an experience which is more primary than reflection and cannot be recaptured completely by reflection. What has to be said here has already been said less explicitly in the first chapter. If man really is a subject, that is, a transcendent, responsible and free being who as subject is both entrusted into his own hands and always in the hands of what is beyond his control, then basically this has already said that man is a being oriented towards God. His orientation towards the absolute mystery always continues to be offered to him by this mystery as the ground and content of his being. To understand man in this way, of course, does not mean that when we use the term "God" in such a statement, we know what this term means from any other source except through this orientation to mystery. At this point theology and anthropology necessarily become one. A person knows explicitly what is meant by "God" only insofar as he allows his transcendence beyond everything objectively identifiable to enter into his consciousness, accepts it, and objectifies in reflection what is already present in his transcendentality.

1. Meditation on the Word "God"

THE EXISTENCE OF THE WORD

It is natural to begin with a brief reflection on the word "God." This is so not merely because, in contrast to a thousand other experiences which can get a hearing even without words, it could be that in this case the *word* alone is capable of giving us access to what it means. But for a much more simple reason we can and perhaps must begin a reflection on God himself with the word "God." For we do not have an experience of God as we have of a tree, another person and other external realities which, although they are perhaps never there before us absolutely nameless, yet they evoke their name by themselves because they simply appear within the realm of our experience at a definite point in time and space, and so by themselves they press immediately for a name. We can say, therefore, that what is most simple and most inescapable for man with regard to the question of God is the fact that the word "God" exists in his intellectual and spiritual existence.

We cannot evade this simple, although ambiguous fact by looking to a possible future and asking if a human race could ever exist in which the word "God" would absolutely disappear. In this case, either the question whether this word has a meaning and refers to a reality outside of itself would not arise any more, or it would arise at a completely new point where what had earlier been the origin of this word would have to achieve presence in a new way and with a new word. In any case, the word exists among us. Its existence is prolonged even by an atheist when he says that there is no God, and that something like God has no specifiable meaning; when he founds a museum without God, raises atheism to the level of a party dogma, and devises other similar things. In this way even the atheist is helping the word "God" to survive longer. If he wanted to avoid that, he would not only have to *hope* that this word would simply disappear in human existence and in the language of society. He would also have to contribute to this disappearance by keeping dead silence about it himself and not declaring himself an atheist. But how is he to do that if others, with whom he must speak and from whose language sphere he cannot completely withdraw, talk about God and are concerned about this word?

The mere fact that this word exists is worth thinking about. When we speak about the word "God" this way, we do not only mean of course the German word. Whether we say *Gott* or "God" or the Latin *deus* or the Semitic *El* or the old Mexican *teotl*, that makes no difference here. It would, however, be an extremely obscure and difficult question to ask how we could know that the same thing or the same person is meant by these different words, because in each of these cases we cannot simply point to a common experience of what is meant independently of the word itself. But for the time being we shall pass over this problem whether the many words for "God" are synonymous.

There are also, of course, names of God or of gods in places where a pantheon of gods is worshipped polytheistically, or where, as in ancient

Israel, the one, all-powerful God has a proper name, Yahweh, because they were convinced that they had quite definite and specific experiences with him in their own history. Without prejudice to his incomprehensibility and hence his namelessness, these experiences characterize him and thus bestow upon him a proper name. But we shall not discuss here these names of God in the plural.

WHAT DOES THE WORD "GOD" MEAN?

The word "God" exists. This by itself is worth thinking about. However, at least the German word says nothing or nothing more than that *about* God. Whether this was always the case in the earliest history of the word is another question. In any case the word "God" functions today like a proper name. One has to know from other sources what or who it means. Usually we do not notice this, but it is true. If we were to call God "Father," for example, or "Lord," or the "heavenly being," or something similar, as happens all the time in the history of religion, then the word by itself would say something about what it means because of its origins in other experiences we have and in its secular usage. But here it looks in the first instance as though the word confronts us like a blank face. It says nothing about what it means, nor can it simply function like an index finger which points to something encountered immediately outside of the word. Then it would not have to say anything about what it means, as is the case when we say "tree" or "table" or "sun."

Nevertheless, because this word is so very much without contour (and it is because of this that the first question has to be: What is this word really supposed to say?) it is obviously quite appropriate for what it refers to, regardless of whether the word may have originally been so "faceless" or not. We can prescind, then, from the question whether the history of the word began with another form of the word. In any case, the present form of the word reflects what the word refers to: the "ineffable one," the "nameless one" who does not enter into the world we can name as a part of it. It means the "silent one" who is always there, and yet can always be overlooked, unheard, and, because it expresses the whole in its unity and totality, can be passed over as meaningless. It means that which really is wordless, because every word receives its limits, its own sound and hence its intelligible sense only within a field of words. Hence what has become faceless, that is, the word "God" which no longer refers by itself to a definite, individual experience, has assumed the right form to be able to speak to us of God. For it is the final word before we become silent, the word which allows all the individual things we can name to disappear into the background, the word in which we are dealing with the totality which grounds them all.

DOES THIS WORD HAVE A FUTURE?

The word "God" exists. We return to the starting point of our reflection, to the plain fact that in the world of words, by which we form our world and without which even so-called facts do not exist for us, the word "God" also appears. Even for the atheist, even for those who declare that God is dead, even for them, as we saw, God exists at least as that which they must declare dead, whose ghost they must banish, and whose return they fear. One could not be at peace about him until the word itself no longer existed, that is, until even the question about him would not have to be asked any more. But it is still there, this word, it is present. Does it also have a future? Marx thought that atheism too would disappear, hence that the very word "God," used in affirmation or in denial, would disappear. Is a future for the word "God" conceivable? Perhaps this question is meaningless because a genuine future is something radically new which cannot be calculated in advance. Or perhaps this question is merely theoretical and in reality it becomes a challenge to our freedom, whether we shall go on saying "God" tomorrow as believers or as unbelievers, challenging each other by affirming, denying or doubting. However the question about the future of the word "God" might be settled, the believer simply sees only two possibilities and no other alternative: either the word will disappear without a trace and leave no residue, or it will survive, one way or another a question for everybody.

REALITY WITHOUT THIS WORD

Consider for a moment these two possibilities. The word "God" will have disappeared without a trace and without an echo, without leaving any visible gap behind, without being replaced by another word which challenges us in the same way, without at least only a question, or better, *the* question even being raised by this word because people do not want to say or hear this word as an answer. What would it be like if this hypothesis about the future is taken seriously? Then man would no longer be brought face to face with the single whole of reality, nor with the single whole of his own existence. For this is exactly what the word "God" does and it alone, however it might be defined phonetically or in its genesis. If the word "God" really did not exist, then neither would these two things exist any more for man, the single whole of reality as such and the single whole of human existence in the mutual interpenetration of both aspects.

Man would forget all about himself in his preoccupation with all the individual details of his world and his existence. *Ex supposito* he would never face the totality of the world and of himself helplessly, silently and anxiously. He would not notice any more that he was only an individual existent, and not being as such. He would not notice that he only considered questions, and not the question about questioning itself. He would not notice anymore that he was only manipulating in different ways different aspects of his existence, and never faced his existence in its unity and totality. He would remain mired *in* the world and *in* himself, and no longer go through that mysterious process which he *is*. It is a process in which, as it were, the whole of the "system" which he is along with his world reflects deeply about itself in its unity and totality, freely takes responsibility for itself, and thus transcends and reaches beyond itself to that silent mystery which seems like nothingness, and out of which he now comes to himself and his world, affirming both and taking responsibility for both.

Man would have forgotten the totality and its ground, and at the same time, if we can put it this way, would have forgotten that he had forgotten. What would it be like? We can only say: he would have ceased being a man. He would have regressed to the level of a clever animal. We can no longer say so readily today that man exists when an earthly being walks upright, makes fire, and fashions stone into tools. We can only say that man exists when this living being in reflection, in words and in freedom places the totality of the world and of existence before himself in question, even if he might become helplessly silent before *this* one and total question. Perhaps it would even be conceivable, and who can know for sure, that the human race, although it would survive biologically and technologically, would die a collective death and regress back into a colony of unusually resourceful animals. Whether this is a real possibility or not, the believer who uses the word "God" would not have to dread this would-be "utopia" as a disavowal of his faith.

For he is familiar with a merely biological consciousness and, if we want to call it such, an animal intelligence in which the question about the totality has not arisen and for which the word "God" has not become part of its destiny. Nor would he be all that confident about saying what such a biological intelligence can accomplish without entering into that destiny which is characterized by the word "God." But man really exists as man only when he uses the word "God" at least as a question, at least as a negating and negated question. The absolute death of the word "God," including even the eradication of its past, would be the signal, no longer heard by anyone, that man himself had died. As we said, perhaps such a collective death is conceivable. This would not have to be any more extraordinary than the death of an individual person and of a sinner. When the question would no longer exist, when the question would simply have died and disappeared, then naturally one would no longer have to give an answer, but neither could he give a negative answer. Nor could this lacuna, if one conceived of it as a possibility, be made an argument that what is meant by "God" does not exist, because if it were, one would have to give an answer, although only a negative answer, to this question. Hence the fact that the question about the death of the word "God" can be raised shows again that the word "God" still survives even in and through the protest against it.

THE SURVIVAL OF THE WORD "GOD"

The second possibility to be considered is: the word "God" will survive. Every individual in his intellectual and spiritual existence lives by the language of all. He has his ever so individual and unique experience of existence only in and with the language in which he lives, from which he does not escape, and whose verbal associations, perspectives and selective a prioris he appropriates, even when he protests against them and when he is himself involved in the ever-ongoing history of language. One has to allow language to have its say because one has to use it to speak and use it to protest against it. A final and basic trust cannot reasonably be denied it if one does not want to be absolutely silent or contradict himself. Now the word "God" exists in the language in which and from which we live and accept responsibility for our existence.

But it is not just some accidental word which appeared suddenly in language at some arbitrary moment and at another disappeared again without a trace, like "phlogiston" and other words. For the word "God" places in question the whole world of language in which reality is present for us. For it asks about reality as a whole and in its original ground. Moreover, the question about the totality of the world of language exists in that peculiar paradox which is proper precisely to language because language itself is a part of the world, and at the same time it is the whole of it as known. When language speaks of anything it also expresses itself, itself as a whole and in relation to its ground, which is distant but present in its distance. It is precisely this that is pointed to when we say "God," although we do not mean thereby identically the same thing as language itself as a whole, but rather its empowering ground. But for this very reason the word "God" is not just any word, but is the word in which language, that is, the self-expression of the self-presence of world and human existence together, grasps itself in its ground. This word *exists*, it belongs in a special and unique way to our world of language and thus to our world. It is itself a reality, and indeed one that we cannot avoid. This reality might be present speaking clearly or obscurely, softly or loudly. But it is there at least as a question.

THE ORIGINAL WORD SPOKEN TO US

At this point and in this context we are not yet concerned with how we respond to this word and this event, whether we accept it as pointing to God himself, or whether in despairing rage we refuse to allow this word to make demands upon us, because, as part of the world of language, it would force us, who are also a part of the world, to face the totality of the world and of ourselves without being able to be the whole or to master it. And at this point we are also leaving entirely open the question how this original totality is defined and related to the world of plurality and to the multiplicity of words in the world of language.

At this point we can only call attention to one thing somewhat more clearly than before, since it touches upon the topic of the word "God" directly. If we understand correctly what has been said about the word "God" up to now, then it is not the case that each of us as an individual thinks "God" in an active process and that *in this way* the word "God" enters into the realm of our existence for the first time. Rather we *hear and receive the word "God."* It comes to us in the history of language in which we are caught whether we want to be or not, which poses questions to us as individuals without itself being at our disposal. The history of language which is given to us, and in which the word "God" occurs as a question to us, is in this way an image and likeness of what it announces. We should not think that, because the phonetic sound of the word "God" is always dependent on us, therefore the word "God" is also our creation. Rather it creates us because it makes us men.

The real word "God" is not simply identical with the word "God" which appears in a dictionary lost among thousands and thousands of other words. For this dictionary word "God" only represents the real word which becomes present for us from out of the wordless texture of all words through their context and through their unity and totality, which itself exists and is present for us. This real word confronts us with ourselves and with reality as a whole, at least as a question. This word exists. It is in our history and makes our history. It is a word. For this reason one can fail to hear it, with ears, as scripture says, which hear and do not understand. But it does not cease to exist because of that. In antiquity Tertullian's insight about the *anima naturaliter Christiana,* that is, the soul that is Christian from its origins, is derived from the inescapability of the word "God." It exists. It comes from those origins from which man himself comes. Its demise can be thought of only along with the death of man himself. It can still have a history whose changing forms we cannot imagine in advance precisely because it is what keeps an uncontrollable and unplanned future open. It is our opening to the incomprehensible mystery. It makes demands on us, and it might irritate us because it disturbs the peace of an existence which wants to have the peace of what is clear and distinct and planned.

It is always open to Wittgenstein's protest, which bids us to be silent about things which we cannot speak about clearly. Notice, however, that he violates this rule in formulating it. The word itself agrees with this maxim if correctly understood. For it is itself the final word before wordless and worshipful silence in the face of the ineffable mystery. It is the word which must be spoken at the conclusion of all speaking if, instead of silence in worship, there is not to follow that death in which man becomes a resourceful animal or a sinner lost forever. It is an almost ridiculously exhausting and demanding word. If we were not hearing it *this way,* then we would be hearing it as a word about something obvious and comprehensible in everyday life, as a word alongside other words. Then we would have heard something which has nothing in common with the true word "God" but its phonetic sound. We are familiar with the Latin expression *amor fati,* the love of one's destiny. This resolve in the face of one's destiny means literally "love for the word that has been uttered," that is, for that *fatum* which is our destiny. Only this love for what is necessary liberates our freedom. This *fatum* is ultimately the word "God."

2. The Knowledge of God

TRANSCENDENTAL AND A POSTERIORI KNOWLEDGE OF GOD

What we are calling transcendental knowledge or experience of God is an *a posteriori* knowledge insofar as man's transcendental experience of his free subjectivity takes place only in his encounter with the world and especially with other people. To that extent the scholastic tradition is correct when it emphasizes against ontologism that man's *only* knowledge of God is an a posteriori knowledge from the world. This is still true even with verbal revelation because this too has to work with human concepts. Hence our transcendental knowledge or experience has to be called a posteriori insofar as every transcendental experience is mediated by a categorical encounter with concrete reality in our world, both the world of things and the world of persons. This is also true of the knowledge of God. To that extent we can and we must say that all knowledge of God is an a posteriori knowledge which comes from and through encountering the world, to which, of course, we ourselves also belong.

The knowledge of God is, nevertheless, a *transcendental* knowledge because man's basic and original orientation towards absolute mystery, which constitutes his fundamental experience of God, is a permanent existential of man as a spiritual subject. This means that the explicit, conceptual and thematic knowledge, which we usually think of when we speak of the knowledge of God or of proofs for God's existence, is a reflection upon man's transcendental orientation towards mystery, and some degree of reflection is always necessary. It is not, however, the original and foundational mode of the transcendental experience of this mystery. It belongs necessarily to the very nature of human knowledge that thought is self-reflexive, that we think of a concrete object *within* the *infinite* and apparently empty horizon of thinking itself, that thinking is conscious of itself. We must get used to taking account of the fact that when we think and when we exercise freedom we are always dealing with more and always have to do with more than that which we are talking *about* in our words and concepts, and that *with which* we are occupied here and now as the concrete object of our activity. If one cannot see both the distinction *and* the unity in this bipolarity in knowledge and in freedom, that is, objective consciousness and subjective consciousness, or, as Blondel puts it, willed will and willing will, then basically he cannot see the point of what we are saying: that *speaking* of God is the reflection which points to a more original, unthematic and unreflexive knowledge of God.

We become conscious of ourselves and of the transcendental structures that are given with our subjectivity only in the fact that the world presents itself to us concretely and in quite definite ways, and hence in the fact that we are involved in the world both passively and actively. This is also true of the knowledge of God. In this sense it is not a knowledge which is grounded entirely in itself. But neither is it simply a mystical process within our own personal interiority, nor, in the light of this, does it have the character of a personal, divine self-revelation. But the a posteriori character of the knowledge of God would be misunderstood if we were to overlook the transcendental element in it and understand the knowledge of God after the model of an a posteriori knowledge whose object comes entirely from without and appears in a neutral faculty of knowledge. In the knowledge of God a posteriority does not mean that we look out into the world with a neutral faculty of knowledge and then think that we can discover God there directly or indirectly among the realities that present themselves to us objectively, or that we can prove his existence indirectly.

We are oriented towards God. This original experience is always present, and it should not be confused with the objectifying, although necessary, reflection upon man's transcendental orientation towards mystery. This does not destroy the a posteriori character of the knowledge of God, but neither should this a posteriority be misunderstood in the sense that God could simply be indoctrinated from without as an object of our knowledge.

This unthematic and ever-present experience, this knowledge of God which we always have even when we are thinking of and concerned with anything but God, is the permanent ground from out of which that thematic knowledge of God emerges which we have in explicitly religious activity and in philosophical reflection. It is not in these latter that we discover God just as we discover a particular object of our experience within the world. Rather, both in this explicitly religious activity directed to God in prayer and in metaphysical reflection we are only making explicit for ourselves what we already know implicitly about ourselves in the depths of our personal self-realization. Hence we know our subjective freedom, our transcendence and the infinite openness of the spirit even where and when we do not make them thematic at all. We also know them when such a conceptual, objectifying thematization and verbal expression of this original knowledge perhaps does not succeed at all, or succeeds very imperfectly and distortedly. Indeed we even know them when we refuse to engage at all in such a process of thematization.

For this reason the meaning of all explicit knowledge of God in religion and in metaphysics is intelligible and can really be understood only when all the words we use there point to the unthematic experience of our orientation towards the ineffable mystery. And just as it is of the nature of transcendent spirit, because it is constituted in an objective world, always to offer along with this objectivity the possibility, both in theory and in practice, of running away from its own subjectivity, from taking responsibility for itself in freedom, so too a person can also hide from himself his transcendental orientation towards the absolute mystery which we call God. As scripture says (Rom. 1:18), he can in this way suppress the most real truth about himself.

The individual realities with which we are usually dealing in our lives always become clearly intelligible and comprehensible and manipulable because we can differentiate them from other things. There is no such way of knowing God. Because God is something quite different from any of the individual realities which appear within the realm of our experience or which are inferred from it, and because the knowledge of God has a quite definite and unique character and is not just an instance of knowledge in general, it is for these reasons very easy to overlook God. The concept "God" is not a grasp of God by which a person masters the mystery, but it is letting oneself be grasped by the mystery which is present and yet ever distant. This mystery remains a mystery even though it reveals itself to man and thus continually grounds the possibility of man being a subject. There can then follow from this ground, of course, the so-called concept of God, explicit language about him, words and what we mean by them and try to say to ourselves reflexively, and certainly a person ought not to avoid the effort involved in this process of reflexive conceptualization. But in order to remain true, all metaphysical ontology about God must return again and again to its source, must return to the transcendental experience of our orientation towards the absolute mystery, and to the existentiell practice of accepting this orientation freely. This acceptance takes place in unconditional obedience to conscience, and in the open and trusting acceptance of the uncontrollable in one's own existence in moments of prayer and quiet silence.

Since the original experience of God is not an encounter with an individual object *alongside of* other objects, and since in the human subject's transcendental experience God is absolutely beyond us in his transcendence, we can speak of God and the experience of God, and of creatureliness and the experience of creatureliness only *together*, in spite of the difference of what is meant in each instance.

It could be asked at this point: But if these two things are connected in this way, then are we only able to say something about what God is *for us*, and not able to say anything about what God is *in himself?* But if we have understood what is meant by the absolutely unlimited transcendentality of the human spirit, then we can say that the alternative of such a radical distinction between a statement about "God in himself" and "God for us" is not even legitimate. What is meant by the deepest characteristic of the human subject in his freedom and his dependence, and hence in his creatureliness, and what is meant by God himself can be understood only by taking into account that basic situation in which human existence finds itself, a situation in which man is in possession of himself and is radically alienated from himself because of the fact that the mystery addresses him in its absoluteness and remains at a distance as distinct from man. For this reason neither can we form a concept of God in the proper sense and then ask afterwards if it exists in the real order. The concept in its original ground and the reality itself to which this concept refers move beyond us and enter the unknown together.

THE DIFFERENT WAYS OF KNOWING GOD AND THEIR INTRINSIC UNITY

Before we begin to discuss the knowledge of God, we have to reflect briefly on other distinctions in the knowledge of God which are made in traditional theology. *First of all,* it is customary in Catholic theology to speak of a so-called natural knowledge of God in which, as the First Vatican Council said (*D.S.* 3004), God can be known at least in principle by the light of natural reason without revelation in the proper sense. This is an a posteriori knowledge, but this must be understood correctly. *Secondly,* besides this so-called natural knowledge of God the school theology speaks of a knowledge of God by means of what we call the Christian revelation *in word* in the proper sense: a knowledge of God by means of his own revelation. It presupposes the knowledge that such a divine revelation in word has taken place and then asks what God has communicated about himself in this divine revelation, for example, that he absolves man's guilt, that he has a universal, supernatural salvific will for man, that he has created on man's behalf a historically concrete existence for himself in what we call the Incarnation, and so on.

Thirdly, we would perhaps have to speak of a knowledge of God which comes about by means of his self-revelatory *salvific activity* in the history of the human race and in that of the individual. In this knowledge God's action and his existence are known together through the effective witness he gives to himself. Even if one is not interested in mysticism and "visions," he cannot deny a priori that there can be a knowledge of God from and in man's individual and collective personal experience of existence. This does not have to be identified either with what is meant by the natural knowledge of God, nor with what is meant by the universal self-revelation of God in *word* and in the history of revelation understood merely verbally.

In its Constitution on Divine Revelation (*Dei Verbum*, Chapter 1), the Second Vatican Council tried to associate and to link together as closely as possible the historical action in and through which God reveals himself and revelation as divine self-communication in human *word.* Consequently, we can join together in our consideration the third way of knowing God just mentioned and the second, namely, the knowledge of God by means of his own *verbal* revelation in grace. But we shall have to go into this in more detail later.

If it is our intention to discuss the knowledge of God, we are not concerned primarily with the distinctions of school theology. We are aiming rather at a more original unity among these three modes of knowledge in concrete human existence. That is also legitimate from a philosophical starting point. If we reflect upon our knowledge of God as upon a historically constituted transcendental experience which, by the very nature of the situation in which man knows, always implies a philosophical knowledge in the proper sense, but which also cannot in principle be completely recaptured in such knowledge, then we must simply reckon with the fact that this knowledge contains elements which a subsequent theological reflection will appeal to as elements of grace and revelation. Everything which we say here about the knowledge of God is indeed said in words, but it refers to a more original experience. That is both possible and legitimate philosophically. The philosopher too can recognize that his philosophical reflection cannot completely recapture that original knowledge.

What we are referring to here is not a natural philosophical knowledge of God, although it includes an element of this. At least in principle, however, it goes beyond that. What we want to discuss refers to the historically constituted transcendental experience of God which is not supposed to be transposed by our discussion of it merely into metaphysics in a strictly philosophical sense. Our discussion will rather simply appeal to this experience of God. Not only can our discussion of the knowledge of God not take the place of the original, transcendental, and yet historically constituted experience of God, but it is not even intended to be a complete philosophical discussion of it.

The original and fundamental unity of the three ways of knowing God which were mentioned is also completely legitimate for a theological reason. According to the Christian and Catholic understanding, in the concrete order of salvation there is no realization of man's being which does not take place within the dimension of that finalization of man's self-realization towards the immediacy of God which we call grace. And in this grace there is included a moment of revelation in the proper, although transcendental, sense.

In the concrete actualization of existence, therefore, there is no knowledge of God which is purely natural, since even theological knowledge is an activity of man which takes place in freedom. In a subsequent theological reflection I can indeed specify elements in the concrete knowledge of God which I ascribe and can ascribe to nature, to the realization of man's essence as such. But the concrete knowledge of God as a question, as a call which is affirmed or denied, is always within the dimension of man's supernatural determination. From a theological point of view, even the rejection of a natural knowledge of God, an unthematic or thematic atheism, is at the same time always and inevitably the at least unthematic "no" by which a person closes himself to the orientation of human existence towards the immediacy of God. We call this orientation grace, and it is an inescapable existential of man's whole being even when he closes himself to it freely by rejecting it.

To put it in other words: from a theological point of view, the *concrete* process of the so-called natural knowledge of God in either its acceptance or its rejection is always more than a merely natural knowledge of God. This is true when the knowing takes place unthematically in the basic and original self-interpretation of human existence as well as when it is reflexive, thematic knowledge.

The knowledge of God we are concerned with, then, is that concrete, original, historically constituted and transcendental knowledge of God which either in the mode of acceptance or of rejection is inevitably present in the depths of existence in the most ordinary human life. It is at once both natural knowledge and knowledge in grace, it is at once both knowledge and revelation-faith, so that distinguishing its elements is a subsequent task of philosophy and theology, but not really a reflexive act for this original knowledge itself.

TRANSCENDENTAL KNOWLEDGE OF GOD AS EXPERIENCE OF MYSTERY

The knowledge of God we are referring to here is rooted in that subjectivity and free transcendence and in that situation of not being at one's own disposal which we tried at least to sketch. Now this transcendental experience, which is always mediated by a categorical experience of the concrete and individual data of our experience in the world and in time and space (all of our experience, including so-called "secular" experience), may not be understood as a neutral power by which, among other things, God can be known. It is rather the basic and original way of knowing God, so much so that the knowledge of God we are referring to here simply constitutes the very essence of this transcendence.

The transcendence in which God is already known, although unthematically and nonconceptually, may not be understood as an active mastering of the knowledge of God by one's own power, and hence also as a mastery of God himself. For this transcendence appears as what it is only in the self-disclosure of that towards which the movement of transcendence tends. It exists by means of that which gives itself in this transcendence as the other, the other which distinguishes this transcendence from itself and enables it to be experienced as mystery by the subject who is constituted as such by this transcendence. By its very nature subjectivity is always a transcendence which listens, which does not control, which is overwhelmed by mystery and opened up by mystery. In the midst of its absolute infinity transcendence experiences itself as empty, as merely formal, as necessarily mediated to itself by finiteness, and hence as a finite infinity. If it does not want to mistake itself for an absolute subject and divinize itself, it recognizes itself as a transcendence which has been bestowed upon it, which is grounded in mystery, and is not at its own disposal. For all its infinity it experiences itself as radically finite. It is precisely in and through the infinity of its transcendence that it is a transcendence which can grasp its own finiteness and must grasp it.

Transcendence strictly as such knows only *God* and nothing else, although it knows him as the condition which makes possible categorical knowledge, history and concrete freedom. Transcendence exists only by opening itself beyond itself, and, to put it in biblical language, it is in its origin and from the very beginning the experience of *being known* by God himself. The word which says everything by saying "God" is always experienced in its origin and by its very nature as a response in which the mystery, while remaining mystery, offers himself to man.

The unity between transcendence and its term cannot be understood as a unity between two elements related equally to each other, but only as the unity between that which grounds and disposes freely and that which is grounded. It is a unity in the sense of a unity between an original word and the response to it which is made possible by the word. This unity can be described in different ways because the unity as well as the primary and the ultimate element in it can only be expressed helplessly by means of the second and conditioned element, by means of the second and conditioned element which never really comprehends the first element. We can speak of transcendence only by speaking of its term, and we can make the specific nature of the term intelligible only by speaking about the specific nature of transcendence as such.

If we wanted to understand this basic and original knowledge of God in transcendence only from its subjective pole, that is, if we wanted to clarify the nature of transcendence in order to clarify from this vantage point what the term towards which the transcendence moves really is, then we would have the difficulty of having to describe intentionality as such without discussing its term. Besides that, we would also have the burden of having to look for an existentiell mystagogy which would describe and focus the attention of each individual in his concrete existence on those experiences in which he in his individuality had the experience of transcendence and of being taken up out of himself into the ineffable mystery. Since the clarity and persuasiveness of the various individual experiences of this kind—for example, in anxiety, in the subject's absolute concern, in love's unshrinking acceptance of responsibility in freedom, in joy, and so on—vary a great deal in individual persons corresponding to the differences in their historical existence, such a mystagogy into one's own personal and individual experience of transcendence would have to vary a great deal from person to person. Such a mystagogy, in which the individual person is made aware of the fact that this experience of transcendence really takes place repeatedly and without being called such in his immediate involvement with the concrete world, could be possible for the individual person only in individual conversation and in individual logotherapy.

Therefore, we want to attempt a description of this basic and original knowledge of God here by pointing out where this transcendence is directed and what it encounters, or better, what is the source by which it is opened up. But the situation is such that our description of the term or the source of transcendence can only be understood if it calls attention repeatedly to transcendental experience as such, which is so obvious and unobtrusive that it can easily be overlooked.

Even when we look to the term and the source of transcendence in order to call attention to the original and unthematic knowledge of God, the difficulty of bringing this knowledge to awareness is still not overcome. For the names which have been given to the term and source of transcendence in the history of man's reflexive self-interpretation as transcending spirit are very numerous. Nor does each of these names mediate for each individual in the concrete experience of his existence in an equal and equally accessible way a reflexive approach to this original experience of God.

To begin with, this term and source by which transcendence is borne can be called "God." We can also speak of being, of ground, of ultimate cause, of illuminating, revealing logos, and we can appeal to what is meant by a thousand other names. When we say "God" or "primordial ground" or "abyss," then of course such a word is always fraught with images which go beyond what the word really wants to say, and which have nothing to do with what it really means. Each of these notions always has the patina of history on it, including the individual's history, so much so that what is really meant by such a word is hardly discernible any more. When we call God "Father" with the Bible and with Jesus himself, and notice the criticism which this name provokes today, we can understand how a word like this, a word in which Jesus dared to express his ultimate understanding of God and his relationship to God, can be misunderstood or not understood at all.

The philosopher might give further reflection especially to the question of how a transcendental relationship to what he calls being, and a transcendental relationship to God are related and how they are to be distinguished.

Since we want to consider directly only the original, transcendental knowledge of God, which is antecedent to and is not able to be recaptured completely by reflexive ontology, we can take a shorter, although to be sure less cautious, route here, because the hesitant caution of philosophy cannot become a substitute for risking an understanding of existence which is always prior to philosophy.

But this still does not solve the difficulty of what name we should give to the term and the source of our original experience of transcendence. We could, of course, following the venerable tradition of the whole of western philosophy, a tradition to which we are certainly responsible, simply call it "absolute being" or "being in an absolute sense" or the "ground of being" which establishes everything in original unity. But when we speak this way of "being" and "ground of being" we run the deadly risk that many contemporaries can hear the word "being" only as an empty and subsequent abstraction from the multiple experience of the individual realities which encounter us directly. For this reason we want to try to call the term and the source of our transcendence by another name, a name, of course, which cannot claim to be the key which opens every door. But maybe, nevertheless, it clarifies what we mean by circumventing the problematic about "being" which we just mentioned. We want to call the term and source of our transcendence "the holy mystery," although this term must be understood, deepened, and then gradually shown to be identical with the word "God," and although we shall have to revert frequently to other terms which are available elsewhere in the humane and philosophical traditions. We shall have to consider later in a separate reflection why we call this mystery "holy."

We are considering the term of the experience of transcendence and we are defining it as the holy mystery not in order to express it in the most unintelligible and complicated way, but for another reason. For if we were simply to say that "God" is the term of our transcendence, then we would have to be continually afraid of the misunderstanding that we were speaking of God in the way that he is already expressed, known and understood beforehand in an objectifying set of concepts.

If we use a less familiar and less well-defined phrase like "holy mystery," in order to express the term of transcendence and the source from which it comes, then the danger of misunderstanding is somewhat less than when we say: "The term of transcendence is God." We must first describe the experience and the term of the experience together before what is experienced can be called "God."

THE TERM OF TRANSCENDENCE AS THE INFINITE, THE INDEFINABLE AND THE INEFFABLE

The term of our experience of transcendence, for which we first of all have to look for a name, is always present as nameless and indefinable, as something not at our disposal. For every name defines, every name distinguishes and characterizes something by giving what it means a particular name selected from among many names. The infinite horizon, which is the term of transcendence and which opens us to unlimited possibilities of encountering this or that particular thing, cannot itself be given a name. For this name would situate the term among the realities which are understood within the horizon of this term and this source. Indeed we can and must reflect upon the mysterious and the incomprehensible which can never be situated within our system of coordinates, and can never be defined by being distinguished from something else. For that would be to objectify it, to understand it as one object among other objects, and to define it conceptually. Indeed we must express it as something distinct from everything else because, as the absolute ground of every particular existent, it cannot be the subsequent sum of these many individual existents. But all the conceptualizing which we have to do remains true only to the extent that, in this act of defining and expressing objectively the term of transcendence as the act's condition of possibility, once again an act of transcendence towards the infinite term of this transcendence takes place. In the act of reflection, which only intends to reflect upon and objectify transcendence, another original act of transcendence takes place.

Hence this original transcendence's pre-apprehension reaches out towards what is nameless and what originally and by its very nature is infinite. By its very nature the condition which makes possible distinguishing and naming cannot itself have a name. We can call this condition the nameless one or the nameless thing, that which or that who is distinct from everything finite, or the "infinite," but in doing this we have not given the term and source of transcendence a name, but have called it nameless. We have really understood this process of naming only if we understand it as simply pointing to the silence of transcendental experience.

What transcendence moves towards, then, is also indefinable. By the fact that the horizon or the term of transcendence extends beyond our reach and thus offers to knowledge the space for its individual objects of knowledge and love, this horizon or term always and essentially and by its very nature is distinct from anything which appears within it as an object of knowledge. To this extent the differentiation between this ineffable term and the finite is obviously not only a distinction which has to be made, but this differentiation is the *one and original* distinction which is experienced. This is so because it is the condition which makes possible all distinguishing of objects, both from the horizon of transcendence itself and among themselves. But this means that this ineffable term of transcendence is itself indefinable, for as the condition of possibility for all categorical distinguishing and differentiating it cannot itself be differentiated from others by means of the same norms for distinguishing.

It is in the light of the distinction between the transcendental term and individual categorical objects on the one hand, and the differentiation of categorical objects among themselves on the other hand, that we can understand the error involved both in a real *pantheism* as well as in a more popular form of *dualism* which places God and the non-divine simply as two things alongside of each other, a dualism which is also found in religion.

When we say against pantheism that God and the world are different, this statement is radically misunderstood if it is interpreted in a dualistic way. The difference between God and the world is of such a nature that God establishes and is the difference of the world from himself, and for this reason he establishes the closest unity precisely in the differentiation. For if the difference itself comes from God, and, if we can put it this way, is itself identical with God, then the difference between God and the world is to be understood quite differently than the difference between categorical realities. Their difference is antecedent to them because they presuppose as it were a space which contains and differentiates them, and no one of these categorically distinct realities itself establishes its difference from the other or is this difference. Pantheism could therefore be called a sensitivity to (or better, the transcendental experience of) the fact that God is the absolute reality, the original ground and the ultimate term of transcendence. This is the element of truth in pantheism.

Conversely, a religious dualism which in a primitive and naive way understands the difference between God and the reality of the world created by him simply as a categorical difference is basically very unreligious because it does not grasp what God really is, that is, because it understands God as an element within a larger whole, as a part of the whole of reality.

God to be sure is different from the world. But he is different in the way in which this difference is experienced in our original, transcendental experience. In this experience this peculiar and unique difference is experienced in such a way that the whole of reality is borne by this term and this source and is intelligible only within it. Consequently, it is precisely the difference which establishes the ultimate unity between God and the world, and the difference becomes intelligible only in this unity.

These very abstract-sounding things are fundamental for an understanding of God which can have religious meaning for people today. For *that* God really does not exist who operates and functions as an individual existent alongside of other existents, and who would thus as it were be a member of the larger household of all reality. Anyone in search of such a God is searching for a false God. Both atheism and a more naive form of theism labor under the same false notion of God, only the former denies it while the latter believes that it can make sense out of it. Both are basically false: the latter, the notion that naive theism has, because this God does not exist; and the former, atheism, because God is the most radical, the most original, and in a certain sense the most self-evident reality.

The term of transcendence is indefinable because the horizon itself cannot be present within the horizon, because the term of transcendence cannot itself really be brought within the scope of transcendence and thus distinguished from other things. The ultimate measure cannot itself be measured. The limit by which everything is "defined" cannot itself be defined by a still more ultimate limit. The infinite expanse which can and does encompass everything cannot itself be encompassed. But then this nameless and indefinable term of transcendence, which is distinguished from everything else only from its own side, and hence differentiates everything else from itself, and which is the norm for everything and is beyond all other norms, this term becomes that which is absolutely beyond our disposal. It is always present only as that which disposes.

It is beyond the control of the finite subject not only physically, but also logically. The moment the subject would define this nameless term with the help of his formal logic and his ontology, the defining itself takes place by means of a pre-apprehension of that which is supposed to be defined. Ontology is that mysterious process in which the first principles show themselves to be unable to be measured, and man recognizes that he is what is measured. The term of transcendence admits of no control over itself because then we would be reaching beyond it and incorporating it within another, higher and broader horizon. This contradicts the very nature of this transcendence and of the real term of this transcendence. This infinite and silent term is what disposes of us. It presents itself to us in the mode of withdrawal, of silence, of distance, of being always inexpressible, so that speaking of it, if it is to make sense, always requires listening to its silence.

Since we experience the term of transcendence only in the experience of this bottomless and endless transcendence, we have avoided any kind of *ontologism* in the usual sense. For this term is not experienced in itself, but is only known unobjectively in the experience of subjective transcendence. The presence of the term of transcendence is the presence of this transcendence, which is only present as the condition of possibility for categorical knowledge, and not by itself. We can see by this statement (and it is one of the most fundamental statements about the real understanding of God and is a really correct approach to the knowledge of God) that the tendency today to talk not about God, but about one's neighbor, to preach not about the love of God, but about the love of neighbor, and to use not the term "God," but "world" and "responsibility for the world"—we can see that this tendency has an absolutely solid foundation. However, going to the extreme of banishing God and of being radically silent about him is and remains false and does violence to the true nature of Christianity.

But what is correct about all of these statements is the plain fact that we do not know God by himself as one individual object alongside others, but only as the term of transcendence. This transcendence takes place only in a categorical encounter in freedom and in knowledge with concrete reality, which indeed appears as world only vis-à-vis God as absolutely other than world. Hence the term of this transcendence is present only in the mode of otherness and distance. It can never be approached directly, never be grasped immediately. It gives itself only insofar as it points wordlessly to something else, to something finite as the object we see directly and as the immediate object of our action. And for this reason the term of this transcendence is mystery.

THE TERM OF TRANSCENDENCE AS THE "HOLY MYSTERY"

We have already and by way of anticipation called the term of transcendence the *holy* mystery. The reason why we had to call it "mystery" consisted ultimately in the fact that we experience it as that which cannot be encompassed by a pre-apprehension which reaches beyond it, and hence it cannot be defined. But why do we characterize it as the "holy" mystery?

We have already emphasized in the first chapter that when we speak of transcendence we do not mean only and exclusively the transcendence which is the condition of possibility for categorical knowledge as such. We mean also and just as much the *transcendence of freedom, of willing,* and *of love.* This transcendence, which is constitutive of the subject as a free and personal subject of action within an unlimited realm of action, is just as important, and is basically just another aspect of the transcendence of a spiritual, and therefore knowing, and precisely for this reason free subject. Freedom is always the freedom of a subject who exists in interpersonal communication with other subjects. Therefore it is necessarily freedom vis-à-vis another subject of transcendence, and this transcendence is not primarily the condition of possibility for knowing *things,* but is the condition of possibility for a subject being present to himself and just as basically and originally being present to another *subject.* But for a subject who is present to himself to affirm freely vis-à-vis another subject means ultimately to love.

Hence when we reflect here upon transcendence as will and as freedom, we must also take into account the character of the term and source of transcendence as love. It is a term which possesses absolute freedom, and this term is at work in freedom and in love as that which is nameless and which is not at our disposal, for we are completely at its disposal. It is what opens up my own transcendence as freedom and as love. But the term of transcendence is always and originally the source of the mystery which offers itself. This term itself opens our transcendence; it is not established by us and by our own power as though we were absolute subjects. Hence if transcendence moves in freedom and in love towards a term which itself opens this transcendence, then we can say that that which is nameless and which is not at our disposal, and at whose complete disposal we exist, that this very thing is present in loving freedom, and this is what we mean when we say "holy mystery."

For what else would we call that which is nameless, that at whose disposal we exist and from which we are distanced in our finiteness, but which nevertheless we affirm in our transcendence through freedom and love, what else would we call this if not "holy"? And what could we call "holy" if not this, or to whom would the name "holy" belong more basically and more originally than to this infinite term of love, which love in the presence of the incomprehensible and the ineffable necessarily becomes worship.

In transcendence, therefore, dwells the holy, nameless and infinite, disposing but not being disposed, forbidding and distant. And this we call mystery, or somewhat more explicitly, the holy mystery, lest in focusing upon the knowledge element we overlook the transcendentality of freedom and love, and so that both elements remain present in their original and personal unity. The two words "holy mystery," which are understood as a unity, but between which nevertheless there is an intrinsic difference, express equally the transcendentality both of knowledge and of freedom and love.

Every experience of transcendence is a basic and original experience which is not derived from something prior, and it receives this character of being underived and irreducible from what is encountered and becomes manifest in it. The designation of this term of transcendence as the "holy mystery," therefore, does not employ concepts derived from elsewhere and applied extrinsically to this term. It derives them rather from this original "object," which is its own ground and the ground and horizon of the knowledge of it, and which discloses itself in and through transcendental experience itself.

If we have arrived in this way at the basic and original idea of mystery and of the holy, and if it is correct to designate the term of transcendence by this name, there can be no question, of course, of giving a *definition* of the essence of this holy mystery. Mystery is as indefinable as every other transcendental "concept." They do not admit of definition because what is expressed in them is known only in transcendental experience, and transcendental experience, as always and everywhere given antecedently, has nothing outside of itself by which it and its term could be defined.

TRANSCENDENTAL EXPERIENCE AND REALITY

We often speak of the *concept* of God. Hence we express the original term of our unthematic transcendentality subsequently in a concept, a name.

This raises the question whether what is expressed in an essential concept this way is only something in the mind, or is also something real. It must be said right away that it would be the greatest misunderstanding, a misunderstanding which would lose all connection with the original experience, if this term were explained as something in the mind, as an *idea* which human thought established as its own creation. For this term is what opens up and makes possible the process of transcendence. Transcendence is borne by this term, and this term is not its creation.

The basic and original knowledge of what "being" is comes from this act of transcendence, and is not derived from an individual existent which we know. Something real can encounter us only in knowledge, and to state that there is something real which is a priori and in principle inaccessible to knowledge is a self-contradictory statement. The very statement and assertion about something which in principle cannot be experienced brings what is supposed to be absolutely unable to be experienced within the realm of knowledge, for one is thinking about it, and hence it is self-contradictory. It follows from this that what is not yet known and what is merely thought are deficient and secondary modes of being the object of knowledge, modes which in principle are ordered to the real to begin with, because without this presupposition it cannot even be said what is meant by the real as such.

Therefore the term of transcendental and hence of original and encompassing experience and knowledge is posited in this experience and knowledge from the outset as that which is genuinely real, as the original unity of essence and existence. We can and must also say, of course, that the reality of the absolute mystery does not simply disclose itself to finite, transcendental spirit in the same kind of an encounter as we have in sense experience, and it should not be understood after the model of the corporeal experience of an individual, material existent. If we were to think that God is experienced in this way we would have wound up in ontologism, and we have already distinguished what we are saying from that, or we would have asserted something which in fact is not true. The affirmation of the reality of the absolute mystery is grounded for us, who are finite spirits, in the necessity with which the actualization of transcendence as our own act is given for us. This repeats from another point of view what we said about the a posteriori character of the knowledge of God, in spite of and without prejudice to the transcendental nature of the experience of God. If we were not inescapably present to ourselves, if we could ignore the act of transcendence, then we would escape the necessity of affirming the absolute reality of the term of transcendence. But this would also eliminate the possibility of an act in which the reality of this transcendence could be denied or doubted. In the act of transcendence the reality of the term is necessarily affirmed because in this very act and only in it do we experience what reality is.

The term of transcendence, therefore, is the holy mystery as absolute being, or as the existent existing in an absolute fullness of being and possession of being.

REMARKS ON THE PROOFS FOR GOD'S EXISTENCE

We have discussed both the holy mystery, which exists absolutely and which we can call by the familiar name "God," and our transcendence to this holy mystery together. In the original unity of this transcendental experience, the two are mutually dependent on each other for their intelligibility. Therefore we do not need to discuss in any great detail those assertions which are the elaboration of a more original knowledge and which are usually called "proofs for the existence of God." In the same way as ontology at the level of the original self-possession of a knowing and freely self-disposing human existence is related to scientific and reflexive ontology, so is our original experience, which we do not have in concepts and words and to which we can only point in words, related to that knowledge which is had in a reflexive proof for God's existence.

The question whether this process should be called a "proof" is secondary. Although reflexive, scientific knowledge is derivative and secondary and can never completely recapture the original experience, it is nevertheless altogether necessary and required. But this reflexive and thematic knowledge of God which is conceptualized objectively and works with concepts is not the primary and most basic and original knowledge, nor can it replace the latter.

As we have already said, a reflexive proof for God's existence is not intended to communicate a knowledge in which a previously and completely unknown and therefore also indifferent object is presented to people from without, an object whose significance and importance for them becomes evident only subsequently and through further determinations which are ascribed to the object. If the proofs are understood in this way, it could be objected to begin with that nothing is known of God. And then how could it be shown that one *must* be concerned about this question? But theology, ontology, the natural knowledge of God, and so on, all of these can appear with the claim to be taken seriously by everyone only if and insofar as they can show the listener that he already has something to do with this question.

A theoretical proof for the existence of God, then, is only intended to mediate a reflexive awareness of the fact that man always and inevitably has to do with God in his intellectual and spiritual existence, whether he reflects upon it or not, and whether he freely accepts it or not. The peculiar situation of giving the grounds subsequently for something which actually does the grounding and is already present, namely, the holy mystery, is what constitutes the specific character, the self-evident nature, and the difficulty of giving a reflexive proof for God's existence. That which does the grounding is itself grounded, as it were, and what is present in silence and without a name is itself given a name.

The point of the reflexive proofs for the existence of God is to indicate that all knowledge, even in the form of a doubt or a question or even a refusal to raise the metaphysical question, takes place against the background of an affirmation of the holy mystery, or of absolute being, as the horizon of the asymptotic term and of the questioning ground of the act of knowledge and of its "object." It is a relatively secondary question what this nameless and distant presence is called, whether the "holy mystery" or "absolute being," or, bringing into the foreground the freedom aspect of this transcendence and the personal structure of the act, the "absolute good," the "personal and absolute Thou," the "ground of absolute responsibility," the "ultimate horizon of hope," and so on. In all the so-called proofs for the existence of God the one and only thing which is being presented and represented in a reflexive and systematic conceptualization is something which has already taken place: in the fact that a person comes to the objective reality of his everyday life both in the involvement of action and in the intellectual activity of thought and comprehension, he is actualizing, as the condition which makes possible such involvement and comprehension, an unthematic and non-objective pre-apprehension of the inconceivable and incomprehensible single fullness of reality. This fullness in its original unity is at once the condition of possibility both for knowledge and for the individual thing known objectively. As such a condition of possibility it is always affirmed unthematically, even in an act which denies it thematically.

The individual person, of course, experiences this fundamental and inescapable structure best in that basic situation of his own existence which occurs with special intensity for him as an individual. If, therefore, he is really to understand this reflection on "proofs" for God's existence, the individual person must reflect precisely upon whatever is the clearest experience *for him:* on the luminous and incomprehensible light of his spirit; on the capacity for absolute questioning which a person directs against himself and which seemingly reduces him to nothing, but in which he reaches radically beyond himself; on annihilating anxiety, which is something quite different from fear of a definite object and is prior to the latter as the condition of its possibility; on that joy which surpasses all understanding; on an absolute moral obligation in which a person really goes beyond himself; on the experience of death in which he faces himself in his absolute powerlessness. Man reflects upon these and many other modes of the basic and transcendental experience of human existence. Because he experiences himself as finite in his self-questioning, he is not able to identify himself with the ground which discloses itself in this experience as what is innermost and at the same time what is absolutely different. The explicit proofs for God's existence only make thematic this fundamental structure and its term.

The experience that every act of judgment takes place as an act which is borne by and is moved by absolute being, which does not live by the grace of our thought, but is present as that by which thought is borne and not as something produced by thought, this experience is made thematic in the metaphysical principle of causality. This must not be confused with the functional law of causality in the natural sciences. According to this law, for every phenomenon as "effect" there is coordinated another phenomenon of quantitative equality as "cause." When understood correctly the metaphysical principle of causality is not an extrapolation from the scientific law of nature, nor is it an extrapolation from the causal thinking that we use in everyday affairs. It is grounded rather in the transcendental experience of the relationship between transcendence and its term. The metaphysical principle of causality, which is applied in the traditional proofs for the existence of God, is not a universal principle which is applied in these proofs to a particular, individual instance alongside of others, although even many scholastic philosophers understand it this way. Rather it only points to the transcendental experience in which the relationship between something conditioned and finite and its incomprehensible source is immediately present, and through its presence is experienced.

We do not need to treat in detail here the usual proofs for the existence of God in the theology and Christian philosophy of the schools. We need not discuss these proofs, be they cosmological, theological, kinetic, axiological, deontological, noetic or moral proofs. For all of these proofs only designate certain categorical realities in human experience and place them explicitly within the realm of that human transcendence within which alone they can be understood. They trace all of these categorical realities and the act of knowing them back to the condition of possibility which is common both to this knowledge and to this reality together. To that extent the different proofs for God's existence can really only clarify the one proof for the existence of God from the different points of departure for the same transcendental experience.

3. God as Person

ANALOGOUS LANGUAGE ABOUT GOD

We can speak about transcendental experience only by means of what is secondary to it. For this reason we always have to speak about it in the language of "on the one hand . . . and on the other hand" and "not only . . . but also." This way of speaking about God comes from the fact that whenever we make this original, transcendental orientation to God explicit and thematic, we have to speak about God by means of secondary and categorical concepts which are contraries within the realm of the categorical. When we say that God is the innermost reality by which a finite subject and the categorical reality which confronts him are borne from within, and say at the same time that God holds sway in absolute and untouchable self-possession and that his reality is not simply the function of being the horizon for our existence, then this "on the one hand . . . on the other hand," this dialectical, bipolar statement, which can never be conceptually synthesized into a higher synthesis, is not the original experience. It results rather from the fact that the original experience of transcendence must be transposed and made thematic, it must as it were be incorporated into its own realm as an individual object.

All of the statements that we just made about God are meant in the sense that that upon which every reality is based and grounded in its innermost self discloses itself on the one hand in what is based and grounded, and can be named from the latter. Otherwise a relationship between the ground and what is grounded cannot even be conceived. On the other hand, however, this ground is given only as ground, and hence it cannot be incorporated into a common and antecedent system with what is grounded. A relation to this ground is real and is always conscious of transcendence and the origins of transcendence in and from absolute mystery. Hence a statement about this mystery is always an original statement caught in an irresolvable tension between the categorical origin of our reflexive statement and its attaining that towards which the statement is really pointing, namely, the term of transcendence. It is a tension which is not produced by us at a logically subsequent midpoint between a univocal "yes" and an equivocal "no." It is rather a tension which we ourselves as spiritual subjects originally *are* in our self-realization, and which we can designate by the traditional term "analogy" if we understand what this word means in its original sense.

Hence we may not understand the word "analogy" as a hybrid between univocation and equivocation. When I call a desk "desk" I have used a univocal concept, that is, I relate it to this piece of furniture in the same sense because I have left out individual differences and have abstracted from them. Hence I apply a univocal predication in exactly the same meaning. If, on the other hand, I call the money which I must pay the state "tax" *(Steuer)*, and use the very same word to designate what you can steer a boat with (*Steuer* = rudder), then the word *Steuer* has a completely different sense in these instances, an equivocal sense. There are two concepts here which in our understanding have nothing to do with each other.

In the school philosophy the so-called analogy of being is frequently presented as though it were a subsequent midpoint between univocation and equivocation. It is as though one had to say something about God, but then would see that he cannot really say that because the original understanding of the content of the statement comes from elsewhere, from something which does not have much to do with God. Hence analogous concepts have to be formed which are a middle ground between the univocal and the equivocal.

But this is not true. Transcendence is the more original in relation to individual, categorical, univocal concepts. For transcendence, that is, this reaching beyond towards the unlimited horizon of the whole movement of our spirit, is precisely the condition of possibility, the horizon, and the basis and ground by means of which we compare individual objects of experience with one another and classify them. This transcendental movement of the spirit is the more original, and this is what is designated as analogy in another sense. Analogy, therefore, has nothing to do with the notion of a secondary, inexact middle position between clear concepts and those which designate two completely different things with the same phonetic sound.

Rather, because transcendental experience is the condition which makes possible all categorical knowledge of individual objects, it follows from the nature of transcendental experience that the analogous statement signifies what is most basic and original in our knowledge. Consequently, however familiar equivocal and univocal statements are to us from our scientific knowledge and from our everyday dealings with the realities of experience, they are deficient modes of that original relationship in which we are related to the term of our transcendence. And this original relationship is what we are calling analogy: the tension between a categorical starting point and the incomprehensibility of the holy mystery, namely, God. We ourselves, as we can put it, exist analogously in and through our being grounded in this holy mystery which always surpasses us. But it always constitutes us by surpassing us and by pointing us towards the concrete, individual, categorical realities which confront us within the realm of our experience. Conversely, then, these realities are the mediation of and the point of departure for our knowledge of God.

ON THE PERSONAL BEING OF GOD

The statement that God is a person, that he is a personal God, is one of the fundamental Christian assertions about God. But it creates special difficulties for people today, and rightly so. When we say that God is a person, and this in a sense which as yet has nothing to do with the question about the so-called three persons in God, then the question about the personal character of God becomes a twofold question: we can ask whether God in his own self must be called a person; and we can ask whether he is person only in relation to us, and whether in his own self he is hidden from us in his absolute and transcendent distance. Then we would have to say that he is a person, but that he does not by any means for this reason enter into that personal relationship to us which we presuppose in our religious activity, in prayer, and in our turning to God in faith, hope and love. We shall not have touched the real difficulties which such an assertion about God as person creates for people today until we have discussed explicitly the relationship between God and man, the self-communication of God to man in grace as the transcendental constitution of man.

If we prescind from these difficulties for the time being, then the assertion that God is a person, is the absolute person who stands in absolute freedom vis-à-vis everything which he establishes as different from himself, this assertion is really self-evident, just as much as when we say that God is the absolute being, the absolute ground, the absolute mystery, the absolute good, the absolute and ultimate horizon within which human existence is lived out in freedom, knowledge and action. It is self-evident first of all that the ground of a reality which exists must possess in itself beforehand and in absolute fullness and purity this reality which is grounded by it, because otherwise this ground could not be the ground of what is grounded, and because otherwise the ground would ultimately be empty nothingness which, if the term is really taken seriously, would say nothing and could ground nothing.

Of course the subjectivity and personhood which we experience as our own, the individual and limited uniqueness through which we are distinguished from others, the freedom which has to be exercised only under a thousand conditions and necessities, all of this signifies a finite subjectivity with limitations which we cannot assert with these limitations of its ground, namely, God. And it is self-evident that such an individual personhood cannot belong to God, who is the absolute ground of everything in radical originality. If, then, we wanted to say that in this sense God is not an individual person because he cannot experience himself as defined in relation to another or limited by another, because he does not experience any difference from himself, but rather he himself establishes the difference, and hence ultimately he himself is the difference vis-à-vis others, then we are correct in saying that personhood in this sense cannot be asserted of God.

But if we proceed this way, then we could do the same with regard to every transcendental concept which is applied to God. When I say that God is the original meaning, the ground, the absolute light, the absolute being, and so on, then I have to know what ground, meaning, and so on are supposed to mean, and I can make all of these assertions only in an analogous sense. This means that I can make them only within that movement in which the comprehending subject allows his comprehension, as it were, to flow into the holy, ineffable and incomprehensible mystery. If anything at all can be predicated of God, then the concept of "personhood" has to be predicated of him. Obviously, the statement that "God is a person" can be asserted of God and is true of God only if, in asserting and understanding this statement, we open it to the ineffable darkness of the holy mystery. Obviously, precisely as philosophers we know what this statement means more concretely and more exactly only if, following an ultimate maxim of genuine philosophizing, we do not fill the philosophical a priori in its empty formality and formal emptiness arbitrarily, or arbitrarily leave it empty, but rather allow this formal assertion to receive its content from our historical experience. In this way we allow God to be person in the way in which he in fact wants to encounter us and has encountered us in our individual histories, in the depths of our conscience, and in the whole history of the human race.

Hence we must not make the formal emptiness and empty formality of the transcendental concept of person, which is asserted of God, into a false god, and refuse from the outset to allow him to fill it through personal experience in prayer, in one's personal and individual history where God draws close to us, and in the history of Christian revelation. From this perspective a certain religious naiveté, which understands the personhood of God almost in a categorical sense, has its justification.

The ground of our spiritual personhood, which in the transcendental structure of our spiritual self always discloses itself as the ground of our person and at the same time remains concealed, has thereby revealed itself as person. The notion that the absolute ground of all reality is something like an unconscious and impersonal cosmic law, an unconscious and impersonal structure of things, a source which empties itself out without possessing itself, which gives rise to spirit and freedom without itself being spirit and freedom, the notion of a blind, primordial ground of the world which cannot look at us even if it wants to, all of this is a notion whose model is taken from the context of the impersonal world of things. It does not come from that source in which a basic and original transcendental experience is really rooted: namely, from a finite spirit's subjective and free experience of itself. In its very constitution a finite spirit always experiences itself as having its origins in another and as being given to itself from another—from another, therefore, which it cannot misinterpret as an impersonal principle.

4. Man's Relation to His Transcendent Ground: Creatureliness

With regard to the topic of creatureliness as the characterization of our relationship to God, at this point we only have to consider it in its basic and ultimate and very formalized characteristics. For this relationship to God is expressed completely only in and through the whole of the Christian message. With regard to these very formal and fundamental characteristics, we shall discuss first of all the relationship itself insofar as it can be characterized in its ultimate nature as a relationship of creatureliness.

At this point we are perhaps justified in prescinding from the question whether, first of all, this is a purely philosophical assertion in which assertion and object are both merely natural, or, secondly, whether we are indeed dealing with a philosophical assertion by a philosophical subject, but one where the object of the assertion is a reality for which God's action in grace is co-constitutive, although it can be so interpreted only subsequently and theologically, or, thirdly, whether this assertion of our creatureliness belongs completely to the realm of revealed theology even with regard to the object which is asserted and the subject doing the asserting. In school theology the question comes up again and again whether the teaching of the First Vatican Council that God can be known by the so-called light of natural reason also refers to God insofar as he is not only some primordial ground of the world, but the creator of the world in the strict sense, that is, whether our creatureliness in the strict sense also belongs to the data which, according to the teaching of Vatican I (*D.S.* 3004), can be known by the light of natural reason. Vatican I does not answer this question. It does indeed teach that God is the creator of all things, and that he has created and continues to create them out of nothing. But Vatican I says nothing about whether this assertion can be a merely philosophical assertion, or whether it can be made only within the framework of revelation, and hence of God's personal self-communication.

CREATURELINESS:
NOT A PARTICULAR INSTANCE OF A CAUSAL RELATIONSHIP

In any case, in our transcendental experience, which necessarily and inescapably orients us towards the ineffable and holy mystery, we experience what creatureliness is and we experience it immediately. The term "creatureliness" interprets this original experience of the relationship between ourselves and God correctly. Analogously to a statement we have already made, and developing it a bit further, we can say that creatureliness does not signify a particular instance of a universal causal relationship between two realities. It is not a relationship which is also found elsewhere, although a bit differently. In the first instance and originally creatureliness refers to a relationship whose nature we can discover only within transcendental experience as such. We cannot discover it in the relationship of one thing being grounded on or in another thing alongside of it, nor in the empirical phenomenon which consists in one phenomenon within the realm of our categorical experience having a functional connection with another phenomenon.

If we were to think that creatureliness is an extrapolation from such a functional relationship between two categorical realities which we meet within the realm of our experience, then right off we would have missed the point of what creatureliness means. Precisely what creatureliness is not is one instance among many of a causal or functional relationship between two things, both of which exist within some superimposed unity. Creatureliness expresses an absolutely unique relationship which occurs only here and therefore has its own unique place, a relationship which is mediated to us only in transcendental experience as such. Just as the metaphysical principle of causality cannot be regarded as an extrapolation from the functional law of causality in the natural sciences, so too creatureliness cannot be regarded or understood as an instance or an application or an extrapolation or an intensification of such a categorical, causal or functional relationship.

Hence what it really means to have a created origin is experienced basically and originally in the process of transcendence. This means that in the first instance the terms "creatureliness," "being created" or "creation" do not point back to an earlier moment in time at which the creation of the creature in question once took place. They mean rather an ongoing and always actual process which for every existent is taking place now just as much as at an earlier point of time in his existence, although this ongoing creation is that of an existent extended *in time.* In the first instance, then, creation and creatureliness do not mean a momentary event, namely, the first moment of a temporal existent, but mean the establishing of this existent and his time itself, and this establishing does not enter into time, but is the ground of time.

CREATURELINESS AS RADICAL DIFFERENCE FROM AND RADICAL
DEPENDENCE ON GOD

To understand what is meant by creatureliness as a person's fundamental relationship to God, let us begin with the transcendental experience of it. As a spiritual person, man implicitly affirms absolute being as the real ground of every act of knowledge and of every action, and affirms it as mystery. This absolute, incomprehensible reality, which is always the ontologically silent horizon of every intellectual and spiritual encounter with realities, is therefore always infinitely different from the knowing subject. It is also different from the individual, finite things known. It is present as such in every assertion, in all knowledge, and in every action.

Proceeding from this basic starting point, we can accordingly define from two points of view the relationship between both the knower and the known as finite existents, and the absolutely infinite: as the absolute and the infinite, God must be absolutely different. Otherwise he would be an object of our knowledge and comprehension, and not the ground of such comprehension. He is and remains so even when he is named and objectified in metaphysical and conceptual reflection. For this reason, then, he cannot be in need of the finite reality called "world," because otherwise he would not really be radically different from it, but would be part of a larger whole as in the understanding of pantheism. Conversely, the world must be radically dependent on God, without making him dependent on it as a master is dependent on his servant. It can have absolutely nothing which is independent of him, any more than the totality of things in the world in their unity and variety can be known without the pre-apprehension of spirit's transcendence towards God. This dependence must be established freely by God, because as finite and as coming to be it cannot be necessary. Moreover, the necessity of what has been established, if such a necessity did exist, could originate only in some necessity in God to establish it, a necessity which would allow the world to be made a necessity of God, and hence would not allow him to be independent of the world. This radical dependence must be ongoing, and therefore not just affect the first moment, for what is finite is related now and always to the absolute as its ground.

Christian doctrine calls this unique relationship between God and the world the createdness of the world, its creatureliness, its ongoing being-given to itself by a personal God who establishes it freely. This establishing, then, does not have some material already at hand as its presupposition, and in this sense it is "out of nothing." Basically creation "out of nothing" means to say: creation totally from God, but in such a way that the world is radically dependent on God in this creation. Nevertheless, God does not become dependent on the world, but remains free vis-à-vis the world and grounded in himself. Wherever we find a causal relationship of a categorical kind in the world, it is indeed the case that the effect is by definition dependent on its cause. But strangely enough this cause is itself also dependent on its effect, because it cannot be this cause without causing the effect. This is not the case in the relationship between God and creatures, for otherwise God would then be an element *within* our categorical realm of experience, and not the absolutely distant term of the transcendence within which an individual finite thing is known.

RADICAL DEPENDENCE ON GOD AND GENUINE AUTONOMY

God establishes the creature and its difference from himself. But by the very fact that God establishes the creature and its difference from himself, the creature is a genuine reality different from God, and not a mere appearance behind which God and his own reality hide. The radical dependence and the genuine reality of the existent coming from God vary in direct and not in inverse proportion. In our human experience it is the case that the more something is dependent on us, the less it is different from us, and the less it possesses its own reality and autonomy. In the realm of the categorical, the radical dependence of the effect on the cause and the independence and autonomy of the effect vary in inverse proportion.

But when we reflect upon the real transcendental relationship between God and a creature, then it is clear that here genuine reality and radical dependence are simply just two sides of one and the same reality, and therefore they vary in direct and not in inverse proportion. We and the existents of our world really and truly are and are different from God not in spite of, but because we are established in being by God and not by anyone else. Creation is the only and unique and incomparable mode which does not presuppose the other as the possibility of an effective movement outwards, but rather creates this other as other by the fact that it both retains it as its creation and sets it free in its own autonomy, and both in the same proportion.

Of course the idea of creation can ultimately be understood and assimilated only by one who has not only had the experience of his own freedom and responsibility in the depths of his existence, a freedom and responsibility which is valid before God and in our relation to God, but has also freely accepted it in an act of his freedom and in reflection. What it really means to be something other than God and nevertheless to have come from him radically and in one's deepest self, what it means to say that this radical dependence grounds autonomy, all of this can be experienced only when a spiritual, created person experiences his own freedom as a reality, a freedom coming from God and a freedom for God. Not until one experiences himself as a free subject responsible before God and accepts this responsibility does he understand what autonomy is, and understand that it does not decrease, but increases in the same proportion as dependence on God. On this point the only thing that concerns us is that man is at once independent and, in view of what his ground is, also dependent.

TRANSCENDENTAL EXPERIENCE
AS THE ORIGIN OF THE EXPERIENCE OF CREATURELINESS

The place where we have the basic and original experience of creatureliness is not in a sequential series of phenomena elapsing in empty temporality, but in a transcendental experience in which the subject along with his time itself is experienced as being borne by an incomprehensible ground. The teaching of Christian faith, therefore, always expresses this creatureliness in the context of a prayerful experience of one's own autonomous and responsible reality, which is totally in the hands of and at the disposal of the absolute mystery which is not at our disposal, and which in this way becomes precisely our own responsibility. Creatureliness, then, always means both the grace and the mandate to preserve and to accept that tension of analogy which the finite subject is; to reflect upon and understand and accept himself as what is truly real, as having responsibility for himself and at the same time being absolutely dependent on and oriented towards the absolute mystery as his future.

Hence the subject in his tension and his analogy will always be tempted to let go of one of the two moments in this indispensable unity. A person either understands himself as only an empty appearance through which the divinity acts out its own eternal drama, runs away from his responsibility and his freedom, at least in the direction of God, and shifts responsibility for himself and his existence onto God in such a way that his burden no longer in truth really remains his own; or, and this is the other possibility of this misunderstanding, he understands the truth and the genuine reality which we are in such a way that they no longer truly come from God but have their meaning independently of him, so that God becomes a partner of man in a false sense. This false sense consists in thinking that the difference between him and us and hence the possibility of a real partnership is not established by him, but is antecedent to him and our relationship to him.

EXPERIENCE OF CREATURELINESS AS DENUMINIZING THE WORLD

The Christian teaching that the world is created, and this creation takes place primarily and originally in the establishment of the free subjectivity of finite persons, does not see here a strange and almost inexplicable exception to the general rule of things. The significance of this teaching lies rather in the fact that it demythologizes and denuminizes the world, and this is decisive for the Christian understanding of existence and of the world, and not only for the modern feeling about existence.

Insofar as the world, established by God in his freedom, does indeed have its origin in him, but not in the way in which God possesses himself, it really is not God. It is seen correctly, therefore, not as "holy nature," but as the material for the creative power of man. Man experiences his creatureliness and encounters God in it, not so much in nature, in its stolid and unfeeling finiteness, but in himself and in the world only as known by him and as freely administered in the unlimited openness of his own spirit.

This observation, of course, does not give a complete description of the proper relationship between man and "nature" as his environment. This relationship has many other characteristics which are not brought out by speaking of denuminizing the world. This relationship itself also has a history whose possibilities we are experiencing today, and not only in a positive sense. In spite of its importance, however, we cannot go into this question any further here.

5. Finding God in the World

THE TENSION BETWEEN A TRANSCENDENTAL STARTING POINT AND
HISTORICAL RELIGION

The question about finding God and his activity with us in our concrete, historical experience in the world creates special difficulties today. We have been considering God up to now as the creative ground of everything which can encounter us within the ultimate horizon which he himself is and which he alone forms. As he who cannot be incorporated along with what is grounded into a system which encompasses them both, we saw him as always transcendent, as the presupposition of everything which exists, and therefore as someone who cannot be thought of as one of these existents, that is, as someone comprehended or comprehensible by us. But this seems to have as its consequence the very thing which constitutes perhaps the basic difficulty which people have today with the concrete practice of religion.

As ineffable and incomprehensible presupposition, as ground and abyss, as ineffable mystery, God cannot be found in his world. He does not seem to be able to enter into the world with which we have to do because he would thereby become what he is not: an individual existent alongside of which there are others which he is not. If he wanted to appear in his world, he apparently would immediately cease to be himself: the ground of everything which appears but which itself does not appear. By definition God does not seem able to be within the world. If someone says too quickly that he does not need to, that he is always to be thought of as beyond the world, he has probably not yet felt this really radical difficulty. The difficulty consists in the fact that by definition God does not seem to be able to be where by definition we are. Every objectification of God, as localized in time and space, as definable in the here and now, seems by its very nature not to be God, but something which we have to derive as a phenomenon from other phenomena in the world which can be specified or must be postulated.

But religion as we know it, as a religion of prayer for God's intervention, as a religion of miracles, as a religion with a salvation history differentiated from other history, as a religion in which there are supposed to be certain subjects with the fullness of divine power as distinguished from other subjects, as a religion with an inspired book which comes from God, as a religion with a particular word which is supposed to be God's word as distinguished from other words, as a religion with definite prophets and bearers of revelation authorized by God, as a religion with a Pope who is called vicar of Jesus Christ (and the term "Jesus Christ" functions here more or less the same as the term "God"), all religion of this kind declares phenomena existing within our experience as definite and exclusive objectifications and manifestations of God. Consequently, in this way God as it were appears within the world of our categorical experience at quite definite points as distinguished from other points.

Such a religion seems incompatible with our transcendental starting point, which, on the other hand, we cannot abandon if we want to talk about God at all today. As it is practiced by people in the concrete, religion always and inevitably seems to say: "God is here and not there," or "This is in accordance with his will and not that," or "He has revealed himself here and not there." As practiced in the concrete, religion seems neither willing nor able to avoid making God a categorical object. Religion which does avoid this seems to evaporate into a mist which perhaps does exist, but in practice it cannot be the source of religious life. Conversely, our basic starting point seems to say that God is everywhere insofar as he grounds everything, and he is nowhere insofar as everything that is grounded is created, and everything which appears in this way within the world of our experience is different from God, separated by an absolute chasm between God and what is not God.

Although we have expressed it in very formal terms, here perhaps lies the basic difficulty for all of us today. All of us, even the atheist who is troubled and terrified by the agonizing nothingness of his existence, seem to be able to be religious in the sense that we reverence the ineffable in silence, knowing that there is such a thing. It strikes us only too easily as an irreligious indiscretion, almost as bad taste vis-à-vis this silent and religious reverence before the absolute mystery when we not only talk about the ineffable, but when beyond that we point our finger as it were at this or that particular thing among the usual pieties within the world of our experience and say: there is God. It is obvious that the historical, revealed religion which Christianity is experiences its most fundamental and universal threat from this difficulty. To do justice to this difficulty we must proceed carefully and in several steps.

IMMEDIACY TO GOD AS MEDIATED IMMEDIACY

It is easy to see that however it is to be understood more exactly, either there can be no immediacy to God in his own self at all, or it cannot be impossible just because of the fact that it is mediated in some sense. If there is any immediacy to God at all, that is, if we really can have something to do with God in his own self, this immediacy cannot depend on the fact that the non-divine absolutely disappears. There can, of course, be a religious fervor which almost lives by the basic sentiment that God appears by the fact that the creature disappears. This feeling that one must vanish, as it were, if God is to become manifest is a completely understandable sentiment which is attested to repeatedly in the Old Testament. The naively religious person who imagines God in a categorical way has no difficulty with this, of course, no more than he sees a difficulty in the fact that he has freedom although he is a creature of God even in his freedom, both as faculty and as act. But the moment we experience that we come radically from God, that we are dependent on him to the last fiber of our being, then the realization that we also have freedom vis-à-vis God is truly something which is not all that self-evident.

If immediacy to God is not to be an absolute contradiction right from the start, it cannot depend on the fact that what is not God absolutely disappears when God draws near. As God he does not have to find a place by having something else which is not him make room. For at least the presence of God as the transcendental ground and horizon of everything which exists and everything which knows (and this is a presence of God, an immediacy to him) takes place precisely in and through the presence of the finite existent.

Mediation and immediacy are not simply contradictory. There is a genuine mediation of immediacy with regard to God. And when according to the understanding of Christian faith the most radical and absolutely immediate self-communication of God in his very own being is given to us, namely, in the immediate vision of God as the fulfillment of the finite spirit in grace, this most radical immediacy is still mediated in a certain sense by the finite subject experiencing it, and thereby also experiencing itself. The finite subject does not disappear in this most immediate manifestation of God and is not suppressed, but rather it reaches its fulfillment and hence its fullest autonomy as subject. This autonomy is at once both the presupposition and the consequence of this absolute immediacy to God and from God.

Something finite as such, insofar as it appears as a definite, individual thing within our transcendental horizon, cannot represent God in such a way that, by the very fact that it is given, the very self of God is also present in a way which goes beyond the possibility of mediation in our transcendental experience. Prescinding from the fact that transcendental experience and its orientation to God can be mediated by every categorical existent, we must insist that a definite, individual thing within our transcendental horizon cannot mediate God in such a way that, simply by the fact that *it* is given, this presence of God over and beyond his transcendentality could have the kind of character which we seem to presuppose in a popular interpretation of religious phenomena. This is precluded simply by the absolute difference which necessarily obtains between the holy mystery as the ground, and everything which is grounded. The individual existent in its categorical individuality and limitations can mediate God to the extent that in the experience of it the transcendental experience of God takes place. But it is admittedly still not clear why and to what extent this kind of mediation should belong to one particular categorical existent rather than to another. And not until we can explain this can there be something like a concrete religion which is practiced in the concrete with its categorical religious realities.

THE ALTERNATIVE: "DEVOTION TO THE WORLD"
OR TRUE SELF-COMMUNICATION OF GOD

Hence the problem which confronts us is still unresolved. For given our presuppositions, it seems that religion is respect vis-à-vis the categorical structures of the world insofar as all of these together have a transcendental orientation towards their primordial ground, and in this kind of "religion" God really plays only an indirect role. This is the one alternative. This alternative could be called man's devotion to and respect for the world, the world in its own proper structures, including its interpersonal structures, in the knowledge that this world has an ultimate orientation towards its transcendental ground and abyss called "God." What would be left as genuine religion is a divinely encompassed "devotion to the world." One person would worship nature as divine; another would experience the world as the location and site for his own self-liberation and his own active self-understanding; a third would perhaps be a scientist who perceives reality as beautiful in the truth he has discovered. All of this would be conceivable in the context of an ultimate relation to the ineffable and silent source and term of everything, which in fear and trembling and before the final silence could be called "God." This would describe what could perhaps be called "natural religion," "natural" because it is very difficult to distinguish clearly here between nature and supernatural grace in their mutual relationship.

Or is religion really more than "devotion to the world"? Is there the possibility of an immediacy to God in which, without him ceasing to be really himself by being made a categorical object, he no longer appears merely as the ever-distant condition of possibility for a subject's activity in the world, but actually gives himself, and this in such a way that this self-communication can be received? We shall show that the essence of this "supernatural" religion and the primary and essential difference between this religion and what we just called "natural religion" cannot be subsumed under a univocal concept of religion. At this point we must state that, at least in Christianity, there can be a "presence" of God as the condition and object of what we are accustomed to call religion in the usual sense only insofar as the representation of this presence of God (in human word, in sacrament, in a church, in a revelation, in a scripture, and so on) can essentially be nothing other than something categorical which points to the transcendental presence of God. If indeed God is to remain himself even in being mediated to us, if he is to be present to us in mediated immediacy as the one infinite reality and as the ineffable mystery, and if in this sense religion is to be possible, then this event must take place on the basis of transcendental experience as such. It must be a modality of this transcendental relationship, and this relationship does allow for an immediacy to God. Moreover, the categorical appearance and concreteness of this immediacy cannot be given in its categorical finiteness as such, but only in its character of pointing to the modality of this transcendental relationship to God which gives immediacy.

Later we shall have to ask more precisely what is the exact nature of *this* mode of a transcendental relationship of man to God. In answering this question it will be shown that the Christian interpretation of the transcendental experience of God consists in the fact that the holy mystery is present not only as a remoteness and distance which situates us in our finiteness, but also in the mode of an absolute and forgiving closeness and of an absolute offer of himself, all of which takes place of course only by grace and in the freedom of God communicating himself. When all of this has been shown, then we shall have to ask why such an immediacy to God does not surpass from the outset every other conceivable, categorically mediated religious presence of God as it is apparently understood by concrete religions, by a religion of miracles, of powerful interventions of God in the world, by a religion of the prayer of petition, of a covenant, of definite sacramental signs and so on in which grace takes place. We shall have to explain why all of these things, which in the usual self-understanding of religion are recognized as the presence and proclamation of God in history, are a real presence of God in his own self, and hence as really grounding religion, only if and insofar as these appearances of God in our world and in time and space are the concrete and historical actualizations of God's transcendental self-communication. Otherwise they would be miracles and not the signs of the historical revelation of God.

GOD'S ACTIVITY IN AND THROUGH SECONDARY CAUSES

Moreover, we must repeat here what Thomas Aquinas said when he emphasized that God works through secondary causes. Of course this statement has to be understood as having a variable meaning. God's immediacy, his being mediated, his presence and his absence, all of these are variable notions because spirit as transcendence is not a characteristic of every existent in the world. But here our primary concern is the statement of Thomas just mentioned. If it is not to be made innocuous, the statement says that God causes *the* world, but not really *in the* world. It says that the chain of causality has its basis in him, but not that by his activity he inserts himself as a link in this chain of causes as one cause among them. The chain itself as a whole, and hence the world in its interconnectedness, and this not only in its abstract, formal unity but also in its concrete differentiation and in the radical differences among the various elements in the whole of the world's reality, this is the self-revelation of its ground. And he himself is not to be found immediately within this totality as such. For the ground does not appear within what is grounded if it is really the radical and hence the divine ground, and is not a function in a network of functions. If, then, there is nevertheless to be an immediacy of God to us, if we are to find him in his own self here where we are in our categorical world of time and space, then this immediacy both in itself and in its categorical, historical objectification must be embedded in this world to begin with. Then the concrete immediacy of God to us as is presupposed by and takes place in concrete religions must be a moment in and a modality of our transcendental and at the same time historically mediated immediacy to God.

A special "intervention" of God, therefore, can only be understood as the historical concreteness of the transcendental self-communication of God which is already intrinsic to the concrete world. Such an "intervention" of God always takes place, first of all, from out of the fundamental openness of finite matter and of a biological system towards spirit and its history, and, secondly, from out of the openness of the spirit towards the history of the transcendental relationship between God and the created person in their mutual freedom. Consequently, every real intervention of God in his world, although it is free and cannot be deduced, is always only the becoming historical and becoming concrete of that "intervention" in which God as the transcendental ground of the world has from the outset embedded himself in this world as its self-communicating ground.

It is a fundamental problem for a contemporary understanding of Christianity how God can really be God and not simply an element of the world, and how, nevertheless, in our religious relationship to the world we are to understand him as not remaining outside the world. The dilemma of the "immanence" or "transcendence" of God must be overcome without sacrificing either the one or the other concern. In our considerations up to now we have already met at least twice the formal structure of this peculiar relationship between transcendental beyondness and categorical accessibility. We have understood our irreducible subjectivity as well as our freedom and responsibility as fundamental human existentials which we always experience and which of course objectify themselves constantly in the concrete and in time and space, but which nevertheless are not something tangible which can be taken and defined as an object alongside of other objects.

Analogously and ultimately for the same reasons, the same formal relationship of tension obtains when we ask whether God appears in his world in a tangible way, whether, for example, he hears prayers or works signs, intervenes in history with his power, and so on. When to the extent that we are religious persons we answer these questions in the affirmative, this does not mean however that what is immediately tangible in this "intervention" does not exist in a functional relationship with the world or that it could not be explained causally. Outside of a religious and transcendental relationship to God and in certain circumstances it might not be able to be incorporated into this functional relationship because of the fact that it is disregarded as something not yet explained and as something justifiably left out of account, but not because it is in principle removed from the causal relationships of the world. The categorical presence of God means only that when the subject really remains subject with his transcendental religious experience and lives out his subjectivity in this way, then these objectifications of God's intervention have a valuable role within this transcendental experience of God. This role indeed really belongs to these phenomena in themselves, but *only insofar as* they really and truly exist within this subjective context, and therefore they can also be recognized in the special character which belongs to them only within this context.

Let us clarify what is meant by an example which is among the most modest ways in which God intervenes in his world, and so admittedly it cannot and does not intend to represent completely the more specific mode of a higher form of divine "intervention." A "good idea" strikes me which has as its consequence an important decision which proves to be valid and objectively correct. I regard this good idea as an inspiration of God. May I? I might be led to this judgment by its suddenness or by the impossibility of finding a causal or functional explanation for the origin of this good idea. But my judgment is not ultimately justified by such a subjective impression. On the contrary, I have the right, and even the obligation to explain this sudden idea, to trace it back to associations that I am not conscious of or to a physiological and psychological constitution which perhaps cannot be analyzed exactly at the moment, to regard it as a function of myself, of my history, of my world of people and of things, of the world as such. Hence I might explain it, that is, incorporate it along with all the concrete characteristics which it has in particular into the totality of the world which is not God. To this extent, therefore, I cannot see in this "good idea" any special presence of God in the world, any "intervention of God."

But the moment I experience myself as a transcendental subject in my orientation to God and accept it, and the moment I accept this concrete world in all its concreteness and in spite of all the functional interconnectedness of all of its elements, accept it as the concrete world in which my concrete relationship to the absolute ground of my existence unfolds historically for me and I actualize it in freedom, then within this subjective, transcendental relationship to God this "good idea" receives objectively a quite definite and positive significance. Hence I can and must say: it is willed by God in this positive significance as a moment of the one world established in freedom by its ground as the world of my subjective relationship to God, and in this sense it is an "inspiration" of God. Of course it could be objected against this that in this way everything can be regarded as a special providence, as an intervention of God, presupposing only that I accept the concrete constellation of my life and of the world in such a way that it becomes a positive, salvific concretization of my transcendental relationship to God in freedom. But against this objection we can simply ask the counter-question: Why, then, may this not be the case?

If and insofar as something is incorporated positively, not just in theory, but in the concrete exercise of freedom, into one's free relationship to God as the objectification and mediation of this relationship, it is in fact an inspiration, a mighty deed, however small, of God's providence, as we are accustomed to call it in religious terms. It is a special intervention of God. But this subjective and in fact correct response of mine in freedom to this or that particular constellation within the realm of my freedom, a constellation which, though functionally explainable, concretely mediates my relationship to God, depends, in spite of the subjective nature of my own decision and response, on factors which can be favorable or unfavorable, and in this difference are not simply and absolutely subject to my disposal.

But to this extent we can and must regard, and rightly so, a particular situation which works out for the good—as distinguished from another situation, which could have been, but is not—as in fact a special providence of God, as his intervention, as his favorable hearing, as a special grace, even if the opposite situation, handled by a correct response in human freedom, could have been made such a special act of God, but in fact was not. Because the subject's response in freedom is itself really and truly for the subject himself something given to him, without it losing thereby the character of the subject's own responsible and accountable action, a good decision along with everything which it presupposes as its mediation correctly has the character of an intervention of God, even though this takes place in and through human freedom, and hence can be explained functionally to the degree that the history of freedom can be explained, namely, insofar as it is based on elements objectified in time and space.

· III ·

Man as a Being Threatened Radically by Guilt

1. The Topic and Its Difficulties

G uilt and sin are without doubt a central topic for Christianity. For it understands itself as a religion of redemption, as the event of the forgiveness of guilt by God himself in his action on us in Jesus Christ, in his death and resurrection. Christianity understands man as a being whose free, sinful acts are not his "private affair" which he himself can absolve by his own power and strength. Rather, however much man's free subjectivity is responsible for them, once they are done they can be really overcome only by God's action. To that extent any introduction to the idea of Christianity would be deficient if it did not discuss man's guilt and forlornness, the necessity of deliverance from radical evil, redemption and the need for redemption.

When such notions as "redemption," the "need for redemption," "salvation," and "deliverance from evil" are used, it is advisable to begin with not to attach a temporal sequence to them. Whether we can fall into sin or have fallen into sin, whether redemption is an "existential moment" in our existence or a process that can be located in time following another process, namely, guilt, all of these are in any case secondary questions. We shall have to repeat again and again that we cannot interpret this world in a Christian way by saying that formerly there was a very evil world burdened with guilt, and that by the redemption of Jesus Christ it then became essentially different in an empirical and tangible way. When we speak of man's guilt, of his forlornness, of the necessity for a deliverance from evil, of redemption and the need for redemption, then at least methodologically we have to say first of all that such notions may not be connected in a temporal sequence.

90

THE OBSCURITY OF THE QUESTION FOR PEOPLE TODAY

The topic, "man as a being threatened radically by guilt," is undoubtedly burdened today with a special difficulty: we cannot say that people today are bothered in a very immediate way and at a clear and tangible level of their consciousness by the question whether and how as sinners in their individual histories of salvation and its opposite they find a merciful God, or how they are justified by God and before God. The normal person today does not fear God in this sense, and the question of his individual justification, which was, once with Augustine and then again at the time of the Reformation, the question on which the church was to survive or perish, this question does not bother people today very much or maybe even not at all.

It might be the case, of course, that in the depths of an individual's conscience and at really decisive points in an individual's personal history it is a very different matter. But judging by first impressions, in everyday life people today have no clear consciousness that they stand before God burdened by guilt and blame which cannot be shifted and as people deserving condemnation, but who nevertheless are saved by the incalculable miracle of God's pardon, by God's grace alone, and are accepted by God. This is the way Luther thought and felt in his immediate experience, and so did Pascal. We cannot really say that *we* still feel this way in any immediate sense. The modern social sciences have a thousand ways and means to "unmask" the experience of man's guilt before God and to demolish it as a false taboo.

People today do not indeed have a particularly positive impression of their own moral dispositions and those of others. They experience all of their finiteness and fragility and ambiguity in the area of moral norms, too. But if they want they can regard very many moral norms as mediated by society, as taboos that it is worth seeing through and getting rid of. However, it is not the case that then the experience of morality as such disappears. It need not be called morality, it need not be subsumed under a conception taken from bourgeois morality. But it cannot be denied that man is responsible, that he is accountable, that at least in certain dimensions of his existence he has the experience of being able to come and of actually coming into conflict with himself and his original self-understanding. Even someone who would fight against all of these experiences as something which only plunges people into neurotic anxiety would do that once again with the ardor of something which he *must* do.

By transcendental necessity, therefore, man is a *moral being*. It is vis-à-vis this demanding reality, this "ledger of his existence" that he experiences his finiteness, his fragility, his ambiguity. But what follows from this continually experienced difference between what one should be and what one is? To be sure, people have experienced evil of apocalyptic proportions in the world, and, armed with the sharp eye of the psychologist, the analyst and the sociologist, they do not quite trust themselves all the way. But precisely because of this skeptical and sober attitude they no longer muster today in the face of good and evil the same ardor with which the message of guilt and its forgiveness used to be preached. They see what is called guilt as a part of that universal misery and absurdity in human existence in respect to which man is not subject but object, and this all the more so as biology, psychology and sociology investigate the causes of what is called moral evil. A person today, then, is more likely to have the impression that God has to justify the unhappy condition of the world before man, that man is the sacrifice and not the cause of the condition of the world and of human history. This is still true even when the wrong seems indeed to be caused by man as a free subject, but this agent is once again the product of his nature and of his social situation.

People today, therefore, are more likely to have the impression that God has to be justified rather than that man himself is unjust and has to be justified by God and before God. This also means that death, when it is still recognized as having a serious existentiell and religious meaning, is hardly if at all seen as the moment when the good or evil condition of the individual person, a condition for which he can never shirk responsibility, comes inexorably to light. It is not understood as judgment, but either as the point at which all of the confusion of human existence is finally resolved, or as the final and naked climax of the absurdity of existence, for which there is no resolution.

But basically the difficulty which we have described and which is typical of our age can only be a challenge for a person to mistrust seriously his own average sentiments, which to be sure are not simply the self-evident norm for everything, to face the message of Christianity about man as sinner, and to ask himself whether this message is not ultimately saying something which he in his false innocence is not hearing, although he should be hearing it in the innermost center of his existence and in his conscience. Nor is a flight into false innocence avoided by retreating to the notion that all of existence is absurd, or by interpreting all of these oppressive and alienating situations as signs of friction in a development which basically is still going forward.

We must at least be open to the possibility that in the message of Christianity at least as much truth about the understanding of human existence becomes audible as a person can hear by himself when he just tries to listen to the voice of his own conscience or to the voice of his own particular age's interpretation of the times.

THE CIRCLE BETWEEN THE EXPERIENCE OF GUILT AND FORGIVENESS

But in addition to this difficulty which is typical of our age there is a more fundamental problem: there is question whether the topic can be treated at all at this point. It could be said that an understanding of the real nature of guilt is not possible until we have discussed the absolute and forgiving closeness of God in and through his self-communication; or that the real truth about a person's guilt can come home to him only when he experiences forgiveness and his deliverance from this guilt. For it is only in a radical partnership with and immediacy to God in what we call grace and God's self-communication that a person can grasp what guilt is: closing oneself to this offer of God's absolute self-communication. It is only in the process of forgiveness to which a person opens himself and accepts that he can understand what the guilt is that is being forgiven. For part of guilt is the fact that the punishment which it brings with it consists precisely in its blindness to its own false nature.

With regard to this fundamental difficulty, there is an irresolvable circle between the experience of guilt and the experience of the forgiveness of this guilt. The two are always dependent on each other in coming to a full understanding of what they really mean. The ultimate and radical nature of guilt itself lies in the fact that it takes place in the face of a loving and self-communicating God, and only when a person knows this and makes this truth his own can he understand the depths of guilt. To this extent, in understanding both of them there is a circle in which they throw light on each other. But because we have to discuss the mutually conditioning elements in this circle in temporal sequence, we have to talk about them one after the other although we know that we have correctly understood the first only after we have discussed the second. And a possible sequence is to speak first of guilt and then of its forgiveness.

2. Man's Freedom and Responsibility

Man's freedom and responsibility belong to the existentials of human existence. Since freedom is situated at the subjective pole of human existence and its experience, and not within what is categorically given, the essential nature of this freedom does not consist in a particular faculty of man alongside of others by means of which he can do or not do this or that through arbitrary choices. It is only too easy to interpret our freedom this way, an interpretation based on a pseudo-empirical understanding of freedom. But in reality freedom is first of all the subject's being responsible for himself, so that freedom in its fundamental nature has to do with the subject as such and as a whole. In real freedom the subject always intends himself, understands and posits himself. Ultimately he does not do *something*, but does *himself*.

FREEDOM IS RELATED TO THE SINGLE WHOLE OF HUMAN EXISTENCE

This means two things. First of all, freedom is related to the single whole of human existence, although this single whole exists in spatial extension and temporal duration. Freedom as the capacity of the subject to decide about himself in his single totality is not of course a faculty which is situated behind a merely physical, biological, exterior and historical temporality of the subject. That would be a gnostic conception of freedom, and there is a very profound and objective reason for this error. Even so deep a spirit and so committed a Christian as Origen gave in to this temptation partially, and understood concrete, historical life as the evil and secondary reflection of a freedom which has really affirmed itself and decided about itself prehistorically and in a completely different and pre-corporeal realm of existence.

Freedom is the capacity of the one subject to decide about himself in his single totality. It cannot simply be divided up into individual pieces, as it were. It is not a neutral faculty which does this at one time and something else at another. But nevertheless, as the freedom of the subject about himself and towards himself and from himself as a single whole, this freedom is not a freedom which lives behind a merely physical, biological, exterior and historical temporality of the subject. Rather it actualizes itself as this subjective freedom in a passage through the temporality which freedom itself establishes in order to be itself. Such a conception of freedom is of course much more nuanced, much more complex and much less unambiguous than the primitive, categorical conception of freedom as a capacity to do this or that arbitrarily. It is also more complex and more difficult in its ambiguity than a gnostic conception of freedom. But it happens to be the case that in a genuine ontological anthropology, what is complex and difficult and by no means radically unambiguous in its unity and identity is also true. Freedom is freedom in and through history and in time and space, and precisely there and precisely in this way is it the freedom of the subject in relation to himself.

The unity of the single actualization of existence in freedom is not indeed an immediate, empirical, individual and categorically identifiable datum of our experience. This unity, and hence the real essence of subjective freedom, is antecedent to the individual acts and events of human life as the condition of their possibility, just as human subjectivity is not the subsequent sum of the individual, empirical realities of human life. Freedom, then, is not a capacity to do this and then that with the capacity itself remaining neutral, so that the results of these individual acts would then be added together subsequently. Since the acts themselves are past, they would continue to exist only in God's reckoning and in man's, and in this way they would once again be placed on freedom's account subsequently. Freedom is not like a knife which always remains the same in its capacity for cutting, and in cutting always remains the same knife. Although it exists in time and in history, freedom has a single, unique act, namely, the self-actualization of the single subject himself. The subject's individual acts must always and everywhere be mediated objectively in the world and in history, but he intends one thing and he actualizes one thing: the single subject in the unique totality of his history.

FREEDOM AS THE FACULTY OF FINAL AND DEFINITIVE VALIDITY

There is a further misunderstanding which extends into the world of religious notions and brings false problems with it. Freedom is not the capacity to do this and then that, in such a way that the second is the opposite and the undoing of the first, so that if this process were to continue on in physical time uninterrupted by itself, its fulfillment could only be understood as an extrinsic interruption of this series of individual, so-called free acts, a series which of itself would extend into infinity. It would be interrupted, namely, by the fact that the realm for this eternally ongoing freedom would be taken away from it extrinsically by God in death.

But freedom is not the capacity to go on eternally in an eternally new process of disposing and redisposing. Freedom has rather a necessity about it which is not connected with physical necessity in the usual sense. For freedom is a capacity of subjectivity, and hence of a subject who is not an accidental point of intersection in a chain of causes extending indefinitely forward and backward, but is rather what cannot be so derived. Freedom therefore is not the capacity to do something which is always able to be revised, but the capacity to do something final and definitive. It is the capacity of a subject who by this freedom is to achieve his final and irrevocable self. In this sense and for this reason freedom is the capacity for the eternal. If one wants to know what finality is, then he must experience that transcendental freedom which is really eternal because it establishes something final, and in a finality which by its very nature can no longer be other nor wants to be other.

Freedom does not exist so that everything can always become different, but so that something can really become final and ineradicable. Freedom is, so to speak, the capacity for establishing something necessary, something which lasts, something final and definitive, and wherever there is no freedom, there is always just something which by its nature goes on generating itself, and becoming something else and being reduced to something else in its antecedents and consequences. Freedom is the event of something eternal. But since we ourselves are still coming to be in freedom, we do not exist with and behold this eternity, but in our passage through the multiplicity of the temporal we are performing this event of freedom, we are forming the eternity which we ourselves are and are becoming.

TRANSCENDENTAL FREEDOM AND ITS CATEGORICAL OBJECTIFICATIONS

As the coming to be in freedom of the finality of the subject, this freedom is a transcendental freedom and a transcendental experience of freedom. It is, then, an element in the subject himself which the subject cannot make conscious and objectify directly in its own self. Hence this freedom is not an individual, empirical datum which the a posteriori anthropologies could point to alongside of other objects. When we begin to reflect upon freedom, this act on the subjective pole is itself once again freedom, and in this act of looking for and reflecting upon an earlier freedom, we can always find as it were only the objectifications of this freedom. These objectifications as such can again be functionally derived forwards and backwards, upwards and downwards in the multiplicity of the world of objective experience, so that freedom can no longer be found. But at the same moment freedom itself has been exercised again on the subjective pole of this act of looking for objectified freedom. By its very nature as an act of the subject, therefore, freedom does not take place in the individualizing, isolating and so observable, empirical world of the individual sciences. For basically nothing is free there except the subject doing the science, and in this kind of science he is always concerned with something other than the subject himself. We have already experienced that we are free and what freedom really means when we begin to ask reflexively about it.

None of this denies, of course, but rather it positively implies that man is a being who in a multiplicity of ways is subject to necessity. Moreover, the assertion that man is a being who is always conditioned and derivative and manipulated by his environment does not simply refer to a regional and definable realm of his existence alongside of which there is the realm of freedom. Rather, these two aspects can never be separated completely in the concrete person. For whenever I act freely as a subject, I always act into an objective world, I always, as it were, leave my freedom and enter into the necessities of this world. And whenever I experience, recognize, analyze and connect these necessities, I am doing this as a free subject, and at least the act of knowing something necessary is a subjective act which the subject himself actively does, is responsible for and takes upon himself freely. All of this is being asserted in the most radical way when we emphasize that freedom is not a categorical, individual datum of human experience which is immediately and empirically observable in time and space.

With regard to individual free actions in his life, the subject never has an absolute certainty about the subjective and therefore moral quality of these individual actions because, as real and as objectified in knowledge, these actions are always a synthesis of original freedom and imposed necessity, a synthesis which cannot be resolved completely in reflection. In his original, transcendental experience of himself as subject, therefore, the subject knows indeed who he is. But he can never objectify this original knowledge in a definite, thematic, propositional knowledge *of absolute certainty* when he makes statements in order to express himself, and in order to judge with respect to himself who and what he has become through the concrete mediation of his categorical actions. The free subject is always present to himself in his origins and in his freedom, and at the same time he is distant from himself in his freedom because of the objective factors through which he must necessarily be mediated to himself.

3. The Possibility of a Decision against God

The point of our reflections upon the essence of subjective freedom is to show that the freedom to dispose of oneself is a freedom vis-à-vis the subject as a whole, a freedom for something of final and definitive validity, and a freedom which is actualized in a free and absolute "yes" or "no" to that term and source of transcendence which we call "God." And at this point, insofar as this is possible at all in a more philosophical and anthropological analysis, we are for the first time getting close to an insight into what guilt means in its theological sense.

UNTHEMATIC AFFIRMATION OR DENIAL OF GOD IN EVERY FREE ACT

Freedom or subjectivity, which is the "object" of freedom itself, freedom for something of final and the definitive validity, and freedom for or against God are all interconnected. For transcendence towards the distant presence of the absolute mystery which offers itself to us is the condition which makes subjectivity and freedom possible. It is only because this horizon of absolute transcendentality which we call "God" is the source and the term of our spiritual movement that we are subjects at all, and hence free. For wherever there is no such infinite horizon, such an existent is locked up within itself in a definite and intrinsic limitation, without knowing this explicitly itself, and for this reason it is not free either.

Now it is decisive for our question that this freedom as "yes" or as "no" implies a freedom vis-à-vis its own horizon. Freedom which is mediated in a human, historical and objective way and in concrete personhood is, of course, always and also freedom with respect to a categorical object. Freedom takes place as mediated by the concrete world which encounters us, and especially by the world of other persons, even when this freedom intends and wants to be freedom vis-à-vis God immediately and thematically. Even in the act of such a thematic "yes" or "no" to God, this "yes" is not affirmed immediately to the God of original and transcendental experience, but only to the God of thematic, categorical reflection, to a God in concepts, maybe even only to a God in false gods, but not immediately and exclusively to the God of transcendental presence.

But since in every act of freedom which is concerned on the categorical level with a quite definite object, a quite definite person, there is always present, as the condition of possibility for such an act, transcendence towards the absolute term and source of all of our intellectual and spiritual acts, and hence towards God, there can and must be present in every such act an *unthematic "yes" or "no"* to this God of original, transcendental experience. Subjectivity and freedom imply and entail that this freedom is not only freedom with respect to the object of categorical experience within the absolute horizon of God, but it is also and in truth, although always in only a mediated way, a freedom which decides about God and with respect to God himself. In this sense we encounter God in a radical way everywhere as a question to our freedom, we encounter him unexpressed, unthematic, unobjectified and unspoken in all of the things of the world, and therefore and especially in our neighbor. This does not preclude the necessity of making this thematic. But this latter does not give us our original relationship to God in our freedom, but rather it makes thematic and objectifies the relationship of our freedom to God which is given with and in the original and essential being of the subject as such.

THE HORIZON OF FREEDOM AS ITS "OBJECT"

Now why is the transcendental horizon of our freedom not only the condition of possibility for freedom, but also its real "object"? Why are we dealing in freedom not merely with ourselves, why are we dealing not only with the world of our fellow man and the world of other persons either in a way which does justice to reality or is destructive of reality, and all within the infinitely vast horizon of transcendence from out of which we encounter ourselves and our world of persons and things in freedom? Why beyond this is this horizon also "object" of this freedom in our "yes" or "no" to it? In the latter case this horizon by definition is once again the condition of possibility for a "no" to itself, and hence this horizon can at the same time be affirmed necessarily and inescapably as the condition of possibility for freedom, and also denied as unthematic "object." Consequently, there is in the act in which freedom says "no" a real and absolute contradiction by the fact that God is affirmed and denied at the same time. How is it that this ultimate contradiction is at the same time distant from itself and relativized into temporality by the fact that such an actualization of the self in a "yes" or "no" to God is necessarily objectified in the finite material of our lives and their temporal and objective extension, and is mediated by this material? This is the question.

THE POSSIBILITY OF ABSOLUTE CONTRADICTION

We have to affirm the real possibility of such an absolute contradiction in freedom. One can of course deny it or have doubts about it. These denials and doubts occur in the popular theology of everyday life whenever it is said that it is inconceivable to hold any other position except that the infinite God in his sovereign objectivity could assess the slight aberration of a finite reality, an offense against a concrete and merely finite essential structure only for what it is, namely as something finite. The "will" against which such a sin really offends is only the finite reality willed by God, and an offense against God's will beyond that would in a false way make God's will into an individual, categorical reality alongside of the thing he wills. Looking at the matter from this point of view, where would we really find that radical seriousness in free decisions which Christian faith acknowledges for at least human existence in its totality?

On the contrary, in these free actions within the categorical reality of our experience which contradict the essential structure of this reality which exists within the horizon of transcendence, there is the possibility of offending against the ultimate term of this transcendence itself. If this possibility did not exist, then basically there would be no real subjectivity in freedom. Freedom would not be characterized by the fact that it is about the *subject* himself, and not about this or that thing. If freedom is about the subject, because the subject is transcendentality; if the individual existents within the world which encounter us within the horizon of transcendence are not events within a horizon which itself remains untouched by what is within the horizon; if rather these concrete realities are the historical concreteness of the transcendence by which our subjectivity is borne, then freedom vis-à-vis the individual existents which encounter us is always and also a freedom vis-à-vis the horizon, the ground and the abyss which allows these realities to become an intrinsic element in our freedom.

THE FREEDOM TO SAY "YES" OR "NO" TO GOD

Because and to the extent that the term and the source of transcendence cannot be a matter of indifference to the subject as knower, to the same extent and for the same reason freedom originally and inevitably has to do with God. Freedom is the freedom to say "yes" or "no" to God, and therein and thereby is it freedom in relation to oneself. If the subject is borne by his transcendental immediacy to God, then really subjective freedom which disposes of the subject as a whole and in a final and definitive way can occur only in a "yes" or "no" to God because it is only in this way that the subject as such and as a whole can be affected. Freedom is the freedom of the subject in relation to himself in his final and definitive validity, and in this way it is freedom for God, however little this ground of freedom might be thematic in an individual act of freedom, and however much, as it were, this God with whom we have to do in our freedom might be appealed to and sought after explicitly and thematically in human words and in human concepts.

In addition to this there is a second aspect which we can only indicate here by way of anticipation. If the historical concreteness of our transcendence in grace includes more than what we have said about it so far, if it also consists in the offer of God's self-communication to us, and in the absolute closeness of this holy mystery as communicating itself and not refusing itself, then freedom in transcendence and in its "yes" or "no" to its ground receives an immediacy to God in and through which it becomes in the most radical way a capacity to say "yes" or "no" to God. This radical way would not yet be given with the abstract, formal concept of transcendence towards God merely as the distant and remote horizon of the actualization of existence, and for this reason neither does it only need to be deduced from this merely distant and remote horizon of our transcendence.

As a being of freedom, therefore, man can deny himself in such a way that he really and truly says "no" to God himself, and indeed to God himself and not merely to some distorted or childish notion of God. To God himself, not merely to some inner-worldly norm of action which we rightly or wrongly call "God's law." Corresponding to the essence of freedom, such a "no" to God is originally and primarily a "no" to God in the actualization of human existence in its single totality and in its single and unique freedom. Such a "no" to God is not originally merely the moral sum which we calculate from individual good or evil deeds, whether we treat all of these acts as having equal value, or whether we believe that in this sum what matters is only the temporally last individual act in our lives, as though this were of absolute importance merely because it is temporally the last, and not insofar as it recapitulates in itself the act of freedom of a whole life in its single totality.

THE HIDDENNESS OF DECISION

Since freedom is the content of a subjective, transcendental experience and not a datum that can be isolated in our objective and empirical world, in our individual existence we can never point by ourselves with certainty to a definite point in our lives and say: precisely here and not somewhere else a really radical "yes" or "no" to God took place. But although we cannot do this because we cannot objectify in this way our original, transcendental and subjective freedom, we know that the entire life of a free subject is inevitably an answer to the question in which God offers himself to us as the source of transcendence. We know moreover that such an answer can also be a radical "no" to this silent, at once present and absent holy mystery, and to this mystery wanting to give itself in absolute closeness through grace. But the peculiar nature of this transcendental presence of God as the very thing which freedom is all about shows how and why this "no" can take place hidden in something harmless, in a situation where something insignificant in the world mediates this relationship to God. In certain circumstances it is possible that nothing is hidden beneath an

apparently very great offence because it can be just the phenomenon of a
pre-personal situation, and behind the facade of bourgeois respectability
there can be hidden a final, embittered and despairing "no" to God, and
one that is really subjectively done and not just passively endured.

"YES" AND "NO" TO GOD ARE NOT PARALLEL

Since freedom's "no" to God is based on a transcendental and necessary
"yes" to God in transcendence and otherwise could not take place, and
hence since it entails a free self-destruction of the subject and an intrinsic
contradiction in his act, for this reason then this "no" must never be
understood as an existential-ontological parallel possibility of freedom
alongside of the possibility of a "yes" to God. This "no" is one of freedom's
possibilities, but this possibility of freedom is always at the same time
something abortive, something which miscarries and fails, something
which is self-destructive and self-contradictory. Such a "no" can give the
appearance that the subject really and radically asserts himself only by this
"no." This appearance can be given because the subject affirms in freedom
a categorical goal absolutely, and in doing this he then misses everything
else absolutely, instead of giving himself over unconditionally to the ineffable and holy mystery. This mystery is not at our disposal, but rather we exist
at its unconditional disposal.

But however much such a "no" can have the appearance of an absolute
act, however much, when looked at categorically, it might represent the
absoluteness of a decision better than a "yes" to God, it is not for this
reason of equal right and stature in relation to a "yes" to God. For every
"no" always derives the life which it has from a "yes" because the "no"
always becomes intelligible only in light of the "yes," and not vice versa.
Even the transcendental possibility of freedom's "no" lives by that necessary "yes." All knowledge and every free act lives by the term and the source
of transcendence. But we have to allow for such a real impossibility and
self-contradiction in this "no": the contradiction, namely, that this "no"
really closes itself and says "no" to the transcendental horizon of our
freedom, and at the same time lives by a "yes" to this God.

ON THE INTERPRETATION OF ESCHATOLOGICAL STATEMENTS

This of course does not explain the possibility of a radical, subjective,
resolute and definitive "no" to God. We shall have to allow this possibility
to exist as the "mystery of evil." In the most radical and existentell uniqueness which he is, man has to reckon with the fact that this mystery of evil

is not only a possibility in him, but that it also becomes a reality, and indeed not insofar as a mysterious, impersonal power breaks into his life as a destructive fate. Rather this possibility of a "no" to God himself can become a reality in him in the sense that in his subjectivity, which he cannot distinguish from himself and shirk responsibility for, he really is evil, and he understands this evil as what he is and what he definitively wants to be. By interpreting and maintaining really subjective freedom in this most radical way, the Christian doctrine about the possibility of such guilt as a "no" to God ascribes to the individual one of these two ultimate possibilities of his existence as really and truly his own.

But at least in principle this Christian teaching says nothing about the question in what concrete individual and to what extent in the human race as a whole this possibility has become reality. The Christian message says nothing about whether in some people or in many people evil has become an absolute reality defining the *final end and result* of their lives. Both conscience and the Christian message, which does not allow us to abbreviate what conscience tells us, teach us about our possibilities and our tasks, they situate us in the process of deciding about our existence. But they do not tell the individual how his own individual history or the history of the whole human race is in fact going to turn out. Nor do the scriptural descriptions of the end-times have to be regarded as conclusive eye-witness accounts of what is some day going to be. If we apply correctly an exact hermeneutic of eschatological statements, these scriptural descriptions of the end both of the individual person and of the whole human race can be understood as statements about the possibilities of human life, and as instructions about the absolute seriousness of human decision.

In real theology we do not have to break our heads over such questions as whether anyone, and if so how many people suffer eternal loss, or whether anyone, and if so how many people really in fact decide against God in their ultimate and original freedom. We do not need to know that, nor do we have to read scripture that way. Even in his revelation about eschatology God does not say what is going to come later. Rather these eschatological statements are basically statements about man existing *now* insofar as he faces these two possibilities about his future. In this sense, however, the message of Christianity as the radical interpretation of the subjective experience of freedom is absolutely and deadly serious. It says to each one of us, not to someone else, but to me personally: in and through yourself, in and through what you in your innermost depths are and definitively want to be, you can be a person who closes himself into the absolute, deadly and final loneliness of saying "no" to God. Moreover, we can understand all of the portrayals in scripture and tradition of the essence of hell as plastic images and pictures of this ultimate loneliness. Nor do we need to look for anything else there, presupposing only that we do not overlook the fact that by his very nature a spiritual subject is permanently related to the world, and do not overlook the intrinsic contradiction this implies when freedom decides finally and definitively *against* the structures of the reality of the world established by God.

THE POSSIBILITY OF SIN AS A PERMANENT EXISTENTIAL

When a person begins to reflect upon himself, he always encounters himself as having already exercised freedom, as having already exercised freedom even when he takes counsel with himself in a highly reflexive way about a further decision still to be made. This decision of freedom which has already been made is still there even when it is objectified and made reflexive, and this latter is a synthesis of original freedom and the necessities of freedom's material, a synthesis which can no longer be resolved completely by reflection. A future decision, however reflexive, is also co-determined by the previous decision which is impervious to subsequent reflection. The actual situation of a person's freedom, therefore, is not completely accessible to reflection, to an examination of conscience which would be understood as a definitive statement of absolute certainty. A person never knows with absolute certainty whether the objectively guilty character of his actions, which he can perhaps establish unambiguously, is the objectification of a real and original decision of freedom saying "no" to God, or whether it is more in the nature of a manipulation which has been imposed upon him and which he endures, and which has about it the character of necessity. The ultimate nature of this manipulation is not accessible to superficial, empirical observation, but it can be a positive response to God. We never know with ultimate certainty whether we really are sinners. But although it can be suppressed, we do know with ultimate certainty that we really *can* be sinners, even when our bourgeois everyday life and our own reflexive manipulation of our motives appear to give us very good grades.

Since freedom in its original and essential being has to do with the original actualization of existence in its unity and totality, and therefore is not finally and definitively actualized until it has actively passed through the deed of life and into the absolute powerlessness of death, the possibility of sin is an existential which belongs to the whole of a person's earthly life and cannot be eradicated.

The fact that a free subject always continues to be threatened by himself is not the characteristic of a particular phase of life which could be surpassed within this earthly life. Rather this threat is really a permanent existential which we can never eradicate in our single, temporal history. It belongs always and everywhere to the single, total, and yet historical actualization of our single subjective freedom.

THE ABIDING SOVEREIGNTY OF GOD

Everything we have said expresses the radical importance of freedom for a person's final and ultimate self, but this of course does not limit the sovereignty of God vis-à-vis this freedom. For God is not a categorical alternative to this freedom, so that God and freedom would have to struggle with each other for their rightful place. An evil will does indeed contradict God within that difference which obtains between God and a creature in transcendental uniqueness, and this difference separating God and the created subject reaches its real essence and the essence of a subjective existent precisely in the act of freedom. Therefore all other differences between God and a merely pre-personal created existent can only be regarded as deficient modes of this real difference. This difference is affirmed in the act of freedom, in a good act as well as an evil one, because even in a good act, indeed all the more so in a good act, something is established which must have the character of being freely grounded in itself just as much, and indeed even more so, than when something which is morally bad is freely affirmed. But this free, subjective being-a-subject in differentiation from God and establishing one's own final and definitive self is really what is meant in the case of a difference between God and the other. This must not be understood after the model of the difference between two categorical existents. Rather it constitutes that unique and radical difference which exists only between a transcendent subject and the infinite, incomprehensible term and source of this transcendence which we call God.

But this very difference is established by God himself, and hence something which is autonomous and which alone realizes this radical difference between God and creatures entails no limitation of God's sovereignty. For this difference is not something which happens to him, but rather he alone makes it possible. He establishes it, he allows it, he grants it the freedom of its own self-actualization of this differentiation. And therefore in his absolute sovereignty and without contradiction at least from our perspective, God can establish freedom as good or as evil freedom without thereby destroying this very freedom.

The fact that as subjects of a freedom still coming to be we do not know whether or not God has so established all freedom that it will reach a good decision, at least finally and ultimately, is something to be accepted in obedience as a fact we know from experience, just as we have to accept our very existence in obedience.

We experience in our very experience of existence what is here the specific characteristic of freedom in its relationship to God: namely, we experience it as contingent by its very nature and at the same time as something necessary for us. We have neither the possibility nor the right to give back our admission ticket to existence, a ticket which is still used and not allowed to expire even when someone tries to annihilate himself in a suicide attempt. And this curious relationship between something contingent which is necessary for us really just has its prime example when there is established free differentiation from God. It is what is most properly our own and as such it is what God has established.

But if freedom is willed and established by God, and if in this way subjectivity exists without limiting the sovereignty of God, then this entails the possibility and the necessity of a free decision vis-à-vis God because this is what constitutes the essence of freedom. At this point we cannot go into the question whether and how this freedom can be accounted for in those peripheral cases where a person exists on a merely biological level, cases in which we do not recognize any concrete possibility of accounting for subjectivity, for example, the mentally handicapped who, at least by our normal standards, never seem to come to the use of reason. But we cannot understand something fundamental which is experienced at the center of existence in terms of such peripheral cases. Each one of us is endowed with his own freedom, and in this situation the Christian and theological assertion that man is a free subject takes on for us in the concrete an inescapable importance and a radical seriousness.

4. "Original Sin"

THE WORLD OF PERSONS AS THE REALM OF FREEDOM'S ACTUALIZATION

If the Christian doctrine about the possibility of radical guilt in human existence is really to be understood, then we must also consider that man precisely *as* free subject, and not merely *in addition* to this, is a being in the world, in history, and in a world of persons. But this means that he always and inevitably exercises his personal, inalienable and unique acts of freedom in a situation which he finds prior to himself, which is imposed on him, and which is ultimately the presupposition of his freedom. It means that he actualizes himself as a free subject in a situation which itself is always determined by history and by other persons.

This situation is not only an exterior situation which basically does not enter into the decision of freedom as such. It is not the external material in which an intention, an attitude or a decision is merely actualized in such a way that the material of this free decision then drops off this decision, as it were. Rather freedom inevitably appropriates the material in which it actualizes itself as an intrinsic and constitutive element which is originally co-determined by freedom itself, and incorporates it into the finality of the existence which possesses itself in its freedom.

The eternal validity of the free subject in and through his freedom is the final and definitive validity of his earthly history itself, and therefore it is also intrinsically co-determined by the elements imposed on it which have constituted the situation of the free subject in time. It is co-determined by the free history of all the others who constitute his own unique world of persons. However much it defends radically against making our own historical decision in freedom innocuous, the Christian interpretation of this situation of the free subject says that this situation, determined by his personal world, inevitably bears the stamp of the history of the freedom of all other men, and this precisely for the individual in his free subjectivity and in his most personal and individual history. Consequently, the guilt of others is a permanent factor in the situation and realm of the individual's freedom, for the latter are determined by his personal world.

The corporeality and objectification of each individual's original decision of freedom participates in the essence of this original free decision, and this is true whether the decision was good or bad. But they are not simply the original goodness or evil of this subjective, original free decision. They only participate in it, and therefore they are inevitably characterized by ambiguity. For while history is still going on, it always remains obscure whether they really are the historical, corporeal objectification of a definite good or evil free decision, or whether it only looks this way because this objectification has arisen only out of pre-personal necessities.

Moreover, this objectification of a free decision is always open to and capable of further determination. For the objectification of one person's free decision which has had an effect on the objectivity of a shared situation of freedom can become an intrinsic moment in the free decision of another.

In this latter decision this objectification can acquire a completely different character without ceasing for this reason to be the result of the first free action.

OBJECTIFICATIONS OF ANOTHER'S GUILT

According to Christian teaching objectifications of guilt are a part of these already existing elements in the situation of an individual's freedom. This seems to sound at first like something perfectly obvious. For every person has the impression that he has to decide about himself and to find himself and God in a world which is co-determined by guilt and by the guilty refusals of others. He knows from his own transcendental experience that there is freedom, and that this freedom objectifies itself in the world, in history, in time and space. He knows that such freedom includes the possibility of a radically evil decision, and he presumes that in this undoubtedly very inadequate and sorrowful world there are to be found objectifications of really subjectively evil decisions which have actually taken place.

This opinion is very natural. But if we think about it carefully and correctly, outside of the possibility of an absolute experience of one's own subjective evil objectifying itself in the world, it can really only claim to be probable at most. We could assume, first of all, that there has indeed always been the pressing and threatening possibility of really subjective evil in the world, but that this possibility has not become reality. We could assume that unfortunate situations which are detrimental to freedom and which always have to be worked through in the development of the human race never arise out of a really subjectively evil decision, but that they are the early stages of a development which begins from far below and moves upwards, and is not yet finished. We could assume that perhaps there have necessarily been evil decisions of freedom objectifying themselves in the world, but that they are then improved and transformed by a subsequent change in this same subjective freedom, so that they no longer have any adverse significance for others which would constitute an essential obstacle to a good decision in freedom by these others.

All of these possibilities might appear very improbable. To a person who in a subjectively honest judgment faces himself not only as a possible sinner, but as a real sinner, it might appear absurd to assume that in the whole history of the human race he alone is such a sinner merely because he only has the possibility of judging about himself, while this possibility is not assured with regard to others, or at least not with the same clarity and certainty. It might strike such a person who has really experienced his own subjective guilt as absurd to believe that he and he alone has brought something evil into this world by his actions in freedom, something which he can no longer intercept completely and undo.

All of man's experience points in the direction that there are in fact objectifications of personal guilt in the world which, as the material for the free decisions of other persons, threaten these decisions, have a seductive effect upon them, and make free decisions painful. And since the material of a free decision always becomes an intrinsic element of the free act itself, insofar as even a good free act which is finite does not succeed in transforming this material absolutely and changing it completely, this good act itself always remains ambiguous because of the co-determination of this situation by guilt. It always remains burdened with consequences which could not really be intended because they lead to tragic impasses, and which disguise the good that was intended by one's own freedom.

ORIGINAL AND PERMANENT CO-DETERMINATION BY OTHERS' GUILT

But this human experience, which is really quite obvious, is prevented from becoming innocuous by the message of Christianity and its assertion that this co-determination of the situation of every person by the guilt of others is something universal, permanent, and therefore also original. There are no islands for the individual person whose nature does not already bear the stamp of the guilt of others, directly or indirectly, from close or from afar. And although this is an asymptotic ideal, there is for the human race in its concrete history no real possibility of ever overcoming once and for all this determination of the situation of freedom by guilt. Throughout its history the human race can indeed, and always will strive anew to alter this situation of guilt, and even do this with very real successes and as an obligation, so that to neglect this obligation would itself be radical guilt before God. But according to the teaching of Christianity this striving will always remain co-determined by guilt, and even a person's most ideal, most moral act of freedom enters tragically into the concrete in an appearance which, because co-determined by guilt, is also the appearance of its opposite.

By rejecting an idealistic as well as a communistic optimism about the future, Christianity believes not only that it is giving witness to the truth, but also that it is performing the best service for a "better world" here and now. It believes that it has offered the world adequate moral imperatives and obligations extending all the way to responsibility before God and to the risk of *eternal* guilt. It believes that its historical pessimism is also the best service towards improving the world here and now, because the Utopian idea that a world functioning in perfect harmony can be created by man himself only leads inevitably to still greater violence and greater cruelty than those which man wants to eradicate from the world. Such a pessimism, of course, can become the excuse for not doing anything, for offering people the consolation of eternal life, and really for offering a religious attitude not only as the opiate of the people, but also as an opiate for the people. But this does not alter the fact that the radical realism which comes to expression in the pessimism of Christianity as we have formulated it with respect to the situation of our freedom is true, and that therefore it may not be disguised.

THE CHRISTIAN TEACHING ABOUT "ORIGINAL SIN"

Such a universal, permanent and ineradicable co-determination of the situation of every individual's freedom by guilt, and then of course of every society's too, is conceivable only if this ineradicable co-determination of the situation of freedom by guilt is also *original*, that is, is already imbedded in the origin of this history to the extent that this origin of the single history of the human race is to be understood as established by man. The universality and the ineradicable nature of the co-determination of the situation of freedom by guilt in the single history of the human race implies an original determination of this human situation by guilt already present at the beginning. It implies an "original sin."

"Original sin" does not mean of course that the original, personal act of freedom at the very origin of history has been transmitted to subsequent generations in its moral quality. The notion that the personal deed of "Adam" or of the first group of people is imputed to us in such a way that it has been transmitted on to us biologically, as it were, has absolutely nothing to do with the Christian dogma of original sin.

We arrive at the knowledge, the experience and the meaning of what original sin is, in the first place, from a religious-existential interpretation of our own situation, from ourselves. We say first of all: we are people who must inevitably exercise our own freedom subjectively in a situation which is co-determined by objectifications of guilt, and indeed in such a way that this co-determination belongs to our situation permanently and inescapably. This can be clarified by a very banal example: when someone buys a banana, he does not reflect upon the fact that its price is tied to many presuppositions. To them belongs, under certain circumstances, the pitiful lot of banana pickers, which in turn is co-determined by social injustice, exploitation, or a centuries-old commercial policy. This person himself now participates in this situation of guilt to his own advantage. Where does this person's personal responsibility in taking advantage of such a situation co-determined by guilt end, and where does it begin? These are difficult and obscure questions.

In order to arrive at a real understanding of original sin, we begin with the fact that the situation of our own freedom bears the stamp of the guilt of others in a way which cannot be eradicated. But this means that the universality and the inescapability of this co-determination by guilt is inconceivable if it were not present at the very beginning of mankind's history of freedom. For if it were not present, hence if this determination of our situation by guilt were only a particular event, then the radical nature of this recognition of a universal and ineradicable co-determination of the situation of our freedom by guilt could not be maintained. We have to understand this co-determination of the situation of human freedom by guilt as imbedded in the origin of history itself. The universality and ineradicable nature of the co-determination of the situation of freedom by guilt in the single history of the human race implies in this sense an "original sin" as it is called by its traditional name.

"ORIGINAL SIN" AND PERSONAL GUILT

"Original sin" in the Christian sense in no way implies that the original, personal act of freedom of the first person or persons is transmitted to us as our moral quality. In "original sin" the sin of Adam is not imputed to us. Personal guilt from an original act of freedom cannot be transmitted, for it is the existentiell "no" of personal transcendence towards God or against him. And by its very nature this cannot be transmitted, just as the formal freedom of a subject cannot be transmitted. This freedom is precisely the point where a person is unique and no one can take his place, where he cannot be analyzed away, as it were, either forwards or backwards or into his environment, and in this way escape responsibility for himself. For Catholic theology, therefore, "original sin" in no way means that the moral quality of the actions of the first person or persons is transmitted to us, whether this be through a juridical imputation by God or through some kind of biological heredity, however conceived.

In this connection it is obvious that when the word "sin" is used for the personal, evil decision of a subject, and when on the other hand it is applied to a sinful situation which derives from the decision of another, it is being used only in an analogous sense, and not in a univocal sense. Now we could ask in a critical way why the church's theology and preaching use a word which can be so easily misunderstood. We would have to answer, first of all, that what is permanent and valid about the dogma of original sin, and its existentiell meaning could certainly be expressed without this word. On the other hand, however, we have to take account of the fact that there is and has to be a certain amount of standardization in the terminology of theology and preaching, that the history of the formulation of this experience of faith did in fact take this course, and that this word is there and cannot be abolished privately and arbitrarily by some individual.

In preaching and in catechesis, therefore, we should not begin immediately with this word, which then has to be modified with a great deal of effort afterwards. We should rather acquire enough theology so that, starting with experience and with a description of the existentiell human situation, we can talk about the *matter itself* without using this word. Only at the end would we have to indicate that this very actual reality of one's own life and one's own situation is called "original sin" in ecclesiastical language.

Then it would be clear from the beginning that with regard to freedom, responsibility, the possibility of expiation and the modes of expiation, and the conceivability of the consequences of guilt which we call punishment, in all of these respects in any case "original sin" is essentially different from what we mean when we speak of personal guilt and sin, and understand them as possible or as actual from the perspective of the transcendental experience of freedom in ourselves.

"ORIGINAL SIN" IN THE LIGHT OF GOD'S SELF-COMMUNICATION

The nature of original sin must be understood correctly and only from an understanding of the effect which the guilt of a particular person or particular persons has on the situation of other persons' freedom. For given the unity of the human race, the fact that man is in the world and in history, and finally the necessity that every original situation of freedom be mediated in the world, there is necessarily such an effect.

Presupposing this basic structure of an act of freedom as being in the world and as co-determining the situation of others' freedom, what is specific about the Christian doctrine of original sin consists in two things:

1. The determination of *our own* situation by guilt is an element within the history of the freedom of the human race, an element which is imbedded in its beginning, because otherwise the universality of this determination of the situation of freedom and of the history of the freedom of all men by guilt is not explained.

2. The *depths* of this determination by guilt, which determines the *realm* of freedom and not freedom as such immediately, must be measured by the theological essence of the sin in which this co-determination of the human situation by guilt has its origins.

If this personal guilt at the beginning of the history of the human race is a rejection of God's absolute offer of himself in an absolute self-communication of his divine life, and we shall be treating this in detail later, then the consequences as a determination of our situation by guilt are different than they would be if it had merely been the free rejection of a divine law within the horizon of God himself. This divine self-communication, which is called the grace of justification, is what is most radical and most deep in the existential situation of human freedom. As divine grace it lies prior to freedom as the condition of possibility for freedom's *concrete* action. *Self*-communication of the absolutely *holy* God designates a quality sanctifying man prior to his free and good decision. Therefore the *loss* of such a sanctifying self-communication assumes the character of something which *should not be,* and is not merely a diminishing of the possibilities of freedom as can otherwise be the case in the instance of a "hereditary defect."

Since there is such a loss for the human race as the "descendants of Adam" in the situation of its freedom, we can and must speak of an original *sin,* although merely in an analogous sense of course, even though we are dealing with an element in the *situation* of freedom and not in the freedom of an individual as such. How this individual responds to this situation co-determined by a guilty act at the beginning of the history of the human race is a matter for his freedom to decide, however threatening and pernicious this situation is, and especially that freedom which is exercised vis-à-vis God's offer of himself. In spite of the guilt at the beginning of the human race, God's offer of himself always remains valid because of Christ and in view of him, although it is no longer present because of "Adam" and from "Adam," and hence no longer from a guiltless beginning of the human race. Even in this situation co-determined by guilt, it remains just as radical an existential in the situation of human freedom as what we call "original sin."

An understanding of what "original sin" means, then, is based on two factors. First of all, it is based on the universality of the determination by guilt of *every* person's situation, and this factor includes the original nature of this determination by guilt in the history of the human race, for this is implied in the universality. Secondly, it is based on the reflexive insight, deepening with the history of revelation and salvation, into the nature of the relationship between God and man. This factor includes the specific nature of the conditions of possibility for this relationship which are implied in the relationship, and also the special depths of guilt if and when there is guilt, and, if there is guilt, what kind of guilt is implied by a rejection of the sanctifying offer of himself which God makes to man.

ON THE HERMENEUTICS OF SCRIPTURAL STATEMENTS

Both the fact and the nature of what we call "original sin," therefore, can be arrived at from man's experience of himself in the history of salvation insofar as this history has reached its culmination in Christ. From this perspective it is also clear that the biblical teaching about original sin in the Old and New Testaments indicates phases of development which are clearly different from each other. The universality of the consequences of sin could not develop into a knowledge of original sin until reflexive knowledge about immediacy to God was radicalized in the instance of a positive relationship to him. The biblical story about the sin of the first person or first persons in no way has to be understood as an historical, eyewitness report. The portrayal of the sin of the first man is rather an aetiological inference from the experience of man's existentiell situation in the history of salvation to what must have happened "at the beginning" if the present situation of freedom actually is the way it is experienced, and if it is accepted as it is. If this is the case, then it is also clear that with regard to the visual representation of these events in the primeval beginnings of the human race, everything which cannot be arrived at by this aetiological inference from the present situation to its origins belongs to the mode of representation and the mode of expression, but not to the content of the assertion. The assertion might be couched in the form of a myth, since this is a completely legitimate mode of representation for man's ultimate experiences, nor can it be replaced radically by some other mode of expression. Even the most abstract metaphysics and philosophy of religion must work with visual images which are nothing else but abbreviated and faded elements of mythology.

Original sin, therefore, expresses nothing else but the historical origin of the present, universal and ineradicable situation of our freedom as co-determined by guilt, and this insofar as this situation has a history in which, because of the universal determination of this history by guilt, God's self-communication in grace comes to man not from "Adam," not from the beginning of the human race, but from the goal of this history, from the God-Man Jesus Christ.

THE "CONSEQUENCES OF ORIGINAL SIN"

Insofar as the situation of our freedom is inescapably co-determined by guilt, and this guilt touches everything which exists as individual elements within this situation of freedom, it is also clear that man's whole encounter in freedom with the world of persons and things which determine him would be different if this situation were not co-determined by this guilt. To this extent, toil, ignorance, sickness, pain and death as we encounter them in the concrete are undoubtedly characteristics of our human existence which would not be present in an existence without guilt *in the same way* that we actually experience them.

In this sense we can and must say that these existentials are the consequence of original sin. But this does not say conversely that everything which confronts us in these characteristics of man's individual and collective history is absolutely nothing else but the consequence of sin, nor that we can form a concrete image of the opposite existentials as they would appear in a realm of existence free of guilt. It is to be taken for granted that man without guilt would also have lived out his life in and through freedom and into something final and definitive, and in this sense would have "died." It is obvious that we cannot imagine concretely this mode of existence moving towards its fulfillment without being touched by guilt. All of the scriptural statements about this are and remain asymptotic attempts to indicate what existence would be like without guilt, a situation which no one has experienced in the concrete, but which we have to postulate if we do not want to shift the blame for our sinfulness and for the co-determination of our situation by sin onto God.

If the essence of sin is an actualization of transcendental freedom in rejection of God, then it can be actualized by a person even when the theoretical and practical mediation of this transcendental freedom is very modest. Just as in the first act in which man appears as man, perhaps when he made fire or used tools and this achievement seemed to exhaust his limits as man, he was already a transcendent being or else he cannot be called man, so too even in the most primitive cultural conditions we must acknowledge in this being the possibility of a "yes" or "no" to God which Christian doctrine acknowledges in the "first man" (or men). Since such a rejection of God must be understood from the perspective of the origin of human freedom as an act of basic and original self-interpretation, and not as one act among many others, neither is there any need to think of man in his innocence as living in a historical paradise for a longer period of time, and to reject what is really meant in Genesis as a mere myth.

·IV·

Man as the Event of God's Free and Forgiving Self-Communication

W hat the Christian message is really all about comes to expression for the first time here in this fourth chapter of our reflections. What was said in the first three chapters was indeed the presupposition without which the Christian message about man would not be possible. But by itself it was not yet so specifically Christian that anyone who accepts these assertions as his own self-understanding could already be called a Christian on the level of an explicit and reflexive profession of faith.

But now we are coming to the innermost center of the Christian understanding of existence when we say: Man is the event of a free, unmerited and forgiving, and absolute self-communication of God.

1. Preliminary Remarks

ON THE NOTION OF "SELF-COMMUNICATION"

When we speak of God's self-communication we should not understand this term in the sense that God would say something *about* himself in some revelation or other. The term "self-communication" is really intended to signify that God in his own most proper reality makes himself the innermost constitutive element of man. We are dealing, then, with an *ontological* self-communication of God. However, this term "ontological," and this is a second possible misunderstanding, should not be understood merely in an objectivistic sense, objectified and reified, as it were. A self-communication of God as personal and absolute mystery to man as a being of transcendence signifies from the outset a communication to man as a spiritual and personal being. First of all, then, we want to avoid both misunderstandings, that of a mere word *about* God, although perhaps spoken by God, as well as that of a self-communication of God which is reified and understood entirely after the manner of a thing.

116

STARTING POINT IN THE CHRISTIAN MESSAGE

It could be objected against the possibility of speaking about the free and forgiving self-communication of God at this point that this insight comes only as a result of the history of salvation and revelation which has its irreversible climax in the God-Man, Jesus Christ. But we shall not discuss this until the fifth or even the sixth chapter of our reflections. But it is legitimate, nevertheless, to reflect at this point upon the real origin and center of what Christianity really is and mediates and means: precisely this absolute and unmerited, and after the third chapter we must add, forgiving self-communication. For when we as historical beings come to an understanding of ourselves, we do this by grasping our past from out of the event of our present.

In order to see what the central theme of this fourth chapter means, then, let us begin a bit differently than we did before with the explicit message of Christianity. To be sure, the Christian message is the result of a long development in the history of man and his spirit. A Christian interprets it correctly as a history of salvation and of an ongoing revelation of God which has reached its climax in Christ. But even in this latter phase in which, according to Christian convictions, this history has reached its proper and highest self-understanding and a point of irreversibility, this message confronts *us*, and no or e can deny that our own historical situation is such that we have the obligation, if indeed we are historical beings, to listen to this message, and to agree with it or to reject it explicitly and responsibly.

2. What Does the "Self-Communication of God" Mean?

THE GRACE OF JUSTIFICATION AND THE "BEATIFIC VISION"

Now the Christian message says in the doctrine of the so-called "grace of justification," and especially in the doctrine of man's fulfillment in the vision of God, that man is the event of an absolute and forgiving *self-communication* of God. "Self-communication" is meant here in a strictly ontological sense corresponding to man's essential being, man whose being is being-present-to-himself, and being personally responsible for himself in self-consciousness and freedom.

God's self-communication means, therefore, that what is communicated is really God in his own being, and in this way it is a communication for the sake of knowing and possessing God in immediate vision and love. This self-communication means precisely that objectivity of gift and communication which is the climax of subjectivity on the side of the one communicating and of the one receiving.

In order to understand our central thesis in this reflection, the doctrine of grace and the doctrine of the final vision of God must be understood within Christian dogmatics in the closest possible unity. For the themes in the doctrine of grace, namely, grace, justification and the divinization of man, are understood in their real nature only in the light of the doctrine of the supernatural and immediate vision of God, which according to Christian dogmatics is man's end and fulfillment. And conversely: the ontological nature of the doctrine of the immediate vision of God can be grasped in all its radicality only if it is understood as the natural fulfillment of that innermost and really ontological divinization of man which comes to expression in the doctrine of the justifying sanctification of man through the communication of the Holy Spirit to him. What grace and vision of God mean are two phases of one and the same event which are conditioned by man's free historicity and temporality. They are two phases of God's single self-communication to man.

THE TWOFOLD MODALITY OF GOD'S SELF-COMMUNICATION

At this point it is already clear from our general anthropology that God's self-communication to man as a free being who exists with the possibility of an absolute "yes" or "no" to God can be present or can be understood in two different modalities: in the modality of the antecedent situation of an offer and a call to man's freedom on the one hand, and on the other hand in the once again twofold modality of the response to this offer of God's self-communication as a permanent existential of man, that is, in the modality of an acceptance or in the modality of a rejection of God's self-communication by man's freedom.

That the acceptance of God's self-communication must be based upon and is based upon God's offer itself, and hence that the acceptance of grace is once again an event of grace itself, this follows from the ultimate relationship between human transcendence as knowledge and freedom and the term and source by which this transcendence is opened and upon which it is based. It follows further and essentially that the created act of accepting God's self-communication allows what is accepted to remain really divine, and does not reduce it to something created only if this created, subjective act is once again borne by God who is communicating himself and being accepted. And it follows still further that the concrete act of freedom precisely in its concrete goodness and moral rectitude must once again be understood as coming from and being empowered by the origin of all reality, and hence by God.

GOD'S SELF-COMMUNICATION AND ABIDING PRESENCE AS MYSTERY

What do we mean by God's self-communication more precisely? To explain this we must look once again to the essence of man which becomes present basically and originally in transcendental experience. Here man experiences himself as a finite, categorical existent, as established in his difference from God by absolute being, as an existent coming from absolute being and grounded in absolute mystery. The fact that he has his origin permanently in God and the fact that he is radically different from God are in their unity and mutually conditioning relationship fundamental existentials of man.

When we say now that "man is the event of God's absolute self-communication," this says at the same time that on the one hand God is present for man in his absolute transcendentality not only as the absolute, always distant, radically remote term and source of his transcendence which man always grasps only asymptotically, but also that he offers himself in his own reality. The transcendental term of transcendence and its object, its "in-itself," coincide in a way which subsumes both—term and object—and their difference into a more original and ultimate unity which can no longer be distinguished conceptually. And when we say that God is present for us in an absolute self-communication, this says on the other hand that this self-communication of God is present in the mode of closeness, and not only in the mode of distant presence as the term of transcendence, a closeness in which God does not become a categorical and individual being, but he is nevertheless really present as one communicating himself, and not only as the distant, incomprehensible and asymptotic term of our transcendence.

Divine self-communication means, then, that God can communicate himself in his own reality to what is not divine without ceasing to be infinite reality and absolute mystery, and without man ceasing to be a finite existent different from God. This self-communication does not cancel out or deny what was said earlier about the presence of God as the absolute mystery which is essentially incomprehensible. Even in grace and in the immediate vision of God, God remains God, that is, the first and the ultimate measure which can be measured by nothing else. He remains the mystery which alone is self-evident, the term of man's highest act, the term by which this act is borne and made possible. God remains the holy One who is really accessible only in worship. God remains the absolutely nameless and ineffable One who can never be comprehended, and hence not through his self-communication in grace and immediate vision either; who never becomes subject to man; who can never be incorporated into a human system of coordinates of either knowledge or freedom.

On the contrary: in this very event of God's absolute self-communication the Godness of God as the holy mystery becomes radical and insuppressible reality for man. The immediacy of God in his self-communication is precisely the revelation of God *as* the absolute mystery which remains such. But the fact that this can happen, that the original horizon can become object, that the goal which man cannot reach can become the real point of departure for man's fulfillment and self-realization, this is what is expressed in the Christian doctrine which says that God wants to give man an immediate vision of himself as the fulfillment of his spiritual existence. This is what is expressed in the Christian doctrine which says that in grace, that is, in the communication of God's Holy Spirit, the event of immediacy to God as man's fulfillment is prepared for in such a way that we must say of man here and now that he participates in God's being; that he has been given the divine Spirit who fathoms the depths of God; that he is already God's son here and now, and what he already is must only become manifest.

THE GIVER HIMSELF IS THE GIFT

It is decisive for an understanding of God's self-communication to man to grasp that the giver in his own being is the gift, that in and through his own being the giver gives himself to creatures as their own fulfillment.

Of course this divine self-communication, in which God makes himself a constitutive principle of the created existent without thereby losing his absolute, ontological independence, has "divinizing" effects in the finite existent in whom this self-communication takes place. As determinations of the finite existent itself, these effects must be understood as finite and created. But the real thing about this divine self-communication is the relationship between God and a finite existent, and this can and must be understood as analogous to a causality in which the "cause" becomes an intrinsic, constitutive principle of the effect itself.

THE MODEL OF FORMAL CAUSALITY

If God himself in his own most proper and absolute reality and glory is the gift itself, then perhaps we can speak of a relationship of *formal* causality as distinguished from efficient causality. At least within the realm of our own categorical experience, in efficient causality the effect is always different from the cause. But we are also familiar with formal causality: a particular existent, a principle of being is a constitutive element in another subject by the fact that it communicates itself to this subject, and does not just cause something different from itself which is then an intrinsic, constitutive principle in that which experiences this efficient causality. We can reflect on this kind of formal causality in order to clarify what we want to say here. In what we call grace and the immediate vision of God, God is really an intrinsic, constitutive principle of man as existing in the situation of salvation and fulfillment.

As distinguished from the intrinsic, essentially constitutive causes which are found elsewhere in our experience, this intrinsic, formal causality is to be understood in such a way that the intrinsic, constitutive cause retains in itself its own essence absolutely intact and in absolute freedom. The ontological essence of this self-communication of God or the possibility of this self-communication of God remains obscure in its uniqueness. The possibility of this self-communication is an absolute prerogative of God, since only the absolute being of God can not only establish what is different from himself without becoming subject to this difference from himself, but can also at the same time communicate himself in his own reality without losing himself in this communication.

Therefore the ontological essence of this self-communication can be conceptualized reflexively only by a dialectical and analogous modification of other concepts which are familiar to us from elsewhere. If, then, one wants to bother with such an analogous application of ontic concepts at all, there is available for this kind of an analogous statement about God's self-communication the notion of an intrinsic, formal causality as distinguished from an outward-directed efficient causality. In this mode of conceptualization it can then be said that in this self-communication God in his absolute being is related to the created existent in the mode of formal causality, that is, that he does not originally cause and produce something different from himself in the creature, but rather that he communicates his own divine reality and makes it a constitutive element in the fulfillment of the creature.

The intrinsic intelligibility and the ontological justification for understanding the notion of self-communication this way is found in the transcendental experience of the orientation of every finite existent to the absolute being and mystery of God. In transcendence as such, absolute being is the innermost constitutive element by which this transcendental movement is borne towards itself, and is not just the extrinsic term and extrinsic goal of a movement. Precisely for this reason this term is not an element in this transcendental movement of such a kind that it would have its existence and meaning only in this movement. Rather, while it is what is innermost in this movement, it also remains absolutely beyond and absolutely untouched by this transcendental movement.

GOD'S SELF-COMMUNICATION
FOR THE SAKE OF IMMEDIATE KNOWLEDGE AND LOVE

When understood in this way, the essence and the meaning of God's self-communication to a spiritual subject consists in the fact that God becomes immediate to the subject as spiritual, that is, in the fundamental unity of knowledge and love. Ontological self-communication must be understood as the condition which makes personal and immediate knowledge and love for God possible. But this very closeness to God in immediate knowledge and love, to God who remains absolute mystery, is not to be understood as a strange phenomenon which is added to another reality which is understood in a reified way. It is rather the real essence of what constitutes the ontological relationship between God and creatures.

In connection with the Christology to be developed later we shall have to show further that creation as efficient causality, that is, as the free establishment by God of what is other precisely as other, must be understood as the presupposition which makes this free self-communication possible, and as its deficient mode, although it is conceivable by itself. It can be made still clearer in Christology that this self-communication of God to what is not God implies the efficient causation of something other and different from God as its condition. Later we shall have to show that basically such a creative, efficient causality of God must be understood only as a modality or as a deficient mode of that absolute and enormous possibility of God which consists in the fact that he who is *agape* in person, and who is by himself the absolutely blessed and fulfilled subject, can precisely for this reason communicate himself to another.

If being is being-present-to-self, if the essence of an existent insofar as it has being is personal self-possession and inner luminosity, if every lesser degree of existence can only be understood as a deficient, delimited and reduced mode of the presence of being, then the ontological self-communication of God to a creature is by definition a communication for the sake of immediate knowledge and love. And conversely of course the parallel is also true: the true and immediate knowledge and love of God in his own self necessarily implies this most real self-communication of God.

THE ABSOLUTE GRATUITY OF GOD'S SELF-COMMUNICATION

This also means that this kind of self-communication by God to a creature must necessarily be understood as an act of God's highest personal freedom, as an act of opening himself in ultimate intimacy and in free and absolute love. Christian theology therefore understands this self-communication as absolutely gratuitous, that is, as "unmerited," and indeed with respect to every finite existent, and prior to any and every sinful rejection of God by a finite subject. Consequently, God's self-communication as a triumph over the sinful rejection of creatures must not only be understood as forgiving grace, but even prior to this it is the gratuitous miracle of God's free love which God himself makes the intrinsic principle and the "object" of the actualization of human existence.

Therefore God's self-communication in grace and in fulfillment in and through the immediate vision of God is characterized in Catholic theology as "supernatural." This notion is supposed to give expression to the fact that this self-communication of God is an act of the most free love, and indeed also with respect to the finite, spiritual existent already established in being by creation. Even with respect to the created subject presupposed as already existing, God's self-communication is a further miracle of his free love which is the most self-evident thing of all, and at the same time it cannot be logically deduced from anything else.

GRATUITOUS DOES NOT MEAN EXTRINSIC

The doctrine that grace and fulfillment in the immediate vision of God are supernatural does not mean that the supernatural "elevation" of a spiritual creature is added extrinsically and accidentally to the essence and the structure of a spiritual subject of unlimited transcendence. In the concrete order which we encounter in our transcendental experience and as interpreted by Christian revelation, the spiritual creature is constituted to begin with as the possible addressee of such a divine self-communication. The spiritual essence of man is established by God in creation from the outset because God wants to communicate himself: God's creation through efficient causality takes place because God wants to give himself in love. In the concrete order man's transcendence is willed to begin with as the realm of God's self-communication, and only in him does this transcendence find its absolute fulfillment. In the only order which is real, the emptiness of the transcendental creature exists *because* the fullness of God creates this emptiness *in order* to communicate himself to it. But precisely for this reason this communication is not to be understood in a pantheistic or gnostic way as a natural process of emanation from God. It is to be understood rather as the freest possible love because he could have refrained from this and been happy in himself. This most free love is such that in free graciousness it creates the emptiness which it wants freely to fill.

Therefore this self-communication of God to spiritual creatures can and must be called supernatural and gratuitous even prior to sin, without thereby introducing into man's single reality a multi-leveled dualism. In the one and only concrete, real order of human existence, what is most intrinsic to man is God's self-communication at least as an offer, and as given prior to man's freedom as the condition of its highest and obligatory actualization. Moreover, this very thing which is most intrinsic and which alone is self-evident is God, the mystery, the free love of his divine self-communication, and hence the supernatural. This is so because in the concrete order man is himself through that which he is not, and because that which he himself is, inescapably and inalienably, is given to him as the presupposition and as the condition of possibility for that which in all truth is given to him as his own in absolute, free and unmerited love: God in his self-communication.

REMARKS ON THE CHURCH'S TEACHING

What we have said so far about God's self-communication is attested to in holy scripture and in the official teaching of the church when they say that the justified person truly becomes a child of God; that in him as in a temple dwells the very spirit of God as a really divine gift; that he participates in the divine nature; that he will see God face to face as he is in himself, and not as mediated by mirrors or likenesses or enigmas; that what he will one day possess and be he already has now in all truth, although only in a hidden way, namely, in the grace of justification as a pledge and as contained in a living kernel.

All of these statements and others like them may not be understood as hyperbolic descriptions of some state or other of salvation and blessedness. What is decisive about the New Testament message is rather that the circle of inner-worldly powers and forces has been broken by an act of the one and living God, who is *God* and not some numinous power, and broken open to the real immediacy of God himself. In biblical terms we no longer have to do with principalities and powers, with false gods and angels, with the vast pluralism of our own origins, but rather with the one and living God who radically transcends all of these other things. We have to do with him who alone can be called by this name which is not really a name. As distinguished from all the powers and forces however numinous, he is present for us in immediacy in his Holy Spirit who has been given to us, and in him who is called "son" in an absolute sense because he was with God in the beginning and is God himself.

CHRISTIANITY AS THE RELIGION OF IMMEDIACY TO GOD IN HIS SELF-COMMUNICATION

Christianity can be a relationship to God which is distinguishable and distinct from and radically surpasses every other religion only if it is a profession of faith in this immediacy to God. This immediacy allows God really to be God even in and through his true self-communication, to be a God who does not give some numinous, mysterious gift which is different from himself, but who gives himself.

Indeed the statement that we have to do with God in his own self and in absolute immediacy bids us give ourselves over unconditionally to the nameless One, to the unapproachable light which has to appear to us as darkness, to the holy mystery which appears and remains all the more as mystery the nearer it comes. Indeed this statement bids us see all paths as leading to where there are no paths, to ground all reasons where there is no ground, to understand all proofs as pointing to the incomprehensible, and never to think that we can establish once and for all some point around which we could organize an absolute system of coordinates which incorporates everything. Indeed this statement bids us surrender ourselves to the ineffable and holy mystery and to accept it in freedom, the mystery which becomes ever more radical for us the more it communicates itself, and the more that we allow this self-communication to be given to us in what we call faith, hope and love. But in the truth of God's absolute self-communication, in which he is at once giver and gift and the ground of the acceptance of the gift, it is also said to us that whoever loses himself completely finds himself in the presence of infinite love. It is said that whoever sets out upon the infinite path shall arrive, and indeed has already arrived, and that those who open themselves to absolute poverty and death and to all of their horror shall find that these are nothing but the beginning of infinite life.

What we can say by way of explaining grace and the immediate vision of God, then, does not give a categorical explanation of some definite thing which exists alongside of other things, but rather it gives expression to the nameless God as someone given to us. What is expressed, therefore, only repeats the naming of God in a quite definite, transcendental way, and points again to our transcendental experience which is beyond words. But it does this in such a way that now we can also say not only that this experience always has its most radical possibility ahead of it, but also that it will attain it, indeed that in the movement towards this attainment it is already borne by the self-communication of the future towards which this process is moving as to its absolute fulfillment. The doctrine about this grace and its fulfillment, therefore, bids us keep ourselves radically open in faith, hope and love for the ineffable, unimaginable and nameless absolute future of God which is coming, and bids us never close ourselves before there is nothing more to close, because nothing will be left outside of God, since we shall be wholly in God and he shall be wholly in us.

3. The Offer of Self-Communication as "Supernatural Existential"

Up to this point we have taken as our starting point the explicit teaching of Christian faith. But even if we are clear about the fact, and we shall be discussing this in the next chapter, that a person learns the ultimate and clearly formulated truth about his existence from the explicit teaching of revelation formulated officially by the church, and this he hears "from without" in human words, and even if we are clear about the fact that he does not form such an interpretation of his existence all by himself and just from his own interpretation of his private experience, one could still have the impression, nevertheless, that the statement that man is the event of God's absolute self-communication is addressed to him from without merely on the conceptual level, and that it does not really express for him in the explicitness of reflexive words what man himself truly is, and what he himself experiences in the depths of his existence. But this is not the case.

THE STATEMENT ABOUT GOD'S SELF-COMMUNICATION AS AN ONTOLOGICAL STATEMENT

The statement, "man is the event of God's absolute self-communication," does not refer to some reified objectivity "in man." Such a statement is not a categorical and ontic statement, but an ontological statement. It expresses in words the subject as such, and therefore the subject in the depths of his subjectivity, and hence in the depths of his transcendental experience.

Christian teaching, which becomes conceptual in reflexive, human words in the church's profession of faith, does not simply inform man of the content of this profession from without and only in concepts. Rather it appeals to reality, which is not only said, but also given and really experienced in man's transcendental experience. Hence it expresses to man his own self-understanding, one which he already has, although unreflexively.

In order to understand this thesis we must first of all consider that the thesis proposed here about the innermost and ultimate characteristic of our basic statement that man is the event of God's absolute self-communication does not refer to a statement which is valid only for this or that group of people as distinguished from others, for example, only for the baptized or the justified as distinguished from pagans or sinners. Without prejudice to the fact that it speaks of a free and unmerited grace, of a miracle of God's free love for spiritual creatures, the statement that man as subject is the event of God's self-communication is a statement which refers to absolutely all men, and which expresses an existential of every person. Such an existential does not become merited and in this sense "natural" by the fact that it is present in *all* men as an existential of their concrete existence, and is present prior to their freedom, their self-understanding and their experience. The gratuity of a reality has nothing to do with the question whether it is present in many or only in a few people.

What we said about God's self-communication being supernatural and unmerited is not threatened or called into question by the fact that this self-communication is present in *every* person at least in the mode of an offer. The love of God does not become less a miracle by the fact that it is promised to all men at least as an offer. Indeed only what is given to everybody realizes the real essence of grace in a radical way. Something gratuitous which is given to one and denied to another is really by its very nature something which falls within the realm of possibility for everyone precisely because it is given to one and is denied to another to whom it could also have been given. Hence such an understanding satisfies only the notion of something unmerited by the individual, but not the notion of something supernatural which essentially transcends the natural.

The supernatural, then, does not cease to be supernatural if, at least in the mode of an offer to man's freedom, it is given to everyone who is a being of unlimited transcendentality as a fulfillment essentially transcending the natural. In this sense everyone, really and radically *every* person must be understood as the event of a supernatural self-communication of God, although not in the sense that every person necessarily accepts in freedom God's self-communication to man. Just as man's essential being, his spiritual personhood, in spite of the fact that it is and remains an inescapable given for every free subject, is given to his freedom in such a way that the free subject can possess himself in the mode of "yes" or in the mode of "no," in the mode of deliberate and obedient acceptance or in the mode of protest against this essential being of his which has been entrusted to freedom, so too the existential of man's absolute immediacy to God in and through this divine self-communication as permanently offered to freedom can exist merely in the mode of an antecedent offer, in the mode of acceptance and in the mode of rejection.

The mode in which God's self-communication is present with respect to human freedom does not nullify the real presence of this self-communication as something offered. For even an offer merely as antecedently given or as rejected by freedom must not be understood as a communication which could exist, but does not. It must rather be understood as a communication which has really taken place, and as one by which freedom as transcendental is and remains always confronted really and inescapably.

THE SELF-COMMUNICATION
AS THE CONDITION OF POSSIBILITY FOR ITS ACCEPTANCE

God's self-communication is given not only as gift, but also as the necessary condition which makes possible an acceptance of the gift which can allow the gift really to be God, and can prevent the gift in its acceptance from being changed from God into a finite and created gift which only represents God, but is not God himself. In order to be able to accept God without reducing him, as it were, in this acceptance to our finiteness, this acceptance must be borne by God himself. God's self-communication as offer is also the necessary condition which makes its acceptance possible.

If, then, man is to have something to do with God as God is in his own self, and if in his freedom he is to open or close himself to God's self-communication without this response reducing God himself to the level of man, then God's self-communication must always be present in man as the prior condition of possibility for its acceptance. This is true insofar as man must be understood as a subject who is capable of such an acceptance, and therefore is also obligated to it. And conversely: without prejudice to its gratuity, God's self-communication must be present in every person as the condition which makes its personal acceptance possible. This presupposes only that the possibility of such a personal acceptance of God is acknowledged in principle for man because God in his universal salvific will has offered and destined this fulfillment not only for some, but for all men, a fulfillment which consists in the fully realized acceptance of this divine self-communication.

MAN'S SUPERNATURALLY ELEVATED TRANSCENDENTALITY

It follows from this that God's offer of himself belongs to all men and is a characteristic of man's transcendence and his transcendentality. Therefore God's self-communication as an offer, and as something given prior to man's freedom as a task and as the condition of freedom's highest possibility, also has the characteristics which all of the elements in man's transcendental constitution have.

Such an element in man's transcendental constitution is not the object of an individual, a posteriori and categorical experience of man *alongside of* other objects of his experience. Basically and originally man does not encounter this supernatural constitution as an object. The supernatural constitution of man's transcendentality due to God's offer of self-communication is a modality of his original and unthematic subjectivity. Hence this modality can at most, if at all, be made thematic in a subsequent reflection and objectified in a subsequent concept. Such a supernatural transcendentality is just as inconspicuous and can be just as much overlooked, suppressed, denied and falsely interpreted as everything else which is transcendentally spiritual in man. This antecedent self-communication of God which is prior to man's freedom means nothing else but that the spirit's transcendental movement in knowledge and love towards the absolute mystery is borne by God himself in his self-communication in such a way that this movement has its term and its source not in the holy mystery as eternally distant and as a goal which can only be reached asymptotically, but rather in the God of absolute closeness and immediacy.

THE EXPERIENCE OF GRACE AND ITS HIDDENNESS

Therefore God's self-communication in grace, as a modification of transcendence in and through which the holy mystery, that mystery by which transcendence is intrinsically opened and borne, is present in its own self and in absolute closeness and self-communication, cannot by simple and individual acts of reflection and psychological introspection be differentiated from those basic structures of human transcendence which we tried to present in the second chapter of our reflections. The absolutely unlimited transcendence of the natural spirit in knowledge and freedom along with its term, the holy mystery, already implies by itself such an infinity in the subject that the possession of God in absolute self-communication does not really fall outside of this infinite possibility of transcendence, although it remains gratutious. Therefore the transcendental experience of this abstract possibility on the one hand and the experience of its radical fulfillment by God's self-communication on the other cannot be clearly and unambiguously differentiated simply by the direct introspection of an individual as long as the history of freedom in its acceptance or rejection is still going on, and hence as long as this fulfillment through self-communication has not yet reached its culmination in the final and definitive state which we usually call the immediate vision of God.

Transcendental experience, including its modality as grace, and reflection upon transcendental experience are no more the same thing conceptually than self-consciousness and objectified, thematic knowledge of something which we are conscious of are the same thing. In our case there are two special reasons why God's self-communication in grace as a modification of our transcendentality is not reflexive and cannot be made reflexive. First, on the side of the addressee of this self-communication, because of the unlimited nature of the subjective spirit already in its natural state; and, secondly, on the side of God's self-communication, because of the unfulfilled state of this self-communication, that is, because it has not yet become the vision of God.

We can describe the transcendental experience of God's self-communication in grace, or, to put it differently, the dynamism and the finalization of the spirit as knowledge and love towards the immediacy of God, which dynamism is of such a kind that, because of God's self-communication, the goal itself is also the very power of the movement (we usually call this movement grace), we can describe this experience along with the essence of this spiritual dynamism adequately only by saying: in grace the spirit moves within its goal (because of God's self-communication) towards its goal (the beatific vision). Consequently, it cannot be concluded from the impossibility of identifying it directly and with certainty in individual reflection that this self-communication of God is absolutely beyond the subject and his consciousness, and is postulated *only* by a dogmatic theory imposed on man from without. What we are really dealing with is a transcendental experience which gives evidence of itself in human existence and is operative in that existence.

We can only appeal here to those individual experiences which a person has and can have of God's self-communication. They cannot indeed be recognized with *unambiguous* and reflexive certainty within an individual's experience, prescinding from possible exceptions, but they are nevertheless not simply and absolutely nonexistent for reflection.

Even if by simple introspection and by making his original, transcendental experiences thematic individually a person could not discover such a transcendental experience of God's self-communication in grace, or could not express it by himself with unambiguous certainty, nevertheless, if this theological and dogmatic interpretation of his transcendental experience is offered to him by the history of revelation and by Christianity, he can recognize his own experience in it. He can find in this interpretation the confidence to interpret what is ineffable in his own experience in accordance with it, and to accept the infinity of his own obscure experience without reservation and without limitation. He can see the legitimacy of his existentiell decision, and can resolutely and courageously accept this synthesis of his original, transcendental experience and its a posteriori, theological interpretation by Christianity, a synthesis which basically cannot be analyzed completely in reflection, but which has already been achieved.

In this sense we can say without hesitation: a person who opens himself to his transcendental experience of the holy mystery at all has the experience that this mystery is not only an infinitely distant horizon, a remote judgment which judges from a distance his consciousness and his world of persons and things, it is not only something mysterious which frightens him away and back into the narrow confines of his everyday world. He experiences rather that this holy mystery is also a hidden closeness, a forgiving intimacy, his real home, that it is a love which shares itself, something familiar which he can approach and turn to from the estrangement of his own perilous and empty life. It is the person who in the forlornness of his guilt still turns in trust to the mystery of his existence which is quietly present, and surrenders himself as one who even in his guilt no longer wants to understand himself in a self-centered and self-sufficient way, it is this person who experiences himself as one who does not forgive himself, but who is forgiven, and he experiences this forgiveness which he receives as the hidden, forgiving and liberating love of God himself, who forgives *in that* he gives himself, because only in this way can there really be forgiveness once and for all.

How strong such a transcendental experience of the absolute closeness of God in his radical self-communication might be, and how localized it might be at definite points in the time and space of a person's individual history, or how weak it might be and diffused in a more general and basic disposition; how much it might be the experience of every individual independently of everybody else, or how much it is shared in by the individual himself only in view of and by participating in the religious experience of stronger and holier people, all of these are questions of secondary importance.

The only point we are making here is this: the individual experience of individual persons and the collective religious experience of the human race, both of them together in a kind of mutual unity and mutual interpretation, make it legitimate for us to interpret man, when he experiences himself in the most various ways as the subject of unlimited transcendence, as the event of God's absolute and radical self-communication.

The experience which we are appealing to here is not primarily and ultimately the experience which a person has when he decides explicitly and in a deliberate and responsible way upon some *religious* activity, for example, prayer, a cultic act, or a reflexive and theoretical occupation with religious themes. It is rather the experience which is given to every person prior to such reflexive religious activity and decisions, and indeed perhaps in a form and in a conceptuality which seemingly are not religious at all. If God's self-communication is an ultimate and radicalizing modification of that very transcendentality of ours by which we are subjects, and if we are such subjects of unlimited transcendentality in the most ordinary affairs of our everyday existence, in our secular dealings with any and every individual reality, then this means in principle that the original experience of God even in his self-communication can be so universal, so unthematic and so "unreligious" that it takes place, unnamed but really, wherever we are living out our existence.

When a person in theoretical or practical knowledge or in subjective activity confronts the abyss of his existence, which alone is the ground of everything, and when this person has the courage to look into himself and to find in these depths his ultimate truth, there he can also have the experience that this abyss accepts him as his true and forgiving security. It makes it legitimate for him and gives him the courage to believe that the interpretation of this experience by mankind's history of salvation and revelation, that is, the interpretation of this experience as the event of God's radical self-communication, expresses the ultimate depths of and the ultimate truth about this apparently so ordinary experience. Of course this kind of an experience also has its more prominent moments: in the experience of death, of radical authenticity, of love, and so on. There one notices more clearly than elsewhere that he reaches beyond this individual moment and comes into the presence of himself and of the holy mystery. And in its interpretation and explanation of this, the ultimate truth of Christianity about God's self-communication says only that this movement does not merely bring us into the presence of a remote, infinite and unencompassable distance, but rather that this mystery communicates itself to us.

Insofar as a person still exists in a situation of freedom which is still coming to be; insofar as the situation of his freedom is always a situation co-conditioned by guilt because of what we call "original sin"; insofar as when a person begins to reflect, in his reflection he never stands before the pure possibility of a previously completely neutral freedom, but always before a freedom which has already been freely exercised; and insofar as a person can never reflexively and conclusively judge this freedom of his which has already been exercised, it follows that transcendental experience is always ambivalent and can never be recaptured completely in human reflection. Man experiences himself as a subject who never knows exactly how in and through his own freedom he has understood and manipulated the objectifications within the realm of his freedom which have been co-conditioned by guilt, who never knows exactly whether he has made them the manifestation of his own original sinful decision, or made them the crucifying suffering involved in overcoming guilt.

Man experiences himself at the same time as a subject who experiences the event of God's absolute self-communication, as a subject who has already responded in freedom with a "yes" or "no" to this event, and who can never bring the concrete and real mode of his response to the level of reflection completely. Hence in this fundamental question of his existence, which he has already answered subjectively, he always remains ambiguous for himself in his reflection. He remains a subject who actualizes the subjectivity of his gratuitously elevated transcendence in his a posteriori and historical encounter with his world of persons and of things, an encounter which is never completely at his disposal. And he actualizes it in his encounter with a human thou in whom history and transcendence find their one actualization together and in unity, and there he finds his encounter with God as the absolute Thou.

4. Towards an Understanding of the Doctrine of the Trinity

Although there will perhaps be an opportunity to discuss the Christian doctrine of the Trinity in connection with our efforts to reach an understanding of the doctrine of the Incarnation, let us try here at this point to reach an initial understanding of the Christian doctrine of the Trinity from what has just been said.

THE PROBLEM OF CONCEPTUALIZATION

With all due respect to the church's official and classical formulation of the Christian doctrine of the Trinity, and taking for granted an acceptance in faith of what is meant by these formulations, we still have to admit that the assertions about the Trinity in their catechetical formulations are almost unintelligible to people today, and that they almost inevitably occasion misunderstandings. When we say with the Christian catechism that in the one God there are three "persons" in the unity and unicity of one nature, in the absence of further theological explanation it is almost inevitable that whoever hears this formula will understand by the word "person" the content which he associates with this word elsewhere.

The terms which the church used in earlier times in an extraordinarily powerful theology and in its process of conceptualization continue to have a history, and this history is not simply at the autonomous disposal of the church. It is directed not only by the church, but also by other histories of human language and concepts, and by the history of the human spirit. Consequently, it is altogether possible for such a term to take on a content which carries with it at least the danger that its application to the old formulations, which are quite correct in themselves, puts a false and a mythological construction on these formulations which cannot be assimilated.

This situation is not surprising, for when Christian doctrine uses the terms "hypostasis," "person," "essence" and "nature" to express the divine Trinity, it is not employing concepts which are clear and unambiguous in themselves and which are applied here in all their clarity. Rather, in order to express what was meant, these concepts were to some extent distinguished from one another in the church's language only very slowly and with great difficulty, and they were defined according to these norms of usage, although the history of the defining process shows that there would also have been other possibilities for expressing asymptotically what was meant. When in our secular use of language today we speak of one "person" as distinct from another person, we can hardly avoid the notion that in order that they be persons and be different, there is in each of these persons its own free center of conscious and free activity which disposes of itself and differentiates itself from others, and that it is precisely this which constitutes a person. But this is the very thing which is excluded by the dogmatic teaching on the single and unique essence of God. This unicity of essence implies and includes the unicity of one single consciousness and one single freedom, although of course the unicity of one self-presence in consciousness and freedom in the divine Trinity remains determined by that mysterious threeness which we profess about God when we speak haltingly of the Trinity of persons in God.

THE PROBLEM WITH A "PSYCHOLOGICAL THEORY OF THE TRINITY"

With regard to the imposing speculations in which, since the time of Augustine, Christian theology has tried to conceive of the inner life of God in self-consciousness and love in such a way that we acquire presumably a certain understanding of the threefold personhood of God, an understanding which portrays, as it were, an inner life of God completely unrelated to us and to our Christian existence, perhaps we can say that ultimately they are not really all that helpful. A "psychological theory of the Trinity," however ingenious the speculations from the time of Augustine down to our own time, in the end does not explain precisely what it is supposed to explain, namely, why the Father expresses himself in Word, and with the Logos breathes a Spirit which is different from him. For such an explanation must already presuppose the Father as knowing and loving himself, and cannot allow him to be constituted as knowing and loving in the first place by the expression of the Logos and the spiration of the Spirit.

Even if we prescind from these difficulties, the fact remains that such psychological speculation about the Trinity has in any case the disadvantage that in the doctrine of the Trinity it does not really give enough weight to a starting point in the history of revelation and dogma which is within the *historical and salvific* experience of the Son and of the Spirit as the reality of the divine self-communication to us, so that we can understand from this historical experience what the doctrine of the divine Trinity really means. The psychological theory of the Trinity neglects the experience of the Trinity in the economy of salvation in favor of a seemingly almost gnostic speculation about what goes on in the inner life of God. In the process it really forgets that the countenance of God which turns towards us in this self-communication is, in the trinitarian nature of this encounter, the very being of God as he is in himself, and must be if indeed the divine self-communication in grace and in glory really is the communication of God in his own self to us.

THE TRINITY IN THE HISTORY AND ECONOMY OF SALVATION
IS THE IMMANENT TRINITY

But if conversely we make the presupposition and hold to it radically that
the Trinity in the history of salvation and revelation *is* the "immanent"
Trinity, because in God's self-communication to his creation through grace
and Incarnation God really gives himself, and really appears as he is in
himself, then with regard to that aspect of the Trinity in the economy of
salvation which is given in the history of God's self-revelation in the Old
and New Testaments we can say: in both the collective and individual
history of salvation there appears in immediacy to us not some numinous
powers or other which represent God, but there appears and is truly present
the one God himself. In his absolute uniqueness, which ultimately nothing
can take the place of or represent, he comes where we ourselves are, and
where we receive him, this very God himself and as himself in the strict
sense.

Insofar as he has come as the salvation which divinizes us in the innermost center of the existence of the individual person, we call him really and
truly "Holy Spirit" or "Holy Ghost." Insofar as in the concrete historicity
of our existence one and the same God strictly as himself is present for us
in Jesus Christ, and in himself, not in a representation, we call him "Logos"
or the Son in an absolute sense. Insofar as this very God, who comes to us
as Spirit and as Logos, is and always remains the ineffable and holy mystery,
the incomprehensible ground and origin of his coming in the Son and in
the Spirit, we call him the one God, the Father. Insofar as in the Spirit,
in the Logos-Son, and in the Father we are dealing with a God who gives
himself in the strictest sense, and not something else, not something different from himself, we must say in the strictest sense and equally of the Spirit,
of the Logos-Son and of the Father that they are one and the same God
in the unlimited fullness of the one Godhead and in possession of one and
the same divine essence.

Insofar as the modes of God's presence for us as Spirit, Son and Father
do not signify the same modes of presence, insofar as there really are true
and real differences in the modes of presence for us, these three modes of
presence for us are to be strictly distinguished. Father, Son-Logos and Spirit
are first of all not the same "for us." But insofar as these modes of presence
of one and the same God for us may not nullify the real self-communication
of God as the one and only and same God, the three modes of presence
of one and the same God must belong to him as one and the same God,

they must belong to him in himself and for himself.

Hence the assertions that one and the same God is present for us as Father, Son-Logos and Holy Spirit, or that the Father gives himself to us in absolute self-communication through the Son in the Holy Spirit are to be understood and made in the strict sense as assertions about God *as he is in himself*. For otherwise they would basically not be assertions about God's self-communication. We may not duplicate these three modes of God's presence for us by postulating a different presupposition for them in God, and we do this by developing a psychological doctrine of the Trinity which is different from these modes of presence. In the Trinity in the economy and history of salvation and revelation we have already experienced the immanent Trinity as it is in itself. By the fact that God reveals himself for us in the modes we indicated as trinitarian, we have already experienced the immanent Trinity of the holy mystery as it is in itself, because its free and supernatural manifestation to us in grace manifests its innermost self. For the absolute identity of the Trinity with itself does not signify a lifeless and empty homogeneity. Rather, this identity includes in itself as the nature of divine life the very thing which encounters us in the trinitarian nature of his coming to us.

We are only trying to indicate here an initial approach towards an understanding of the Christian doctrine of the Trinity. In spite of its own problems, perhaps this approach still allows us to avoid many misunderstandings about this doctrine, and to show positively that the doctrine of the Trinity is not a subtle theological and speculative game, but rather is an assertion which cannot be avoided. It is only through this doctrine that we can take with radical seriousness and maintain without qualifications the simple statement which is at once so very incomprehensible and so very self-evident, namely, that God himself as the abiding and holy mystery, as the incomprehensible ground of man's transcendent existence is not only the God of infinite distance, but also wants to be the God of absolute closeness in a true self-communication, and he is present in this way in the spiritual depths of our existence as well as in the concreteness of our corporeal history. Here lies the real meaning of the doctrine of the Trinity.

·V·

The History of Salvation and Revelation

1. Preliminary Reflections on the Problem

The divinized transcendentality of man, who actualizes his essence in history and only in this way can accept it in freedom, has itself a history in man, an individual and a collective history. This transcendentality, as borne, empowered and fulfilled by the divinizing self-communication of God, this transcendentality *takes place;* it does not simply exist. It is for this reason that we said that man is the *event* of the free, unmerited and forgiving self-communication of God in absolute closeness and immediacy. And this is the ground and the thematic, the beginning and the end of man's history.

Christianity is not an indoctrination into certain conditions or facts or realities which are always the same, but is the proclamation of a history of salvation, of God's salvific and revelatory activity on men and with men. And because God's activity is directed to man as a free subject, Christianity at the same time is also the proclamation of a history of salvation and its opposite, of revelation and the interpretation of it which man himself makes. Consequently, this single history of revelation and salvation is borne by God's freedom and man's freedom together and forms a unity.

Fundamentally Christianity makes the claim that it is salvation and revelation for every person; it makes the claim that it is a religion of absolute value. It declares that it is salvation and revelation not only for particular groups of people, not only for particular periods of history in the past or in the future, but for *all* people until the end of history. But at first glance such an absolute claim is not compatible with Christianity saying simultaneously of itself that it is an historical religion. Something historical seems by definition incapable of making absolute claims of any kind. This raises the question how the historical nature of Christianity, which it maintains is one of its radical and essential characteristics, is compatible with its claim to be absolute and universal and to have a mission to evangelize all men. If ultimately we can speak of God in a sense which is recognizable and is to be taken seriously only insofar as our relationship to him is really understood to be transcendental, then the question becomes all the more critical why there can be something like a history of salvation and revelation. For this presupposes that God in his salvific and revelatory activity occupies a quite definite position in time and space within our experience. It could be objected that what is historical cannot be God, and that what is God cannot be historical. For the historical is always something concrete, something particular, something which exists as individual within a larger context. But God is the primordial ground and abyss of all reality who always lies beyond everything which can be conceived.

What then can still take place in a history of salvation and revelation if always and everywhere and from the very beginning God with his absolute reality has already communicated himself as the innermost center of everything which can be history at all? If we are already moving within our goal, what more can really take place in this history as the history of divine salvation and revelation except the manifestation of God in the beatific vision? To put it in biblical terms: if God as he is in himself has already communicated himself in his Holy Spirit always and everywhere and to every person as the innermost center of his existence, whether he wants it or not, whether he reflects upon it or not, whether he accepts it or not, and if the whole history of creation is already borne by God's self-communication in this very creation, then there does not seem to be anything else which can take place on God's part. Then the whole history of salvation and revelation as we understand it in the categorical and particular terms of time and space does not seem to be able to be anything else but the process of limiting and mythologizing and reducing to a human level something which was already present in its fullness from the outset. Hence the question whether and in what sense there can be a history of revelation and salvation is one of the most difficult and fundamental questions Christianity faces.*

*A short note is in order here: the following pages of this fifth chapter coincide perhaps more than is usual elsewhere with formulations to be found in the first chapter of *Die Grundlagen heilsgeschichtlicher Dogmatik* by A. Darlap (vol. 1 of *Mysterium Salutis*, edited by J. Feiner and M. Löhrer [Einsiedeln: Benziger Verlag, 1965]). This is explained by our close collaboration in a variety of theological endeavors.

2. The Historical Mediation of Transcendentality and Transcendence

HISTORY AS THE EVENT OF TRANSCENDENCE

To move toward a solution of this problem with regard to the history of revelation and salvation, let us begin with a proposition from metaphysical anthropology: man as subject and as person is a historical being in such a way that he is historical precisely *as* a transcendent subject; his subjective essence of unlimited transcendentality is mediated *historically* to him in his knowledge and in his free self-realization. Hence man realizes his transcendental subjectivity neither unhistorically in a merely interior experience of unchanging subjectivity, nor does he grasp this transcendental subjectivity by means of an unhistorical reflection and introspection which is possible in the same way at every point in time. If in fact the realization of transcendentality takes place historically, and if on the other hand true historicity —which must not be confused with just being in time and space physically or with the temporal duration of a physical or biological phenomenon or with a series of free acts which remain particular—has its ground and the condition of its possibility in the transcendentality of man himself, then the only way to reconcile these two facts is to say that history is ultimately the history of transcendentality itself; and conversely, man's transcendentality cannot be understood as a capacity which is given and lived and experienced and reflected upon independently of history.

We are beginning with the proposition, therefore, that transcendence itself has a history, and that history itself is always the event of this transcendence. For on the one hand we have to say that modern consciousness, which takes history with radical seriousness, both backward into the past and forward into the future, certainly cannot make sense out of a transcendentality in man which would be absolutely ahistorical. On the other hand, following the whole and lengthy tradition of the West which is still valid today, we have to say: the moment that history, towards the past or towards the future, no longer grasps its transcendental depths as the condition which makes genuine history possible, this very history itself also becomes blind. It has to be admitted that transcendence can be possessed only in a mediating relationship to the past and to the future, but it must equally be said that this history and this historical relationship experience their own historicity and their true history only if the transcendental conditions of possibility for such history are always taken into account. Indeed we can say that the ultimate thing about history itself is that it is the history of man's transcendentality. This also means that man's transcendentality along with its term and its source is not reached alongside history, so that history would then be degraded to some kind of a spectacle in which man is also involved, although he could find what is really eternal about his reality alongside and independently of his history. Transcendence itself has its history, and history is in its ultimate depths the event of this transcendence.

This is true not only of the individual history of an individual person, but also of the history of social units, of peoples and of the one human race, whereby we are presupposing that in the origin, unfolding and goal of its history mankind forms a unity. The unity of mankind itself is once again not something fixed and unchangeable which moves through history, but it too has a history. The "supernatural existential" also has a history. If it is in this way that man is a being of subjectivity, of transcendence, of freedom and of a mutual relationship with the holy mystery which we call God; if he is the event of God's absolute self-communication, and if he is all of this always and inescapably and from the very beginning; and if *as* such a being of divinized transcendence he is at the same time a historical being both individually and collectively, then it follows that this ever-present and supernatural existential, in and through which he is oriented towards the holy mystery and towards God's absolute self-communication as an offer to man's freedom—this existential itself has a history individually and collectively, and this is at once the single history of both salvation and revelation.

This history of salvation, therefore, is history *on God's part.* The transcendental structures of this single history of each individual and of the human race are historical insofar as, even as permanent and inescapable, they are grounded in God's free and personal self-communication. This history is also free on God's part insofar as, in accordance with the basic relationship between creator and creature, the beginning of this history, even though it is dependent on man's freedom, it is nevertheless an event of God's freedom which can give itself or refuse to give itself. Insofar as this history is the history of God's freedom and of man's, and insofar as there exists therefore a concrete dialectic in history, both individual and collective, between the presence of God as giving himself in an absolute self-communication, and the absence of God as always remaining the holy mystery, this expresses what the history of salvation and revelation really means. The historicity of the history of salvation on God's part and not only on man's part, a history which really is the one true history of God himself, and a history in which the unchanging and untouchable God manifests his power to enter into the time and the history which he as the Eternal One has created, this historicity of course is experienced most clearly and comes to light most clearly in Christianity's fundamental dogma of the Incarnation of the Eternal Logos in Jesus Christ.

This history of salvation is also a history *on the part of man's freedom*, since God's personal self-communication as the ground of this history addresses the created person precisely in his freedom. We cannot distinguish clearly in our own experience when this divine and human history of salvation is in fact a history of salvation and not a history of its opposite. There is never a salvific act of God on man which is not also and always a salvific act of man. There is no revelation which could take place in any other way except in the faith of the person hearing the revelation. To this extent it is clear that the history of salvation and revelation is always the already existing synthesis of God's historical activity and man's at the same time, because the divine and the human history of salvation cannot be understood as joining together in a kind of synergistic cooperation. Once again, God is the ground of man's act of freedom, and in his own act he burdens man with the grace and the responsibility for his own accountable acts. The divine history of salvation, therefore, always appears in the human history of salvation; revelation always appears in faith. And conversely: they always appear in what man experiences as most his own, in what he receives as given to him as his very own by the God of his transcendence who is at once distant and close. This transcendence of man, which necessarily exists in history because of man's historicity as subject, and which is constituted as it is in the concrete by God's self-communication, is the history both of salvation and of revelation.

3. The History of Salvation and Revelation as Coextensive with the Whole of World History

THE HISTORY OF SALVATION AND WORLD HISTORY

The fact that the history of salvation is coexistent with the whole history of the human race (which is not to say identical, for in this single history there is also guilt and the rejection of God, and hence the opposite of salvation) no longer poses any special problem today for the normal interpretation of Christianity. Anyone who does not close himself to God in an ultimate act of his life and his freedom through free and personal sin for which he is really and subjectively guilty and for which he cannot shirk responsibility, this person finds his salvation.

The history of the world, then, means the history of salvation. God's offer of himself, in which God communicates himself absolutely to the whole of mankind, is by definition man's salvation. For it is the fulfillment of man's transcendence in which he transcends towards the absolute God himself. Therefore the history of God's offer of himself, offered by God in freedom and accepted or rejected by man in freedom, is the history of salvation or its opposite. All other history which can be or has been experienced empirically is really history in the strict sense, and not just the "history of nature," only insofar as it is also a genuine moment in this history of salvation and its opposite, only insofar as it is the concrete, historical actualization of the acceptance or rejection of God's self-communication, although it is always subject to the judgment of God which has not yet been experienced but will one day be revealed.

Corresponding to man's essence as transcendence and history, such a history of salvation has essentially two moments which mutually condition each other: it is the event of God's self-communication as accepted or rejected by man's own basic freedom; and this moment of God's self-communication, which seemingly is merely transcendent and trans-historical because it is permanent and always present, belongs to this history and takes place within it. This self-communication is a moment in the history of salvation insofar as the self-communication and the freedom of its acceptance and rejection, which is really exercised in the concrete, historical corporeality of man and of mankind, come to appearance there. They are known by man in this appearance, even on the level of reflection to some extent, at least initial reflection, and they come to expression, although in images and likenesses.

There belongs to the history of salvation, therefore, not merely a word coming from God and *about* God in his history, there belong not merely sacramental signs of God's grace in the broadest sense and the historical development of these symbols, rites, likenesses and signs, there belongs not only religious institutions and the historical development of these religious social structures, but there also belongs the event of the self-communication of God himself. For this event of God's self-communication is indeed transcendental, but precisely *as transcendental* it is a real history. Just as in Christian theology the Holy Spirit as communicated belongs to the essence of the church, just as mediated grace belongs to the essence of the sacraments, just as the interior act of God on man in faith belongs to the complete essence of God's word in revelation, so too there belongs to the essence and to the reality of the history of salvation, on the one hand, the transcendental event of God's self-communication to man and the original, free act of accepting or rejecting God's self-communication, which act can never be recaptured completely in reflection and can never be identified completely and unambiguously in history, and there belongs, on the other hand, the concreteness of man's history in which he actualizes this acceptance or rejection in freedom. This history takes place neither in an ahistorical and only apparently existential interpretation of man's interiority, nor is this history of salvation historical merely in the sense that what is experienced tangibly in the world would already be salvation history without its ongoing self-transcendence into the holy mystery of God who is communicating himself.

Insofar as basically at least there is nothing historically tangible in man's existence which could not be the material and the concrete corporeality of transcendental knowledge and freedom, the history of salvation as such is necessarily coexistent with all history. Wherever human history is lived and suffered in freedom, the history of salvation and its opposite are also taking place, and hence not merely where this history is actualized in an explicitly religious way in word and in cult and in religious societies. Indeed there is never transcendence which is not accompanied by some degree of reflection, however limited, because every transcendental experience must be mediated objectively. But the mediation of this experience of transcendence does not necessarily have to be an explicitly religious mediation. Consequently, the history of salvation and its opposite is not confined to the history of true and false religion strictly as such. Rather it also encompasses the apparently merely profane history of mankind and of the individual person, presupposing only that transcendental experience is actualized there and historically mediated.

THE UNIVERSAL HISTORY OF SALVATION
IS ALSO THE HISTORY OF REVELATION

The universal history of salvation, which as the categorical mediation of man's supernatural transcendentality is coexistent with the history of the world, is also and at the same time the history of *revelation*. This too, then, is coextensive with the whole history of the world and of salvation. This statement will appear surprising at first to the Christian who likes to have the history of revelation begin with Abraham and Moses, that is, with the history of the Old Testament covenant, and who usually recognizes beyond that only a primeval revelation in paradise. A popular understanding of Christianity usually and carelessly identifies the explicit history of revelation in the Old and New Testaments and the writing down of this in the scriptures of the Old and New Testaments with the history of revelation as such. Later we shall have to reflect upon the distinction between this special, Christian history of revelation and the universal and supernatural history of revelation, and also upon its own proper value and significance. But the point here, first of all, is that not only the history of salvation, but also the history of revelation in the proper sense takes place wherever the individual and collective history of the human race is taking place.

But notice: also where an *individual* salvation and human history is taking place. To be sure, as historical beings in a community we are always related to others, related to their history and to their experience even in our salvation and in our individual existence. But it would be a primitive and ultimately false conception of the individual's history of faith if we were to think that it is not in a true and theological and very radical sense a moment in and a part of the real history of revelation. But here the main point is the statement that the history of revelation in the human race is coextensive with the whole history of the world's freedom.

Hence we must first of all consider and evaluate the thesis that the history of salvation and revelation takes place wherever individual and especially collective human history is taking place. This is not meant merely in the sense that there is a history of the so-called "natural revelation" of God in the world and through the world. A "natural revelation" also has its history. This is present in the history of the religious and philosophical knowledge of God, both individual and collective, although this history and the history of natural revelation strictly as such cannot simply be identified. For in the concrete history of man's knowledge of God causes are at work which are due to grace, and hence they have to do with revelation in the strict sense, and these causes are present as moments in this concrete history of man's knowledge of God. But we are not really talking about this history of the natural revelation of God when we say that there is a universal history of revelation which is coextensive with the history of mankind and of salvation.

As we understand it, when God comes to us in his freedom, in his absolutely and radically supernatural grace in what we have called the offer of God's self-communication, the God of supernatural salvation and of grace is already at work. Consequently, man can never even begin to have anything to do with God or to approach God without being already borne by God's grace. In the concrete, of course, there are sinful rejections of God by man, and there are false, depraved and inadequate interpretations by man of the relationship between God and man. In this sense there are abominations and false religions in the history of religion. But there is no history of religion which is the founding of religion by man alone, so that God then, fixed categorically in time and space, would come to meet this activity of man as its confirmation or as its condemnation and judgment.

Because of the self-communication of God which is present in man as an existential, the history of religion is always a true (although not yet historically fulfilled) or a false religion of man which exists in the supernatural order of grace, and is borne and founded and made possible by God, and exists in the mode of acceptance or of rejection of this God.

Now the history of mankind as understood in this way, the history of man's spirit and of his freedom, the thematic or unthematic history of his salvation as coextensive with the history of the world, this history is also in the proper sense the history of supernatural *revelation*. It has its ultimate ground in God's supernatural self-communication to man in grace, and it is in service of God's self-communication to man in grace. Hence it signifies supernatural, verbal revelation of a state of affairs which is beyond the realm of man's merely natural knowledge. This is not to say, however, that this state of affairs is not accessible to man's transcendental and gratuitously elevated experience, and would therefore be communicable merely through human propositions which come "from without" and are caused by God only in this way.

THE FOUNDATION OF THE THESIS IN THE DATA OF CATHOLIC DOGMATICS

The postulate of such a history of revelation can be grounded, first of all, in some data which is really taken for granted in Catholic dogmatics. We shall appeal to this data in order to show that, contrary to a superficial self-interpretation, when Christianity is interpreted exactly according to its own self-understanding it understands itself as the process by which the history of revelation reaches a quite definite and successful level of historical reflection, and by which this history comes to self-awareness historically and reflexively, a history which itself is coextensive with the whole history of the world.

According to the Christian view of things, even though a person is co-conditioned by original sin in his situation of salvation and sin, he always and everywhere has the genuine possibility of encountering God and achieving salvation by the acceptance of God's supernatural self-communication in grace, a possibility which is forfeited only through his own guilt. There is a serious, effective and universal salvific will of God in the sense of that salvation which the Christian means by his own Christian salvation. In Catholic dogmatics God's salvific will is characterized as universal in contrast to the pessimism in Augustine or in Calvinism; that is, it is promised to every person regardless of where or at what time he lives, but this does not just mean that a person in some way or other is kept from being lost. It means rather salvation in the proper and Christian sense of God's absolute self-communication in absolute closeness, and hence it also means what we call the beatific vision. This very salvation is made possible for every person even within the infralapsarian situation of original sin, and it can be forfeited only through his own personal guilt.

But this salvation takes place as the salvation of a free person, as the fulfillment of a free person as such, and hence it takes place precisely when this person in fact actualizes himself in freedom, that is, towards his salvation. It never takes place without the involvement of this person and the involvement of his freedom. A person who actualizes himself in freedom, and a salvation which would merely be a reified state produced objectively by God alone *on* the person, are mutually contradictory notions. A salvation not achieved in freedom cannot be salvation. If, then, by virtue of God's universal and serious salvific will such salvation occurs even outside the explicit history of the Old and New Testaments, if it occurs everywhere in the history of the world and of salvation, then this history of salvation takes place by being accepted in freedom. But this is not possible without it being accepted as known. In understanding this statement one should not suppose that the only way in which something can really and truly be known is by that categorical knowledge objectified in words and concepts and propositions which we usually presuppose when we speak of "knowing." A person knows infinitely more about himself, and knows about himself in a much more radical way than merely by this objectified and verbalized knowledge which can, as it were, be written down in a book. The identification of knowledge as self-consciousness with conceptually and propositionally objectified knowledge is a misunderstanding. Our postulate about the universality of salvation and revelation can also be clarified further by references to other dogmatic teachings of Catholic Christianity.

Because of God's universal salvific will, a Christian has no right to limit the actual event of salvation to the explicit history of salvation in the Old and New Testaments, despite the theological axiom which has been current from the time of the Fathers down to our own times, namely, that outside the church there is no salvation. The Old Testament as a scripture giving witness to God's salvific activity is aware of such salvific activity of God outside the history of the old covenant, and is aware of a real covenant between God and the whole human race. The Old Testament covenant is only a special instance of the former which has reached a special level in the historical consciousness of Israel. The Old Testament is aware of holy pagans who are pleasing to God. The New Testament is also aware of a salvific efficacy of the grace of Christ and his Spirit which does not coincide with the initiatives of the visible witnesses to Christ who were explicitly and historically authorized by Christ. The official church of Christ has its origins in and is borne by this efficacy. But it is a self-evident axiom for the New Testament and for the later teaching of the church that salvation takes place only where there is *faith* in the word of God revealing himself in the proper sense of the term. Church teaching even explicitly rejects the idea, although not in a definitive way, that a merely philosophical knowledge, and hence a merely "natural" revelation, is a sufficient basis for such faith or for a person's justification.

If, then, there can be salvation and hence also faith everywhere in history, then a supernatural revelation of God to mankind must have been at work everywhere in the history of the human race. It must have been at work in such a way that it actually touches every person and effects salvation in him through faith, every person who does not close himself to this revelation by a failure to believe through his own fault.

SUPPLEMENTARY THEOLOGICAL AND SPECULATIVE FOUNDATION

These reflections which proceed directly from propositions of the church's faith can be further strengthened and deepened by a more speculative theological reflection. And such a reflection can at the same time further clarify how this universal but still supernatural revelation and history of revelation can be understood in such a way that its existence does not contradict the simple facts of the history of the human spirit and of religion, and of man's secularity, but rather appears in harmony with the history of revelation and salvation in the Old and New Testaments. This latter is the only thing we are usually accustomed to think of when we speak of the history of revelation and salvation without further qualification.

We have discussed the fact that, according to the dogmatic teachings of Christianity, man's transcendence is "elevated" by God's self-communication as an offer to man's freedom. This happens in such a way that the spiritual movement of man in his transcendental knowledge and freedom is oriented towards the absolute immediacy of God, towards his absolute closeness, towards that immediate possession of God's very self which finds its full actuality in the beatific vision of God face to face. We said about this at the time that this reality is a datum of man's transcendental experience, that this statement about God's self-communication is not an ontic statement which only asserts a reified state of affairs which lies beyond man's personhood, his consciousness, his subjectivity and his transcendentality. The statement that God's self-communication to man always and everywhere means an ontological reality does not of course mean that, prescinding from exceptional cases, this reality as ontologically present is present in man in such a way that this datum can be brought to reflexive presence with indisputable clarity and certainty merely by the process of individual introspection. Something of which we are transcendentally conscious and something which can be brought to the level of transcendental reflection and differentiated reflexively and with certainty from other moments in man's transcendentality are not the same thing either conceptually or in reality. We can prove very clearly in other instances too that such a distinction is not simply a subterfuge, but that it really belongs to the primary data of man's transcendental subjectivity.

But the supernaturally elevated, unreflexive but really present, and transcendental experience of man's movement and orientation towards immediacy and closeness of God, that is, the experience as such prior to being made thematic reflexively and historically, must be characterized as real revelation throughout the whole history of religion and of the human spirit. Nor can it in any way be identified with so-called natural revelation. This transcendental knowledge, which is present always and everywhere in the actualization of the human spirit in knowledge and freedom, but present unthematically, is a moment which must be distinguished from verbal and propositional revelation as such. But it deserves nevertheless to be characterized as God's self-revelation. This transcendental moment in revelation is a modification of our transcendental consciousness produced permanently by God in grace. But such a modification is really an original and permanent element in our consciousness as the basic and original luminosity of our existence. And as an element in our transcendentality which is constituted by God's self-communication, it is already revelation in the proper sense.

The school theology which bears a Thomistic stamp expresses this situa-

tion by saying: wherever our acts of an intentional kind are elevated ontologically by supernatural grace, by the Spirit of God, these acts always and
necessarily have a supernatural, a priori formal object which cannot be
reached as formal object by a merely natural act, although in certain
circumstances it can be reached as content.

The divine causation of the a priori horizon of our knowledge and
freedom must be characterized as a specific and original mode of revelation,
indeed even as the mode upon which all other revelation is based. This is
true however little this horizon might itself be represented thematically and
conceptually, this horizon within which and towards which we actualize our
existence with its categorical objectivity.

According to the common Christian teaching about the revelation which
is usually designated simply as *the* revelation, that is, the revelation of the
Old and New Testaments, such a revelation is really heard both with regard
to its content and to its mode only if it is heard in faith, that is, through
the grace of God, and hence only if it is heard in the power of God's
self-communication and in grace's "light of faith." Consequently, there
corresponds to the objective supernaturality of a revealed proposition a
divine and subjective principle for hearing this proposition in the subject
who is able to hear it. Only when God is the subjective principle of the
speaking and of man's hearing in faith can God in his own self express
himself. For otherwise every expression of God would cross, as it were, the
radical boundary separating creatures from God and would become subject
to finiteness, humanness and merely human subjectivity. A proposition
never appears only as an individual proposition all by itself on the *tabula
rasa* of a consciousness, but is always dependent on man's transcendentality, on the a priori horizon of his understanding, and on his universal
language field. Hence even if the objective proposition is produced by God,
if it enters into a *merely* human subjectivity without this subjectivity itself
being borne by God's self-communication, then the supposed word of God
is a human word before we notice it. The a posteriori proposition of verbal
revelation which comes in history can be heard only within the horizon of
a divinizing and divinized a priori subjectivity. Only then can it be heard
in the way that it must be heard if what is heard is seriously to be called
the "word of God."

The subject's a priori luminosity in his transcendentality can and must
be called knowledge, although this a priori knowledge is actualized only in
the a posteriori material of the individual reality which encounters us.

Likewise, this a priori, supernatural and divinized transcendentality can and must be called revelation prior to its illumination of the individual, a posteriori objects of experience in historical revelation.

ON THE CATEGORICAL MEDIATION OF SUPERNATURALLY ELEVATED TRANSCENDENTALITY

There is still the further question whether the concrete experience of this supernatural horizon can take place only in material which is specifically religious, and which is offered by that historical and defined revelation which we are usually accustomed to call revelation in an absolute sense. Usually, one would easily be inclined to answer this question in the affirmative. This would suggest explicitly or implicitly that this supernatural transcendentality can come to self-presence and self-awareness only if and insofar as there occurs a synthesis of our supernatural a priority with specifically religious material, that is, only if we use the word "God," only if we speak of God's law, only if we explicitly want to do God's will, and hence only if we are involved in an explicitly sacral and religious realm.

But however much this seems to be the case, it is basically false. For if man's transcendentality is really mediated to itself by all the categorical material of his a posteriori experience, then, presupposing that a free subject in his transcendentality is acting, the only correct understanding is that supernaturally elevated transcendentality is also mediated to itself by any and every categorical reality in which and through which the subject becomes present to itself. It is not the case that we have nothing to do with God until we make God conceptual and thematic to some extent. Rather there is an original and unthematic experience of God, although it is nameless, whenever and to the extent that subjectivity and transcendentality are actualized. And correspondingly, man's supernatural transcendentality is already mediated to itself, although in an unobjectified and unthematic way, whenever a person appropriates himself as a free subject in the transcendentality of his knowledge and his freedom.

We are presupposing, then, that this categorical and necessary historical mediation of our transcendental and supernatural experience in and through the categorical material of our history takes place not only in the specifically and thematically religious material of our motivation, our thought and our experience, but everywhere. In this sense the world is our mediation to God in his self-communication in grace, and in this sense there is for Christianity no separate and sacral realm where alone God is to be found. Even though a categorical objectivity is in the first instance and explicitly profane, it can be adequate for the mediation of our supernaturally elevated experience which we are rightly calling revelation. If this were not the case, it would be impossible to see why even a moral act whose immediate and thematic formal object is an object of natural morality could be a supernaturally elevated act in someone who is baptized. But it is impossible to deny this, for the Christian understanding of existence presumes that in practice it is to be taken for granted that, presupposing man's supernatural elevation in grace, the entire moral life of a person belongs within the realm of supernatural salvific activity, and that the observance of the natural moral law is supernaturally elevated and salvific in itself, and not only as a precondition and as an extrinsic consequence.

We can say further that without such a presupposition the possibility of salvation for *all* men would no longer be intelligible. But such a possibility of salvation is taught explicitly and very clearly by the Second Vatican Council in a variety of places (see, for example, *Lumen gentium*, 16; *Gaudium et spes*, 22; *Ad gentes*, 7; *Nostra aetate*, 1ff.). In view of the spatial extension and especially the temporal duration of the history of the human race as we know it today, we can no longer seriously assume without making arbitrary postulates that all men have been in contact with concrete, historical, verbal revelation in the narrowest sense, and hence with the explicit tradition of a primeval revelation in paradise or with the biblical revelation in the Old or New Testaments, and that they must have been in contact in order to be able to believe and thus achieve their salvation. But salvific activity without faith is impossible, and faith without an encounter with God revealing himself personally is a contradiction in terms.

In the concrete, then, there remains no other conceivable possibility but a faith which is simply the obedient acceptance of man's supernaturally elevated self-transcendence, the obedient acceptance of his transcendental orientation to the God of eternal life. As an a priori modality of consciousness, this orientation has the character of a divine communication. This transcendental, supernatural experience, which in itself and in the mode in which it takes place satisfies the notion of a divine revelation, and therefore in its history constitutes a history of revelation, does indeed need a historical, categorical mediation. But this mediation does not necessarily and everywhere have to make this transcendental experience explicit and thematic *as* the effect of supernatural, revelatory activity by God.

4. On the Relationship between the History of Universal, Transcendental Revelation and Special, Categorical Revelation

As God's real self-communication in grace, therefore, the history of salvation and revelation is coexistent and coextensive with the history of the world and of the human spirit, and hence also with the history of religion. Because there is self-transcendence on man's part through God's ontological and revelatory self-communication, the history of revelation takes place wherever this transcendental history has its history, and hence in the whole history of man. Up to now we have postulated this history of revelation and salvation in a more a priori way, but where and how it takes place in man's history and how this universal, supernatural history of revelation allows for the necessity along with itself, or better, within itself, of that history of revelation which is usually called the history of revelation in an absolute sense are two questions which we can now consider and answer together.

THE ESSENTIAL AND NECESSARY HISTORICAL SELF-INTERPRETATION OF SUPERNATURAL, TRANSCENDENTAL EXPERIENCE

Supernatural, transcendental experience has a history, and does not just occur again and again as embedded in history, for transcendental experience as such has a history which is identical with the history of man, and does not just occur at certain points in this history.

In order to see from this vantage point the relationship, the necessity and the difference between this transcendental history of salvation and revelation and the categorical, particular and official history of salvation, two things especially have to be taken into account. First, the categorical history of man as a spiritual subject is always and everywhere the necessary but historical and objectifying self-interpretation of the transcendental experience which constitutes the realization of man's essence. Secondly, this realization of man's essence does not take place alongside the events of historical life, but within this historical life. The categorical, historical self-interpretation of what man is takes place not only, and not even in the first instance, by means of an explicit anthropology formulated in propositions. It takes place rather in the whole history of man, in what he does and what he suffers in individual life; in what we call simply the history of culture, of society, of the state, of art, of religion, and of the external, technical and economic mastery of nature. It is here that this historical self-interpretation of man takes place, and not just when the philosophers begin to do anthropology. The theoretical reflection in a metaphysical or theological anthropology which we usually call man's self-interpretation and self-explanation is indeed necessary. But it is nevertheless bound to this total history of mankind and is a relatively secondary moment.

This self-interpretation must be understood as taking place in genuine history, and not as a biological, deterministic evolution. It is history, and therefore freedom, risk, hope, reaching out to the future and the possibility of failure. And it is only in all of this and in this way that man possesses his transcendental experience as event, and with it his own essential self. This essential self cannot be possessed subjectively alongside the actualization of history. Therefore this self-interpretation of transcendental experience in history is essential and necessary. It belongs to the very constitution of transcendental experience, although these two elements are not simply the same thing in an identity which is given from the outset.

If, then, history exists in this way as the necessary and objectifying self-interpretation of transcendental experience, then there is a revelatory history of transcendental revelation as the necessary and historical self-interpretation of that original, transcendental experience which is constituted by God's self-communication. This historical self-communication of God can and must be understood as the history of revelation. For this history is the consequence and the objectification of this original self-communication of God which reveals God. It is its interpretation and hence its very history. We have no choice, then, but to call the history of the explicit self-interpretation of transcendental, supernatural experience in the life of the individual and of mankind, and in the propositional, theological anthropology which follows upon this experience, we have no choice but to call it the history of revelation.

ON THE NOTION OF A CATEGORICAL
AND SPECIAL HISTORY OF REVELATION

The categorical history of revelation, in an unthematic way and through everything which takes place in human history, can indeed be the historical mediation of the transcendental, supernatural experience of God as supernatural revelation. But the history of the transcendental revelation of God will necessarily show itself again and again to be a history which is taking place in an irreversible direction towards a highest and comprehensive self-interpretation of man. Consequently, it will be ever more intensely an explicitly religious self-interpretation of this supernatural, transcendental and revelatory experience of God.

From this perspective we can now say: where such an explicitly religious and categorical history of revelation as the history of transcendental revelation through God's self-communication knows itself to be willed positively and to be directed by God, and is assured of the legitimacy of this knowledge in ways which are offered by this history, there we have the history of revelation in the sense which is usually associated with this word. To be sure, this mode of the history of revelation is only a species, a segment of the universal, categorical history of revelation. It is the most successful instance of the necessary self-interpretation of transcendental revelation, or better, it is the full realization of the essence of both revelations and their single history, both transcendental and categorical revelation in the unity and purity of their essence.

Admittedly this still leaves us with a concept of the categorical history of revelation which does not simply coincide unambiguously and exclusively with the Old and New Testament history of revelation. We have not come that far yet. For what we have just given as a kind of definition of the categorical history of revelation in the narrower sense, a definition which is therefore applicable unambiguously to the Old and New Testaments, does not necessarily have to apply only to the Old and New Testaments. When we say that in the word of God which he proclaims an Old Testament prophet really satisfies the narrower definition of what we are calling the categorical history of salvation, a definition based on the fact that this history knows itself to be a history of salvation explicitly willed and directed by God, this still does not answer the question whether this has not also occurred outside the Old and New Testament history of revelation.

If the transcendental and supernatural experience of God necessarily interprets itself historically, and therefore forms a categorical history of revelation, and if this is present everywhere, then this also means that such a history is always a history of revelation which is provisional and not yet completely successful, and which is still seeking itself, and it means especially that it is a history of revelation which is permeated and made obscure and ambiguous by man's guilt in a situation which is co-conditioned by guilt.

Therefore the history of revelation in the usual and especially the full sense of the term is found where this self-interpretation of God's transcendental self-communication in history succeeds, and where with certainty it reaches its self-awareness and its purity in such a way that it correctly knows itself to be guided and directed by God, and, protected by him against clinging tenaciously to what is provisional and to what is depraved, it discovers its own true self.

This is not to say that revelation in such essential purity is found *only* within the realm of the Old and New Testaments. At least in individual salvation history, there are no reasons against but many reasons for saying that in such an individual history of salvation and revelation there are moments of history in which the divine origins and the absolute correctness of a self-interpretation of the transcendental experience of God become manifest and achieve certainty about themselves.

But also in the collective history of mankind and in the history of its religion outside the economy of salvation in the Old and New Testaments, there can be such brief and partial histories within this categorical history of revelation in which a part of this self-reflection and reflexive self-presence of universal revelation and its history is found in its purity. But usually they will lack any tangible continuity among the various moments in these partial histories as far as we can see. In a history of guilt and of false religion they will always be shot through with a history of erroneous, sinful or merely human interpretations of this original transcendental experience which is present thematically and unthematically everywhere in history.

Whatever in fact might be the situation with regard to this possibility, in principle it need not be denied. It presupposes only that this categorical history of revelation is understood or can be understood as a self-interpretation of the revelatory and transcendental experience of God. If this interpretation is correct, it must be understood as positively willed and directed by God because of his real salvific will. "Direction" is understood here not as adventitious and coming from without, but rather as the immanent power of this divine self-communication. As coming freely from God and as given to man in history, it is of course a real and genuine history whose concrete course cannot be deduced a priori from some abstract principle. Rather, just like man's historical self-interpretation in other areas, it must be experienced, suffered and accepted in history itself.

The Christian historian of religion does not have to understand the non-Christian history of religion outside the Old and New Testaments merely as a history of man's religious activity, nor merely as depraved examples of man's potentialities for establishing religion. He can observe and describe and analyze the phenomena in the history of non-Christian religions without reservations, and interpret them with regard to their ultimate intentions. If he sees the God of the Old and New Testament revelation also at work there, however primitive they might be or however depraved, and these things of course do exist in the history of religion, he is in no way prejudicing Christianity's absolute claims.

Since, however, there is obviously also a history of the opposite of salvation, he must not overlook this history and the history which is contrary to revelation within the history of the human race and of religious phenomena. But when and where he discovers the history of real and genuine and supernatural revelation, which of course cannot be complete because it can only be complete in Jesus Christ, the crucified and risen one, his findings are not to be rejected a priori and dogmatically because of Christianity's absolute claims. He is rather simply cautioned to do his work in the history of religion objectively, and to see man as he really is: the being who always and everywhere stands before the claim of God's self-communication in grace, and who is always and everywhere a sinner who receives this grace of God in his history and again and again allows it to become depraved through his own fault. This of course raises the question about the concrete criteria for drawing distinctions.

JESUS CHRIST AS THE CRITERION

Not until the full and unsurpassable event of the historical self-objectification of God's self-communication to the world in Jesus Christ do we have an event which, as an eschatological event, fundamentally and absolutely precludes any historical corruption or any distorted interpretation in the further history of categorical revelation and of false religion. We shall have to supply the theological foundations of this assertion in the next chapter. In Jesus Christ, the crucified and risen one, then, we have a criterion for distinguishing in the concrete history of religion between what is a human misunderstanding of the transcendental experience of God, and what is the legitimate interpretation of this experience. It is only in him that such a discernment of spirits in an ultimate sense is possible.

It is in fact also true that with regard to the actual situation of the Old Testament history of revelation too, it is only in Christ that we Christians have the possibility of making a radical distinction between the categorical history of revelation in the full sense and in its purity, and the formation of human substitutes for it and misinterpretations of it. If as historians and scientists of religion, and independently of our faith in Jesus Christ, we tried in an impartial and purely historical way to transpose ourselves back into the Old Testament and the religious phenomena which are attested to historically there, we would have no ultimate criterion for distinguishing from the perspective of the essence of God's transcendental self-communication what is a pure and legitimate manifestation and historical objectification of this divine self-communication and what is an abbreviated, human corruption of it. We would also have to distinguish here more precisely (but once again this is impossible without taking Jesus Christ into account) between what would be legitimate there as a provisional objectification at a particular time of the transcendental experience of God, which, although it is only a provisional interpretation, does have an intrinsic dynamism towards the full revelation in Jesus Christ, and what was really a corruption even when measured against the Old Testament situation at the time.

THE FUNCTION OF THE BEARERS OF REVELATION

Although the possibility and the actuality of a history of salvation and revelation which is found outside of reflexive Christianity is beyond doubt, there still remains the possibility of allowing for a special "official" history of revelation along with a universal, categorical history of salvation and revelation which is the self-interpretation of the transcendental, supernatural experience of God. This special history then is really identical with the Old and New Testament history. This categorical history of revelation in the Old and New Testaments can and must be understood as the valid self-interpretation of God's transcendental self-communication to man, and as the thematization of the universal categorical history of this self-communication, which of course does not necessarily have to be made thematic always and everywhere in a sacral way. Those persons who were the original bearers of such a revealed communication from God and whom we characterize as *prophets* in the traditional terminology are to be understood as persons in whom the self-interpretation of this supernatural, transcendental experience and its history takes place in word and in deed. Hence something comes to expression in the prophets which fundamentally is present everywhere and in everyone, including ourselves who are not called prophets.

A self-interpretation and historical objectification of man's supernatural transcendentality and its history need not and may not be explained as a merely human and natural process of reflection and objectification. For we are dealing with the self-interpretation of that reality which is constituted by the personal self-communication of God, and hence by God himself. If it interprets itself historically, then God interprets himself in history, and the concrete human bearers of such a self-interpretation are authorized by God in a real sense. This self-interpretation is not a subsequent process, but rather is an essential, historical moment within this supernatural transcendentality which is constituted by God's self-communication. Looked at from both God's side and man's side, it is not a static reality, but has its own history in the history of mankind. The historical objectification and self-interpretation of God's transcendental self-communication, therefore, is governed by the same absolute and supernatural salvific will of God and by the same supernatural salvific providence as that divine self-communication through which man is constituted in his concrete essence, and from out of which he enters into his most real history, into the history of this transcendental self-communication, into the history of salvation and revelation.

In theological terms the "light of faith" which is offered to every person, and the light by which the "prophets" grasp and proclaim the divine message from the center of human existence is the same light, especially since the message can really be heard properly only in the light of faith. Once again, this light is nothing else but the divinized subjectivity of man which is constituted by God's self-communication. Of course the notion of the prophetic light implies that historical and concrete configuration of the light of faith in which the transcendental experience of God is *correctly* mediated by concrete history and its interpretation. Looked at theologically and correctly, the prophet is none other than the believer who can express his transcendental experience of God correctly. Perhaps as distinguished from other believers, it is expressed in the prophets in such a way that it becomes for others too the correct and pure objectification of their own transcendental experience of God, and it can be recognized in this correctness and purity.

The notion of such a special, categorical revelation as we have just outlined it and the notion of a revelatory event which takes place in a prophet and is destined for others presuppose, of course, that not absolutely everybody is the prophetic voice of such a categorical and historical self-interpretation of God's transcendental revelation through self-communication. It presupposes rather that many receive and must receive such a self-interpretation from other individuals, not because they do not have this transcendental experience of God, but because it belongs to man's essence that his own experience of himself, both in the realm of the human and in the realm of grace, is realized in the history of man's interpersonal communication.

A self-interpretation which really succeeds and finds a living form takes place among men in such a way that particular people, their experiences and their self-interpretation become a productive model, an animating power and a norm for others. This does not relativize the prophet. For this very self-interpretation which takes place in a pure objectification is the history of the transcendental self-communication of God himself. For this reason it is not only a gnoseological history of pure theory, but is a reality of history itself. As existing in an interpersonal world, a person arrives concretely at his own self-interpretation, however much it comes from within and enters within, only within the self-interpretation of his interpersonal world, and by participating in and receiving from the tradition of the historical self-interpretation of those people who form his interpersonal world from out of the past and through the present into the future.

A person always forms his own secular self-understanding only within a community of persons, in the experience of a history which he never makes alone, in dialogue, and in experience which reproduces the productive self-interpretation of other people. Therefore in his religious experience, too, man is always an interpersonal being, and this extends to the ultimate uniqueness of his subjectivity. The historical self-interpretation of one's own religious existence is not a solipsistic affair, but takes place necessarily in and through the historical experience of the religious self-interpretation of one's own world, of one's own "religious community." Its creative and unique figures, its prophets, succeed in a special way in objectifying historically the transcendental self-communication of God in the material of their history by the power of this self-communication of God. Consequently, they succeed in making possible the self-discovery in history of transcendental religious experience for other members of such a historical, interpersonal world.

There is no real difficulty in the fact that this implies something of a fluid boundary between believing prophets and "mere" believers. Insofar as there is question of establishing a critical norm for and the legitimacy of the success of the historical self-interpretation of the transcendental experience of God in the historical words and deeds of a prophet, there can always still be an "absolute" difference between prophets and "simple believers." Such a criterion and such a legitimacy do not belong to every such self-interpretation in each and every believer by himself. In any case they cannot be established for others because "signs" do not accompany every self-interpretation, and we shall have to discuss the sense and the function of these signs as a criterion of legitimacy. Where such a self-interpretation of the transcendental, supernatural experience of God takes place, an interpretation which is legitimate and destined for many others, there we have an event in the history of revelation in the *full* and usual sense of the term. There these events have sufficient continuity among themselves, and sufficient causal connections and relationships. There individual self-interpretations, which are therefore limited in their theme and in their depth, form a unity with others, and hence form a structure which is consistent and which binds the individual interpretations together.

THE ORIENTATION TOWARDS UNIVERSALITY
IN THE PARTICULAR AND SUCCESSFUL HISTORY OF REVELATION

Perhaps we have said enough to clarify the characteristics, the relationship and the difference between the universal, both transcendental and categorical history of revelation, and the particular, regional history of revelation. They do not exclude each other, but rather mutually condition each other. The former, the universal history of revelation, both transcendental and categorical, reaches its complete essence and its full historical objectification in the particular, regional, categorical history of revelation. This is not to say that the former history of revelation may be overlooked because the latter exists. If the particular, categorical history of revelation, in which transcendental revelation is interpreted for a spatially or temporally defined group of people, is conceivable simply because in other areas of life as well there are spatially, temporally and culturally limited self-interpretations of man in particular cultures and in limited epochs, nevertheless every correct self-interpretation of man's supernatural transcendentality as the fundamental element in the constitution of every person's existence has a fundamental meaning for all men. Every correct, regionally or temporally limited historical self-interpretation of man's supernatural relationship to God has therefore an intrinsic dynamism towards universalism, towards the mediation of an ever more adequate religious self-understanding for all men, although it might not be aware of this dynamism.

To what extent this fundamentally universal determination of a regionally or temporally limited categorical history of revelation is in fact operative under God's salvific providence, and in what explicit and tangible way or in what historical anonymity this takes place, these things of course can only be learned a posteriori from history itself, and cannot be deduced in an a priori way. If the "prophets" who appear in such a particular history of salvation and the religious institutions which are thereby founded have an "authority" vis-à-vis the individual person in his own religious self-interpretation, then we can and must also speak of an "official" particular, categorical history of revelation.

5. On the Structure of the Actual History of Revelation

In order to clarify a little further what we have said so far, and to transpose it from abstract concepts into somewhat more concrete and historical terms, let us ask now whether and how the formal concepts we have acquired are appropriate for mediating a notion of the structure of the actual history of revelation, at least in its larger lines. We shall look to the official history of salvation and revelation, namely, to that of the Old Testament as the final preparation for the absolute event of revelation in Jesus Christ.

"PRIMEVAL REVELATION"

Man is constituted by creation and by God's self-communication: through creation he is radically different and distant from God as the absolute and holy mystery, and at the same time through grace he is absolutely close to this mystery. Insofar as man's transcendental constitution, his origins, always involves being situated in a concrete history as in a beginning and within a horizon which is prior to him in his freedom, and insofar as this constitution is both logically and really, although perhaps not temporally and tangibly, antecedent to his free and sinful self-interpretation, we can speak of the beginning of God's transcendental and categorical revelation in paradise, that is, of a primeval transcendental and categorical revelation.

In employing this notion, of course, we can and must for the time being leave completely open the question as to what extent and in what way this "primeval revelation" was mediated to future generations from those who first received it in the world, that is, from "Adam and Eve." Primeval revelation means nothing else but that, when man really existed as man, that is, as subject and as freedom and responsibility, these latter were always ontologically oriented towards the God of absolute closeness through God's self-communication, and his movement began with this finality both in his individual and in his collective history. To what extent this supernatural transcendentality was present reflexively and was already thematic in a religious way is a completely different question which we can leave open, nor for this reason do we have to doubt the real core and meaning of the notion of primeval revelation.

Now insofar as God's salvific will as the offer of self-communication remains operative despite man's guilty rejections at the beginning, and insofar as every person receives his human nature, called by God to self-communication, from the one human race in the unity of its history, we can speak without hesitation of the transmission of this primeval, transcendental revelation. But we can do so only insofar as a person always exists as having his origin in others and in a total history, and insofar as he also receives his gratuitous transcendentality in this history and from this history. In this sense, then, we can speak of the transmission of this primeval, transcendental revelation as such, although it is transmitted through history not because it was received by "Adam," but because his guilt was already encompassed and surpassed by God's absolute will to communicate himself in view of Jesus Christ and because of Jesus Christ.

Whether and to what extent a historical transmission of the primeval categorical revelation took place, and indeed in explicit human words, is another question. For such a transmission undoubtedly does not manifest itself primarily in narrative accounts about the historical beginning of man in his concreteness, but rather in keeping the transcendental experience of God alive, and in the experience that the historical situation is conditioned by guilt. The process of keeping this experience alive can take place in different forms, even in depraved and polytheistic forms, and also without any explicit reference to tradition as such. Nevertheless, this satisfies the notion of revelation and of the communication of revelation insofar as we are dealing with the ongoing transmission of the historical objectification of transcendental revelation, and with the transmission of objectifications of the kind of guilt which is possible only in confrontation with the transcendental revelation of God.

The accounts in the first chapter of Genesis about the beginning of the history of the human race are not to be understood as an eyewitness report about the events of primeval history which was transmitted from the beginning and down through the generations, nor as an eyewitness report which was supplied by God as someone who was, as it were, involved in this primeval history. They are to be understood rather as an aetiology which infers back from the supernatural, transcendental experience of the present to what must have been in the beginning the historical ground of this experience of the present. Consequently, whatever the truth and the primeval historicity of what is inferred, the representation of this beginning which is inferred from the present still works in its presentations and representations with material which is taken from the present of those peoples and those persons who have contributed directly or indirectly to the forming and shaping of these Genesis accounts.

Because such an aetiology always and everywhere takes place to some extent and in some form among historical people through anamnesis, and because therefore the aetiology of a person is always and inevitably dependent, either in agreement or in disagreement, on the aetiology of the world around him and the world previous to him, the statement that man reaches his origins aetiologically does not disagree with the statement that he knows about his origins through primeval revelation and tradition. But it can be understood in such a way that such a tradition can and must appear in the most varied forms, without thereby being *merely* fantasy and mythology in a negative sense, and without ceasing to be, even in the strangest forms of mythological representation, a more or less successful objectification of the transcendental experience of revelation. If one feels that such attempts at self-understanding by man which come from his origins and lead back into his origins are mythological, then we should call his attention to the fact that basically there are no concepts without perception, and that even the most abstract metaphysical language works with images, analogies and representations, with a "conversion to the phantasm," as Thomas Aquinas would say.

IS IT POSSIBLE TO STRUCTURE THE WHOLE HISTORY OF REVELATION?

At first glance at least, although this might also be a bit premature, the history of religion shows that this historical interpretation of transcendental, supernatural revelation comes down to us in such a way that various histories of religion arise in different places in the world and at different times in the history of the human race. Moreover, we are apparently unable to unify these many histories into a structured history of revelation and salvation so that from our vantage point we can see a single and clear direction in its movement. Of course this history in the multiplicity of its histories has a direction from God's vantage point. For theologians and Christians it moves towards Christ, and this can also be at least postulated by those historians and philosophers of history who believe that they can admit in the multiplicity of histories an ultimate meaning which is discernible even within the world, and which can be surmised or gathered from the results of history.

But still the ultimately unifying structure and the exact law of development in this single history of salvation and revelation among the many histories of religion are hardly discernible. Moreover, the different attempts which the historians of religion propose in order to classify and systematize the many religions with regard to their nature and their historical sequence contribute little towards an understanding of the history of revelation prior to the Old Testament and Christian revelation.

Nor does Holy Scripture, especially that of the Old Testament, offer any key which leads to clearer results in this attempt to structure the universal history of revelation within the history of religions. The Old and New Testaments do indeed know that the whole of history stands under God's salvific will and his covenant will, and that it is always co-constituted by guilt. The New Testament is also familiar with the notion of an ever-worsening depravity in the history of mankind and also of religion. Such a history of religion and of the world as existing under the anger and the remoteness of God, under his patience and forbearance, under sin and judgment, not only as a time of widening distance from the purity of the original beginning, but also as a time in which there is no escape from these beginnings, a time of darkness and of guilt, a time of preparation for Christ: all of this is present, but it does not really become clear whether and how this preparation was more than the experience of the need for redemption. Nor does it become clear how such a preparation is to be understood if we remember that the generations of mankind succeed one another, and hence in a certain sense each one must always begin all over again.

Hence the pre-biblical history of revelation and salvation stretches back from us into an obscure and almost structureless past, however much accurate knowledge we might have about non-biblical religions with regard to the variety of their rites, their social institutions, their theories, their restorations and reform movements, and their mutual struggles and influences. In spite of everything we know about the history of religion, this history remains very unstructured as far as the real history of *revelation* goes. If we see the meaning of secular history in a theoretical and practical self-appropriation of man and of the world around him, and hence in the progress of the history of freedom as the capacity for self-determination, for hope, for risk-taking and for love, we do not succeed from this philosophical interpretation of history in incorporating really clear structures and caesurae into the history of the human race.

If we could ever get out of the habit of seeing the moments and caesurae of world history in a naive way from our own individual and so very short lifetime, and hence if we could understand that even a very short epoch, a historical moment, can last several thousand years, it still would not be possible for us to structure the earlier history of salvation and revelation before biblical times, and to clarify the different phases in the course of this history. But if we did get out of this habit, one thing would become clear for us: the whole biblical age from Abraham to Christ shrinks into the brief moment of the inauguration and of the event of Christ. Moreover, insofar as we are Christians, we have the right and the obligation to see it—from the perspective of the Old and New Testaments and with a view to the whole history of revelation which is coextensive with the history of the human race—as the final moment before the event of Christ and as forming a unity along with this event.

We can point out of course that the period of man's existence from his biological beginnings up to recent millennia, in which there seems to be for the first time historical consciousness, explicit tradition, and so on, could be regarded not as a period of history, but as an ahistorical pre-history of the human race. In this pre-history the human race does indeed exist in a mute way and reproduce itself, but it has not yet really taken hold of its existence in the clarity and freedom of history, nor made it the object of its own activity and planning and responsibility. From the viewpoint of secular history we could certainly look at it this way.

But for the theologian, however important such considerations are in many respects, and however much they could also be relevant for theology, they still remain ultimately indecisive. Theologically we have to say, without for this reason being disavowed by the secular sciences: wherever we really find a being of absolute transcendence who places the biological and the interpersonal realm as a whole in question, there we find a man with freedom, with self-determination, and with an immediate boundary with absolute mystery. And wherever this is missing, what we call "man" in a philosophical and Christian and theological sense did not exist, however similar this being may have been to us in other respects. For a theological understanding, therefore, man in this sense necessarily has a history of freedom, of salvation and of revelation, and we can leave the question open here as to what extent he himself made this history thematic in a religious way. But since such a history objectifies and expresses itself corporeally in language, in interpersonal life, in rites, and so on, the notion of a history of freedom, salvation and revelation as real history in the theological sense and in theological terms cannot be excluded even from those periods in which man still seems to have existed in a very ahistorical way in many respects.

It remains the case, then, that it is not possible for us to structure in a more precise, theological way this pre-biblical, immensely long and genuinely historical history of salvation and revelation. Consequently, the whole biblical history of revelation, that is, the particular and "official" categorical history of revelation which is the only one we know about, shrinks to the brief historical moment of preparation for and inauguration of the event of Christ. The time of the so-called biblical patriarchs is either a time whose representatives, who are not really accessible to us historically, say but one thing: the history of the Old Testament covenant has its origins in a universal history of salvation and revelation and it preserves its connection with it, and it must continue to bear its grace and the burden of its guilt in order to bring it totally into Christ; or, the time of the patriarchs before Moses is already the history of the beginnings of this particular and official history of revelation, and is the time of the most proximate historical foreshadowing of the covenant people of Israel, and is this insofar as a certain kernel of historical tradition from the pre-history of Israel was already present in the history of the patriarchs. The fifteen hundred years of the real history of the Old Testament covenant with Moses and the prophets, with all their differences and all their dramatic changes, are still but the brief moment of the very last preparation of history for Christ. For us, then, this Old Testament pre-history of Christ is merely the final and immediate pre-history of Christ himself, since a really theological statement about it which is still valid for us is now possible for us at least only in view of Christ.

This is shown just by the fact that the Old Testament scriptural foundation for such a statement admits of no unified interpretation with regard to its content and its scope except in view of Christ. For except in view of him, this scripture with its slow genesis and the many strata in its tendencies and its theological conceptions could hardly be subsumed under one unified idea, unless it is the idea that a people in its long history knows that it is the partner of the one, living, judging and gracious God, who is the incomprehensible but ever present Lord of its history, and therefore knows that this history is fundamentally open to an unknown but salvific future, and that it is given over to the disposal of the coming God of the future.

It is not the concrete content of this history before Christ in the old covenant which makes it the history of revelation, for nothing really happens in the realm of the categorical which does not also happen in the history of every other people. What makes this history a history of revelation is rather the interpretation of this history as the event of a dialogical partnership with God, and as a prospective tendency towards an open future. These two moments are not interpretations added to this history extrinsically, but are historical moments within what is being interpreted.

But it is this interpretation which constitutes the history as a history of revelation.

It follows from this that such history could also have taken place and has taken place in the history of other peoples, especially since in the concrete the history of Israel was also the history of guilt, of falling away from God, the history of a legalistic ossification of something which was originally religious, and all of this inseparably mixed together. Now if someone says that it is only in the history of the religion of a small Near Eastern people that scripture allows for the knowledge of the continuity and structured sequence of a particular history of revelation, and that we would not have this possibility in other histories of religion with this clarity and certainty, we can readily admit this. But this very interpretation and differentiation of the particular history of salvation in the Old Testament from other particular histories of salvation, and also from everything else which took place in this history, was not possible for the people of the Old Testament themselves in the same way and to the same extent that it is possible for us. They acknowledged without hesitation a salvific relationship between Yahweh and other peoples which had its effects in history.

If, then, the interpretation of the Old Testament history of salvation is possible for us only in view of Christ, because it is only in view of him that its special nature concerns us at all, then it can really have a religious meaning for us only as the most immediate and proximate pre-history of Christ himself, and it is only in this way that it can be our own history of revelation and our own tradition. But this means that basically we have only two fixed points and one dividing line which are really decisive and identifiable in our own categorical history of revelation and salvation: the *beginning* and the *fullness* of salvation history in Christ.

Later we shall have to say from the perspective of Christology and soteriology that this dividing line "Christ" is not a moment which could be followed by other moments in the history of salvation and revelation which are equally radical, except for the final and definitive fulfillment.

Two things should be mentioned by way of conclusion. If compared with the immense duration of the history of the human race we distinguish only very few final caesurae in this secular history, then in certain circumstances the moment of such a caesura, the turning point in history, lasts some thousands of years by our calendar calculations. If we look for the one most decisive caesura in man's two-million-year secular history, the moment of this caesura lies in those thousands of years in which, in a rapidly progressive acceleration, man developed from a being ensconced in nature and immediately threatened by it into a being who lives in an environment which he himself has created and no longer merely accepts; those thousands of years in which he developed into the man who makes himself the object of his own manipulation, who has transformed his numinous environment into a rationally planned and demythologized site for his own plans. Perhaps we are today at the end of this new beginning, and now stand at the end of the so-called modern period. Looked at from the perspective of the whole history of the human race, however, the modern period is only the end of the whole history of culture up to now. We are entering into that realm of history which man has opened for himself.

In this discussion we can leave entirely open the question how long the second period of hominized existence will last, a period now just beginning and coming after a period of natural existence. We can also leave open the question whether this second period will be the brief moment of a catastrophe brought on by man himself, or will be a realm of time, almost ahistorical again, in which man will exist in a nature which has finally been made subject to him, and will be man in a way which we cannot yet concretely imagine. Now it follows from this, if we calmly understand this realm of time as a moment in the coming to be of the history of the human race, and it is but a moment even if it has lasted several thousand years, it follows that the event of Christ must be located within this realm of time. It is only in the light of both elements that we can find a really theological explanation for this one radical caesura between what comes after and what came before.

If we understand the whole realm of time up to now, which we call "historically accessible" history, as a relatively very brief transition, then the place of Christ in this secular history of the world, and of course all the more so in the history of religion which is coextensive with this realm of time, becomes intelligible and becomes correlative to the caesura which has lasted several thousand years. After an almost incalculable sojourn in an almost natural existence, in this caesura mankind becomes conscious of itself, and not only in introverted reflection, art and philosophy, but also in an art and reflection which turns out to the world around it. And at the same time as the history of the human race enters into this period it reaches the God-Man, the absolute historical objectification of its transcendental understanding of God. In this objectification, namely, in Jesus Christ, the God who communicates himself and the man who accepts God's self-communication become irrevocably one, and the history of revelation and salvation of the whole human race reaches its goal. This does not, however, decide the question of individual salvation.

Now man no longer moves towards his goal only transcendentally, but rather this history of mankind also reaches its very goal categorically, and within this goal it actively directs itself towards the final goal. For in this history and within the period of this caesura there is already present the very thing towards which mankind is moving: the God-humanity of mankind in the one God-Man Jesus Christ. Therefore the single and final fundamental caesura in secular history and the final, fundamental caesura in the history of salvation and revelation occur in the same historical moment of transition, even if this moment lasts several thousand years. From both a secular and a theological perspective, man has come to himself, that is, has come to the mystery of his existence, not only in the transcendentality of his beginning, but also in his history. For this reason this moment can really be called the "fullness of time," although for secular history and for theological history this fullness of time is present only in its beginning.

6. A Summary of the Notion of Revelation

"NATURAL" REVELATION AND GOD'S REAL SELF-REVELATION

If God creates something other than himself and thereby creates it as something finite, if God creates spirit which recognizes this other as finite through its transcendence and hence in view of its ground, and if therefore at the same time it differentiates this ground as qualitatively and wholly other from what is merely finite, and as the ineffable and holy mystery, this already implies a certain disclosure of God as the infinite mystery. This is usually called the "natural revelation of God," although this is a misleading term. But this leaves God still unknown insofar as he becomes known only by analogy as mystery, insofar as he becomes known only negatively by way of his preeminence over the finite, and only by mediate reference, but he does not become known in himself by direct immediacy to him. His ultimate and unambiguous relationship to spiritual creatures cannot be known in this way. For in this kind of a natural, transcendental relationship to God the question is still unanswered whether God wants to be for us a silent and impenetrable mystery keeping us at a distance in our finiteness, or wants to be the radical closeness of self-communication; whether he wants to confront our sinful rejection of him in the depths of our conscience and in its categorical objectifications in history as judgment or as forgiveness.

Beyond this "natural revelation," which is really the presence of God as question, not as answer, there is the real revelation of God. This is not simply given with the spiritual being of man as transcendence, but rather has the character of an event. It is dialogical, and in it God speaks to man, and makes known to him something which cannot be known always and everywhere in the world simply through the necessary relation of all reality in the world to God in man's transcendence. This latter is the way we know the question about God and the fact that man is placed in question by this mystery. Rather, presupposing the world and transcendental spirit, the real revelation discloses something which is still unknown for man from the world: the inner reality of God and his personal and free relationship to spiritual creatures.

We do not have to raise the question here whether we as individuals could know by ourselves and with certainty that God *can* express himself in this way or not. Whether the *possibility* of a self-communication of God in grace could be known from man and his transcendence, whether man could interpret his transcendence as the realm of a possible self-communication of God in his own self, or whether he would have said that this realm is indeed given as the condition of possibility for a relationship to the absolute mystery, but could not be fulfilled by God's self-communication without being shattered, these are all questions which we will not treat here. God has in fact revealed himself in this way. And at least from this we know that such a revelation through God's self-communication is in itself *possible*.

This revelation has two aspects, transcendental and historical, which are distinct but belong together. Both are necessary so that revelation can exist at all. These two aspects have a certain variability in their reciprocal relationship.

THE TRANSCENDENTAL ASPECT OF REVELATION

First of all, the historical and personal revelation in word encounters the inner, spiritual uniqueness of man. God communicates himself to it in his own most proper reality as spiritual luminosity, and gives man in his transcendence the possibility to accept this personal self-communication and self-disclosure, to listen and to accept it in faith, hope and love in such a way that it is not brought down to the "level" of finite creatures as such. Rather, as the self-disclosure of God in his very self, it can really "come" into man's midst. For the act of hearing, the acceptance of this self-disclosure and self-communication is borne by God himself through his divinization of man.

This revelation is God giving himself in absolute and also forgiving closeness, so that God is neither the absolute, remote and distant One, nor judgment, although he could be both. Consequently, in this forgiving closeness God gives himself as the inner fulfillment of unlimited transcendentality. The absolutely unlimited question is fulfilled and answered by God himself as the absolute answer.

What we have described in this way is called in Christian terminology sanctifying and justifying grace as a divinizing elevation of man. In this elevation God gives not only something different from himself, but his very own self, and the act of its acceptance is borne by him. Now insofar as, first of all, this grace was offered by God to all times and to all men in view of and in his absolute willing of Jesus Christ, the God-Man, and insofar as it is already effective as an offer, and, as we can hope, although we cannot know for sure, is accepted at least by the majority of men as the final result of the free act of their whole lives; insofar as, secondly, this grace alters man's consciousness and gives him, as scholastic theology says, a new, higher and gratuitous, although unreflexive, formal object, that is, gives him transcendence towards the absolute being of God as beatifying; insofar as, thirdly, at least the horizon of the human spirit as the infinite question is filled by this ineffable self-communication of God with the believing trust that this infinite question is answered by God with the infinite answer which he himself is, it follows that through this grace the event of free grace and of God's self-communication is already given to all times. This inner self-communication of God in grace at the core of a spiritual person is destined for all men, in *all* of his dimensions, because all are to be integrated into the single salvation of the single and total person. Therefore all transcendent subjectivity possesses itself not for itself *alongside* history, but *in* this very history, which is precisely the history of man's transcendence itself.

THE CATEGORICAL, HISTORICAL ASPECT OF REVELATION

God's self-revelation in the depths of the spiritual person is an a priori determination coming from grace and is in itself unreflexive. It is not in itself an objective, thematic expression; it is not something known objectively, but something within the realm of consciousness. But none of this means that this a priori determination exists for itself, and that in this apriority it could only become the object of a subsequent reflection which would have nothing intrinsically to do with the apriority of grace as such. Rather God's gift of himself, the gratuitously elevated determination of man, the transcendental revelation is itself always mediated categorically in the world, because all of man's transcendentality has a history. It takes place in the historical material of a person's life, but does not for this reason become simply identical with it. If, then, this supernatural determination is to take place in the concrete, and especially, if God's self-revelation in grace is to become the principle of concrete action in its objective and reflexive consciousness, and hence also in the dimension of society, then God's non-objective and unreflexive self-revelation in grace must always be present as mediated in objective and reflexive knowledge, regardless in the first instance of whether this is an explicitly and thematically religious mediation or not.

This "mediation" has its history, and it exists within this history under God's direction, which is nothing else but the dynamism of God's transcendental self-communication towards its historical realization and mediation, and hence this mediation is itself God's revelation. The history of the mediation of God's transcendental revelation is an intrinsic moment in the historicity of God's self-disclosure in grace. For by its very nature and not only because of the nature of man, this self-disclosure has a dynamism towards its own objectification, since it is the principle of the divinization of the creature in all of its dimensions.

The attempt is made in every religion, at least on man's part, to mediate the original, unreflexive and non-objective revelation historically, to make it reflexive and to interpret it in propositions. In all religions there are individual moments of such a successful mediation made possible by God's grace, moments when the supernatural, transcendental relationship of man to God through God's self-communication becomes self-reflexive. Through these moments God creates for man the possibility of salvation also in the dimension of his objectivity, his concrete historicity. But just as God has permitted man's guilt, and this guilt has its darkening and depraving effect on all of man's collective and social dimensions, this is also the case in the history of man's objectifying self-interpretation of gratuitous revelation. It is only partially successful, it always exists within a still unfinished history, it is intermixed with error, sinful delusions and their objectifications, and these once again co-determine the religious situation of other people.

Whenever and wherever this objectification of revelation is accomplished for a community of people and not only for the individual existence of an individual as such; when the mediating translation is accomplished in those persons whom we then call religious prophets, bearers of revelation in the full sense, and when it is directed by God himself in the dynamism of his divine self-communication in such a way that it remains pure, although it mediates perhaps only partial aspects of the transcendental revelation; and when this purity of revelation in its objectification by the prophets and our own call by this objectified revelation is shown to be legitimate for us by what we call signs, then we have what is called public, official, particular and ecclesially constituted revelation and its history, we have what we are accustomed to call "revelation" in an absolute sense.

This kind of revelation not only has the character of event and is historical insofar as it is a free decision of God, and insofar as it calls for a free, historical response on the part of every person. This revelation is also historical and particular in the sense that it does not take place everywhere in this official and, as it were, reflexively guaranteed purity. Rather, it has a special history within universal history and within the universal history of religion. Although this universal history and the history of religion themselves always remain the history of revelation, and although this particular history of revelation in its purity and as reflexively guaranteed always has a more remote or a more proximate significance for the history of everyone, the particular history of revelation still remains a moment within the universal history of salvation and revelation, although an immanent moment. In view of the genuine historicity of man who necessarily exists in a world of personal relationships, this is no more surprising than it is surprising that in other areas of man's history there are preeminent historical events which cannot be repeated every day.

THE UNSURPASSABLE CLIMAX OF ALL REVELATION

If history is also the history of what is always unique and unrepeatable, then universal history always contains particular history, and this latter still always remains a moment within the whole universal history. Insofar as this revelation has a history because of the historicity of reflection upon God's self-gift to man in grace—and indeed this history is differentiated within universal history—the history of revelation has its absolute climax when God's self-communication reaches its unsurpassable high point through the hypostatic union and in the incarnation of God in the created, spiritual reality of Jesus for his own sake, and hence for the sake of all of us. But this takes place in the incarnation of the Logos because here what is expressed and communicated, namely, God himself, and, secondly, the mode of expression, that is, the human reality of Christ in his life and in his final state, and, thirdly, the recipient Jesus in grace and in the vision of God, all three have become absolutely one. In Jesus, God's communication to man in grace and at the same time its categorical self-interpretation in the corporeal, tangible and social dimension have reached their climax, have become revelation in an absolute sense. But this means that the event of Christ becomes for us the only really tangible caesura in the universal history of salvation and revelation, and it enables us to distinguish a particular and official history of revelation within the universal history of revelation before Christ.

·VI·

Jesus Christ

We come now to what is most specifically Christian in Christianity, Jesus Christ. Indeed, our reflections thus far say, in effect, that there is also an "anonymous Christianity." According to the Catholic understanding of the faith, as is clearly expressed in the Second Vatican Council, there can be no doubt that someone who has no concrete, historical contact with the explicit preaching of Christianity can nevertheless be a justified person who lives in the grace of Christ. He then possesses God's supernatural self-communication in grace not only as an offer, not only as an existential of his existence; he has also accepted this offer and so he has really accepted what is essential in what Christianity wants to mediate to him: his salvation in that grace which objectively is the grace of Jesus Christ. Since the transcendental self-communication of God as an offer to man's freedom is an existential of every person, and since it is a moment in the self-communication of God to the world which reaches its goal and its climax in Jesus Christ, we can speak of "anonymous Christians." But it still remains true: in the full historical dimension of this single self-communication of God to man in Christ and towards Christ, only someone who explicitly professes in faith and in baptism that Jesus is the Christ is a Christian in the historical and reflexive dimension of God's transcendental self-communication.

This sixth chapter, then, brings our reflections to what is decisively Christian in Christianity. The method of procedure in this section is very difficult because, precisely in view of our previous reflections, in this topic the two moments in Christian theology reach their closest unity and their most radical tension: first, essential, existential-ontological, transcendental theology, which must develop in a general ontology and anthropology an a priori doctrine of the God-Man, and in this way try to construct the conditions which make possible a genuine capacity to hear the historical message of Jesus Christ, and an insight into the necessity of hearing it; and, secondly, plain historical testimony about what happened in Jesus, in his death and resurrection, and about what in its unique, irreducible and historical concreteness forms the basis of the existence and of the event of salvation for a Christian. Consequently, at this point what is most historical is what is most essential.

When we say that at least today an a priori doctrine of the God-Man must be developed in a transcendental theology, this does not mean of course that such an a priori doctrine could be developed temporally and historically prior to the actual encounter with the God-Man. We always reflect upon the conditions of possibility for a reality which we have already encountered. But this does not make such a reflection superfluous. It offers a clearer and more reflexive understanding of what we have encountered as real, and it gives an added legitimacy to our intellectual conviction that we have grasped reality as it is.

We shall develop several lines of reflection which will try to bring home to us the single whole of the Christian doctrine of Jesus Christ under different aspects. These individual reflections cannot and do not intend to avoid overlapping somewhat as they focus on the one reality of Christ from very different vantage points. Hence repetitions which express anew the whole of Christology from ever new approaches will not be avoided, although they make great demands on the patience of the reader.

In connection with this I would call attention right away to the following: in giving a justification for our faith in Christ, the basic and decisive point of departure, of course, lies in an encounter with the historical Jesus of Nazareth, and hence in an "ascending Christology." To this extent the terms "incarnation of God" and "incarnation of the eternal Logos" are the end and not the starting point of all Christological reflection. Nevertheless, we need not exaggerate the one-directional nature of such an ascending Christology. If Jesus as the Christ has ever actually encountered someone, the idea of a God-Man, of God coming into our history, and hence a descending Christology, also has its own significance and power. If in what follows, then, ascending Christology and descending Christology appear somewhat intermingled, this is to be admitted without hesitation at the outset. It need not be a disadvantage, but rather it can serve as a mutual clarification of both of these aspects and both of these methods.

1. Christology
within an Evolutionary View of the World

EXPLANATION AND CLARIFICATION OF THE TOPIC

First of all, the basic issue here is the transcendental possibility in man which enables him to hear something like a message from the one God-Man. Hence the topic is concerned especially with the question of transcendental Christology, or of the transcendental possibility for man to take the question of a God-Man seriously.

We are really asking a transcendental question, but it has a historical concreteness in the hearer, in the questioning subject, and we shall characterize this concreteness as the situation of an evolutionary view of the world. We are aware of course that this is not a very precise characterization. It is within this framework that we have to give expression to the really transcendental nature of the possibility of hearing God's message in our flesh.

We are dealing, therefore, simply with the question of showing the compatibility of one statement within a complex of other statements, horizons of understanding and convictions, and not with the one or the other set of statements by themselves. This means that we are not concerned here in the first instance with a presentation of Catholic Christology, nor with what can perhaps be vaguely designated as an "evolutionary view of the world." Our question is the possibility of coordinating the two. We are presupposing thereby the evolutionary view of the world as a given, and we are asking whether Christology is compatible or can be compatible with it, and not vice versa.

Indeed the more radical question and ultimately the more obvious question for Christian faith would be to ask how an evolutionary view of the world can be justified before Christian faith. But the first question is legitimate nevertheless; in fact it is basically unavoidable for all of us. Although it is a secondary question for him, even the believer asks whether his faith is compatible and at least sufficiently reconcilable with the lifestyle and the horizons of understanding which he shares with his age and with his contemporaries. And this question is legitimate because, as Peter says (1 Pet. 3:15), he has to give an account of his faith not only to himself, but also to the world in which he lives. Moreover, the question is all the more legitimate because his faith does not require him to harbor a radical mistrust of this pluralism in his horizons of understanding, convictions and views of life, a mistrust of that pluralism which he finds as a given and which he cannot synthesize completely into the unity of an absolute system which would include everything which is present in his existence. But if he is aware of this pluralism, he has to ask how in practice he can live as a believer in the concrete world in which he exists.

When we ask, then, whether Christology is or can be compatible with an evolutionary view of the world, we are not trying to deduce the Christian doctrine of Incarnation from an evolutionary view of the world as a necessary consequence and a logical development. Nor are we trying to show that the doctrine of the Incarnation does not stand in a direct and simple contradiction either really or logically to what we can know with certainty in the content of an evolutionary view of the world. For if our intention were to deduce the doctrine of Incarnation as a cogent inference from an evolutionary view of the world, then we would be making an attempt at theological rationalism, an attempt to turn faith, revelation and dogma into philosophy, or to reduce the ultimately irreducible facticity of concrete history into speculation and metaphysics. If our purpose were merely the second alternative, this too would fail to accomplish the real task. For even if the doctrine of the Incarnation of the divine Logos is not directly denied by the contemporary evolutionary view of the world, this doctrine could still be experienced as a foreign body, as something which seems to be absolutely unrelated to the mentality and experience of people today. The task consists, then, in showing an intrinsic affinity and the possibility of a reciprocal correlation between the two without making the Christian doctrine of Incarnation a necessary and intrinsic element within the contemporary view of the world.

Now presupposing a certain initial understanding of the problem we have just posed, it is also clear how difficult, onerous and many-sided the task is. All the problems of reconciling Christian teaching and its interpretation of existence with the life-style and mentality and experience of today's world are rolled up into one and concentrated in our topic. All of the objective and historical difficulties which are conjured up by the phrase "Christianity and the modern spirit" present themselves at this point where we are dealing with the most central and most mysterious assertion of Christianity. At the same time this assertion is about a reality which is said to belong precisely to that dimension which is associated with people today as the one they are most familiar with scientifically, existentielly and affectively, namely, the dimension of the material world and of tangible history. For we are dealing with an assertion which allows God, the reality about whom theology speaks, to be present precisely where man feels at home and in the only place where he feels competent: in the world and not in heaven. It cannot be our task here to discuss the general questions and difficulties which are connected with reconciling Christian religion and modern thought. We must confine ourselves to the special questions which are raised by our more limited problem, although we are aware of the fact that perhaps what most alienates people today from the doctrine of the Incarnation is due to the estrangement people feel today with metaphysical and religious statements in general.

We shall take as our starting point today's evolutionary view of the world, but we are going to presuppose it rather than present it. We shall ask first of all, then, how it sees the relationship between matter and spirit, and hence we are asking about the unity of the world, the unity between the history of nature and the history of man. For we want to take the statement that the Logos became *flesh* really seriously. We do not want to understand this fundamental dogma of Christianity in a mythological way which can no longer be understood and assimilated, nor do we want to explain it in such a way that what it means is really relegated to a realm in which we can risk assertions which no one can prove, but which in any case have absolutely nothing to do with what we otherwise think we know and experience with certainty. But we can only present these further horizons here very briefly, and in doing so we shall touch only upon those correlations and that knowledge which are common to Christianity and common to theology: we are trying to avoid theories which Teilhard de Chardin has made current. If we reach the same conclusions, so much the better, and we do not have to avoid that deliberately. We ourselves only want to reflect here upon what really every theologian could say if he brought his theology to bear upon those questions which are raised by an evolutionary view of the world.

We shall have to bear with a bit of abstractness, and this can perhaps be somewhat of a disappointment to a natural scientist. For it would be understandable if a natural scientist would expect more exact data than can be offered here, and indeed from those scientific findings which are familiar to him. But if we were to make such an attempt, not only would we have to lay claim to scientific knowledge which is accessible to a theologian only at second or third hand, but we would also have to assume all the burdens which are inevitably connected with the interpretations of particular scientific results which are not undisputed. We have enough to do here just with the difficulties which arise in philosophy and theology in connection with these questions.

If we take as our starting point the unity of spirit and matter, and this does not mean homogeneity, then we have to try to understand man as the existent in whom the basic tendency of matter to discover itself in spirit through self-transcendence reaches its definitive breakthrough, so that from this perspective the essence of man himself can be seen within a fundamental and total conception of the world. But it is this very essence of man which, through its free and highest and full self-transcendence into God by means of God's self-communication, a self-transcendence gratuitously made possible for him by God, it is this essence which is "awaiting" its fulfillment and that of the world in what we call in Christian concepts grace and glory.

The permanent beginning and the absolute guarantee that this ultimate self-transcendence, which is fundamentally unsurpassable, will succeed and has already begun is what we call the "hypostatic union."

The God-Man is the initial beginning and the definitive triumph of the movement of the world's self-transcendence into absolute closeness to the mystery of God. In the first instance this hypostatic union may not be seen so much as something which distinguishes Jesus from us, but as something which must occur once and only once when the world begins to enter upon its final phase, which does not necessarily mean its shortest phase. In this phase it is to realize its definitive concentration, its definitive climax and its radical closeness to the absolute mystery which we call God. From this perspective the Incarnation appears as the necessary and permanent beginning of the divinization of the world as a whole. Insofar as this unsurpassable closeness in total openness takes place precisely in relation to the absolute mystery which God is and remains, and insofar as this definitive phase of world history has indeed already begun but is not yet complete, the further course of this phase and its result remain, of course, shrouded in mystery. The clarity and the finality of Christian truth lies in the inexorability of man's deliverance into this mystery, and is not the clarity of comprehending a partial element in man and in his world.

THE UNITY OF ALL CREATED THINGS

The Christian professes in his faith that all things, heaven and earth, the realm of the material and of the spiritual, are the creation of one and the same God. But if everything which exists exists only by having its origin in God, then this means not only that all things in their variety proceed from *one* cause which, because it is infinite and all-powerful, can create the most varied things. It also means that this variety manifests an inner similarity and commonality, and that this variety or differentiation forms a unity in its origin, its self-realization and its determination—that is, it forms a *single* world. It follows from this that it would be unchristian to understand matter and spirit as merely existing alongside each other in fact, and as being basically and absolutely disparate realities in relationship to each other. For Christian theology and philosophy it is to be taken for granted that spirit and matter have more in common than they have differentiating them.

This commonality manifests itself first of all and most clearly in the unity of man himself. According to Christian teaching a human person is not a contradictory or merely provisional composite of spirit and matter, but is a unity which is both logically and really antecedent to the differentiation and distinction of its elements. Consequently, these elements are intelligible precisely in what is proper to them only when they are understood as elements within the *one* person. From this perspective it is clear that it is ultimately only from the single person and therefore only from his or her single self-realization that we know what spirit and matter are, and hence both must be understood as related to each other to begin with. There also corresponds to this the Christian teaching that the fulfillment of the finite spirit which man is must be understood only in the context of the fulfillment of his *whole* reality and the fulfillment of the cosmos, however little we can "imagine" this. In this fulfillment his materiality must not simply be excluded as something merely provisional, however little we are able to form a positive image of materiality in its fulfilled state.

Now natural science as one element within the single whole of man's knowledge knows a great deal "about" matter, that is, it determines ever more exact relationships of a functional kind among the phenomena of nature. But since it abstracts from man, and this is methodologically justified, it can know a great deal "about" matter, but it cannot know *matter itself,* although its knowledge does lead it back to man himself in an a posteriori way. This is really self-evident: the field or the whole cannot be determined by the means by which the parts are determined. It is only in relation to man that we can say what matter is, and not vice versa, that is, going from matter to what spirit is. We are saying here deliberately in relation to "man," and not in relation to "spirit." Otherwise we would be back in the kind of Platonism which is also found in materialism, for it believes just as much as platonic spiritualism does that it has a starting point for understanding the whole and its parts which is independent of man as a single whole. But it is only in man that both of these elements, spirit and matter, can be experienced in their real essence and in their unity.

But beginning with the original experience of the single person of himself we can say: *spirit* is the single person insofar as he becomes conscious of himself in an absolute presence to himself, and indeed does this by the fact that he is always oriented towards the absoluteness of reality as such, and towards its one ground whom we call God. This return to himself and this orientation towards the absolute totality of all possible reality and its single ground condition each other reciprocally. But this orientation does not have the character of being a possession of the known, a possession which empties by seeing through. It has rather the character of being taken possession of, and of being drawn into the infinite mystery. It is only in the loving acceptance of this mystery and in its unpredictable disposal of us that we can genuinely undergo this process, and undergo it in that freedom which is necessarily given with transcendence of every individual thing and of one's own self. Insofar as the single person experiences himself in this way, he can and has to say: I am spirit.

One and the same person grasps both himself and the world around him which is necessarily a part of him as *matter* insofar as this act of returning to self in the experience of this orientation towards the mystery to be accepted in love always and primarily takes place only in an encounter with something individual, with something which manifests itself from its own self, with something which in the concrete is not at our disposal and confronts as an inescapable given. A person experiences both himself and the world which directly encounters him as matter insofar as he experiences his own facticity, experiences himself as someone who is a given and is to be accepted and is not yet comprehended; insofar as in the midst of knowledge as self-possession there stands something which is not himself; insofar as every person includes what is foreign to himself and is not at his own disposal. Matter is the condition which makes possible the objective other which the world and man are to themselves. It is the condition for what we experience immediately as time and space, and this precisely when we are not able to objectify it for ourselves conceptually. Matter means the condition for that otherness which estranges man from himself and precisely in doing so brings him to himself. It is the condition which makes possible an immediate intercommunication with other spiritual existents in time and space and in history. Matter is the ground of the givenness of the other as the material of freedom, and the ground of real communication between finite spirits in mutual knowledge and love.

THE NOTION OF "ACTIVE SELF-TRANSCENDENCE"

Now this relationship of reciprocal conditioning between spirit and matter is not simply a static relationship, but it has itself a history. Man as spirit which becomes present to itself experiences his self-estrangement as extended in time, as nature with a history. He becomes present to himself as one who has already existed in time both in himself and in the world around him, for the world too belongs to him and to his constitution. And conversely: materiality in time as the pre-history of man in his reflexive freedom must be understood as oriented towards the history of the human spirit.

We have tried to understand spirit and matter without separating them, and as mutually related and inseparable elements of the single person, but once again neither are they reducible to each other. This insurmountable pluralism of elements within the *single* person can also be expressed by saying that there is an essential difference between spirit and matter. But this essential difference is not to be understood as an essential difference between two existents which come together only subsequently to their own being and their own essence. It is absolutely important to assert an essential difference between matter and spirit because it is only by doing so that one's view remains open for all of the dimensions of the single person and all of their immeasurable, indeed infinite extension, and also because it is only by doing so that a radical openness towards the ultimate point of identity whom we call God is maintained. This essential difference must not be misunderstood as an essential opposition or as an absolute disparity and mutual indifference between the two. If the *temporal* duration of the relationship between spirit and matter is kept in mind, then without hesitation we can say of the intrinsic relationship between the two that it is of the intrinsic nature of matter to develop towards spirit.

If there is such a thing as becoming at all, and becoming is not just a fact of experience, but it is a fundamental axiom of theology itself, because otherwise freedom and responsibility and the fulfillment of man in and through his own responsible action makes no sense, then the true nature and the true structure of becoming cannot be understood merely as a becoming *different* in the sense that a reality becomes different, but not more. Becoming must be understood as becoming *more*, as the coming to be of more reality, as reaching and achieving a greater fullness of being. But this more must not be understood as simply added to what was there before. Rather it must on the one hand be the effect of what was there before, and on the other hand it must be an intrinsic increase in its own being. But this means that if becoming is really to be taken seriously it must be understood as real *self-transcendence*, as surpassing oneself, as emptiness actively achieving its own fullness.

But if this notion of an active self-transcendence in which an existent and an agent actively achieves a higher perfection of itself which was not there before is not to make nothingness the ground of being and emptiness the source of fullness, in other words, if the metaphysical principle of causality is not to be violated, then this self-transcendence can only be understood as taking place by the power of the absolute fullness of being. On the one hand this fullness of being is to be understood as so *intrinsic* to the finite existent moving towards its fulfillment that this finite existent is empowered to achieve a real and *active* self-transcendence, and it does not simply receive this new reality passively as something caused only by God. On the other hand the inner power of self-transcendence is to be understood at the same time as distinguished from this finite and active existent in such a way that the power of the dynamism which is intrinsic to the finite existent must nevertheless *not* be understood as constitutive of the *essence* of the finite existent. For if the absoluteness of being which gives this power and makes it effective were the essence of the finite agent itself, then this latter would no longer be capable of real becoming in time and in history because it would already possess from the outset the absolute fullness of being as its own.

Perhaps it will suffice here to propose the thesis that the notion of an active self-transcendence in which both "self" and "transcendence" are to be taken with equal seriousness is a logically necessary notion if the phenomenon of becoming is to be maintained. This notion of self-transcendence also includes transcendence into something substantially new, a leap to something *essentially* higher. For, if we were to exclude this and emasculate the notion of self-transcendence, then certain phenomena which occur in natural history could no longer be taken seriously and seen without qualification for what they really are, as for example the procreation by parents of a new person, and not only of a biological nature, and this in something which apparently is in the first instance merely a biological occurrence. But essential self-transcendence is no more an intrinsic contradiction than is simple self-transcendence so long as one allows that it takes place within the dynamism of the power of absolute being which is intrinsic to the finite existent, but is not part of its own essence, that is, it takes place within what is called theologically "God's preservation of and cooperation with" creatures.

Now if this notion is metaphysically legitimate, and if the world is one, and if as one it has a history, and if in this one world not everything is already there from the beginning precisely because it is in the process of becoming, then there is no reason to deny that matter should have developed towards life and towards man. But in no way does this deny or obscure the fact that matter, life, consciousness and spirit are not the same. This distinction does not exclude development if there is becoming, if becoming implies or can imply real self-transcendence of an active kind, and if self-transcendence at least can include essential self-transcendence.

What we are trying to understand here in these a priori reflections as conceptually intelligible is also confirmed by ever more exactly and more comprehensively observed facts in the natural sciences. These sciences indeed no longer have any choice but to conceive of a world in the process of becoming in which man too appears as the product of this world. At this point we have to refer back to our previous reflections on the intrinsic interrelationship between spirit and matter. We also have to take into account the history of the cosmos as it is being investigated and described by natural science today. This history is being seen more and more as an interconnected history of matter, of life and of man. This single history does not exclude essential differences, but rather they are included in the notion of it because history of course is not the continuation of the same thing, but is precisely the coming to be of something new, of something more and not merely of something else. Conversely, neither do these essential differences exclude history because this history results precisely in an essential self-transcendence in which something which existed earlier really surpasses itself in order really and truly both to become something different and to preserve itself.

Insofar, then, as the higher order always embraces the lower as contained within it, it is clear that for the real event of self-transcendence the lower prepares for and is a prelude to this self-transcendence in the unfolding of its own reality and order. In its history it moves slowly towards that boundary which is then surpassed in the actual self-transcendence, that boundary which is not recognized as having been clearly surpassed until there has been a rather clear development of something new. Nor is the boundary itself able to be established exactly and unambiguously. It would be desirable, of course, to show more concretely what common features are found in the process whereby material, living and spiritual beings come to be, and to show more exactly how what is merely material is a prelude in its own dimension to the higher dimension of life, and how this is a prelude to spirit in a progressive approximation to the boundary to be surpassed through self-transcendence. If we really postulate a single history of the whole of reality, we would certainly have to indicate what permanent and formal structures of this entire history are imbedded in matter, life and spirit as common to all of them. It would have to be shown how even the very highest, although it is essentially new, can be understood as a variation of what existed previously.

But if we wanted to accomplish all of this, then the philosopher and the theologian would perhaps have to abandon his own field too much and develop these fundamental structures of the single history of the world by means of the more a posteriori method of the natural sciences. Let me just point out that the theologian not only *can* admit a notion of self-possession in an analogous sense for all material things, the self-possession which reaches its proper essence fully in consciousness or self-consciousness, but also as a good Thomistic philosopher he really *has* to do so. For what he calls the form in every existent is for him also and essentially idea, and the reality which we designate in the ordinary and, in its place, quite correct sense as "unconscious" is from a metaphysical point of view the existent which possesses *only* its *own* idea and is locked in itself. From this perspective it would also be clear that a really higher and more complex organization can also appear as a step towards consciousness and finally towards self-consciousness, although at least *self*-consciousness includes a real essential transcendence of the material vis-à-vis its previous state.

THE FINALITY OF THE HISTORY OF NATURE AND SPIRIT

If man is thus the self-transcendence of living matter, then the history of nature and of spirit form an intrinsic and stratified unity in which the history of nature develops towards man, continues on in him as *his* history, is preserved and surpassed in him, and therefore reaches its own goal with and in the history of man's spirit. Insofar as this history of nature is subsumed in man into freedom, the history of nature reaches its goal in the free history of spirit itself, and remains as an intrinsic, constitutive element in it. Insofar as the history of man still encompasses within itself the history of nature as the history of living matter, in the midst of its freedom it is still based upon the structures and necessities of this material world. Because man is not only a spirit who observes nature, but is also a part of it, and because he is to continue its history, his history is not only a history of culture situated above the history of nature, but is also an active transformation of the material world itself. And it is only through action which is of the spirit and through the life of the spirit which is action that man and nature reach their single and common goal.

In view of man's transcendence towards the absolute reality of God as infinite mystery, and precisely because his goal consists in the infinite fullness of God, this goal is of course hidden from and beyond the power of man himself. It can be reached only in the acceptance of this hiddenness and this distance. Insofar as the history of the cosmos is the history of free spirit, the history of the cosmos as well as the history of man is situated in guilt and trial. But insofar as the history of freedom always remains based upon the antecedent structures of the living world, and insofar as spirit's history of freedom is encompassed by the efficacious and victorious grace of God, the Christian knows that the history of the cosmos as a whole will find its real fulfillment in spite of as well as in and through man's freedom. He knows that as a whole its consummation will also be its fulfillment.

MAN'S PLACE IN THE COSMOS

In spite of the magnificent results and perspectives of science, even the modern natural scientist, and the rest of us too who share this mentality, still remain to a large extent really imprisoned in a pre-scientific as well as a pre-philosophical and pre-theological perspective. For even today he and we along with him usually think at the unconscious and unreflexive level that it belongs precisely to the spirit of natural science to see man as a weak and incidental being who is exposed to a nature which is indifferent to him, until finally he is swallowed up again by a "blind" nature. It is only by a kind of schizophrenia that we have anything like a conception of man's dignity and abiding value and of the unique existence of each person. But the notion that man is an accidental and really unintended product of the history of nature, a caprice of nature, contradicts not only metaphysics and Christian faith, but basically it also contradicts natural science itself. If man does exist, and precisely if he is the "product" of nature, if he appears not just at any time at all, but at a definite point in this development, a point at which he himself can even direct this development at least partially by the fact that he now objectifies it and stands over against what has produced him, and transforms the producer itself, then this very nature becomes conscious of itself *in him.* But then it is directed towards him because "chance" is not a meaningful term for natural science, and the natural scientist infers from the result at least a movement directed towards it.

If we do not see it this way, then it makes no sense at all to see the history of the cosmos and that of man as a single history. But then human thought will sooner or later fall back into a platonic dualism again, for spirit will then have to feel like a stranger who is on earth by chance, and it will not allow itself for long to be disdained and abused as insignificant and powerless. If spirit is not regarded as the goal of nature itself, and if it is not seen that nature finds itself in spirit in spite of all the physical powerlessness of the individual person, then in the long run man will only be able to have validity as the disparate adversary of nature, and he will form this estimate of himself.

Now the specific characteristic of the reality which comes to be in man is his presence to himself and his relationship to the absolute totality of reality and to its original, unfathomable ground as such. There flows from this the possibility of a real objectification of individual objects, and the latter's ability to be detached from an immediate reference to man in the sphere of the merely biological. If this is seen as the goal of the history of the cosmos itself, then we can say without hesitation that the world which has been established finds itself in man and in him makes itself its own object, and that it no longer has a relation to its ground only behind it as the presupposition of itself, but it also has it in front of it as its explicit thematic.

Nor is this assertion invalidated by the possible objection that such a recapitulation of a world which is dispersed in time and space, a recapitulation into itself and into its ground, is found in man only in its very formal and almost empty beginnings. Moreover, we can conceive of non-human, personal spirits (monads) who would accomplish this better. Unlike man they would not be the subjective factor in the world's totality and its self-presence in such a way that at the same time they would also really be a *partial* element of this world. Maybe there are such beings. Christians even know of them and call them angels. But this recapitulating self-presence of the whole or of the cosmos in the individual person and in the action and activity of the human race, however much it is still at its beginnings, is something which can take place many times in an absolutely unique way in each individual person precisely if it takes place in and through a definite partial element existing as something individual within the time and space of the cosmos.

Consequently, it cannot be said that this cosmic self-consciousness could not be human or could take place only once. It takes place in its own unique way in each individual person. The one material cosmos is the *single* body as it were of a *multiple* self-presence of this very cosmos and its orientation towards its absolute and infinite ground. If this cosmic corporeality of countless personal self-consciousnesses in which the cosmos can become present to itself has become self-present only in a very incipient way in the self-consciousness and in the freedom of individual persons, it exists nevertheless in every person as something which can and should come to be. For man in his corporeality is an element of the cosmos which cannot really be demarcated and separated, and he communicates with the whole cosmos in such a way that, in and through the corporeality of man as what is other to spirit, the cosmos really presses forward to this self-presence in spirit.

These beginnings of the self-presence of the cosmos in the spirit of individual persons has a history which is still going on. This takes place individually and collectively in the interior and exterior history of the individual person and of the human race. Again and again we find ourselves under the impression that nothing final will ever come out of this incalculably long and laborious process by which the cosmos finds itself in man. Again and again the process by which the reality of the world becomes conscious of itself in man seems to be aborted. Again and again a kind of secret obstinacy against self-consciousness, a kind of will to the unconscious seems to prevail. But if we presuppose that evolution has any ultimate and one-way direction at all, then the process by which the cosmos becomes conscious of itself in man, in his individual totality and in the freedom which he actualizes, this process must also have a final result. This seems to vanish and to fall back into the mute beginnings of the cosmos and of its dispersion only because we who are situated *here and now* in time and space are utterly incapable of experiencing the final coming to itself of such a monadic unity of the world, incapable of experiencing at our point in time and space the uniqueness of the fully comprehended totality of the cosmos. It must, however, exist. In Christian terminology we usually call it man's final and definitive state, his salvation, the immortality of the soul or the resurrection of the flesh, but in doing so we have to see clearly that, when correctly understood, all of these terms are describing a final and definitive state of fulfillment for the cosmos.

Now according to Christian teaching, this self-transcendence of the cosmos in man towards its own totality and towards its ground does not really and fully reach its ultimate fulfillment until the cosmos is not only something established in existence by its ground, is not only something created, but also receives the immediate self-communication of its own ground in the spiritual creatures which are its goal and its high point. This immediate self-communication of God to spiritual creatures takes place in what we call "grace" while this self-communication is still in its historical process, and "glory" when it reaches fulfillment. Not only does God create something different from himself, but he also gives himself to this other. The world receives God, the infinite and the ineffable mystery, in such a way that he himself becomes its innermost life. The always unique self-possession of the cosmos, which is concentrated in each individual spiritual person in its transcendence towards the absolute ground of its reality, takes place by the fact that the absolute ground itself becomes immediately interior to what is grounded by it.

In this sense the end is the absolute beginning. This beginning is not infinite emptiness or nothingness, but rather is the fullness which alone explains what is shared in and what is beginning, the fullness upon which a process of becoming can be based, and which can really give it the power of a movement towards what is the more developed and at the same time the more interior. In this one-way history in freedom and in action there really is more at the end than the created beginning contains in itself. This beginning, however, is to be distinguished from that absolute beginning which is the absolute God himself in his glory. Precisely because the movement of the development of the cosmos is thus borne from the beginning and in all its phases by a thrust towards greater fullness and interiority, and towards an ever closer and more conscious relationship to its ground, the message that it will reach an absolute immediacy with this infinite ground is present and found in the movement itself. If the history of the cosmos is always and basically a history of the human spirit, a desire to become conscious of itself and of its ground, then immediacy to God in God's self-communication to spiritual creatures, and in them to the whole cosmos, is the appropriate end of this development. As such it can no longer really be disputed in principle, presupposing that this development can reach its own absolute goal at all, and that it is not only as something unattainable that the goal sets the movement in motion.

As particular and biologically conditioned individuals we experience only the most rudimentary beginning of the movement towards this infinite goal. But we are nevertheless constituted in such a way that, as distinguished from animals, in the consciousness with which we wage our biological struggle for existence and vie for our earthly dignity we live and act out of a formal anticipation of the whole. We are even those beings who in the experience of grace, although it is of a non-objective kind, do experience the event of the promise of the absolute closeness of the mystery which grounds everything. And this gives us the right to have the courage to believe in the fulfillment of the ascending history of the cosmos and of each individual cosmic consciousness, a fulfillment which consists in the immediate experience of God in the most real and revealing self-communication.

Because of the very nature of the matter which it is about, this assertion also preserves in the most radical way the ineffable mystery which pervades our existence. For if God himself, who is the inexpressible infinity of mystery, is and will be the reality which is our fulfillment, and if the world does not understand itself in its deepest truth until it abandons itself radically to this mystery, then this message does not say something or other whose content exists alongside of other contents and falls within a common conceptual system of coordinates. It is saying rather that in front of and behind all of the individual things which are to be coordinated and in respect to which the sciences conduct their business, there always stands the infinite mystery, and that in this abyss lies the beginning and the end, and the blessed goal.

A person might declare himself uninterested in this abyss at the beginning and at the end of his existence as though annoyed by the too heavy demands it makes, and he might try to flee to the intelligible clarity of science as the only realm of his existence which is appropriate for him. But this is not allowed, and although he might be capable of it on the surface of his existence and of his objective consciousness, in those depths of the really spiritual person by which everything is borne and nourished he cannot escape the infinite question which encompasses him, and which is the only question which is its own answer. For it exists and has nothing outside itself which could be the answer. It is the question which is its own answer when it is accepted in love. Man is moved by this absolute question. If he enters into this movement, which is the movement of the world and of the spirit, he really comes to himself for the first time, and comes to God and to his goal, the goal in which the absolute beginning itself in its immediacy is our goal.

THE PLACE OF CHRIST IN AN EVOLUTIONARY VIEW OF THE WORLD

It is only from this perspective that the place of Christology in such an evolutionary view of the world can be determined.

We are presupposing, then, that the goal of the world is God's self-communication to it, and that the entire dynamism which God has implanted in the process by which the world comes to be in self-transcendence (and this as intrinsic to it but not, however, as a constitutive element of its own essence) is already directed towards this self-communication and its acceptance by the world. Now how are we to understand more exactly this self-communication of God to every spiritual creature, to all those subjects in which the cosmos becomes conscious of itself and of its relationship to its ground? To understand this we must point out first of all that these spiritual subjects within the cosmos are free.

But this statement presupposes at the same time that the history of the cosmos' becoming self-conscious and becoming itself is always and necessarily a history of the intercommunication of spiritual subjects. For the process by which the cosmos becomes conscious of itself in spiritual subjects must also imply necessarily and above all an intercommunion among these subjects in each of which the whole is present to itself in its own unique way. For otherwise the world's becoming conscious of itself would divide rather than unify.

God's self-communication, then, is a communication to the freedom and intercommunication of the many cosmic subjects. This self-communication is necessarily addressed to a free history of the human race. It can take place only in a *free* acceptance by free subjects, and indeed in a *common* history. God's self-communication does not suddenly become acosmic, directed only to an isolated and individualized subjectivity. It affects the history of the human race and is addressed to all men in their intercommunication, for it is only therein and thereby that the acceptance of God's self-communication can take place historically. Hence the event of this self-communication is to be understood as an event which takes place historically at ever definite points in time and space, and from there it is addressed to others as a call to their freedom. God's self-communication must have a permanent beginning and in this beginning a guarantee that it has taken place, a guarantee by which it can rightly demand a free decision to accept this divine self-communication. This free acceptance or rejection on the part of individual freedoms is not really about the event of God's self-communication as such, but only about the relationship which the spiritual creature assumes towards this self-communication. Admittedly, we usually call self-communication only a self-communication which meets with a free and therefore beatifying acceptance. But we have always emphasized that this self-communication of God necessarily exists either in the mode of its acceptance, which is usually called justification, or in the mode of its rejection, which is called disbelief and sin.

ON THE NOTION OF ABSOLUTE SAVIOUR

From this there follows first of all the notion of *saviour in an absolute sense*. We are applying this title to that historical person who appears in time and space and signifies the beginning of the absolute self-communication of God which is moving towards its goal, that beginning which indicates that this self-communication for everyone has taken place irrevocably and has been victoriously inaugurated. This notion of saviour, or more precisely perhaps *absolute* saviour, does not mean that God's self-communication to the world in its spiritual subjectivity must begin first with him in a *temporal* sense. It can have already begun before the saviour, indeed it can be coexistent with the whole spiritual history of the human race and of the world, and this in fact is the case according to Christian teaching. We are calling saviour here that historical subjectivity in which, first, this process of God's absolute self-communication to the spiritual world as a whole exists *irrevocably;* secondly, that process in which this divine self-communication can be recognized unambiguously as irrevocable; and thirdly, that process in which God's self-communication reaches its climax insofar as this climax must be understood as a moment within the total history of the human race, and as such must not simply be identified with the totality of the spiritual world under God's self-communication.

Insofar as this self-communication is to be understood as free both on the part of God and of the history of the human race, it is perfectly legitimate to employ the notion of an event through which this self-communication and acceptance reaches a point in history which is irrevocable and irreversible. It does so by the fact that the history of this self-communication reaches its real breakthrough and the real essence of what it is. However, with respect to its duration and to the plurality of the history of the human race in time and space, the history of God's self-communication to the human race must not for this reason have already reached its end and its conclusion. In the genuine history of a dialogue in freedom between God and the human race, a point is conceivable at which God's self-communication to the world is indeed not yet concluded, but nevertheless the fact of this self-communication is already given unambiguously, and the success, the victory and the irreversibility of this process has become manifest in and in spite of this ongoing dialogue of freedom. It is precisely this beginning of the irreversible and successful history of salvation which we are calling the absolute saviour, and hence in this sense this beginning is the fullness of time, and it is the end of the previous history of salvation and revelation which was, as it were, still open.

This moment in which the irreversibility of God's historical self-communication becomes manifest refers both to the communication itself and to its acceptance. Insofar as a historical movement lives by virtue of its end even in its beginnings, because the real essence of its dynamism is the desire for the goal, it is completely legitimate to understand the whole movement of God's self-communication to the human race as borne by this saviour even when it is taking place temporally prior to the event of its irrevocable coming to be in the saviour. Of course this presupposes a philosophy or a conception of a final cause which conceives of the creative potency and the power of the goal as that by which the movement towards the goal is borne.

But if we understand history as a *single* history, then even if this history is moving into the openness of the future, precisely for this reason and to this extent it is borne by this future. The goal is not only something which is not at hand and is made or produced or reached in history, but it is also *causa finalis*, the cause or the moving power of the movement towards the goal. The whole movement of this history of God's self-communication lives by virtue of its moving towards its goal or its climax in the event by which it becomes irreversible, and hence precisely by virtue of what we are calling the absolute saviour. Therefore this saviour, who constitutes the climax of God's self-communication to the world, must be at the same time *both* the absolute promise of God to spiritual creatures as a whole *and* the acceptance of this self-communication by the saviour, for otherwise of course history could not have reached its irreversible phase. Only then is there an absolutely irrevocable self-communication on both sides, and only then is it present in the world in a historical and communicable way.

REMARKS ON THE MEANING OF THE ASSERTION OF A HYPOSTATIC UNION

The absolute saviour, that is, the irreversibility of the history of freedom as the self-communication of God which succeeds, is, first of all, a historical moment in God's salvific activity in the world, and indeed in such a way that he is a part of the history of the cosmos itself. He cannot simply be God himself as acting in the world, but must be a part of the cosmos, a moment within its history, and indeed at its climax. And this is also said in the Christological dogma: Jesus is truly man, truly a part of the earth, truly a moment in this world's biological process of becoming, a moment in man's natural history, for he "was born of a woman" (Gal. 4:4). He is a man who just like us receives in his spiritual, human and finite subjectivity the self-communication of God in grace which we assert of all men, and therefore of the cosmos, as the climax of the development in which the world comes to itself absolutely and comes to the immediacy of God absolutely. According to the conviction of Christian faith, Jesus is that person who, in and through what we call his obedience, his prayer and his freely accepted destiny to die, also lived out the acceptance of the grace bestowed on him by God and of the immediacy to God which he possesses as man.

We must not understand the God-Man as though God or his Logos disguised himself, as it were, in order to perform some salvific activity and in order to be able to become known among us here in the world. Jesus is truly man, he has absolutely everything which belongs to a man, including a finite subjectivity in which the world becomes conscious in its own unique, historically conditioned and finite way, and a subjectivity which has a radical immediacy to God in and through God's self-communication in grace, just as it is also present in us in the depths of our existence. This immediacy is based on God's self-communication in grace and glory just as ours is.

The fundamental assertion of Christology is precisely that God became *flesh*, became matter. This is not to be taken for granted, nor did it lie in the "signs of the times" and in the spirit of that age in which the dogma of the Incarnation arose, and in which the "became flesh" of John 1:14 was asserted of the divine Logos for the first time by John against the docetists. If a God, who as spiritual transcendence is understood as simply and absolutely above and beyond the material world, draws close to the world to bring salvation, he would really have to be understood as someone who in virtue of being spirit draws close to *spirit* in the world, encounters it, and then finally he also and secondarily brings about the salvation of the world in this "psychotherapeutic" way, if he does so at all. And this was precisely the understanding of the most dangerous heresy with which Christianity had to struggle in its beginnings, basically from the writings of John on: the understanding of gnosticism.

But Christianity teaches something different, and its teaching does lie in the signs of our times because, if we can put it this way, due to their Christian origins our times are correctly more materialistic than the pre-Christian Greek age in which something finite, something which exists in time and space could only appear as a barrier against God, and not as a mediation to the immediacy of God. According to the true teaching of Christianity, God lays hold of matter when the Logos becomes flesh, and does so precisely at that point of unity at which matter becomes conscious of itself and spirit possesses its own essential being in the objectifications of matter, that is, he does so in the unity of a spiritually human nature.

In Jesus matter is borne by the Logos exactly as the soul is, and this matter is a part of the reality and of the history of the cosmos, a part which can never be understood as detached from the unity of the world. The Logos of God himself establishes this corporeal part of the world as his own reality, both creating and accepting it at the same time. Hence he establishes it as what is different from himself in such a way that this very materiality expresses *him*, the Logos himself, and allows him to be present in his world. His laying hold of this part of the single material and spiritual reality of the world can rightly be understood as the climax of that dynamism in which the self-transcendence of the world as a whole is borne by the Word of God.

For there is no problem in understanding what is called creation as a partial moment in the process in which God becomes world, and in which God in fact freely expresses himself in his Logos which has become world and matter. We are entirely justified in understanding creation and Incarnation not as two disparate and juxtaposed acts of God "outwards" which have their origins in two separate initiatives of God. Rather in the world as it actually is we can understand creation and Incarnation as two moments and two phases of the *one* process of God's self-giving and self-expression, although it is an intrinsically differentiated process. Such an understanding can appeal to a very old "Christocentric" tradition in the history of Christian theology in which the creative Word of God which establishes the world establishes this world to begin with as the materiality which is to become his own, or to become the environment of his own materiality. Such an understanding in no way denies that God could also have created a world without an Incarnation, that is, that he could have denied to the self-transcendence of matter that ultimate culmination which takes place in grace and Incarnation. For although every such essential transcendence of self is the goal of the movement, it is always related to the lower stage as grace, as the unexpected and the unnecessary.

This, then, is what is supposed to be expressed by the Christian dogma of the Incarnation: Jesus is truly man with everything which this implies, with his finiteness, his materiality, his being in the world and his participation in the history of the cosmos in the dimension of spirit and of freedom, in the history which leads through the narrow passageway of death.

That is one side of the question. But now we have to look at the other side too. This same salvific event which the saviour brings must be present in the history of the world in such a way that God's self-communication to all spiritual creatures attains an irrevocable and irreversible character, and that because of a unique and individual history the presence of this self-communication to the whole of spiritual creation becomes manifest. But if we presuppose that this is, as it were, the "normal" fulfillment of the history of the cosmos and of the spirit, without saying thereby that this development *necessarily* has to go so far or has already gone so far, then we have to say that in the limit-idea of this saviour the same notion of a hypostatic union between God and man is implied which constitutes the real content of the Christian dogma of the Incarnation. And we also have to say that this now gives us a concept which makes intelligible to some extent and incorporates into our current world-view the same thing which in traditional Christology is expressed as hypostatic union, as Incarnation.

ON THE RELATIONSHIP BETWEEN
HUMAN TRANSCENDENCE AND HYPOSTATIC UNION

There is perhaps no particular difficulty in conceiving of the history of the world and of spirit as the history of a self-transcendence into the life of God. In its ultimate and highest phase this self-transcendence is identical with an absolute self-communication of God, which signifies the same process as seen from God's side. But such an ultimate and absolute self-transcendence of the spirit into God is to be understood as taking place in *all* spiritual subjects. This follows in an a posteriori way from the dogmatic data of the Christian self-understanding of man. One could think in the first instance, of course, that in itself an essential self-transcendence does not take place in all the "exemplars" which have the same point of departure, but only in a few definite ones, just as in biological evolution there survive alongside the new and higher forms representatives of the lower forms from which the higher forms are derived.

But prescinding altogether from more special theological reasons, this is inconceivable for man because by his very "nature" and by his very essence man is the possibility of transcendence which has become conscious of itself. The realization of this ultimate self-transcendence into immediacy with God cannot be denied to an individual who shares this essence unless he closes himself to it by his own fault. This presupposes only that this self-transcendence towards the immediacy of God takes place at least in one person or in a few persons, and, secondly, that all men form one human race in mutual intercommunication and therefore have a common goal. But in any case Christian revelation says that this self-transcendence is offered to everyone, and that it is a real potentiality of their individual existence which they can close themselves to only through their own fault. Insofar as Christianity knows about grace and glory as the immediate self-communication of God, it also professes that this fundamentally unsurpassable fulfillment is for all men, presupposing of course that they do not reject such a possibility through their own free and personal guilt.

Now how do we incorporate into this basic conception the doctrine about the hypostatic union of a particular, *individual* human nature with the Logos? Is something like this to be understood only as its *own* and still higher level of the self-transcendence of the world into God, as a still higher level of a simply and absolutely new and incommensurably higher kind in God's self-communication to a creature, so that it exists only in one unique "instance"? Or can this hypostatic union, which took place in one single person and which occurs only once in its essential uniqueness, nevertheless be understood precisely as the way in which the divinization of a spiritual creature is and must be accomplished if this self-transcendence of the world into God in spiritual subjectivity through God's self-communication is to take place at all? Is the hypostatic union an absolutely higher level on which the bestowal of grace on a spiritual creature is surpassed, or is it a singular and unique moment in the universal bestowal of grace, which bestowal cannot even be conceived of without the hypostatic union of an individual person?

If the Incarnation were to be regarded as an absolutely different and new level in the hierarchy of the world's reality which simply and only surpasses what existed previously or is to exist, without it being necessary for this "lower" level, then given this presupposition either the Incarnation would have to be able to be seen as a surpassing culmination of the ascending hierarchy of the realities of the world, so that it is incorporated positively to some extent in an evolutionary view of the world, or both notions would have to be abandoned. We would have to abandon the notion that the Incarnation of the Logos is the point of climax in the development of the world towards which the whole world is directed, although in grace and in freedom, and, secondly, we would have to abandon the notion that the Incarnation is compatible with an evolutionary view of the world. The Incarnation cannot be understood as the end and the goal of the world's reality without having recourse to the theory that the Incarnation itself is already an intrinsic moment and a condition for the universal bestowal of grace to spiritual creatures. Such an Incarnation would indeed still appear as the very highest of all the realities of the world because it is a hypostatic union between God and a reality of the world. But this does not yet make it intelligible as the world's end and its goal, as a climax which can be envisaged asymptotically from below. Something like this seems to be possible only by presupposing that the Incarnation itself, in its uniqueness and in the degree of reality which it implies, is to be made intelligible along with God himself as an intrinsic and necessary moment in the bestowal of grace on the whole world, and not just as something decreed by God as the means actually employed for this bestowal of grace.

The precise question, therefore, is whether there is an intrinsic unity between the event of the Incarnation on the one hand, and the self-transcendence of the whole spiritual world into God through God's self-communication on the other. If it can be shown that these two realities not only have an extrinsic, factual relationship to each other, but that by the very nature of both realities they are intrinsically and necessarily related, then in spite of the uniqueness of the Incarnation and in spite of the value and the significance of Jesus Christ for each one of us which this uniqueness implies, the Incarnation does not appear simply as a higher realization of God's self-communication which leaves the rest of the world behind. If we see a relationship of mutual conditioning between the two realities, then we cannot perceive the God-Man simply as someone who enters into our existence and its history from outside, moves it a step further and also brings it to fulfillment in a certain sense, but then nevertheless leaves it behind.

This question is hardly touched upon in traditional theology, although it is of considerable importance for a contemporary understanding of the Incarnation of God. To answer it to whatever extent an answer is possible, the first thing to be pointed out is this: the intrinsic effect of the hypostatic union for the assumed humanity of the Logos consists precisely and in a real sense *only* in the very thing which is ascribed to all men as their goal and their fulfillment, namely, the immediate vision of God which the created, human soul of Christ enjoys. Theology emphasizes that the Incarnation took place "for the sake of our salvation," that it does not really add any increase in reality and life to the divinity of the Logos, and that the prerogatives which accrue *intrinsically* to the human reality of Jesus through the hypostatic union are of the same essential nature as those which are also intended for other spiritual subjects through grace. Theology has also tried to clarify the problem by posing the hypothetical question: if one had to choose, which would be preferable, the hypostatic union without the immediate vision of God, or this vision of God, and it chose to affirm the second alternative.

This also shows how difficult it is to define more exactly the relationship between that fulfillment which Christian faith acknowledges for all men, and that unique fulfillment of human potentiality which we profess as the hypostatic union. And yet a more exact definition of this relationship is required, that is, we have to clarify whether we can understand what we call the Incarnation of the Logos as a concrete moment within the process by which the divinization of all spiritual creatures is realized. If we can, then we have already envisaged this hypostatic union implicitly when we see the history of the cosmos and of the spirit reaching that point at which there occurs the absolute self-transcendence of the spirit into God and the absolute self-communication of God in grace and glory to all spiritual subjects.

The point of the thesis that we are trying to establish is this: although the hypostatic union is a unique event in its own essence, and viewed in itself it is the highest conceivable event, it is nevertheless an intrinsic moment within the whole process by which grace is bestowed upon all spiritual creatures. If this total event of the bestowal of grace on all mankind finds its fulfillment, it must have a concrete tangibility in history. It cannot be sudden and acosmic and purely meta-historical, but rather this fulfillment must take place in such a way that this event emanates in time and space from one point. It must be an irrevocable reality in which God's self-communication is shown to be not a mere conditional and revocable offer, but unconditional and accepted by man, and hence it achieves self-presence in history. But when God brings about man's self-transcendence into God through his absolute self-communication to all men in such a way that both elements constitute a promise to all men which is irrevocable and which has already reached fulfillment in one man, then we have precisely what is signified by hypostatic union.

In this notion of hypostatic union we cannot remain satisfied with the conceptual model of just any kind of unity or any kind of connection between this human, historical and also subjective reality and the divine Logos. Nor have we grasped the real nature of this union adequately by saying that because of this union the human reality can really and truly be asserted of the divine subject of the Logos. For however true this is, the question is precisely why this is possible, and how we are to understand the union which justifies asserting the human reality of the divine in a *communicatio idiomatum*. The assumption of the human and the "union" has the character of a self-communication of God. In this self-communication a human reality is assumed so that the reality of God is communicated to what is assumed, to the humanity, and in the first instance that of Christ. But this very communication which is the purpose of the assumption is a communication in and through what we call grace and glory, and this is what is intended for everyone.

Grace in all of us and hypostatic union in the one Jesus Christ can only be understood together, and as a unity they signify the one free decision of God for a supernatural order of salvation, for his self-communication. In Christ the self-communication of God takes place basically to all men. This is meant not in the sense that they would also have the hypostatic union as such, but rather that the hypostatic union takes place insofar as God wishes to communicate himself to all men in grace and glory. God's unsurpassable self-communication to all men has reached its fullness and is historically tangible in an irrevocable way. Every self-expression of God which is not simply the beatific vision takes place through a finite reality, through a word or through an event which belongs to the finite, created realm. But as long as this finite mediation of the divine self-expression does not represent a reality of God himself in the strict and real sense, it is still basically provisional and surpassable because it is finite. And in this finiteness it is not simply the reality of God himself, and so it can be surpassed by God by establishing something else finite.

If, therefore, the reality of Jesus, in whom as offer and as acceptance God's absolute self-communication to the whole human race "is present" for us, is really to be the unsurpassable and definitive offer and acceptance, then we have to say: it is not only established by God, but it is God himself. But if this offer is itself a human reality as graced in an absolute way, and if this is really and absolutely to be the offer of God himself, then here a human reality belongs absolutely to God, and this is precisely what we call hypostatic union when it is understood correctly. This union is distinguished from our grace not by what has been offered in it, which in both instances, including that of Jesus, is grace. It is distinguished rather by the fact that Jesus is the offer for us, and we ourselves are not once again the offer, but the recipients of God's offer to us.

But the union of the offer with, and its inseparability from, the one who is offering himself to us must be understood in accordance with the specific nature of the offer. If the real offer to us is the human reality itself as graced, in which and from which God offers himself to us in his grace, then the union between the one offering and the offer cannot be understood only as a "moral" unity, as for example between a human word or a mere sign on the one hand and God on the other. It must rather be understood only as an irrevocable kind of union between this human reality and God, as a union which eliminates the possibility of separation between the proclamation and the proclaimer, and hence a union which makes the really human proclamation and the offer to us a reality of God himself. And it is just this that the hypostatic union means, this and really nothing else: in this human potentiality of Jesus the absolute salvific will of God, the absolute event of God's self-communication to us along with its acceptance as something effected by God himself, is a reality of God himself, unmixed, but also inseparable and therefore irrevocable. But to assert this is to assert precisely the offer of the grace of God's self-communication to us.

2. On the Phenomenology of Our Relationship to Jesus Christ

We shall return to the question of our existentiell relationship to Jesus Christ in the ninth section of this sixth chapter, where we want to consider it as Christians in the full sense of the word. But it seems to be advisable at this point in our Christological reflections to say something about the phenomenology of our relationship to Jesus Christ. A transcendental Christology, which we gave some indication of in the last section and which is to be treated somewhat more extensively in the next section, does not begin with the presupposition that we know absolutely nothing in our historical experience about Jesus as the Christ as the absolute saviour. The transcendental Christology which seems to be an option for us today, and which asks about the a priori possibilities which are found in man for an understanding of the dogma about Christ, arises in fact only subsequent to and because of a historical encounter with Jesus as the Christ.

Prior to such a transcendental Christology, therefore, it makes sense to ask and to state quite simply what our actual relationship to Jesus Christ is as it has always been understood by Christianity in its history. After all that was said in the fifth chapter about the relationship between transcendentality and history, perhaps nothing more need be said here about the relationship of mutual conditioning between this section and the following section, which is to deal with the question of a transcendental Christology.

THE STARTING POINT IN AN ACTUAL FAITH RELATIONSHIP

To begin with the relationship which a believing Christian actually has to Jesus Christ is a human starting point for Christology, and therefore it is also a legitimate starting point from the viewpoint of fundamental theology. However necessary a transcendental Christology about the idea of an absolute saviour might be, and however much a Christian is obliged to give an account both to himself and to others of the historical reasons and of the legitimacy of his conviction that he has found the absolute saviour precisely in Jesus Christ, nevertheless he need not and may not act as though he would produce or must produce such a relationship for the first time by means of these reflections. Even if he has to give an account of the reasons for his belief in Jesus Christ to someone who does not believe in Jesus Christ, he can nevertheless reflect first of all upon the faith which he actually has and upon the nature of it. He can and may begin this way because faith precedes theology, and he certainly does not have to think that theological reflection must first construct his faith from out of nothing as it were, or must recapture completely a faith which ultimately after all is based on grace and free decision. Theological reflection does not exist in order to make grace and free decision superfluous. A Christian does not have to think this because nowhere in human existence does theoretical reflection completely recapture an original and living act. This reflection strictly as such may not simply presuppose its result, for otherwise of course it would be a bad and ideological apologetics. But neither does it have to act as though there were no conviction prior to it which has its own certainty in practice and in life. Such a theoretical, and therefore always subsequent, reflection is more honest if it says what it is aiming for right at the beginning.

This relationship to Jesus Christ which we are reflecting upon as something which actually exists is meant in the sense in which it is in fact understood and lived in the Christian churches. A *certain* amount of leeway in delineating the nature of this relationship is of no consequence for our reflection upon it, presupposing only that it is distinguished from a merely historical or a merely "human" relationship to Jesus as can be had by anyone who has heard tell of Jesus of Nazareth.

In describing this Christian relationship, in the first instance at least we do not have to distinguish between what Jesus is in the faith of a Christian "in himself," and what he "means for us." For in their unity these two aspects cannot be completely separated from each other. For, on the one hand, we neither could nor would be concerned about Jesus if he had no "meaning for us," and on the other hand every assertion about his meaning for us implies an assertion about something "in itself." For otherwise, of course, contrary to the fundamental conviction of Christianity, we ourselves would be ascribing this meaning to him by our own power.

THE RELATIONSHIP TO JESUS CHRIST AS ABSOLUTE SAVIOUR

When it is asked how really Christian faith is lived in all of the Christian churches, we can say in a phenomenological description of this common Christian relationship to Jesus Christ: this relationship to Jesus Christ is present in and through the "faith" that in the encounter with him in the unity and totality of his word, his life and his victorious death the all-encompassing and all-pervasive mystery of reality as a whole and of each individual life, the mystery which we call God, "is present" for our salvation, offering forgiveness and divine life, and is offered to us in such a way that God's offer in him is final and irrevocable. Therefore this relationship can also be characterized as a relationship to the absolute and eschatological saviour, which notion will be discussed more in detail later. We can leave open at this point the more exact understanding of what salvation means, namely, the fact that it implies the absolute self-communication of God in himself as the innermost power of our existence and as our goal. We can also leave open the question of the collective and the individual aspects of this salvation, and the question *how* more exactly salvation "is present" in Jesus historically. This question has to take into account the salvific nature of all history and of the activity for which *all* men are responsible in a common history of salvation which is still going on.

We are calling this relationship absolute because we are dealing with the definitive salvation of the whole person and of the human race, and not with a particular situation of man. This absolute relationship to Jesus Christ in history might be interpreted adequately or inadequately in the theological reflection of individual churches or of individual Christians. Its presence in some individual might be hidden in the ultimate, existentiell decision of this individual Christian which cannot be brought to reflection. But wherever it is, there is Christianity. Wherever it is interpreted adequately and legitimately in a profession of faith and hence unites people in this profession, there is ecclesial Christianity. Wherever this relationship is not actualized in history and interpreted as absolute, real explicit Christianity ceases to exist.

This description of the relationship to Jesus Christ, which we are maintaining is common to all Christians, does not deny that there are already many legitimate Christologies in the New Testament and in the history of Christian faith after the New Testament. For the inexhaustible mystery which is hidden in this relationship has been described and can also be described in the future within different horizons of understanding, from different points of departure and with different conceptual tools. When we say that the relationship to Jesus Christ which is common to all Christians can be characterized by the notion of the absolute saviour, this does not deny that this relationship is being described by *one* Christology alongside other actual or possible Christologies and their theoretical reflection. But we are maintaining that with good will all such actual or possible Christologies can recognize themselves in this description.

THE RELATIONSHIP TO JESUS CHRIST IS SELF-VALIDATING

In this relationship to Jesus Christ a person grasps the absolute saviour in Jesus and makes him the mediation of his immediacy to God in his own self, and when it is actualized and understood adequately it contains *in itself* its own validation before the tribunal of man's existence, his conscience and his intellectual honesty. Consequently, as a concrete absolute, which it has to be in order really to be itself, it cannot by definition be produced and constructed "from outside." This does not exclude, but rather includes, first, that it can and must be explained in the mutually conditioning elements of its reality, its understanding and its validation; and, secondly, that there is a possibility of preaching this relationship to non-Christians in apologetics by showing that, in his existence as spirit and as person in grace and in history, man always exists within the hoped-for and actually present circle of this relationship, whether this is known explicitly or not, whether it is accepted or rejected in freedom, and whether the apologist and preacher of this relationship succeeds or not in making clear to another that this relationship does exist.

3. Transcendental Christology

We have already dealt with the subject matter of transcendental Christology in the first section of this sixth chapter. There, however, the predominant horizon of understanding was the contemporary mentality which sees the world from an evolutionary point of view. Therefore it seems advisable to take this topic up again and to develop it somewhat more extensively. We have already discussed the relationship of this section to the topic of the previous section. What is meant by "transcendental Christology" must follow only gradually as we proceed.

SOME OBJECTIONS TO TRANSCENDENTAL CHRISTOLOGY

The following objections do not invalidate the necessary role of a transcendental Christology.

First, it is not invalidated by the fact that by itself it cannot establish a concrete relationship precisely to *Jesus* as the Christ as it was described in the second section of this chapter. For the decisions of practical reason and a relationship to a concrete person in his historical concreteness can never be deduced completely in a transcendental way. But to see this very fact, however, is an operation which belongs to transcendental reason, which shows a person the legitimacy of an historical decision which has its legitimacy in itself and not in the transcendental reflections of theoretical reason.

Secondly, neither is it invalidated by the fact that, although a transcendental Christology per se is a priori to a concrete, historical relationship to Jesus Christ and to the Christology which reflects upon *this relationship* in the way that Christology is traditionally done, nevertheless it is temporally and historically *subsequent* to the usual Christology. Moreover, it cannot appear clearly and explicitly until, on the one hand, man has found this historical and self-validating relationship to Jesus Christ, and, on the other hand, until he has reached the historical era of transcendental anthropology and of transcendental reflection upon his historical nature, and may no longer forget it.

Thirdly, is it not invalidated by the objection that the historical appearance of an absolute saviour, the incarnation of the divine Logos in our history, is an absolute miracle which encounters us and cannot be deduced, and therefore it may not be reached surreptitiously by speculation. However correct the content of this objection is, there does not follow from it any rejection of transcendental Christology, for even the miraculous and the unexpected in history must be able to affect us. Therefore we must be able to ask about the conditions of possibility in us which enable it to affect us, especially since we do not have to presuppose that these conditions must be found only and exclusively in what is called in traditional theological terminology "pure nature." They are rather included in the "supernatural" elevation of "human nature," and because this elevation takes place everywhere and is not absolutely beyond consciousness it can be appealed to by transcendental Christology.

THE IMPORTANCE OF TRANSCENDENTAL CHRISTOLOGY IN OUR AGE

At an age in the history of the human spirit when there is a transcendental anthropology over and beyond a purely empirical, a posteriori and descriptive anthropology, and when it can no longer be overlooked, an explicit transcendental Christology is also necessary, a Christology which asks about the a priori possibilities in man which make the coming of the message of Christ possible. Its absence in the traditional theology runs the risk that the assertions of traditional theology will be deemed simply a mythological (in a pejorative sense) overlay on historical events, or that we shall have no criterion by means of which we are able to distinguish in the traditional

Christology between a genuine reality of faith and an interpretation of it which is no longer capable of mediating the content of faith to us today.

THE PRESUPPOSITIONS OF TRANSCENDENTAL CHRISTOLOGY

A "transcendental Christology" presupposes an understanding of the relationship of *mutual* conditioning and mediation in human existence between what is transcendentally necessary and what is concretely and contingently historical. It is a relationship of such a kind that both elements in man's historical existence can only appear together and mutually condition each other: the transcendental element is always an intrinsic condition of the historical element in the historical itself, and, in spite of its being freely posited, the historical element co-determines existence in an absolute sense. In spite of their unity and their relationship of mutual conditioning, neither of the two elements can be reduced to the other. Their relationship to each other has itself an open history, and the historical element signifies at the same time both what has come down historically and what lies ahead in the future.

As has already been indicated, a transcendental Christology does not necessarily have to go into the question whether the orientation of man which it appeals to and interprets, an inescapable orientation in hope towards an absolute saviour in history, is grounded only in his nature as elevated by the "grace" of God's self-communication, or is already grounded in his spiritual subjectivity by itself as a limit-idea. The latter could be true insofar as this spiritual subjectivity grounds a dialogical relationship to God and hence possibly allows the hope for God's final and definitive offer of himself to arise. We can leave this question open here. Transcendental Christology appeals to a person who (as we know at least from the universal revelation in grace which has become reflexive in Christianity) already has at least unthematically a finality and a dynamism imparted by God himself towards God's self-communication, and it asks him whether he could not appropriate this orientation as his own in freedom and from out of his own inner experience, an experience which unthematically at least belongs to his transcendental constitution.

THE DEVELOPMENT OF A TRANSCENDENTAL CHRISTOLOGY

Given this presupposition we can say: a transcendental Christology takes its starting point in the experiences which man always and inescapably has, even when it takes the form of a protest against them, experiences which cannot satisfy the claim to absoluteness or to absolute fulfillment and salvation in the immediate "objects" which are in the foreground of the experience and through which these experiences are mediated, a claim nevertheless which man inevitably makes in view of these experiences.

From this starting point there also follows the relationship of *mutual* conditioning between Christian theo-logy and Christo-logy. For the fact that the claim of this inescapable experience is not satisfied is also the point at which we experience what is meant by the word "God," that is, we experience it in the hiatus between the unlimited transcendentality of knowledge and freedom on the one hand, and on the other the "object" which is given historically and mediates this transcendentality to itself. From this starting point of transcendental Christology there also follows *one* factor in solving the problem of verification in Christology, although a historical relationship to Jesus as the absolute saviour cannot be validated by this alone.

The procedure of transcendental Christology consists more precisely in the following. First, in an anthropology which we are rather presupposing here and whose approach we are just giving some indication of, although in principle it could be worked out, man is understood as the existent of transcendental necessity who in every categorical act of knowledge and of freedom always transcends himself and the categorical object towards the incomprehensible mystery by which the act and the object are opened and borne, the mystery which we call God. This is true in all of the dimensions of his existence: his knowledge, his subjectivity, his freedom, his interpersonal relations, his relationship to the future, and so on. It is also true of the hiatus characteristic of each of these dimensions individually and of all of them taken together, the hiatus between the unity which is sought after ("reconciliation") and the plurality which is ever present.

Secondly, man is understood as someone who dares to hope (and shows that hope is possible *in* the very act of this courageous hope) that his existence is borne by this all-pervasive mystery not merely as the asymptotic goal and the dynamism of an infinite movement which always remains within the realm of the finite. He hopes rather that this mystery gives *itself* as the fulfillment of the highest claim of existence for the possession of absolute meaning and of the very unity which reconciles everything. Consequently, the finite, the conditional and the plurality which we are inescapably does indeed remain, but nevertheless it participates in the infinite itself, in the unity of the fullness of meaning, in a Thou who is absolutely trustworthy.

Man finds the courage to dare this most radical hope within himself. He accepts it in freedom, he reflects upon it, and he recognizes perhaps that in order for *this* movement to be possible, it must already be borne by the self-communication of its goal as the dynamism towards it, a self-communication of God which is at the same time the real essence of grace and of the process of transcendental and universal revelation. It belongs to one's own experience of transcendence as an act of freedom, to the ever *threatened* character of hope, to one's own "sinfulness," to the personal nature of God and to the fact that essentially he has the character of mystery that this self-communication of God is experienced as an event of God's freedom, a God who can refuse himself, whose offer is in itself ambivalent, for it can be salvation or justice, and it is still in history, its own history and our history.

Thirdly, it belongs to the unity of transcendentality and historicity in human existence that this self-communication of God and the hope for it are necessarily mediated historically. They "appear" in history, and they come fully to man in his categorical consciousness and hence to themselves only in the actualization of human existence in time and space. It is not possible to do so here, but in a theology of revelation we would have to consider more exactly *how* something finite and conditional and provisional can announce the coming of the infinite, the absolute and the definitive, and can awaken hope *precisely for this* without making God himself categorical, and without making him the mere cipher for an "infinite" and open movement towards something always finite. In other words, we would have to consider how God can not only reveal "something" which can be expressed categorically, but can reveal *himself* in a revelation which takes place in categorical words, and do this without making himself finite, without making himself an "idol."

But in any case God as he is in himself can be present revealing himself within the realm of the categorical (and without this neither is there any transcendental presence of God for us) only, first of all, in the mode of *promise*, promise as the ongoing transcendence of the categorical which affirms the starting point of hope and its categorical goal merely as a stage of hope in the absolute sense, affirms it as the mediation of revelation, and hence also negates it as not identical with the real goal of hope; and, secondly, in the mode of *death* as the most radical event of that negation which belongs to the very nature of every historically mediated revelation, and which becomes absolute in death because nothing categorical can any longer be hoped for. Consequently, at that point there remain only two possibilities: hope for "everything," or mere despair.

Fourthly, this most courageous act of hope searches in history for that self-promise of God which loses its ambivalence for the human race as such, becomes final and irreversible, and is the end in an "eschatological" sense. *This* self-promise of God can be understood *either* as fulfillment in an absolute sense, that is, as the establishment of the "kingdom of God"; *or,* if history continues, as a historical event within history which is of such a nature that it makes the promise itself irrevocable without bringing the history of the entire world as a whole to the culmination of complete fulfillment.

Fifthly, the categoriality of God's irreversible offer of himself to the world as a whole, which allows this irrevocable offer to be present historically and which mediates to us the hope which corresponds to *this* offer, can only be a man who on the one hand surrenders every inner-worldly future in death, and who on the other hand in this acceptance of death is shown to have been accepted by God finally and definitively. For an offer of God to a *free* and "exemplary" subject can be shown in a categorical way to be *irreversibly* victorious and eschatologically final only by the fact that it is actually accepted by this free subject. We are presupposing here the anti-individualistic conviction that, given the unity of the world and of history from the viewpoint of both God and the world, such an "individual" destiny has "exemplary" significance for the world as a whole. Such a man with this destiny is what is meant by an "absolute saviour."

It is to be shown later that, if the being and the destiny of this saviour are understood correctly, he can also be expressed correctly by the formulations of the classical Christology of Chalcedon and, from an ecclesial point of view, must be so expressed. It is likewise to be shown later *how* the acceptance of the saviour's radical surrender in death by God can become manifest historically as "resurrection." Moreover, we must also reflect later upon the fact that the "absolute" saviour, as understood in this way in his quasi-sacramental causality as sign, actually has by this very fact the soteriological efficacy which church doctrine asserts of the destiny of Jesus, presupposing that this redemption is not misunderstood in a mythological way as causing some change of mind on God's part.

A transcendental Christology as such cannot presume for itself the task and the possibility of saying that the absolute saviour, whom radical hope in God himself as the absolute future searches for in history, is to be found there, and that he has been found precisely in *Jesus* of Nazareth. Both of these statements belong to the experience of history itself which cannot be deduced. *Today,* however, a person would be blind with regard to this actual history if he did not approach it with that reflexive and articulated hope for salvation which is reflected upon in a transcendental Christology. Transcendental Christology allows one to search for, and in his search to understand, what he has already found in Jesus of Nazareth.

4. What Does It Mean to Say: "God Became Man"?

By its very nature a transcendental Christology will work towards the notion of an "absolute saviour." If it reaches this notion, and if it is shown later that such an absolute saviour can be found precisely in Jesus of Nazareth and only in him, and if he has been found by Christianity, this still does not answer unambiguously the question whether, given what the notion of absolute saviour means, he can be identified with the incarnate, eternal Logos and Son of the Father which Christianity already in the New Testament professed this Jesus to be, or whether the statement about the incarnate Logos of the eternal God is an additional statement going beyond the assertion that Jesus is the absolute saviour. We shall have to consider this for the time being as an open question.

But if we have already begun to do a transcendental, and hence "essential" Christology, then consequently in carrying such an essential Christology further, and prior to the question about an encounter with the historical, concrete Jesus, it makes sense to ask what is really meant when Christianity speaks of an *incarnation of God.* We can pose this question here in the sixth chapter because we are not beginning with the presupposition that we would only know anything about Jesus by means of an historical investigation which we are here and now undertaking for the first time out of historical curiosity, as it were. Rather, as was said in the first section, we are presupposing the faith of Christianity as a given, although it is to be made legitimate later by the work of fundamental theology in a genuinely historical reflection. Nor does this mean that we are arguing in a vicious circle. Hence it seems legitimate to ask at this point what is really meant then by an incarnation of God, without intending to define and limit the question from the outset to an understanding of such an incarnation in the sense of an absolute saviour.

THE QUESTION OF THE "INCARNATION OF GOD"

Let us ask now what the doctrine of Incarnation or God becoming man means. We are still moving within the framework of an essential

Christology, that is, we are not yet asking the question whether there has already existed in history a saviour as we are understanding the term, nor who he is concretely. We are trying to reflect upon the mystery which is called in theological language the mystery of "God becoming man." Here lies the center of the reality from out of which we Christians live, and which we believe. It is only here that the mystery of the divine Trinity is accessible to us, and only here that the mystery of our participation in the divine nature is promised to us in a definitive and historically tangible way. The mystery of the church is only the extension of the mystery of Christ. But in all of the mysteries just mentioned together lies the content of our faith. This mystery is inexhaustible, and compared with it most of the other things we talk about are relatively insignificant. The truth of the faith can be preserved only by doing a theology of Jesus Christ, and by redoing it over and over again. For it is true here too that only he possesses the past who has recaptured it as his own present.

In posing this question we are not trying to prove that the meaning of the Incarnation to be developed here coincides with official church declarations. We are only concerned with the meaning itself. Since the aim of these reflections is to discover what it means to say that God becomes "incarnate," we are dealing from the outset with an essential and "descending" Christology, although such a Christology cannot be developed without repeatedly bringing in considerations from transcendental anthropology. Hence some overlapping with the previous sections is unavoidable and we shall have to make allowance for that.

We are asking: What does it really mean to say that God became man as we profess in our faith? We are asking a quite rudimentary question because it has to be answered in a sufficiently adequate way if we want to maintain that we believe in Jesus Christ. In asking this question, of course, it is also legitimate at the same time to give more emphasis to this or that partial element of the whole answer, to be selective and to stress certain things, for we could never answer the question completely. In our reflections we shall in the first instance presuppose the Church's official answer rather than repeat it explicitly. If we ourselves try to say something about the meaning of these ancient formulas, this does not mean that the ancient formulas which gave an answer to this question should be set aside as obsolete. The church and its faith are indeed always the same throughout their history, for otherwise there would only be disparate events in an atomized history of religion, but not the history of a single church and of a single faith which is ever the same. But since this single and identical church has had a history and still has a history, the ancient formulas of the church are not merely the end of a very long history of faith and dogma. They are also a point of departure, so that in the spiritual movement of setting out from and going back to these formulas lies the only guarantee, or, to put it more cautiously, the only hope, that we have *understood* the ancient formulas. If true understanding is always the process whereby the person understanding becomes open to the incomprehensible mystery, and if this mystery is not a remainder in our knowledge which is still and only provisionally unknown, but is rather the condition which makes it possible to grasp any of the individual elements in our knowledge, and is the all-encompassing incomprehensibility of the original whole, then it is not surprising if a rethinking of this kind has to take place, all the more so when we are trying to understand the comprehensible destiny of the Word of God, who is himself incomprehensible.

THE "WORD" OF GOD

Beginning as early as the prologue of John's Gospel, Christian faith says that the Word of God became flesh, became man (John 1:14). In our reflections we may initially forego saying anything about the subject of the sentence, about this "Word" of God. Such an omission is not without its dangers, for it could be that we would miss the meaning of the Incarnation of the Word of God if our ideas about the Word of God who becomes man are very vague. Since the time of Augustine the theology of the schools has become accustomed to thinking that it is to be taken for granted that any one of the non-numerical three whom we call the persons of the one God-head could become man, presupposing only that this divine person wanted to. On this supposition the "Word" of God in our sentence does not mean much more for understanding the sentence than any divine subject, a divine hypostasis. Then in a classical formulation this sentence would really only say: one of the Trinity became man. On this supposition we would not really need to know anything very clearly about what is proper precisely and exclusively to the *Word* of God in order to understand the sentence which we are dealing with.

But if one follows an older, pre-Augustinian tradition which is found especially in the Greek Fathers and has doubts about this supposition, then we shall not be able simply to forego any attempt to understand the predicate of the sentence from a more exact understanding of its subject.

For if it is contained in the meaning and essence precisely of the Word of God that only *he* and he alone is the one who begins and can begin a human history in case God makes the world his own in such a way that this world is not only his work, a work distinct from himself, but it also becomes his own reality, then it could be that we understand what Incarnation is only when we know what precisely the "Word" of God is, and that we understand adequately what the Word of God is only when we know what Incarnation is.

But it also follows from this that in order to understand the subject of the sentence which we are reflecting upon we must turn precisely to the *predicate* of the sentence. Hence we must first reflect upon the statement: God became *man*. For it is precisely in this statement that we understand for the first time what the Word of God really means. Not because every divine person could become man, but because it is from the statement: God has offered himself to us in immediacy precisely in history and as man, that we grasp that God, the incomprehensible abyss whom we call Father, really has a Logos, that is, really has the possibility of offering his very own self to us in history, and that this God is historically faithful, and in this sense the true One, the Logos.

BECAME "MAN"

The Word of God became *man*. What does it mean to say: "Became man"? We are not yet asking what it means to say that this Word *became* something. We are considering first of all simply *what* it became, namely, man.

Now we could think that in this fundamental dogma of Christianity the noun in the predicate, "man," is easily the most intelligible part of the assertion. For man is what we ourselves are, what we experience in daily life, what has been experimented with and lived out a million times in the history to which we belong, what we are familiar with from the inside, each one in himself, and from the outside, in the world of persons around us. We could go further and say that we know it so well that we can distinguish the contents of its basic structure from accidental modifications, and also from an ultimate, personal self, and then we can call the content of this basic structure or the content of what man is "nature." Then our statement means: The Word of God has assumed an individual human "nature" and in this way become man.

Of course we do know all sorts of things about man. Every day the most varied anthropological sciences make assertions about man. All the arts speak about man. Each one speaks in its own way about this inexhaustible topic. But is man really *defined* by all of this? There are many sciences which are of the opinion that man could be defined, although perhaps only asymptotically and from ever-new approaches which are still incomplete and unfinished. Every pragmatism, every denial of metaphysics must at least in principle understand man in this definable way.

To this we have to say: to define, that is, to give a delimiting formula which enumerates completely the sum of the elements of a particular essence, is obviously possible only when we are dealing with an object or a thing which is really composed of ultimate and primary elements, and indeed of elements which are themselves ultimate and understood in themselves, and hence once again are limited and defined, and this time in themselves. We shall pass over the question whether in this sense there can be any definitions at all in the strict sense. In any case such a definition of man is impossible. He is, as we could readily "define" him, that indefinability which is conscious of itself.

Of course there is much about man which is definable at least to some extent, and all of this occupies, and rightly so, the so-called exact natural sciences which are concerned with anthropology. Man could also be called *zoon logikon, animal rationale,* a rational animal. But before we rejoice at the simple clarity of such a "definition," we would have to ask ourselves what *logikon* really means. But when we do this we wind up in something which is literally boundless. For we can say what man is only if we say what he has to do with and what concerns him. But in the case of man who is a transcendental subject this is something which is boundless, something which is nameless, and ultimately it is the absolute mystery whom we call God. In his *essence,* in his nature, therefore, man himself is the mystery, not because he is in himself the infinite fullness of the mystery which concerns him, which fullness is inexhaustible, but because in his real essence, in his original ground, in his nature he is the poor, but nevertheless conscious orientation to this fullness.

When we have said everything which can be expressed about ourselves which is definable and calculable, we have not yet said anything about ourselves unless in all that is said we have also included that we are beings who are orientated towards the God who is incomprehensible. But this orientation, and hence our nature, is grasped and understood only if we freely allow ourselves to be grasped by the incomprehensible One, and do this by ratifying the act which, while it is itself inexpressible, is the condition of possibility for all conceptualizing expression. Our existence is constituted by the acceptance or rejection of the mystery which we are, we who in our poverty are oriented towards the mystery of fullness. The necessity which we find of having to decide to accept or to reject it, which decision is the *act* of our existence, is the mystery which we are, and this is our nature because the transcendence which we are and which we do brings our existence and God's existence together, and both as mystery.

In this context we must repeat again and again and understand that a mystery is not something which is not yet disclosed and which exists as a second element alongside something which is grasped and comprehended. Understood in this way, mystery is confused with the unknown which has not yet been discovered. Mystery is rather something which exists and confronts us as the unfathomable; it is a given and does not have to be produced. It is not another element of knowledge which is merely temporarily unmastered, but is the horizon which cannot be mastered and which masters all of our understanding, and which allows the other to be understood by being present itself in its silence and in its incomprehensibility. Mystery, therefore, is not something provisional which is done away with or which could in itself be non-mysterious. It is rather the characteristic which always and necessarily characterizes God, and through him characterizes us. This is so very true that the immediate vision of God which is promised to us as our fulfillment is the immediacy of the incomprehensible. It is, then, the shattering of the illusion that our lack of total comprehension is only provisional. For in this vision we shall see in God himself, and no longer merely in the infinite poverty of our transcendence, that God is incomprehensible. But the vision of the mystery in itself, accepted in love, is the beatitude of the creature, and it alone makes the One who is known as mystery the inconsumable thorn bush of the eternal flame of love.

But where have these reflections on the noun "man" in the predicate brought us? We have come very much closer to our topic. For if this is what human nature is, the poor, questioning and in itself empty orientation towards the abiding mystery whom we call God, then we do understand more clearly what it means to say: God assumes a *human* nature as his own. If this indefinable nature, whose limit, that is, its "definition," is this unlimited orientation towards the infinite mystery of fullness, is assumed by God as *his own* reality, then it has reached the very point towards which it is always moving by virtue of its essence. It is its very *meaning*, and not just an accidental side activity which it could also do without, to be given away and to be handed over, to be that being who realizes himself and finds himself by losing himself once and for all in the incomprehensible.

The very thing which necessarily takes place in man in an initial way and which places him before the question whether he wants to have anything, indeed everything or nothing to do with it, this takes place in an unsurpassable way and in the strictest and most radical sense when this nature of man as so understood so gives itself to the mystery of fullness and so empties itself that it becomes the nature of God himself. This is how it happens when we say that the eternal Logos of God himself has assumed a human nature. Seen from this perspective, the Incarnation of God is the unique and *highest* instance of the actualization of the essence of human reality, which consists in this: that man is insofar as he abandons himself to the absolute mystery whom we call God. Anyone who understands correctly what an obediential potency for the hypostatic union means, and what it really means to say that human nature can be assumed by the person of the Word of God, and what such a capacity to be assumed consists in, and anyone who understands that it is only a spiritual and personal reality that can be assumed by God, he knows that this obediential potency cannot be an individual potency alongside other potencies in the structure of human being, but rather is objectively identical with man's essence.

When we try in this way to gain some understanding from man's essence of what Incarnation really means, it should be noted that such a Christology is not a "consciousness Christology" as opposed to an ontological Christology of the substantial union of the Logos with its human nature. It is based rather on the metaphysical insight of a genuine onto-logy that the true being of spirit as such is itself spirit. If we accept this presupposition, then we can readily formulate a genuinely onto-logical counterpart to the traditional Christology, a counterpart which is necessarily coordinate with the traditional ontic Christology. We can then remove from the traditional dogmatic statements the mythological impression that God has set things right on earth in the livery of a human nature which is joined to him only extrinsically, and did this because things could no longer be managed from heaven.

Any idea that this union of God and man has to take place in the case of every man because this union of God and man is the most radical culmination of man's essence is forgetting that historicity and personhood must not be reduced to the level of nature, to the level of what is given always and everywhere. The truth of a divine humanity would be mythologized if it were simply a datum of every person always and everywhere. Such an idea would also overlook the fact that the humanity of God, in which the God-Man as individual exists for every individual person, neither is nor can be graced in itself with a closeness to God and an encounter with God which is essentially different from *the* encounter and self-communication of God which in fact is intended for *every* person in grace, and which has its highest actualization in man in the beatific vision.

Now we must reflect further upon the fact that the Word of God *became* something: "The Word became flesh." Can God become something?

This question has always found an affirmative answer in pantheism or in a philosophy in which God himself is simply "historical." But Christians and really theistic philosophies find themselves in a difficult situation here. They profess that God is the immutable One who *is* in an absolute sense, that is, in the sense of pure act, and who in blissful security and in the self-sufficiency of infinite reality always possesses what he is from eternity to eternity in absolute and in a certain sense unmoved, "serene" fullness. He does not have to become it first or acquire it first. It is precisely when *we* for our part have received the burden of history and of becoming as a grace and a distinction, and regard the necessity of becoming and the possibility of becoming not simply as something merely negative, but as a positive distinction, it is precisely then that we must necessarily profess such a God with an infinite fullness of being. For it is only because he is the immeasurable fullness that the process of becoming in spirit and in nature can be more than the meaningless self-consciousness of an absolute void collapsing into its own emptiness. Neither, therefore, is the Christian profession of an unchangeable and unchanging God in his eternally complete fullness merely the postulate of a particular philosophy. It is also a dogma of faith, as was once again explicitly defined in the First Vatican Council (*D.S.* 3001), and the substance of this is already present in the scriptures of the Old and New Testaments. But still it is true: the Word *became* flesh.

It cannot be denied that at this point the traditional theology and philosophy of the schools gets into a dilemma. It treats first of God as one and three and extols his immutability, his infinite fullness of being possessed always from eternity to eternity, the "pure act" of God. But in this earlier treatise it does not advert to the fact that later in the treatise on "Christ, the Word of God" and "Christ, the man" it has to say: and the Word became flesh. When at this point in Christology it deals with this apparently so vexing problem that God "became" something, it declares that the becoming and the change are on the side of the created reality which is assumed, but not on the side of the eternal, immutable Logos. Without a change in itself, the Logos assumes something which as a *created* reality does become: the human nature of Jesus. Hence all becoming and all history and the laborious effort connected with them still remain on this side of the absolute abyss which separates the immutable, necessary God from the mutable, conditional and historical world in its process of becoming, and which admits of no admixture between them.

But after all this is said it still remains true that the *Logos became* man, that the history of the becoming of this human reality became *his own* history, that our time became the time of the eternal One, that our death became the death of the immortal God himself. However we divide the predicates which are apparently contradictory and of which one part does not seem to be able to be predicated of God, it still remains true that this distribution to two realities, the divine Word on the one hand, and the created human nature on the other, may not let us forget that the one, created reality with its process of becoming is the reality of the Logos of God himself. Hence after we have all the particulars of this division, the whole question begins all over again. It is the question as to how to understand the truth that the assertion of God's immutability may not make us lose sight of the fact that what took place in Jesus as becoming and as history here in our midst, in our space, in our time and world, in our process of becoming, in our evolution and in our history, that this is precisely the history of the Word of God himself, *his own* becoming.

If we face squarely and uncompromisingly the fact of the Incarnation which our faith in the fundamental dogma of Christianity testifies to, then we have to say plainly: God can become something. He who is not subject to change in himself can *himself* be subject to change *in something else.*

Now this gives us a formulation which is not intended to offer a positive insight into the compatibility of the dogma of God's immutability and the possibility of becoming in the eternal Logos, nor a positive solution to the duality of this fundamental Christian assertion. It is a formulation which clearly and seriously maintains both sides of it. If we say that something happened or that a change has taken place only where the created element, the humanity of the Logos is in its own self, and if we see this event only on this side of the boundary which separates God and creature, then we have indeed seen and expressed something which is true, for on our side there does take place in Jesus of Nazareth a process of becoming: beginning, time, death, fulfillment, created reality. But if we say only this, we have overlooked and left unsaid the very thing which ultimately is the precise point of the whole assertion: that this very event we are talking about, this process of becoming, this time, this beginning and this fulfillment is the event and the history of God himself. It is precisely this which has not yet been expressed when we merely say something about the unmixed human nature of the divine Logos. It is ultimately not so important whether one wants to call "change" the thing which is still to be said, namely, that this very event of temporal becoming is really the event of God himself, or whether one avoids this term. If we do call it a change, then we also have to say that the God who is not subject to change in himself can change in something else, can become man.

We may not regard this process by which one changes in something else as a contradiction to God's immutability, nor allow this changing *in* something else to be reduced to asserting a change *of* something else. Here ontology has to be adapted to the message of faith and not be schoolmaster to this message. If the mystery of the Incarnation is transposed into the dimension of the finite alone, the mystery in the strictest sense would really be eliminated. For then it is not particularly exciting that something has become or something is becoming, that something has time and space, a beginning and an end, if it is within our dimension and would be expressed only in and from this dimension. There can, of course, be no absolute mysteries at all in the finite alone as such because in a correct ontology there can always be conceived for something finite an intellect which corresponds to it and which is able to fathom it. The mystery of the Incarnation must be in God himself, and precisely in the fact that, although he is immutable in and of himself, he *himself* can become something in another.

The assertion of God's immutability is a dialectical assertion in the same sense as is the assertion of the unity of God in and in spite of the Trinity, that is, both of these assertions remain in fact really correct only if we immediately add the other two assertions, namely, about the Trinity and about the Incarnation respectively. Nor may we understand one of the assertions as subordinate to the other. Just as through the doctrine of the Trinity we learn that unity, which we think of in the first instance as lifeless sameness, is by no means an absolute ideal, but is also trinity in its highest instance precisely because God is absolute perfection, so too do we learn through the doctrine of the Incarnation that God's immutability, without thereby being eliminated, is by no means simply the only thing that characterizes God, but that in and in spite of his immutability he can truly become something: he himself, he in time. Moreover, this possibility is not to be understood as a sign that he is in need of something, but rather as the height of his perfection. This perfection would be less perfect if he could not become less than he is and always remains.

This brings us to an ontological ultimate which a merely rational ontology would perhaps never suspect. Such an ontology finds it difficult of course to take cognizance of this ultimate, and to insert it as a primal formula right into the primal beginnings and origins of its discourse. The absolute, or, more correctly, the absolute One in the pure freedom of his infinite unrelatedness, which he always preserves, possesses the possibility of himself becoming the other, the finite. He possesses the possibility of *establishing* the other as his own reality by dispossessing *himself*, by giving *himself* away. The primary phenomenon which we must begin with is not the notion of an assumption which presupposes what is to be assumed as already and obviously given, and only destines it for the one assuming. In this conception what is to be assumed never really quite gets assumed because it is repulsed by God's immutability understood in an isolated way by itself, understood statically and undialectically, and what is assumed may never touch him in his immutability.

The primary phenomenon given by faith is precisely the self-emptying of God, his becoming, the kenosis and genesis of God himself. He can become insofar as, in establishing the other which comes from him, he himself *becomes* what has come from him, without having to become in his own and original self. Insofar as in his abiding and infinite fullness he empties himself, the other comes to be as God's very own reality. The phrase is already found in Augustine that God "assumes by creating" and also "creates by assuming," that is, he creates by emptying himself, and therefore, of course, he himself is in the emptying. He creates the human reality *by the very fact that* he assumes it as his own. He, the Logos, constitutes the differentiation from himself by the fact that he retains it as his own, and conversely: because he truly wants to have the other as his own, he constitutes it in its genuine reality. God goes out of himself, he himself, he as the self-giving fullness. Because he can do this, because this is his free and primary possibility, for this reason he is defined in scripture as love.

Therefore his capacity to be creator, that is, the capacity merely to establish the other without giving himself, is only a derived, delimited and secondary possibility which ultimately is grounded in this real and primordial possibility of God, namely, to be able to give himself to what is not God, and thereby really to have his own history in the other, but as his own history. In their innermost essential ground creatures must be understood as the possibility of being able to be assumed, of being the material for a possible history of God. God establishes creatures by his creative power insofar as he establishes them from out of nothing in their own non-divine reality as the *grammar of God's possible self-expression.* Nor can he establish them in any other way even if in fact he were to remain silent, because even God's silence would always once again presuppose ears to hear the silence of God.

THE "WORD" BECAME MAN

From this perspective we could now reach a clearer understanding than we did earlier of why precisely the *Logos* of God became man, and why he alone can become man.

The immanent self-expression of God in its eternal fullness is the condition which makes possible God's self-expression outwards and outside himself, and the latter is the identical revelation of the former. However much the mere establishment of something other and different from God is the work of God the creator as such and without distinction of persons, still the possibility of creation can have its ontological condition and its ultimate ground in the fact that God who is without origin expresses or can express himself within himself and for himself, and thus establishes the original, divine distinction within God himself. If this God expresses his very own self into the *emptiness* of what is not God, then this expression is the outward expression of his immanent Word, and not something arbitrary which could also be proper to another divine person.

It is only from this perspective that we can better understand what it means to say: God's Logos *becomes* man. Of course there are men who are not the Logos himself, namely, we ourselves. Of course there could also be men if the Logos had not himself become man. For if we wanted to deny this, we would be denying the freedom of the Incarnation, the freedom of God's self-communication in grace to the world, and consequently the difference between nature and world on the one hand, and grace or God's self-communication on the other. There can indeed always be the lesser without the greater, although the lesser is always grounded in the possibility of the greater, and not vice versa. To this extent we can readily say: there could be men, that is, the lesser, even if the Logos had not himself become man. But we can and have to say nevertheless: the possibility that there be men is grounded in the greater, more comprehensive and more radical possibility of God to express himself in the Logos which becomes a creature.

If, therefore, the Logos becomes man, then this humanity of his is not something which exists antecedently, but rather is that which comes to be and is constituted in its essence and existence if and insofar as the Logos empties himself. This man is precisely as man the self-expression of God in his self-emptying, because God expresses precisely *himself* if he empties himself, if he discloses himself as love, if he conceals the majesty of his love and manifests himself in the ordinariness of man. If we were not to understand it this way, then ultimately the humanity of the Logos which he has assumed would be a disguise of God, really only a signal which discloses nothing at all of him who is there, except perhaps through human words. But the utterance and the validation of these words could just as well be understood if they were not the words of the incarnate Logos of God himself. But we cannot understand the Incarnation in such a way that the Logos becomes man and then says something about God only by the fact that he *speaks.* For the moment we understand it this way, the Incarnation of God would be superfluous. For God could also call forth and express in some other prophet the words which the man Jesus as the messenger of God says about God. The man Jesus must be the self-revelation of God through who he is and not only through his words, and this he really cannot be if precisely this humanity were not the expression of God.

MAN AS THE CIPHER OF GOD

This is not contradicted by the fact that there are also other men, namely, we ourselves, who are not this self-expression of God becoming other. For "what" he is as the self-expression of the Logos and "what" we are is the same. We call it "human nature." But the unbridgeable difference is constituted by the fact that this "what" in him is spoken as his self-expression, and this is not the case with us. And the fact that he in his reality says exactly what we are renders the content of our essence and of our history redeemed, and opens it into the freedom of God. It says what we are: the utterance in which God could empty himself, could express himself into that empty nothingness which necessarily surrounds him. For he is love and therefore he is necessarily the miracle of the possibility of a free gift, and therefore as love he is the incomprehensibly obvious.

From this perspective we could define man, driving him all the way back to his deepest and most obscure mystery, as that which comes to be when God's self-expression, his Word, is uttered into the emptiness of the Godless void in love. It is also for this reason that the incarnate Logos has been called the abbreviated Word of God. The abbreviation, the cipher of God himself is man, that is, the Son of Man and the men who exist ultimately because there was to be a Son of Man. Man is the radical question about God which, as created by God, can also have an answer, an answer which in its historical manifestation and radical tangibility is the God-Man, and which is answered in all of us by God himself. This takes place at the very center of the absolute questionableness of our being in and through what we call grace, God's self-communication and beatific vision. When God wants to be what is not God, man comes to be. This of course does not define man in terms of the flatness of the ordinary and the everyday, but introduces him into the ever incomprehensible mystery. But he is this mystery. For in this way he becomes precisely someone who participates in the infinite mystery of God, just as a question participates in its answer, and just as the question is borne only by the possibility of the answer itself. We know this by the fact that we recognize the incarnate Logos in our history and say: here the question which we are is answered historically and tangibly with God himself.

From this point we could reach the Christian dogma of the Incarnation of the eternal Logos. If God himself is man and remains so for all eternity; if therefore all theology is eternally anthropology; if it is forbidden to man to think little of himself because he would then be thinking little of God; and if this God remains the insoluble mystery: then man is for all eternity the expression of the mystery of God which participates for all eternity in the mystery of its ground. Even when everything provisional will have passed away, God will still have to be accepted as the unfathomable mystery of beatifying love, unless we might think that we could comprehend God's self-expression outwards, so that both it and we could finally become boring for ourselves. Or unless we think that we could get behind man in any other way except by seeing through him into the blessed darkness of God himself, and there grasp all the more that this finiteness of the incarnate Logos is the finiteness of the infinite Word of God himself. He is the union of the historical manifestation of the question which man is and the answer which God is. He is the union of a question which as a question about God is the manifestation of the answer. This is the union which is meant in Christology.

Because it is the union of the real essence of God and of man in God's personal self-expression in his eternal Logos, for this reason Christology is the beginning and the end of anthropology, and this anthropology in its most radical actualization is for all eternity theology. It is first of all the theology which God himself has spoken by uttering his Word as our flesh into the emptiness of what is not God and is even sinful, and, secondly, it is the theology which we ourselves do in faith when we do not think that we could find Christ by going around man, and hence find God by going around the human altogether. It could still be said of the creator with the Old Testament that he is in heaven and we are on earth. But we have to say of the God whom we profess in Christ that he is exactly where we are, and only there is he to be found. If nevertheless he remains infinite, this does not mean that he is *also* still this, but means that the finite itself has received infinite depths. The finite is no longer in opposition to the infinite, but is that which the infinite himself has become, that in which he expresses himself as the question which he himself answers. He does this in order to open for the whole of the finite of which he himself has become a part a passage into the infinite—no, I should say in order to make himself the portal and the passage. Since their existence God himself has become the reality of what is nothing by itself, and vice versa.

Because in the Incarnation the Logos creates the human reality by assuming it, and assumes it by emptying *himself,* for this reason there also applies here, and indeed in the most radical and specific and unique way, the axiom for understanding every relationship between God and creatures, namely, that closeness and distance, or being at God's disposal and being autonomous, do not vary for creatures in inverse, but rather in direct proportion. Christ is therefore man in the most radical way, and his humanity is the most autonomous and the most free not in spite of, but because it has been assumed, because it has been created as God's self-expression. The humanity of Christ is not the "form of God's appearance" in such a way that it would be an empty and shadowy appearance which would have no validity of its own in the presence of and vis-à-vis the one who appears. By the fact that *God* himself ex-ists, this finite existence of his receives in the most radical way its own validity, power and reality even vis-à-vis God himself.

This shows that every conception of the Incarnation in which the humanity of Jesus would only be the livery of God which he uses to signal that he is present and speaking is a heretical conception. And it is basically this heresy, which was rejected by the church itself in its struggle against docetism, apollinarism, monophysitism and monothelitism, which is perceived today as mythological and is rejected as mythology, and not a really orthodox Christology. We also have to admit that such a mythological understanding of the Christological dogma of our faith can also be present implicitly in very many Christians however orthodox their formulas are, and hence it inevitably provokes a protest against mythology. We would have to ask whether those who think that they have to demythologize Christianity have the same understanding of the doctrine of Christianity as the pious Christians whose piety is mythological. Their demythologizing is based on a crypto-heresy of Christians, and they think that this is the dogma of Christianity and is to be rejected, and if it were, they would be right. But basically they have not rejected the Christian dogma, but a mythological and primitive understanding of it.

But the converse is also true: some who reject the orthodox formulas of Christology because they misunderstand them may nevertheless on the existentiell level actually believe in the Incarnation of God's Word in genuine faith. For if a person really believes with regard to Jesus, his cross and his death that there the living God has spoken to him the final, decisive, comprehensive and irrevocable word, and if with regard to Jesus a person realizes that he is thereby redeemed from all the imprisonment and tyranny of the existentials of a closed and guilty existence which is doomed to death, he believes something which is true and real only if Jesus is the person whom Christian faith professes him to be. Whether he knows it reflexively or not, he believes in the Incarnation of God's Word.

ON THE IMPORTANCE AND THE LIMITS OF DOGMATIC FORMULAS

When we say that basically such a person believes in the Incarnation of God's Word, although he rejects the correct and orthodox Christian formulas because, due perhaps to no fault of his own, he cannot assimilate them, this does not lessen the importance of a formula which is objectively correct and is the ecclesial, sociological basis of the common thought and faith of Christians. But in the actual living out of his existence someone can believe Christologically although he does not adhere to the formulas of some particular objective conceptualization of Christology. The living out of existence does not admit of every position which is logically conceivable, even on the existentiell level. We can say then: anyone who accepts Jesus as the ultimate truth of his life and professes that God has spoken the ultimate word to him in Jesus and in his death, not all the penultimate words which we still have to find ourselves in our own history, but the ultimate word for which he lives and dies, he thereby accepts Jesus as the Son of God as the church professes him to be. This is true whatever the theoretically inadequate or even false conceptualization might sound like in his own formulation of the faith in which he is living out his existence.

Moreover, and we shall be discussing this more extensively in a later section where we treat the question of Jesus in the non-Christian religions, many have already encountered Christ who did not know that they had grasped the very one into whose life and death they entered as into their blessed and redeemed destiny, that they had encountered the very one whom Christians correctly name Jesus of Nazareth. Created freedom is always the risk of the uncalculated which, whether one attends to it or not, lies within the object of choice which is seen. Something *absolutely* unseen and something *wholly* other are not appropriated by freedom when it opts for something definite and something limited. But something unexpressed and unformulated is not therefore also and necessarily something absolutely unseen and unsought for. Now God and the grace of Christ are present as the secret essence of every reality we can choose. Therefore it is not so easy to opt for something without having to do with God and Christ either by accepting them or rejecting them, either by believing or not believing.

Consequently, anyone who, though still far from any revelation explicitly formulated in words, accepts his existence in patient silence (or, better, in faith, hope and love), accepts it as the mystery which lies hidden in the mystery of eternal love and which bears life in the womb of death, is saying "yes" to Christ even if he does not know it. For anyone who lets go and jumps falls into the depths which are there, and not only to the extent that he himself has fathomed them. Anyone who accepts his humanity fully, and all the more so of course the humanity of others, has accepted the Son of Man because in him God has accepted man. And if it says in scripture that whoever loves his neighbor has fulfilled the law, then this is the ultimate truth because God himself has become this neighbor, and hence He who is at once nearest to us and farthest from us is always accepted and loved in every neighbor.

5. On the Theological Understanding of the History of the Life and Death of Jesus of Nazareth

a) Preliminary Remarks

ON THE RELATIONSHIP OF THE PREVIOUS TRANSCENDENTAL INQUIRY TO HISTORICAL EVENTS

In the first section of this chapter where we tried to situate Christology within an evolutionary view of the world, and also in the third and fourth sections where we tried to deepen our transcendental and essential Christology, our concern has only been with the *idea* of a God-Man. We have been asking: Is something like an absolute saviour or a God-Man, and this is what the Incarnation of the eternal Logos in hypostatic union is, is this an idea which is intelligible to some extent, prescinding from the question whether and where this idea has been realized? Of course we have been doing this "essential" and "transcendental" Christology only because in fact we believe that in our own personal lives as Christians we have found this God-Man in Jesus Christ. But the transcendental idea of an absolute salvific event in which God's self-communication to the world as a whole reaches its irreversible historical manifestation and realization is of course something quite different from the statement that here in this concrete man there has taken place what we have considered so far only as an idea.

Earlier we tried to develop from out of man's transcendental essence and his intellectual and spiritual situation today an idea of what notions like "God-Man," "incarnate Logos," and "absolute saviour" can mean. But in this a priori outline of a transcendental Christology we were conscious of the fact that this is possible historically only because Christianity and actual faith in Jesus as the Christ already exist, only because humanity has already had the historical experience of the reality behind this transcendental idea. It is only in reflection upon the experienced fact that the transcendental possibility of such an idea can be made intelligible. We said that the ultimate and decisive question for Christianity is not whether the notion of an absolute saviour or of the historical manifestation of God's absolute and definitive communication and offer of himself to the world is conceivable in principle. The ultimate and decisive question is rather whether this historical offer has already *taken place,* or whether it is only the asymptotic and still ambiguous point towards which our hope strives, and finally whether and why we can truly believe that this event of an absolute mediator of salvation and of the historical concreteness of God's absolute self-communication to the world has taken place precisely and only in Jesus of Nazareth.

THE ACCOUNTABILITY OF OUR FAITH IN JESUS AS THE CHRIST

The topic of this section is the justification, that is, the accountability of this faith in the historical Jesus as the Christ of faith before the tribunal of conscience and of truth, the tribunal which we ourselves are in the concrete situation of our own existence. We have consciously posed the question in the sense just formulated, and hence we are not asking directly: Is the historical Jesus the Christ of faith, and how does he show that he is this Christ? This is the way the question is usually posed in Catholic fundamental theology. It is not of course an illegitimate question insofar as this question about the "objective state of affairs" is implied in the question we are asking about the credibility of our faith in Jesus as the

Christ. But a question which by its very nature challenges and confronts the whole of human existence cannot be posed to begin with as a question for which particular elements of the concrete existence of the subject doing the asking can be put in parentheses.

When I ask a question which really concerns me in my totality, then in asking this question I cannot leave out anything about myself as unimportant. When I ask about salvation for myself, I am necessarily asking about myself in my totality, for this is precisely what the notion of salvation means. Therefore, we are posing the Christological question here about Jesus the Christ as a question about the accountability of each one's own faith in Jesus as the Christ. Hence we are posing it as a question about the accountability of faith, which implies a free decision, as a question about my faith, as a question which places every individual in his concrete existence as a man and as a believer in question, and demands an answer.

The "objective" question, so to speak, which we mentioned above ("Is Jesus the Christ, and how does he show that he is?") is not excluded or minimized by our question: "How do I account for my faith in this Jesus as the Christ?" We are rather presupposing that within such a faith, about whose ground and moral justification we are asking, this objective question too is really found and gives this faith a quite definite structure. Because of this structure, precisely what is "most objective" is disclosed only to the most radical subjective act, and at the same time precisely the "subjective act" knows itself to be empowered and justified by the objective facts. Within the subjective situation which we are presupposing here as accepted by us, and it is precisely as accepted that we are asking about its grounds, we are presupposing the situation of our Western, Christian and ecclesial faith, and even real and absolute faith in Jesus as the Christ. We only have to reflect on our concrete lives to see that we are always making presuppositions, in the first place in order to be able to test them. This characteristically human situation is unavoidable. The reflection "Why can I believe in Jesus as the Christ?" begins with the presupposition that I do believe. This faith as actualized and as always to be actualized anew reflects upon its own intrinsic justification.

THE CIRCULAR STRUCTURE OF FAITH KNOWLEDGE

Now this methodological presupposition raises the question how a person who does not believe in Jesus as the Christ can come to this faith. This question can be raised about the individual history of an individual person who lives in an intellectual and spiritual situation which bears the stamp of Christianity, as well as in a collective sense for peoples who in their whole intellectual and spiritual situation and history seem to live outside the realm of Christianity. With regard to the question how someone enters into a circle of intellectual, spiritual and existentiell knowledge, into a circle whose elements mutually support each other and which ultimately cannot be constructed "synthetically" by the individual himself, let us say here very briefly that there certainly is the phenomenon of a knowledge which exists as a single whole and whose elements do not really have to be constructed subsequently in an artificial and reflexive synthesis. It is a knowledge within whose circle a person experiences himself situated without having constructed this circle synthetically and reflexively himself.

This neither excludes nor declares superfluous the process by which this person can and must justify his experience before the tribunal of conscience and of truth. Nor does it exclude the fact that his being situated in this circle remains a question for moral decision. It is a question at least in the sense of whether a person accepts his being situated in this circle prior to reflection and decision, or whether he rejects it. In the latter case this inherited knowledge might vanish very quickly, and a person might then become blind to the knowledge which was offered to him although he had not really produced and synthesized it. But if there is such a phenomenon in general, and if a person cannot really exist in an intellectual and spiritual way without being involved with this kind of knowledge, which cannot be completely analyzed and reduced to its elements and then put back together again arbitrarily, then this can also be presumed for the knowledge which we are dealing with here in our question.

It follows from the Christian teaching that faith requires grace that at least from the viewpoint of Christian theology we have to be dealing with this kind of knowledge here. Hence it follows that from the viewpoint of Christian dogma we are not proposing the postulate of such a circle arbitrarily, and that to maintain that such a circle cannot be produced artificially by subsequent reflection is not contrary to a reasonable fundamental theology, but rather in accordance with it. For what is meant by the grace of faith as an unconditional presupposition of believing and being able to believe also implies that a moment of synthesis, which ultimately cannot be made completely reflexive, is necessary for faith in order that there can come to exist that unity in which subjective willingness to believe sees the objective ground of faith, and hence this objective ground justifies the willingness to believe which the subject must bring.

This is neither the place nor the occasion to describe in what forms and structures the process of entering into this circle of understanding takes place in an individual or in society. Basically a Christian can do only this:

he can presuppose that an understanding which is offered to the freedom of faith is already present at the center of the listener's being, and he can express in a conceptual articulation for this person the understanding which is already present. If the listener also accepts the Christological assertion explicitly, then the speaker has not really produced this understanding of faith in its original unity, but has only brought it to the conscious level of objective conceptualization. If this reflexive assertion, which is offered to the listener as the interpretation of his already presupposed understanding of faith, is not accepted in an explicit profession of faith, then the speaker has to recognize either that the listener has freely closed himself to an understanding which was offered to him both by grace and by the historical message presented to him in their unity, or that the grace of Christ, which in any case is present and operative in him, has not yet in God's salvific providence produced the *kairos* in which this inner light of grace can find its historical objectification in an explicit faith in Jesus as the Christ. Which of these two alternatives is in fact the case is something which the one who delivers this explicit Christological message cannot judge.

This brief reflection is only intended to show that, although our question about Jesus as the Christ begins from the outset with the situation of the Christology professed and believed in the church, the possibility of justifying the church's Christology to someone who does not yet believe explicitly in Jesus as the Christ is not excluded; rather, if this possibility is understood correctly, it is presupposed.

THE HISTORICAL DIMENSION OF CHRISTIAN FAITH

With this fifth section we are necessarily entering into the area of historical knowledge of events which once took place at a quite definite point in time and space. For the real point of the Christian message lies precisely in the assertion that this Jesus, who died under Pontius Pilate, is none other than the Christ, the Son of God, the absolute saviour. The salvation of all times depends on this historical event, indeed the salvation of each one of us. It is grounded in this historical, unique event, although later we shall have to consider the specific way in which the salvation of *all* is grounded in the historical event of the death and resurrection of Jesus of Nazareth. Although it can be said, and rightly so, that the knowledge of such a historical, salvific event is not known after the manner of neutral "historical" knowledge, but is known always and only through Jesus' self-interpretation, and that the legitimacy of this can be grasped once again only in the circle of faith and through the miracle of the deeds and of the resurrection of Jesus which makes this self-interpretation legitimate, it is true nevertheless that Christology's assertion of faith about Jesus refers to a quite definite historical person and to historical events. Hence it implies historical assertions. These may perhaps be really found only within an assertion of faith, but there at least they are meant in a really historical sense. Therefore the conscience and the intellectual honesty of the believer are faced with the question: In what sense and with what right does he assert and maintain that they are historical events?

THE PROBLEM OF THE UNIVERSAL SIGNIFICANCE OF PARTICULAR HISTORICAL EVENTS

Christological assertions, therefore, also have a historical dimension. But if they do not want to give up this historical dimension and take flight to the dimension of existential philosophy, which apparently is liberated from the burden of history, this means that they are also inevitably burdened with all the difficulties and uncertainties of knowing an event which lies far back in history. This situation is especially burdened in our case because the historical events with which we are dealing here are not of such a nature that despite all of our historical curiosity about their existence, their more exact nature and their interpretation, we can ultimately forget about them. These events are rather of decisive importance for man's existence. They are supposed to concern us really and radically in the innermost center of our existence, but nevertheless they are supposed to be historical events.

But Christian faith regards these quite definite events located in time and space as events to which a person can indeed close himself existentielly in what we call disbelief, but he does this in such a way that these quite definite events in time and space still inevitably and inescapably concern his existence in its innermost core. There exists, therefore, an unavoidable difference and incongruence between the certainty and uncertainty of historical knowledge as such, and the existentiell significance of historical events when they belong to the past and are not experienced simply and immediately in themselves and in their own concreteness. Christianity says that historical events which lie far back in the past still touch my existence, and at the same time it remains true that the more exact historical course of these events is characterized by a certain element of uncertainty, obscurity and ambiguity which is both inevitable and insurmountable.

In earlier times the tradition was simply taken for granted and it determined their own present in a powerful and unquestioned way. They were not as sensitive as we are to this discrepancy and incongruence between the historicity and the existentiell significance of past events. But from the time of the Enlightenment theology and philosophy have been asking repeatedly how something historical can be existentielly and unambiguously significant, and whether salvation, that is, we ourselves in our ultimate ground and in our totality, can be dependent on a historical truth and reality, or whether we can only be dependent on something whose transcendental necessity or immediate verifiability is evident from the exact sciences. Faith as such of course presupposes these historical events to be absolutely true and real. But at least in a Catholic understanding of faith, there belongs among the elements of faith at least to some extent a moment of reflection about whether the events which faith posits absolutely are known historically, and whether this historical knowledge as such can be justified before the tribunal of conscience and of truth. In this respect the incongruence between the merely relative verifiability of historical knowledge as such on the one hand, and the absolute, existentiell significance of historical events and the absoluteness of faith on the other cannot in principle be resolved.

THE INEVITABLE INCONGRUENCE BETWEEN RELATIVE HISTORICAL
CERTAINTY AND ABSOLUTE COMMITMENT

In order to understand that, in spite of this lesser degree of certainty about historical events, such a claim by historical events can nevertheless be justified, it is of the greatest importance to see that basically and in general a person cannot live out his existence without calmly accepting the inevitability of such an incongruence between the relative certainty of his historical knowledge on the one hand and the absoluteness of his commitment on the other, and without tolerating this in his own existence. By accepting these historical facts calmly, courageously and confidently, and indeed with the awareness that he himself would still have lived out his existence in a morally good way should he have erred in his historical knowledge, he comes to the insight that one cannot escape the possibility of error by means of an existentiell abstention vis-à-vis historical facts merely because one cannot reach any absolute, historical certitude about them. Always and everywhere in the absolute and irreversible decisions of his life a person is involved with historical facts about whose existence and nature he possesses no absolute, theoretical certitude. There exists everywhere and inevitably in life this incongruence between the absolute commitment which is inevitably demanded of a person on the one hand, and theoretical certainty about the facts which this person is involved with in such a commitment on the other. This situation belongs inevitably to the essence of freedom.

By its very nature freedom always decides absolutely, since even the act of abstaining is once again an absolute decision. This latter decision is itself made on the basis of knowledge which is not absolute. This is still true even when such a decision follows on the basis of transcendental, metaphysical insights. For even here the reflexive decision is conditioned by an interpretation of transcendental experience or of the original metaphysical insight, by an interpretation which cannot strip off its historical conditioning. Even when such an interpretation, however precise and metaphysically astute, only intends to articulate the ultimate necessities of reality, it does its work with linguistic materials which are contingent and conditioned.

If, therefore, in our case the historical knowledge of Jesus, of his self-interpretation and of the justification he gives for it is burdened with many problems, uncertainties and ambiguities, this fact is to be readily admitted and it is no reason to abstain from an absolute commitment to him and to the salvific significance of his reality for us. For even such a cautious abstention would be a decision, an act of saying "no" to him, and the reasons for this "no" which can be objectified in historical knowledge would be weaker than those for a positive commitment to him and to his claim. It is to be emphasized here, of course, that the evidence for this final judgment still has to be furnished. And obviously we have to admit that, in spite of well-founded historical knowledge about Jesus and his claim, in our case the distance between historical foundation and responsive commitment is the largest distance conceivable. For this historical knowledge as such cannot be essentially more cogent than any other historical knowledge which makes existentiell claims upon us to an essentially lesser degree. But the commitment which we are dealing with here as distinguished from other consequences which follow from historical knowledge is simply absolute because it concerns the very salvation of the whole person.

b) Observations From Hermeneneutics And Fundamental Theology On The Problem Of Historical Knowledge Of The Pre-Resurrection Jesus

TWO THESES

First, the faith which would grasp in Jesus the absolute saviour cannot be uninterested a priori in the history of Jesus before the resurrection and in his self-understanding. Otherwise "faith" would create the Christ of salvation "on the occasion of" Jesus of Nazareth. This Christ would then be mythological, sustained by "faith" rather than sustaining and empowering faith. The statement is correct that we cannot write a biography of Jesus, because all of the assertions about Jesus in the New Testament which have come down to us in history were formulated as faith assertions about the Christ of salvation, but it does not justify a priori the conclusion that we know nothing about Jesus historically, or only things which are and remain theologically unimportant. We can know much about Jesus historically, and indeed things which have theological relevance, with of course a historical "certainty" or "probability" which neither can nor must produce the absoluteness of faith. How much we can know is an a posteriori question which always has to be asked and answered anew. Later we shall treat separately the specific nature of the historical knowledge of the resurrection of Jesus which by the nature of the case is unique.

Secondly, taking into account the legitimate difference between what a subject is precisely *as* subject, and not as a mere thing, and how and to what extent a subject is capable of verbal self-reflection (in which difference, however, the two may not be understood as mutually and absolutely indifferent to each other) taking this difference into account we can say on the one hand that the self-understanding of the pre-resurrection Jesus may not contradict in an historical sense the Christian understanding of his person and his salvific significance, but that on the other hand it must not be required *a priori and with certainty* (in order to recognize in Jesus the Christ of faith) that in itself and especially for us his pre-resurrection self-understanding already coincides positively and unambiguously with the content of Christological faith. Hence his resurrection may not simply be understood as God putting his seal upon a claim of the absolute saviour which was already present fully and unambiguously *before* the resurrection. This thesis allows more latitude in the inquiry into the historical Jesus from the viewpoint of dogmatic theology. It is not however prejudiced in favor of a negative or a minimalistic understanding of Jesus' self-understanding before the resurrection.

We have just formulated these theses with regard to problems in hermeneutics and fundamental theology in order to prepare specifically for the question about the historical Jesus as saviour. Perhaps they can also be treated somewhat more extensively and in a larger context, for they touch on topics which could also be treated in the more general context of justifying the faith of a religion with a historical revelation.

CHRISTIAN FAITH REFERS TO THE CONCRETE HISTORY OF JESUS

It is often said today in the discussion about Jesus as the Christ of faith that we cannot know anything about the historical Jesus, or at least we cannot know anything relevant to faith and theology. We know only the witness of faith which the people of apostolic times and especially the authors of the New Testament writings have borne to Jesus as the Christ. We can never get beyond this testimony by trying in a neutral study of history to discover something about Jesus which would both be important for faith and theology, and would still be attributable to him both "in himself" and for us, independently of the faith testimony of the first witnesses. Hence we merely have the choice of accepting this faith of the first witnesses without further questions, or of rejecting it. Basically, then, the same thing can also be said about the testimony of faith of those who preached Jesus as the Christ later, and hence of the testimony of the church. In all of these instances the Christ of faith is an absolute, final datum in the disciples, and to want to go beyond this to a Jesus of history is impossible to begin with, and even contradictory.

At most a few historical trivialities could be established in this way, for example, that there was a Jesus of Nazareth, that he came into conflict with the religious and political officials of his time for reasons which are not quite clear any more, and therefore finally ended his life on the cross. But everything which goes beyond this is so very much the matter and content and object posited by faith, for which no further reasons can be given, that the content of this faith with regard to historical events, and especially with regard to the resurrection of Jesus, no longer admits of any further justification. Instead, this faith in its formal and existential structure is the real and only legitimate criterion for deciding what historical and factual content is really to be counted as part of its essence and what is not. All content of an historical nature which cannot be reached by this approach to the essence of faith is not essential for faith, and cannot be the object of a genuine article of faith.

Such an understanding has the advantage of course of freeing us to begin with from every historical difficulty. In such a conception faith itself is the first and last thing in an undifferentiated simplicity. Faith does not contain within it an element distinguishable from itself which would ground it. And if it still makes occasional historical statements, these could not cause any misgivings even for the most radical historical sceptic.

But this attempt to emancipate oneself from the burden of history is the first misgiving that one can voice. However one might interpret transcendentality and existentiality more exactly, and make them the real ground of his faith, we cannot *in principle* possess them without a reference to real history. The degree to which such a history is included in the actualization of genuine transcendentality, and of an existential faith which is understood merely in a transcendental way, might vary greatly in different individuals, but there is no one who could actualize his transcendentality without it being mediated by history.

Beyond this we also have to say that the genuine Christianity of the New Testament understood itself differently than this approach does. It knew itself to be a faith which was related to a definite historical event, and which did not itself simply posit this event or create it in faith, but rather it receives its justification and foundation from this event. This assertion is not to be proven here in detail. It follows from everything which has to be said later about the self-interpretation of Jesus, his death and his resurrection as the content of Christian faith. In all of this the historical event of Jesus including what we call miracle and resurrection appears in the self-interpretation of the Christian faith of the first community not merely as an object which faith creates for itself, but also as the *ground* of faith through which faith knows itself to be given and to be justified before the tribunal of truth and conscience in the believer.

ON THE RELATIONSHIP BETWEEN THE OBJECT AND THE GROUND OF FAITH

Someone might reject as impossible such a relationship between faith and historical events whereby the historical event makes faith legitimate. But then he should no longer say that he still has *the* Christian faith as Christianity has understood it in all ages. Otherwise he would at least have to show clearly that a rejection of the relationship between faith and the ground of faith as we understand it is unambiguously necessary. This, however, is impossible.

To understand this view we have to go back a bit further. First of all, we are distinguishing more explicitly and clearly than before between the *object* of faith and the *ground* of faith. This distinction, however, is a formal and not a material distinction, since in practice and in the concrete every ground of faith is also an object of faith, although the converse relationship is not true, that is, not every object of faith is a ground of faith. Jesus' self-interpretation, for example, which we have transcribed by the notion of an absolute saviour, belongs perhaps almost exclusively to the object of faith, and a ground of faith different from it must be found for it. This is not to deny that this self-interpretation in its historical uniqueness and content corresponds to our prior transcendental search for the historically unambiguous and definitive manifestation of our supernatural, transcendental experience of God's absolute self-communication. Indeed it corresponds in such a way that this self-interpretation of Jesus can also show the ground of its credibility within itself. But the validity of this latter would be so difficult to transmit from one person to another if there were no other grounds of faith that we want to maintain the basic distinction between the ground and the object of faith in spite of this very important qualification which is not really treated in the theology of the schools.

According to Christianity's understanding of faith in all ages, including that of the New Testament, there belongs to the grounds for believing in Jesus as the Christ what we call the miracles and mighty deeds of Jesus, and especially his resurrection. We are not yet raising the question whether in the concrete we can still recognize today a ground of faith in the miracles and mighty deeds of Jesus which have come down to us in history, and these as distinct from the resurrection, or whether today we have to concentrate our question about the grounds of faith upon the question of the resurrection. We would do this not because of apologetical anxieties, but for theological considerations yet to be explained. Nor are we asking yet how and why the two grounds of faith just mentioned, Jesus' miracles and mighty deeds on the one hand, and his resurrection on the other, are essentially different from each other. Nor are we asking at this point in our inquiry whether and how people at the time of Jesus could recognize these grounds of faith as historical events, and whether and with what differences from the knowledge of the direct New Testament witnesses such knowledge as a ground faith is possible for us, a knowledge which is related either to the miracles and to the resurrection of Jesus, or only to the latter. What we are maintaining at this point is that the miracles and mighty deeds of Jesus and his resurrection do have such a function in the self-interpretation of Christian faith, and that at least in the Catholic church Christian faith regards these realities not only as something which is believed, as an object of faith, but also as grounds of faith.

When, therefore, we assume for the miracles and mighty deeds of Jesus and for his resurrection the function of grounding faith, this is not to maintain that such knowledge induces and justifies faith from outside as it were. When we reject a faith which has no grounds as an unchristian conception of faith, this does not mean that the ground of faith is extrinsic to faith itself and must be grasped independently of faith. Such an extrinsic relationship between faith and the ground of faith need not be assumed because this is by no means the only conceivable way in which a ground of faith can be distinguished from an object of faith, and can exercise the function of grounding the object. Some fundamental considerations based upon Christian dogma stand opposed to defining the relationship in this extrinsic way, and not just considerations based on the actual experience of people today, their historical scepticism, and so on. It is quite conceivable that the ground of faith is reached only *in* faith, but nevertheless can exercise a true grounding function within it, and is not only an object of faith posited arbitrarily or because of the formal essence of faith.

Therefore it is not scepticism about whether historical knowledge has the function of grounding faith that is the real reason why we reject this extrinsic relationship between the ground and the object of faith. Ultimately it is dogmatic reasons that are decisive. Basically they have been valid and they would also be valid today even if we were less sceptical about the purely historical value of our knowledge of Jesus of Nazareth than is perhaps necessary in our contemporary situation. There are dogmatic reasons against such an extrinsic relationship, for the Catholic doctrine of faith maintains that faith and the knowledge of faith are not possible without grace, and that they entail the personal and *free* assent of the believing subject. A real and effective grasp of the historical grounds of faith takes place only within the process of faith itself in grace and in freedom. Hence they exercise their function of grounding faith as an element within faith and in the circle of a relationship of mutual conditioning between the transcendental experience of grace and the historical grasp of events which ground faith.

ON THE DIFFERENT MEANINGS OF "HISTORY"

Along with this appeal to the historical events which engender faith, there is in fact also present in Holy Scripture always an appeal to the experience of the Spirit of God, which we interpreted earlier as the finalization of human existence towards the immediacy of God through God's self-communication. Without this an assent of faith is ultimately impossible. Presupposing this relationship of mutual conditioning in which the grace of faith opens one's eyes to the credibility of particular historical events, and presupposing conversely that these events on their part make one's entering into the transcendental experience of grace legitimate, then we can acquire a correct understanding of the otherwise very obscure, but much used and not unimportant distinction between salvation history *(Geschichte)* and the merely historical *(historisch)*. Salvation history strictly as such must belong to the dimension which we call the history of man in a very objective and real sense, and it is also affirmed as real and objective in the assertion in which faith grasps its object and its ground together in a free act and decision borne by grace. But this salvation history as the ground of faith does not have to be called "historical" *(historisch)* insofar as it does not have to make and does not make the claim that it is also accessible to a knowledge which is not interested in faith, and in this sense is merely neutral and profane historical knowledge.

Therefore history in the first sense *(Geschichte)* as distinguished from the second *(historisch)* would then be something in the "objective" reality and world and history of man which is grasped and *only* grasped within an existentielly committed assent of faith. History in the second sense would be something which could also be grasped outside of such faith knowledge by merely profane history *(Historie)*.

THE FAITH OF THE FIRST WITNESSES AND OUR FAITH

When we emphasize in this way that the relationship between historical events which ground faith and faith itself comes to existence within faith, this is true for the first witnesses who had an immediate historical experience of Jesus as well as for us, the later generations of believers. This difference between the object and the ground of faith and, despite this, the immanence of both elements within faith itself, is valid first of all, then, for the first witnesses of faith. They too reach the salvation history event which really grounds faith only within faith. This is not a sad and regrettable calamity for faith, but rather it follows from the very nature of faith because and insofar as it is a total and existentiell decision in freedom. Faith, therefore, can reach that by which it is grounded and borne only in this freedom, that is, in the act of faith itself. To this extent the experience of faith and the experience of the ground of faith are no different for the first disciples than they are for us.

This does not simply make us equal to them and independent of them. This does not deny that our faith is grounded in the faith of the first witnesses, but rather this is implied in our understanding. The significance for our faith of the faith of the first disciples, and the significance of the faith of the generations of believers coming between them and us lies not only in the transmission of historical materials which we then turn again into a ground and an object of faith by ourselves alone in an absolutely new, autonomous and independent act of faith. Rather the faith of the first witnesses and the faith of the generations who have brought the faith of the first witnesses down to us is an element in the grounds of our faith.

The coming to faith of the first witnesses as an experience of the successful combination of a gratuitous transcendental disposition to believe on the one hand, and the grasping of particular historical events as the historical mediation of this transcendental disposition to believe on the other hand, is in a positive sense for us subsequent believers one of the elements which grounds our own faith. This does not mean, however, that the relationship of mutual conditioning between the original salvific event which grounds faith and the faith of the first witnesses is no longer accessible to us. On the contrary: insofar as we are given courage by their faith and believe their testimony, we enter ourselves into the structure of their faith and can by all means say with them, and correctly, that *because* Christ is risen, I believe.

SALVIFIC KNOWLEDGE IS POSSIBLE
ONLY WITHIN THE COMMITMENT OF FAITH

Insofar as this thesis is directed precisely to faith in Jesus Christ, the reasons for it cannot be furnished until we ask ourselves later with what right we can justify Jesus' interpretation of himself as the absolute saviour, the saviour vindicated as such by his resurrection. By the very nature of the case, such a relationship in general between the ground and what is grounded cannot be understood in any other way except within the circle of the one faith. For by definition salvific knowledge concerns an object which touches and lays claim to the whole person. If in general there must be a correspondence between the type of knowledge and the object of knowledge, a correspondence which is antecedent to the concrete act of knowledge in each instance, then it is clear to begin with that the salvific knowledge of a salvific object, a knowledge which we call faith, can be reached only by the whole person in the commitment of his whole existence. Hence it is clear to begin with that in this case there can be no point of his existence which stands outside of this act of knowledge.

If this salvific knowledge is nevertheless also historical knowledge, then the historical object is necessarily an object which can appear only in this salvific, historical knowledge which as faith involves the whole person. And yet it is that which grounds this faith because faith, in spite of its gratuitous transcendentality, must necessarily be grounded by history if salvation is not to take place beyond the dimension in which man lives his life and possesses his spiritual transcendentality. Such a relationship of mutual conditioning will not surprise anyone who has once understood in a really reflexive and existentielly clear way that even the most profane historical reality is not really given unless it is recognized. And this also brings it under the law of a subjective apriority without which nothing at all can be known, although this apriority is not always identical with the gratuitous transcendentality in which and from out of which alone a person can grasp something which is of salvific significance.

We emphasized earlier how the thesis that, without lessening its function as ground, the salvific, historical object is given only in the act of faith itself, does not eliminate the possibility of articulating the grounds of faith to nonbelievers. This becomes even clearer when we note that the articulation of the grounds of faith for a "nonbeliever" is done by a believer who knows this reflexively. Intentionally or unintentionally, in his articulation of the grounds of faith he brings into play his own faith in its successful combination of the gratuitous transcendental disposition to believe and the historical experience which mediates this. In this way, and in a form which implies far more than some kind of learned or historical indoctrination, he appeals to the experience which is already present in the other person unreflexively, either as freely although unthematically accepted already, or as offered to freedom as a genuine possibility.

ON THE DISTINCTION BETWEEN ARTICULATIONS OF THE OBJECT OF FAITH
AND OF THE GROUND OF FAITH

However much we have emphasized that the data of salvation history are found only within the gratuitous miracle of faith itself, nevertheless, to go back to something we said earlier and clarify it, statements about the realities of faith and statements about the salvific events which ground faith are not simply and always identical. This difference follows not only from the different *objective* quality of the realities we are referring to, but this difference between a salvific, historical reality as the ground of faith and as the object of faith also follows from the mode of our own historical knowledge. This too constitutes a difference with regard to realities which belong to the same historical dimension as far as their own objective nature goes.

For example, the infancy narratives about Jesus belong in themselves to the same historical dimension as the last supper. They even belong more radically to the historical reality of Jesus than his resurrection, which is a reality of a quite special nature because, although it does indeed have to do with the concrete, historical Jesus in himself and not only with our articulation of faith, it makes an assertion about a reality which as such no longer belongs to the dimension of our historical, empirical world. This is clear of course just from the fact that only the believers shared in the experiences of the resurrection, while his enemies did not.

The accounts from which we can acquire historical knowledge about Jesus of Nazareth, if we can acquire it at all, are the accounts of the New Testament, and hence accounts which are one and all faith assertions. In relation to us, therefore, it can readily be the case that an assertion in such an account is accessible to us only as a faith assertion, and we are not able to reach this content of faith as a partial ground of faith as well, while another assertion presents a content of faith and at the same time reveals a ground of faith. It can be the case here that the assertion about a mere content of faith without its own ground of faith does refer to an historical event, but one whose historicity, however, is no longer accessible to us as an element in the ground of faith. For example, the faith assertion about the virgin conception of Jesus might refer beyond this to an event in the dimension of history. But if we ask whether the account of it in the infancy narratives about Jesus in the New Testament also allows us to grasp in the faith testimony of the account the grounds of this faith just as much as do the mighty deeds of Jesus or his resurrection, we may calmly answer this question in the negative. Even presupposing our faith and our readiness to believe, it is not possible for us to differentiate in such an account by means of an historical inquiry the ground of faith and the content of faith.

Even presupposing the circle we mentioned, we have the right and the obligation in reading the New Testament accounts to distinguish whether the details in each instance furnish us with a content of faith, or beyond this also furnish us with grounds of faith. When fundamental theology makes this inquiry, there is no need to judge the *historical* value of the texts for us as the same for all the texts. In view of this it is obvious, and very important for our reflections, that the number of texts and the scope of their assertions is much less in an inquiry of fundamental theology than is the number and the scope of the content of the texts which give witness to New Testament faith. This distinction still has to be made even when we read all of these assertions as believers and within the circle of our own faith.

We do not abandon this circle between faith and the grounds of faith when we ask: In a historical inquiry what can be established with sufficient certainty about those events which are not only objects of faith but also grounds of faith? Concretely, did Jesus know himself to be the absolute saviour, and can it be maintained with sufficient certainty before the tribunal of conscience and of truth that such a claim is known by historical inquiry? We do not abandon the circle we established in this kind of an inquiry by fundamental theology. For we are not denying that this sufficient historical knowledge is really disclosed only to someone who grasps it in a total act of knowledge, and does this in such a way that it is taken up into the absolute act of faith, and its per se very relative certainty becomes adequate in the act of faith itself. But, conversely, in spite of the existence of the circle we mentioned the distinction between texts which offer only the content of faith and texts which offer historical grounds of faith must be maintained. Texts significant for fundamental theology and texts significant for dogmatic theology have a different character both with regard to their number and their scope. The perspectives and inquiries of fundamental theology and history on the one hand and dogmatic theology and salvation history on the other are not identical, even though or just because they are both envisaged within the circle of the one faith.

This basic distinction justifies the believer in proceeding very rigorously when he inquires in fundamental theology about our historical knowledge of realities which ground faith and are not just the content of faith. Since the believer too has to distinguish between the content of faith and the grounds of faith, he is completely justified in examining rigorously assertions offered in the New Testament as the grounds of faith, and in trying to come up with a minimum of such knowledge. Even the traditional fundamental theology and apologetics emphasize that they have to maintain and want to maintain with sufficient certainty that the "substance" of the New Testament accounts is historical, but they do not maintain in an assertion of fundamental theology strictly as such that everything that goes beyond this substance is historical. In earlier times presumably this "substance" of historical knowledge in fundamental theology, a substance necessary for a faith which knows that it is mediated historically, was estimated too generously in the concrete, perhaps far too generously. But this was not a fundamental mistake. And we always have to reckon with the possibility that in a false kind of skepticism this historical substance which grounds the faith is estimated too modestly.

THE MINIMAL HISTORICAL PRESUPPOSITIONS OF AN ORTHODOX CHRISTOLOGY TO BE ESTABLISHED BY FUNDAMENTAL THEOLOGY

It follows from our reflections that in fundamental theology we really only have to prove that two theses are historically credible in order to establish in fundamental theology the grounds of faith for orthodox Christianity's whole Christology.

First, Jesus saw himself not merely as one among many prophets who in principle form an unfinished line which is always open towards the future, but understood himself rather as the *eschatological* prophet, as the absolute and definitive saviour, although the more precise question what a definitive saviour means and does not mean requires further reflection.

Secondly, this claim of Jesus is credible for us when, from the perspective of our transcendental experience in grace of the absolute self-communication of the holy God, we look in faith to that event which mediates the saviour in his total reality: the resurrection of Jesus. If we succeed in what follows in proving that these two theses are credible, then we have accomplished everything which in the first instance has to be accomplished in fundamental theology. All other assertions about Jesus as the Christ can be left to faith itself as the content of faith.

We do not have to presuppose in fundamental theology that the New Testament testimony has to be found equally reliable in each and every detail. We are justified in not getting ourselves into the dilemma that either an account has to merit belief in all its details, or it is to be absolutely rejected. The answer to a question in fundamental theology about the reliability of the sources for the life and self-understanding of Jesus and for the justification of his claim obviously cannot reach any more than a judgment of "substantial" historicity. This answer cannot and may not imitate the judgment of faith about the absolute inerrancy of scripture by estimating the value of the sources for fundamental theology to be of equal weight everywhere. A differentiation of the sources with regard to their historically verifiable reliability is therefore necessary and legitimate. The exact sense of what the "substantial" reliability of the sources means can only follow from a positive investigation of the individual sources. In the accounts of the historical life of Jesus up to his death we can calmly reckon with the fact that, because they are kerygmatic testimonies of faith and not secular biography, they are always partially shaped by the judgment of faith about Jesus arrived at with the resurrection.

c) The Empirical Concrete Structure Of The Life Of Jesus

THE NATURE OF OUR PROCEDURE

When we now ask what we know about the life and the self-interpretation of the historical Jesus of Nazareth, there can be no question, in what we have called an "introduction to the idea of Christianity" on a first level of reflection, of doing exegesis in detail and with the tools of contemporary historical science in order to answer the question: What do we know with

sufficient historical certainty or probability about this Jesus from the historical sources which are at our disposal? Such a task does not belong to the
first level of reflection, because this would necessarily demand too much of
the author as well as of the reader of this initial introduction. Consequently,
neither *can* this be the task of the first level of reflection upon the legitimacy of Christian faith in Jesus as the Christ. On this level of reflection
we are entirely justified in presupposing the results of original and scientific
exegesis and of the history of the life of Jesus, at least with regard to the
results which these historical sciences pass on to us as sufficiently certain
or probable. Everything which is said in what follows, therefore, is said in
reference to these sciences and their results, and with the claim that this
reference is verified by these sciences.

Of course these exegetical sciences have not simply produced results
which they acquired with absolute unanimity and which were formulated
by all of these sciences in complete agreement. But something like this is
not to be expected in historical science to begin with. Moreover, the
conditional nature of these historical sciences, the differences of opinion
among them, and the fact that it is assumed that on the average their results
are somewhat fluid are not reasons for us to refuse absolute commitment
to the historical because this is the only way it is known. Hence we are only
reporting in summary fashion what we can maintain is able to be known
and is known about Jesus of Nazareth from exegesis with a sufficiently good
conscience.

A SUMMARY IN THESIS FORM

What follows, then, can be presented without hesitation as elements in our
historical knowledge of Jesus, prescinding for the moment from the ultimate nature of his self-understanding:

1. Jesus lived in and was part of the religious milieu of his people and
the historical situation in which he found himself. In general he accepted
it as legitimate and willed by God, and he took part in this religious life
which included temple and synagogue, law and customs, feasts and holy
scriptures, priests and teachers. To this extent he intended to be a religious
reformer, not a radical religious revolutionary. How and to what extent his
message and his demanding interpretation of his religious heritage and
milieu did represent a radical "revolution" is another question.

2. He was a radical reformer. As a reformer he broke the lordship of the
law which in fact put itself in God's place, although this was not the real
intention of the law nor, to note in passing, was it interpreted this way by

Paul. He fought against legalism in order to move beyond a mere ethic of pious sentiments, and beyond a justification by works which was supposed to give man security against God. He knew himself to be radically close to God, and for him God was not an empty symbol of man's importance, but was the ultimate reality who was simply taken for granted as part of life. It is precisely for this reason that he was someone who saw himself in radical solidarity with social and religious outcasts, because his "Father" loved them. He resolutely accepted the struggle which his attitude and his activity provoked on the part of the religious and social establishment. But in his own eyes he was not directly a social critic in the sociological sense.

3. While at first he hoped for a victory in his religious mission in the sense of a "conversion" of his people, the experience grew ever stronger in him that his mission was bringing him into mortal conflict with the religious and the political society.

4. But he faced his death resolutely and accepted it at least as the inevitable consequence of fidelity to his mission and as imposed on him by God.

5. His radical preaching and his exhortation to reform were intended as a call to conversion in and because of the closeness of God's kingdom, and were intended to gather disciples who "follow" him. *For the time being* we shall prescind here from the question whether these disciples were assenting to something which ultimately was independent of Jesus himself, or whether the "thing" for which he recruited them, that is, the imminent kingdom of God, was inseparably present precisely with him. Jesus did not think that everyone then and everyone in every age could follow him *only* through an *explicit* social and critical involvement for the underprivileged and the outcasts. This negative statement does not deny that *everything* which we do and do not do has social relevance even when it is not intended as such and perhaps has this relevance *only* unintentionally, and that consequently the whole theology of Jesus can also be read as "political" theology.

6. From a *historical* point of view a great deal has to be left open in an inquiry about the pre-resurrection Jesus: whether he had a verbalized messianic consciousness; which of the over fifty names given to Jesus in the New Testament corresponds most nearly or exactly to his self-understanding; whether perhaps the title "Son of Man" in New Testament Christology belongs among the very words of Jesus, or whether this cannot be proven; whether, at least for a time, Jesus thought in terms of a possible difference between himself and a future Son of Man; whether and to what extent and in what sense the pre-resurrection Jesus explictly ascribed a

soteriological function to his death beyond what is implied in the assertion of thesis four; whether and in what sense in his expectation of the imminent coming of God's kingdom he foresaw before the resurrection his disciples as a new community to be established and as established, as a new Israel made up of those who believed in him, and whether and in what sense he intended this and institutionalized it.

d) On The Basic Self-Understanding Of The Pre-Resurrection Jesus

THE TRULY HUMAN SELF-CONSCIOUSNESS OF JESUS

Jesus had a human self-consciousness which may not be identified in a "monophysitic" way with the consciousness of the divine Logos. In the latter case the human reality of Jesus would then ultimately be directed passively by the consciousness of the Logos like a puppet of the divine subject who alone would be active, although in the livery of man. Like every other human consciousness, the human self-consciousness of Jesus stood at a created distance from God in freedom, in obedience and in worship. Besides this, the difference between the human self-consciousness and God, which forbids us to understand this human self-consciousness as a double of the divine consciousness, is shown by the fact that during his public life Jesus first had to learn (here as always we are talking about the objectified and verbalized consciousness of Jesus) that because of the hardness of heart of his listeners the kingdom of God did not come in the way that he had thought it would at the beginning of his preaching.

Without prejudice to the ultimate continuity of his consciousness of a radical and unique closeness to God, an unreflexive consciousness in the depths of his being which continued throughout the whole history of his life (as is shown in the unique nature of his behavior towards the Father), the objectifying and verbalizing self-consciousness of Jesus has a history. It shares the horizons of understanding and the conceptualizations of his milieu, and in regard to himself, not just in "condescension" to others. It learns and it has new and surprising experiences. It is threatened by ultimate crises of self-identity, although once again they remain encompassed by the consciousness that even they are hidden in the will of the "Father," but they are not for this reason any less acute.

THE PROBLEM OF THE "IMMINENT EXPECTATION"

Jesus objectified and verbalized his unique relationship to God for himself and for his listeners by means of what we usually call apocalyptic, an imminent expectation and an eschatology of the present. Since apocalyptic can be understood as a conceptual framework characteristic of Jesus' time, and since an eschatology of the present furthers rather than hinders an understanding of the importance of Jesus, the real problem is posed by what is called the "imminent expectation." The problem lies in the fact that we ourselves make a brief *temporal* interval before the coming of God's kingdom the decisive point of this expectation, while Jesus himself denied this and yet expressed an imminent expectation. *If* we ignore the question left open by Jesus about the ultimate meaning of "soon" in the coming of the day of Yahweh, then because this "soon" and the knowledge that the day was unknown were not synthesized into a higher unity in the consciousness of Jesus we may speak of an "error" in the imminent expectation of Jesus. In this "error" Jesus would only have shared our lot, since to "err" in this way is better for historical man, and hence also for Jesus, than to know everything in advance.

But if we presuppose and preserve the more correct notion of "error" in the sense of existential ontology, there is no reason to speak of an error of Jesus in his imminent expectation. A genuine human consciousness *must* have an unknown future ahead of it. The imminent expectation of Jesus was for him the *true* way in which he had to realize in his situation the closeness of God which calls for an unconditional decision. Only someone who thinks in a false and ahistorical existentialism that he is able to decide for or against God beyond time and history can be surprised at this objectification of the situation of a salvific decision, although he himself has to and may objectify it in a *somewhat* different way corresponding to *his own* experience.

JESUS' MESSAGE ABOUT GOD'S KINGDOM AS THE DEFINITIVE
PROCLAMATION OF SALVATION

Jesus, then, proclaimed the imminence of "God's kingdom" as the "now" present situation of an absolute decision for or against salvation. But *this* situation is present precisely by the fact that God offers to everyone as a sinner *salvation* and nothing less. Hence God does not merely establish an ongoing ambivalent situation for man's freedom, but rather decides this by his own act precisely in favor of man's salvation. In doing so he does not dispense man from his own responsibility for salvation, nor does he harmonize into a "system" the call to a free conversion *and* the proclamation of the victorious existence of the kingdom of grace for sinners.

To this extent it is true and need not be glossed over that Jesus proclaimed the kingdom of God and not himself. This man Jesus is the perfect man in an absolute sense precisely because he forgot himself for the sake of God and his fellow man who was in need of salvation, and existed only in this process of forgetting. Hence a statement of Jesus about himself, which there are of course and inevitably so, is conceivable to begin with only *if* and because it appears as an unavoidable element in *that* closeness of God's kingdom which Jesus proclaims as taking place now for the first time. The "function" of Jesus reveals his "essence." This closeness of God as the closeness of a salvation which prevails victoriously may not be understood in the consciousness of Jesus as a situation which is *always* equally present like a permanent existential in man, and which can at most be forgotten and suppressed and therefore must always be preached anew. It becomes present with Jesus and his proclamation in a new, unique and unsurpassable way.

It is not easy to say why this is so, and indeed according to the preaching of the pre-resurrection Jesus and independently of his death and his resurrection. Presupposing them of course would make the problem much easier and offer a quite different solution. Is what is being expressed in this proclamation of Jesus simply his relationship to God, which he does not find in others but would mediate to them insofar as they are capable of it? Would the kingdom have come quite "quickly" in full glory if the message of Jesus had not been rejected? Did he in any case "have" to preach on that hypothesis? Because of the condemnation, death and resurrection of Jesus, we have to say that this whole problem *by itself* is no longer an immediate and existentiell problem for us, and that consequently we cannot expect a final solution. Later we shall have to return to this question once again very briefly.

In any case Jesus' proclamation of that closeness of God's kingdom which is present for the first time with him as the situation of our decision is also true for us (in spite of our uncertain calculation of a lengthy history of mankind still ahead) insofar as, first, through his death and his resurrection a situation for decision is present which, with respect to the *irreversibility* of God's offer of salvation, was not present before, although the whole of history was already directed towards it in a hidden way and in a hope against all hope; and secondly, insofar as this situation of salvation is always of very short duration for the individual person, who can never lose himself in the crowd of all mankind.

THE CONNECTION BETWEEN THE MESSAGE AND THE PERSON OF JESUS

The closeness of God's kingdom, which did not always exist but does "now" and in a new presence as the victorious situation of man's salvation, a situation of radical conversion or *metanoia*, is for the pre-resurrection Jesus already inseparably connected with his person. This thesis can be gathered historically from the sources, at least with regard to the behavior of the synoptic Jesus, taking into account and applying all of the principles and methods (especially of form criticism and redaction criticism), and also taking into account a theology of community. This is possible and would have to be shown in detail by exegetes, especially by pointing out that Jesus made the decision at the last judgment dependent on a decision vis-à-vis his own person. Christian exegesis is in agreement about this today, although non-Christian exegesis either denies it or explains it as a personal error of the earthly Jesus. The only presupposition of this thesis is that one does not maintain a priori that Jesus *could not* have asserted such an identity of the imminent coming of God's kingdom with his proclamation and his person, and makes allowance for the fact that for the later community to ascribe this function to Jesus is even more difficult to explain.

If the objection is made that the resurrection experience of the community explains this connection, then we would have to ask the counter-question: Why then would the experience that a person merely was still alive after his death allow someone to ascribe to him a function which the person himself never claimed for himself? But it is evident that the "resurrection" was understood as the victory and the divine vindication of a claim which seemed to have been radically disavowed in death. But what claim? The claim merely of one of the prophets and religious reformers by whom the content of the message was indeed proclaimed, but precisely as completely independent of the preacher himself? But in that case, since the validity of the message is already presupposed, and since they were familiar enough with the fate of prophets which ended in death, and did not have to doubt the claim of the message itself on that account, it is impossible to see a reason for ascribing precisely to *this* one prophet a victory in death if his message were independent of his person. These reflections, however, are not supposed to take the place of the historical proof of the thesis, but only to clarify the context within which the proof has to be evaluated.

We have to explain the sense and the scope of this thesis somewhat further. We have spoken of an inseparable connection between the closeness of God's kingdom preached by Jesus as *new* and his "person." But taking into account what was said above concerning Jesus' message about the kingdom, we can formulate the thesis more cautiously at first: the pre-resurrection Jesus thought that this new closeness of the kingdom came to be *in and through* the totality of what he said and what he did. This gives us a twofold advantage.

First, it is easier to understand how Jesus could identify the kingdom of God with himself before there was a place in this theology (of his) for his death and his resurrection. And, secondly, it is easier to understand why the focus and the center of his preaching was this kingdom of God and not directly himself. It has to be added immediately that with this closeness of God's kingdom, which Jesus proclaimed as new and as not yet present until then, we are not dealing with a merely relatively greater closeness than before, which could again be surpassed by a still greater closeness and urgency in God's call, and hence could be replaced. This understanding, which would correspond to that of any prophet who always knows, or would have to know at least in principle from his basic understanding of God, that he will be succeeded by another prophet who speaks a new and different word of God—this understanding becomes impossible just by the fact of Jesus' imminent expectation. He is the final call of God, and after him no other follows or *can* follow because of the radical nature in which God, no longer represented by something else, promises *himself*.

But this thesis, as formulated in this more cautious way, is anything but something to be taken for granted. For how and why is the presence of what is proclaimed dependent on its proclamation? Is it because otherwise nothing is known about what is proclaimed, and hence it cannot become effective because the unknown cannot be accepted in freedom? But if this is the answer, we would have to explain why then without precisely *this* proclamation nothing would be known about what is proclaimed. And further: What should this new and unsurpassable closeness of the coming of God's kingdom consist in if indeed it would not be known without the proclamation of Jesus, but nevertheless it would in itself be present independently of his proclamation? How would it be made intelligible in the religious experience of Jesus that he knew of a new closeness in the coming of God's kingdom if he informs people who simply do not know, and tells them something which indeed did not always exist prior to this proclamation, but which in itself would still have taken place independently of it? But where, when and how is this experienced by Jesus himself? If one makes this presupposition that the proclamation of Jesus was necessary because of otherwise unanswerable questions, and if on this supposition of a merely gnoseological necessity for Jesus' proclamation of the kingdom one reflects honestly and soberly, then one has to say that he proclaimed nothing really "new," but only proclaimed the old anew, although in a prophetic and radical way. And in fact his "originality" is doubted in a variety of ways.

Hence nothing is left but to say: Jesus experienced a relationship to God which he experienced as new and unique in comparison with other men, but which he nevertheless considered to be exemplary for other men in their relationship to God. He experienced his new and unique "relationship of sonship" to the "Father" as significant for all men by the fact that in this relationship God's closeness to all men has now come to be in a new and irrevocable way. In his unique and yet for us exemplary relationship to God, the pre-resurrection Jesus can experience the new coming of God's kingdom as grounded in his person, and hence he can know that this coming is inseparably connected with his proclamation precisely as *his* proclamation.

This does not deny that all of this becomes ultimate and radical both in itself and for us only through his death and his resurrection. But it becomes intelligible how Jesus could already have known and experienced himself as the absolute saviour before the resurrection, although this self-interpretation becomes ultimately credible for us through the resurrection, and is thereby also revealed for the first time in its ultimate depths. Jesus experiences in himself that radical and victorious offer of God to him which did not exist before in this way among "sinners," and he knows that it is significant, valid and irrevocable for *all* men. According to his own self-understanding he is already before the resurrection the one sent, the one who inaugurates the kingdom of God through what he says and what he does in a way that it did not exist before, but now does exist *through* him and *in* him. At least in this sense the pre-resurrection Jesus already knew himself to be the absolute and unsurpassable saviour.

e) The Relationship Of The Pre-Resurrection Jesus To His Death

The pre-resurrection Jesus went to meet his death freely and, on the level of his explicit consciousness, deemed it at least the fate of a prophet. In his eyes this fate did not disavow his message or himself, although it brought him to experience them in an inconceivably new and unforeseen way. Rather this fate remained hidden in the intention of God which Jesus knew to be a forgiving closeness to the world. This would have to be established historically in more detail, or shown to be something which is to be taken for granted from the nature of the events. If one maintains this as a minimal historical assertion, we can leave open here the historical question whether the pre-resurrection Jesus himself already interpreted his death explicitly as an "expiatory sacrifice" for the world; or whether he saw it as a necessary act of obedience demanded by the will of the Father in the sense of the "death of a just man"; or whether such an interpretation is post-resurrection and correct theology; or whether these alternatives are too clumsy and too simple to begin with.

From the viewpoint of fundamental theology this minimal assertion is sufficient. For, in the first place, by freely accepting the fate of death Jesus surrenders himself precisely to the unforeseen and incalculable possibilities of his existence; and, secondly, Jesus maintains in death his unique claim of an identity between his message and his person in the hope that in this death he will be vindicated by God with regard to his claim. But this means that his death is an atonement for the sins of the world and was adequately consummated as such. This presupposes that the Pauline doctrine of redemption is understood as a legitimate but secondary interpretation of the fact that in the death and resurrection of Jesus God's salvific will reaches its historical manifestation as victorious and irreversible, and thereby is itself definitively present in the world. Hence this presupposes, in other words, that this "expiatory sacrifice" itself is interpreted in a theologically correct way and is not misinterpreted as "changing the mind" of an angry God.

f) Miracles In The Life Of Jesus And Their Weight In Fundamental Theology

QUESTIONS ON THE IMPORTANCE OF THE MIRACLES OF JESUS
FOR OUR RELATIONSHIP TO HIM IN FAITH

Mighty deeds, signs and wonders are reported to us in the gospel accounts of the life of Jesus. We can presuppose here that historical criticism cannot simply eliminate these mighty deeds of Jesus as a whole from the life of Jesus as later fictions. Jesus was a miracle-worker to some degree and extent, and he perceived in his deeds a sign of the fact that a new closeness of the kingdom of God had come through him.

But the question for us is this: What importance do these "miracles" have for *our* faith relationship to Jesus as the absolute saviour? This can be broken down more exactly into the following specific questions:

First, what is left of these miracles as far as historical facts go if in historical criticism we have to reckon with the fact that the gospel accounts have "embellished" these mighty deeds of Jesus somewhat, although some historical basis is not to be doubted?

Secondly, how are we to interpret more exactly what is then still left, since, for example, sudden cures of the sick do not have to be interpreted immediately and automatically as miracles worked directly by God himself in the sense of classical fundamental theology.

Thirdly, on the supposition that the first two questions are answered or not answered, and prescinding from the resurrection, is it absolutely required of a Catholic fundamental theology to assign to the miracles within the life of Jesus an indispensable function in making the claim of Jesus before the tribunal of conscience and truth legitimate *for us today?*

A Catholic fundamental theology has to respect the First Vatican Council and cannot simply be satisfied with a sweeping dismissal of these questions. Hence we shall have to treat them somewhat more extensively.

OFFICIAL CHURCH TEACHING
AND THE CONTEMPORARY HORIZON OF UNDERSTANDING

If we answer first of all with the tradition of the church, and especially with the fundamental theology of the nineteenth and twentieth centuries and the teaching of Vatican I, we have to say that the claim of Jesus upon our faith in him as the Messiah and as the definitive inbreaking of God's kingdom is made legitimate by his miracles and his resurrection. This is the answer of Vatican I (cf. *D.S.* 3009). If it also refers to prophecies besides this, we do not have to maintain this differentiation in its own right here. Even in view of this, we can say that, however little this traditional teaching prescinds from the miracles within the life of Jesus, it still does not oblige us strictly to regard these miracles by themselves and without the resurrection as a cogent justification of Jesus' claim, and indeed cogent for us today. To the extent that this official church teaching is binding, it refers globally to the miracles of Jesus, and hence includes his resurrection. It does not prevent us from making distinctions within this whole with respect to the importance in fundamental theology of the individual elements within the whole.

This assertion of traditional Catholic fundamental theology, and of the Christian and Catholic self-understanding and self-interpretation of faith, raises of course a host of problems and, as has to be faced honestly, more than *one* stumbling block for people today. These people, and this includes ourselves, certainly do not automatically find it easy to understand the resurrection of Jesus as a *ground* of faith even when they are ready to recognize the resurrection as an *object* of faith. Even as an object of faith, it might still appear to them as a desperately courageous risk of their faith. We shall treat this more extensively in the next section.

But with regard to the miracles in general which are reported in the life of Jesus, however religious people today are personally and however much human respect they have for religious realities and for the belief in miracles in other people and in other times, including right down into our own time, still they can readily think that they do not quite understand what a miracle is really supposed to be. They could regard something like this only as a piece of mythology which, with the best will in the world, no longer fits into the rational and technical world which is now our world. Perhaps they could not really conceive of a God who would have to work with miracles in order to save man. They could have no choice but to doubt the historical verifiability of miracles in the life of Jesus, or to explain them somehow or other in such a way that for them they do not necessarily have to be understood as the direct and mighty deeds of God himself which interrupt all the laws of nature. They will say further that they are surprised that they are expected to find it probable that there should have been more miracles in earlier times than they discover within the scope of their own lives and within the realm of experience of contemporary times.

Moreover, it is a theological problem how the miracles in the life of Jesus are related to *the* miracle in an absolute sense, namely, to his resurrection. For it is obvious that in the New Testament's understanding the miracles within the pre-resurrection life of Jesus and the miracle of the resurrection are not simply juxtaposed extrinsically. Rather, the resurrection of Jesus occupied without a doubt a unique place in the apostolic foundations of the faith in the original community, and it was not aligned with the rest of the miracles of the historical Jesus. It seems that these miracles, which are reported very naturally in the life of Jesus, appear nevertheless in the apostolic preaching only on the periphery. They are not really used as an argument in apologetics and in "fundamental theology," but rather are narrated in the portrayal of a concrete picture of Jesus and his life.

ON THE GENERAL NOTION OF MIRACLE

Let us try first of all to say something about the general notion of miracle, although in doing so it will turn out that the universality of a homogeneous or univocal concept of miracle can only be maintained with very many reservations and qualifications.

First of all, it is very clear in the New Testament to begin with that these miracles in the life of Jesus may not be seen as miraculous demonstrations which are *totally* extrinsic to the reality which they are supposed to give witness to and make legitimate. It is not the case that basically every miracle, just so long as it carries with it its own divine origin, can give witness to every truth or reality, just so long as this reality exists and the miracle-working God adds this miracle to it. A miracle in the New Testament is a *semeion,* a sign, that is, the manifestation of God's salvific activity in grace and in revelation. The "sign" is an intrinsic element in the salvific act itself and belongs to this salvific act of God. It is its manifestation in historical tangibility, the outermost layer as it were in which the revelatory and salvific act of God reaches into the dimension of our corporeal experience. Consequently, such a "sign" in its own nature and structure is essentially and necessarily dependent on and conditioned by the respective nature of that which is to be disclosed by the "miracle." And since this is not always the same thing, this also allows the miracle in a real history of salvation to become quite different in each instance insofar as the structure of the miracle also participates in the historical process of the history of salvation and revelation as such.

Therefore by the very nature of a miracle, and this is also attested to in the New Testament, it is to be expected a priori that if there are miracles, they are not simply and always of the same kind. Basically this can also be readily said of their frequency. Hence miracles do not only have an inner variability, but also and by their very nature they are "miracles" in the first instance for *a definite addressee,* and this is very important. They are not *facta bruta* but an address to a knowing subject in a quite definite historical situation. Miracles which just happened, but which did not intend to say anything to anyone, and in which God would, as it were, merely correct the objective course of the world, are an absurd notion to begin with.

MIRACLES AND THE LAWS OF NATURE

From this perspective it can perhaps also be said that the notion of miracle as an occasional suspension of the laws of nature by God is extremely problematical. Insofar as God is different from the finite world and has omnipotent freedom over the world, the notion of miracle as an interruption of the laws of nature can be valid. If with the formula that in miracles God suspends the laws of nature in a particular instance one intends to state nothing else but the fact, which certainly belongs to the Christian concept of God, that God exists in sovereign freedom, omnipotence, and domination vis-à-vis this world and in *this* sense is not bound by the laws of nature, then it can indeed be said: miracles are something like an interruption of the laws of nature.

But if in this way some sense might be found in this traditional formula about the nature of miracles, this still does not yet justify this meaning of the concept, nor does it show that it can be used in grounding the knowability of miracles as signs, as the manifestation of God's salvific activity in the dimension of our earthly experience. This follows just from the fact that, according to the experience of the New Testament and of the church, perhaps most miracles which occur in the actual history of salvation and revelation as signs which ground faith can never or extremely rarely be shown certainly and positively to be a suspension of the laws of nature, even when they are shown to have really taken place historically. We are still prescinding here from the resurrection of Jesus because ontologically it is an instance which is *sui generis*.

There are different things which have to be considered in order to see why and how we can, if not dispute, at least do without the notion of a suspension of the laws of nature without thereby denying or endangering a correct understanding of the reality of miracles or their sign function in grounding faith. First of all, for our modern experience and interpretation of the world, every stratum, every dimension, of reality is constructed from the lower to the higher, that is, from the more empty and indetermined to the more complex and full, and it is open for the higher dimension. The higher dimension implies in its own reality the lower dimension as an element of itself, and subsumes it into itself in the Hegelian sense, both preserving it and surpassing it. It does not therefore violate the laws of the lower dimension, no more than the higher can be understood only as the more complex instance of the lower and be explained by it. The specific nature, the radical irreducibility and the essential novelty of man vis-à-vis merely biological, physical and chemical nature do not imply that, insofar as man in his reality subsumes into himself the material, the chemical, the physical and the animal-psychological, he must for this reason alter this reality in its own structure. We can say rather that the dimension of the material and biological is subsumed into freedom without having to be altered in its own structures, because it is open to begin with to this higher sphere and is multivalent.

Therefore the world of the material and the biological, as an intrinsic element of historical spirit, can become the manifestation of it. By its own intrinsic nature, and because of its indetermination and further determinability, the lower material and biological world can be integrated into the higher order without losing its own laws and structure because of this integration. In the actualizations of his corporeal spirit, for example, man is never merely an animal, but in what takes place in his corporeal spirit (which can never be broken down completely into what is merely spiritual and what is only biological and material) the laws of biochemistry or of general biology or of animal behavior in a merely negative sense do not therefore have to be abolished or suspended. Vis-à-vis what is merely biological, the miraculous (that is, the fact that the meaning of man's corporeal spirit cannot be derived from the lower) is accomplished by man precisely by the fact that he takes the reality and the law of the merely biological into his service.

To this extent the "miraculous" is constituted by the fact that the higher order cannot be derived from the lower order in which the higher order comes to appearance. This appearance manifests the essence of the lower and of the higher order together, without the two aspects being able to be completely separated from each other. It requires a certain intuition and a certain trusting self-involvement in order to see the higher in the appearance of the lower, and in order to withstand the temptation to reduce the higher into the lower and to overlook the qualitative leap.

Now this relationship, which is all-pervasive in a world which is stratified and plural and yet forms a unity, also obtains between the dimension of man's "nature" as a reality which can be established objectively and expressed in the natural sciences, and the dimension of freedom and of the unique, of the creative and the unforeseeable. This relationship between two dimensions, of which the higher cannot be derived from the lower, and yet appears in it and expresses itself in it by its own means, obtains not only between the material and the biological spheres of man on the one hand, and the spiritual and personal in general and in the abstract on the other hand. It also obtains between this sphere of man's spiritual and personal historicity in general, and the sphere of the concrete, individual person in his freedom and his ever unique decisions. The ever unique situation of a person's decision must be able to manifest itself in the situation of the historical in general, of interpersonal experience. There it must be able to make its call to the individual person tangible. There it must be able to give a sign of the correctness of the decision which is always unique.

MIRACLES FROM THE PERSPECTIVE OF
THE RELATIONSHIP BETWEEN GOD AND WORLD

If we are introducing here a concept of miracle which legitimately reaches beyond the question of an interruption of the laws of nature, not because we are skeptics but because of the very nature of miracle, we are only bringing into play what we said about the actual relationship between God and his created world. God is not only someone who creates a world different from himself with its structures and laws and its own dynamism, and establishes it permanently outside of himself, its creative ground; in his free and supernatural self-communication God has also made himself the ultimate and highest dynamism of this world and its history. Consequently, the creation of the other has to be understood to begin with as a moment within this divine self-communication to the other, a moment which God's self-communication presupposes as the condition of its own possibility insofar as it constitutes in this world created *ex nihilo sui et subjecti* the addressee of this self-communication of God.

Now looked at from this perspective, the laws of nature as well as the general structures of the historical must be understood to begin with as the structures of this precondition which the free and personal self-communication of God creates as the condition of its own possibility. The law of nature and also of history must be regarded from this vantage point as an element within grace, that is, within God's self-communication, and hence also as an element within the history of revelation and salvation. From this perspective and hence precisely from a theological vantage point, and not merely because of a modern, rational skepticism, there is no reason why this presupposition would then have to be abolished and suspended if God's self-communication is to come to appearance in its own presupposition, the very presupposition which this very self-communication creates for itself, or, in other words, if a miracle is to appear as a sign of God's salvific act in a way which corresponds to this historical phase of God's self-communication.

In view of these reflections perhaps we may say: a miracle takes place in the theological sense, and precisely not in the sense of a preternatural marvel, when for the eyes of a spiritual person who is open to the mystery of God the concrete configuration of events is such that there participates immediately in this configuration the divine self-communication which he already experiences "instinctively" in his transcendental experience of grace, and which on the other hand comes to appearance precisely in the "miraculous," and in this way gives witness of its presence.

MIRACLE AS CALL

With regard to the relationship of such a manifestation to the reality in which and from out of which this manifestation is formed, the element of the extraordinary or of the "wonder-ful" may be very variable. This depends on the significance of that to which such a manifestation is calling and that for which it is to make a personal decision legitimate. It is sufficient if, measured by the total situation of the person in question, it performs the function of a call in such a way that this person in his situation is morally obliged to obey this sign. It can readily be the case, then, that the sign function of a particular manifestation is present for a particular person without it therefore also having to be valid for another person. Viewed in the abstract, an "answer to a prayer" does not have to go beyond physical or biological possibilities in a demonstrable way, but it can nevertheless have a sign function for a particular person in God's existentiell call.

We must always keep in mind that a miracle is not simply intended to be an event within a neutral world of things which would have to be equally accessible and meaningful for everyone. It is rather a call into the uniqueness of the concrete situation of a particular person. In functioning as a call, and this belongs to the very nature of a miracle, this function cannot always and in principle depend upon the fact that the "miracle" can be shown to be an interruption of the laws of nature or to go beyond every statistical probability. A sudden cure from sickness, for example, can in a concrete situation be an existentiell argument for God's existence or for his love, an argument which in the concrete is binding for the concrete person. This presupposes that the person does not think with absolute certitude prior to the miracle that he has to hold that there is no God. But if this person is convinced that he has to reckon with the fact that God does exist, that the course of the world does make sense, and that the structure of his own existence is meaningful, then in certain circumstances such a cure can imply a moral obligation to act in accordance with its meaning as a call. It is not the case that there would be no such demand until this cure is shown positively to be an interruption of the laws of nature. If a person did not act this way in a case like this, he would not be making his decision from out of the totality of the concrete situation of his existence.

When we regard miracles in this way as an event which can be encountered within the range of our human experience, we are presupposing with regard to the nature of a miracle as sign that a person is inwardly open to the fact that his existence is ultimately not at his own disposal, and that he has the capacity to perceive the concrete meaning of his existence. This latter can never be completely reduced to universal laws, but retains its claim to meaning and the question of its meaning even when, measured by universal laws, "everything comes about naturally." The uniqueness of spiritual and personal existence can never be understood completely as a function of the universal, although the concrete element of this existence does not by any means for this reason have to be situated absolutely beyond the realm of universal laws and appear as an interruption of these universal laws.

A miracle, therefore, presupposes a person who is willing to allow himself to be called in the depths of his existence, who is free and open to the singularly wonder-ful in his life. This really does accompany the whole surveyable world of experience constantly, and at the same time goes beyond it: in that characteristic inner expansiveness and many-sided openness of man's spirit-filled nature by virtue of which he has a basic receptiveness for what is beyond the world of his experience, for intimacy with God. Of course he has to continually open himself anew to this intimacy by breaking through all of the ossifications and entrapments of the world and simply giving free rein to the original expansiveness of his being. This he does by a willingness to believe and by having ears for God, and by an honest affirmation of his finite existence which makes him conscious of the ultimate ambiguity and ambivalence of the horizons which are within his control. This keeps alive in him that humble and receptive wonder in which he accepts the events of the world of his experience in its concreteness. If he scrutinizes them responsibly, they offer themselves as a call, and he knows that he is empowered and obligated by them to an historical dialogue with God. Holy Scripture is also familiar with this fundamental willingness in man to believe as a presupposition for the experience of a miracle, for Jesus always says: "Your faith has made you whole."

The natural scientist does not need to have this openness to the "wonderful" as a scientist. In his method he has the right to explain everything, that is, to want to understand everything as the consequence of universal laws. As a scientist, therefore, he can ignore what he cannot explain positively as something not yet explained, or as something of no interest to him as a scientist. The only presupposition for all of this is that in his methological abstinence the natural scientist is conscious of the fact that this method of his is an a priori delimitation vis-à-vis the total horizon and the total structure of his ever unique existentiell existence, and that he is conscious of the fact that he can never be *just* a natural scientist. For in the actualization of his existence he has already gone beyond this a priori methodological limitation, and as a moral agent he can never make decisions *only* according to the laws of the exact sciences by themselves.

THE VARIOUS MIRACLES OF JESUS
AND THE UNIQUE MIRACLE OF HIS RESURRECTION

From these general considerations about the nature and function of miracles, about the presuppositions that enable them to be experienced, and about their character as a call, it is clear that in our discussion of the legitimacy of Jesus' claim the question about the miracles in his life is from the outset a question about the sign and wonder character of the event of the reality and of the life of Jesus *as a whole*. But this means for us in the concrete that we have to ask about the resurrection of Jesus because, if it is credible, then of course it is *the* miracle in the life of Jesus in which the real significance of this life coalesces in radical unity and becomes manifest for us. In saying this we are not denying the importance of the miracles which Jesus worked in his earthly life, although it does have to be said that as categorical, individual miracles they are further removed from us. They were calls for those who experienced them immediately within the totality of their existentiell situation which, in relation to these individual miracles, is not our situation.

Because the individual miracles in the life of Jesus are further removed from us in their importance and in their ability to be known than is the resurrection, since the resurrection speaks to us immediately because of its character as an answer to the question about the meaning of everything, we do not have to go into the individual miracles in the life of Jesus here. We can only say that these miracles as a whole cannot be eliminated historically from the life of Jesus because they are presupposed by sayings of Jesus which are beyond doubt; in addition, they are not denied, for example, even in the Talmudic sources.

We can limit ourselves, therefore, to the question of the resurrection of Jesus and its historical credibility because this calls us in an essentially more radical way than the individual miracles in the life of Jesus. For in the resurrection there is the very closest identity between salvific sign and salvific reality, more so than in any other conceivable miracle, and it appeals to our hope for salvation and for resurrection, a hope which we have with transcendental necessity.

6. The Theology of the Death and the Resurrection of Jesus

a) Preliminary Remarks

In this section I do not intend to present the theology of the death and resurrection of Jesus which is already found and is explicitly developed in

Paul, John and the Letter to the Hebrews, nor that which is found in the official teaching of the church. Neither is treated thematically until the seventh section, and there both can be treated at the same time. It is true that there are differences among the New Testament Christologies and soteriologies, and between them and the new and conceptually different Christologies in the official teaching of the church. But the difference between the "late" New Testament Christology and soteriology (and by this I mean the theology of the New Testament authors, which includes explicit Logos theology, the doctrine of pre-existence, the Johannine "I" sayings, the explicit application of titles of exaltation, explicit soteriologies, and so on) and the Christology and soteriology in the official teaching of the church does not offer any greater difficulties or any difficulties of a different kind than does the difference between the earthly Jesus and his death and his resurrection in the consciousness of the first witnesses on the one hand, and these later New Testament Christologies on the other. This is especially true since the difference mentioned second is the more important difference.

Taken as a whole the mutual transpositions back and forth between the New Testament Christologies and soteriologies and the Christology in the official teaching of the church is not an especially difficult problem for us today, however long and complicated the history of the transposition of the "late" New Testament Christologies and soteriologies into the subsequent conciliar Christology was. The legitimacy of the "late" New Testament Christologies and soteriologies vis-à-vis the Jesus of history and the original experience of his person and his fate involves the same difficulty and urgency as is the case with regard to the conciliar Christology. Therefore we shall be concerned here in the first instance and prior to the later New Testament Christologies and soteriologies only with the question of the Christology which is found in the first experience of the disciples with the crucified and risen Jesus.

Our concern here is first of all to establish the intellectual presuppositions of the core of that original experience of Jesus as the Christ, and then the core of this original experience itself. This experience is the original, indeducible and first revelation of Christology which is then articulated and interpreted more reflexively in the "late" New Testament and in the official teaching of the church. To inquire in this way back behind the explicit New Testament Christology does not mean that in doing so we may not also allow ourselves to be guided by this developed Christology. One gets to know the blossom from the root *and* vice versa. The fact that such a return to the original revelation as an event and as a faith experience always and inevitably brings with it its own theological interpretation is not an objection against this procedure. For the circle between original experience and interpretation is not to be eliminated, but is to be recaptured as intelligibly as possible.

b) Intellectual Presuppositions For Discussing The Resurrection

THE UNITY OF THE DEATH AND RESURRECTION OF JESUS

The death and resurrection of Jesus can be understood only if the intrinsic relationship of the two realities and their unity are kept clearly in view. In this context the "temporal" interval between the two events is not indeed to be denied here insofar as it can make any sense at all given the non-temporal nature of what happens in the resurrection, but ultimately it is not important. The death of Jesus is such that by its very nature it is subsumed into the resurrection. It is a death into the resurrection. And the resurrection does not mean the beginning of a new period in the life of Jesus, a further extension of time filled with new and different things. It means rather and precisely the permanent, redeemed, final and definitive validity of the single and unique life of Jesus who achieved the permanent and final validity of his life precisely through his death in freedom and obedience. From this perspective, if the fate of Jesus has any soteriological significance at all, this significance can be situated neither in the death nor in the resurrection taken separately, but can only be illuminated now from the one and now from the other aspect of this single event.

THE MEANING OF "RESURRECTION"

We miss the meaning of "resurrection" in general and also of the resurrection of Jesus to begin with if our original preconception is the notion of a resuscitation of a physical, material body. The resurrection which is referred to in the resurrection of Jesus as distinguished from the resuscitation of the dead in the Old and New Testaments means the final and definitive salvation of a concrete human existence by God and in the presence of God, the abiding and real validity of human history, which neither moves further and further into emptiness, nor perishes altogether. In this respect death (and without death there is no final and definitive validity) is precisely the essential renunciation and the radical relinquishing of any imaginary model of the "how" of this finality, whether this model is related to the "body" or to the "spiritual soul" of this single human existence. An empty tomb as such and by itself can never testify to the meaning and to the existence of a resurrection. Although it is not necessarily to be disputed, we can prescind here from the question to which stratum in the tradition of the resurrection of Jesus the empty tomb belongs, and what significance it has in this tradition. Resurrection does not mean to begin with a salvifically neutral survival of human existence, but means its salvation and its acceptance by God. What the situation is of those whose final state is one of loss is another question which should not be settled cheaply by constructing a salvifically neutral concept of resurrection.

From this perspective it is also clear that person and cause ("cause" in the sense of that to which one is dedicated) may not be separated in the discussion of resurrection and in the interpretation of this term. The term "resurrection" has to be interpreted, and already is interpreted in the New Testament, because we must avoid the misunderstanding that resurrection is a return to life and existence in time and space as we experience it. For when it is misunderstood in this way, resurrection could not be the salvation which is in God's hands, incomprehensible and known only in hope. If it is not idealized ideologically, the real "cause" of a person is the thing which is actualized and realized in the concrete existence of the person. Hence it is the validity of the person himself in its abiding validity.

If someone wanted to say, therefore, that the resurrection of Jesus means that his "cause" did not end with his death, we would have to refer both positively and critically to what we just said in order to avoid an idealistic misunderstanding of this "cause" of Jesus. As a result of this misunderstanding, the survival of this cause would only be the validity and effectiveness of an "idea" which goes on generating itself. We would have to ask further how then on this account it would still be clear that at least during his life and in his self-interpretation the cause of Jesus would have been inseparably bound up with his person if *he* simply would have perished, as this account seems to suggest, and there would survive merely the cause which would no longer be truly *his*. This too should be emphasized: if the resurrection of Jesus is the permanent validity of his person and his cause, and if this person and cause together do not mean the survival of just any person and his history, but mean the *victoriousness* of his claim to be the absolute saviour, then *faith* in his resurrection is an intrinsic element of this resurrection itself. Faith is not taking cognizance of a fact which by its nature could exist just as well without being taken cognizance of. If the resurrection of Jesus is to be the eschatological victory of God's grace in the world, it cannot be understood without faith in it as something actually and freely arrived at, and it is only in this faith that its own essential being is fully realized.

In *this* sense we not only can but must say that Jesus is risen into the faith of his disciples. But this faith into which Jesus is risen is not really and directly faith in this resurrection, but is that faith which knows itself to be a divinely effected liberation from all the powers of finiteness, of guilt and of death, and knows itself to be empowered for this by the fact that this liberation has taken place in Jesus himself and has become manifest for us. We shall discuss this later, but if faith counts as our hope in our "resurrection," then faith believes in *this* resurrection primarily of Jesus himself, and does not substitute for his resurrection a faith for which there can no longer be specified any "content." This is true however much ultimately *fides qua* and *fides quae*, the act of faith and the content of faith, might be inseparably connected, and however much every act of faith as the absolute freedom of the subject which comes from God and tends towards God is already at least implicitly the content of faith in one's own resurrection. This is the point which we shall take up next.

c) Transcendental Hope In The Resurrection As The Horizon For Experiencing The Resurrection Of Jesus

SUMMARY THESIS

An act of hope in one's own resurrection is something which takes place in every person by transcendental necessity either in the mode of free acceptance or of free rejection. For every person wants to survive in some final and definitive sense, and experiences this claim in his acts of freedom and responsibility, whether he is able to make this implication of the exercise of his freedom thematic or not, and whether he accepts it in faith or rejects it in despair. Now "resurrection" is not an additional assertion about the fate of a secondary *part* of man, an assertion which could not be known in hope from a primordial understanding of man. Resurrection is rather the term which, in view of man's concrete situation, promises the abiding validity of his single and entire existence. Resurrection of the "flesh" which man *is* does not mean resurrection of the body which man *has* as a part of himself. If, then, a person affirms his existence as permanently valid and redeemable, and does not fall into the misunderstanding of a platonic anthropological dualism, then he is affirming his resurrection in hope.

It should not be objected that this presupposes a quite definite anthropology which too few people share in their actual self-understanding in order to be able to function so simply as the presupposition for asserting a transcendental hope in the resurrection. For we are not understanding man here in some special sense alongside other and not inconceivable senses, but we are taking man in a very "unphilosophical" sense as he is and as we find him in his *unity*. For belief in resurrection does not prejudice the more precise question *how* the "parts" and "elements" of man which are not explicitly distinguished will exist in his final state. It only forbids in a *negative* sense the exclusion of particular elements of man from the outset as of no consequence for his final state. It does not therefore determine in a positive sense anything more precisely about the nature of this final state for each of the individual "elements" taken by itself.

The assertion of a transcendental hope in resurrection does not deny that we are more successful in actually objectifying this self-understanding in the light of the experience of the resurrection of Jesus. The circle between transcendental and categorical experience is operative everywhere. This transcendental hope in resurrection is the horizon of understanding for experiencing the resurrection of Jesus in faith. For when it is not suppressed, this transcendental hope in resurrection necessarily seeks the historical mediation and confirmation in which it can become explicit. And it thereby acquires the precise characteristic of an *eschatological* hope which is aroused by a fulfilled hope. Basically, then, it can only be a question of whether this transcendental hope in resurrection is still simply *looking* in history to see whether it can encounter a risen one, or whether he "already" exists and as such can be experienced in faith. If this is the only legitimate alternative, and hence if what is appropriate for man is *either* the promise which is still simply outstanding, *or* life within a hope which has already experienced fulfillment, then he does not need to be skeptical and close himself to the witness of others that Jesus lives, that he is risen.

KNOWLEDGE OF ONE'S OWN DEATH

What was summarized briefly here might be explained somewhat further especially since, compared with its importance, we went into this topic only rather briefly in our earlier chapters on Christian anthropology.

Let us begin once again right at the forefront, that is, with ourselves, with as little philosophy as possible, and with the hope that what is said appeals to an experience in man which he does not escape even if he suppresses it, and even if words can express it only indirectly, very imprecisely and from a distance. Man faces his own death, and he knows this. As distinguished from the demise of an animal, this knowledge is itself a piece of his dying and of his death because it constitutes the precise difference between the death of a man and the demise of an animal, because only man exists always and inescapably confronted with his end, with the totality of his existence, with its temporal end. Only man possesses his existence unto this end. Hence the question can only be what this death, which is constantly staring us in the face, tells us about ourselves, what this existence unto death is really all about.

ANTHROPOLOGICAL REFLECTIONS ON DEATH
AND THE FINALITY OF EXISTENCE

Of course this death and this life unto death can be suppressed. One can explain that to be occupied with this end is an aberration which should not be yielded to. But even this explanation once again summons up the knowledge of death at least for the one who needs such an explanation. Hence the question is whether in death itself one is still someone for whom his life and his death are of some concern. The deceased is no longer the concern of the survivors as far as anything can be established "empirically" —this much is certain. The deceased is whisked out of the business which we are about. But what happens to someone who vanishes this way? "I" might allow myself to be spared this question with regard to others, but I cannot ignore it with regard to myself, for I know that I have to die. And if I do ignore something which so truly concerns me, I have already made my decision.

Perhaps it may not really be all that clear that in death "it's all over." For perhaps what is left over from the tragedy which we call human life is not just an overwhelming respect for the "law of the conservation of energy." For there certainly existed previously a metabolism which now might take other paths after medical death, and which is directed a little less unambiguously in the definite direction of maintaining the biological system. But a few other things also existed previously: a person with love, fidelity, pain, responsibility, freedom. By what right really does one maintain that everything is over? Why should it really be "over." Because we do not notice anything any more? This argument seems a little weak! All that really follows from it is that the deceased no longer exists for me, the survivor. But does he therefore no longer exist for himself? Does he have to exist for me? Would it be conceivable that he could have had his "reasons" to be transformed in such a way that what has come to be no longer plays a role among us?

If we look at this life of ours, it is of itself not of such a nature that one would like to go on forever here; of itself it strives towards a conclusion to its present mode of existence. Time becomes madness if it cannot reach fulfillment. To be able to go on forever would be the hell of empty meaninglessness. No moment would have any importance because one could postpone and put everything off until an empty later which will always be there. Nothing could ever elude anyone, and everything would thus proceed into the emptiness of absolute weightlessness. When someone has died, therefore, nothing could be more obvious. But when the deceased is gone, can his real self not continue to exist, transformed and transposed beyond physical time and space? For it always was more than the mere interplay of the "elementary particles" of physics and biochemistry. For it was love and fidelity, and perhaps also sheer ordinariness, and other similar things which come to be in time and space, but do not reach fulfillment there.

WHAT DO "AFTERLIFE" AND "ETERNITY" MEAN?

We may not understand the existence which arises out of death as a mere "continuation" in the characteristic dispersion and the indetermined openness of temporal existence, an openness which can be determined ever further, and thus is really empty. In this respect death marks an end for the whole person. Anyone who simply allows time to "continue" for man's soul beyond his death so that new time arises gets into insuperable difficulties both in the understanding and in the existentiell actualization of the true finality of man which takes place in death. But anyone who thinks that "with death everything is over" because man's time does not really continue, because time which once began must also end, and finally because a time which spins on endlessly in its empty course into something ever new which constantly annuls the old is really impossible and more terrible than hell, this person is thinking in the conceptual framework of our empirical temporality just as much as the person who has the soul "continue." In reality "eternity" comes to be in time as its own mature fruit. Eternity does not really come "beyond" the experienced time of our biological life in time and space and continue this time, but rather it subsumes time by being released from the time which *came to be* temporarily, and came to be so that the final and definitive could be done in freedom.

Eternity is not an incalculably long-lasting mode of pure time, but a mode of spirit and freedom which have been actualized in time, and therefore it can be grasped only from a correct understanding of spirit and freedom. Time which does not endure as the seedbed of spirit and freedom does not offer any eternity. But we get into difficulty because the final and time-conquering state of man's existence which has been actualized in spirit and in freedom has to be taken out of time, and yet in conceiving this final state we almost unwillingly think of it as an endless continuation. Just as in modern physics, we have to learn to think of eternity without imagining it, and in this sense demythologize it and say: through death there comes to be the final and definitive validity of man's existence which has been achieved and has come to maturity in freedom. It is what has come to be as the liberated, final validity of something which was once in time and which came to be as spirit and freedom in order to be. Cannot what we call our life, therefore, be a brief flash in a process in which there comes to be in freedom and responsibility something which is, and definitively is, because it is of value to be what it is? And this happens in such a way that becoming ceases when being begins, and we do not notice anything of it because we ourselves are still in the process of becoming.

Truly we cannot limit reality to something whose existence even the dullest and most superficial person has neither the desire nor the possibility of denying. Surely there is more. Just as there are scientific instruments to establish a "more" in reality in the sphere of the material world, so too without instruments, but not without the higher development of the spirit, there are experiences which grasp that eternity which does not extend as a temporal continuation "beyond" our life, but rather is imbedded in the time of freedom and responsibility as the realm where they come to be in time. In the temporal duration of life which is to end completely, eternity is actualizing itself towards its fulfillment. Anyone who has ever made a morally good decision in a matter of life and death, radically and uncompromisingly, so that absolutely nothing redounds to him from it except the presumed goodness of this decision, he has already experienced in this decision the eternity which we mean here. If he then reflects upon it afterwards and tries to transpose this original experience into theory, he might arrive at false interpretations and even go so far as to doubt or deny "eternal life." Perhaps he might even think that he can make an absolutely and radically free decision which profits him nothing only if he does not even hope for eternal life. Then of course he has not understood this eternal life as the finality and definitiveness of his freedom, but as a continuation in which he would be rewarded with something other than the free act of his whole existence.

If for a great variety of reasons a person is not able afterwards to interpret reflexively the experience of eternity which he has had in time and in his freedom, or if from an objective point of view he interprets it falsely, although perhaps existentielly and *in* his own act of freedom he interprets it correctly, this is indeed regrettable, because it brings with it the danger of evading such total moral decisions, but it changes nothing in the original experience itself.

THE EXPERIENCE OF IMMORTALITY: NATURE OR GRACE?

Now it is not necessary here to differentiate in reflection between what in this experience belongs to man's spiritual and immortal nature, and what is grace, that is, the presence of the eternal God which for the Christian interpretation of existence reaches its culmination in Jesus Christ, who was hung on a cross and there triumphed. In order that the reflections we just made might avoid the false appearance of a rationalistic proof for the "immortality of the soul," we can assume that the experience which we are appealing to here draws its power and its life from that supernatural self-communication of God in grace which gives the eternity-making act of moral freedom its ultimate and radical depths. But given the reciprocal, although variable, relationship of conditioning between the transcendental experience of grace and the experience of salvation history, it follows immediately that we have the right and the obligation at least to look and see whether this transcendental experience in grace of our eternal validity as moral persons has not become concrete and tangible in salvation history; whether it is not confirmed by the categorical experience of salvation history. Since we ourselves have still to die, this confirmation can be found of course only in the experience of the final and definitive fulfillment of another person.

From the perspective of a genuine anthropology of the concrete person, in this question we are neither justified nor obliged to split man into two "components" and to affirm this definitive validity only for one of them. Our question about man's definitive validity is completely identical with the question of his resurrection, whether the Greek and platonic tradition in church teaching sees this clearly or not. This presupposes, of course, that we do not understand this resurrection as a return to time and space as we know it. By definition the fulfillment of man neither is nor can be in time and space, because this world of time and space as such is the realm where personal freedom and responsibility come to be, but it is not the realm where this personal responsibility achieves final validity.

Looking at the matter this way we have to say: the transcendental experience of the expectation of one's own resurrection, an experience man can reach by his very essence, is the horizon of understanding within which and within which alone something like a resurrection of Jesus can be expected and experienced at all. These two elements of our existence, of course, the transcendental experience of the expectation of one's own resurrection, and the experience in faith of the resurrection of Jesus in salvation history, mutually condition each other. Except in view of the resurrection of Jesus, perhaps we would not in fact manage to interpret ourselves correctly in this experience of our own. But it is also true conversely that one can really experience the resurrection of Jesus only if he is a person who has already had this kind of experience himself.

d) On Understanding The Resurrection· Of Jesus

FAITH IN THE RESURRECTION OF JESUS AS A UNIQUE FACT

There is faith in the resurrection of Jesus, and this indeed is a unique fact. This in itself is worth thinking about. This uniqueness exists although there are enough people, including the murdered "prophets," whom we would like to experience as alive. Does not the reason for this uniqueness lie in the fact that the reason itself is unique and simple and thus "true," and hence that it is not that accidental combination of disparate experiences and reflections which represents the cause of errors? Anyone who denies the resurrection of Jesus (unless he has misunderstood it to begin with and then correctly rejects this misunderstanding) would have to ask himself this question—that is, he would have to answer the question why the error he is asserting does not occur more frequently, even though the causes it presupposes are continually present.

THE UNITY OF THE APOSTOLIC EXPERIENCE
OF THE RESURRECTION AND OUR OWN

From the New Testament on, Christian doctrinal tradition says correctly that with regard to faith in the resurrection of Jesus all of us are and remain dependent on the testimony of predetermined witnesses who "saw" the risen Lord, and that we could believe in the resurrection of Jesus only because of this apostolic witness and in dependence on it. Consequently, even the theology of mysticism, for example, denies to the mystics to whom Jesus "appears" the character of being resurrection witnesses, and denies to their visions any equality with the appearances of the risen Jesus to the apostles. All of this is correct and of decisive importance: our faith remains tied to the apostolic witness.

But for various reasons, however, this dependence would be interpreted falsely if we wanted to understand it after the secular model of other kinds of "faith" in an event at which one was not present himself, but which one accepts nevertheless because someone who assures him that he has experienced it seems to be "credible." For first of all and *on the one hand,* the weight of such secular testimony is essentially dependent on the extent to which the recipient of the testimony is in a position to evaluate the credibility of the witness from similar experiences which he had had himself. Hence if the testimony of the apostles about the resurrection were to be judged *only* according to the secular model of a witness's statement, it would have to be rejected as incredible, even if it could not be explained how it arose given the undeniable honesty and unselfishness of the witnesses. But the presupposition for employing this model in our question is not applicable. We ourselves do not stand simply and absolutely outside of the experience of the apostolic witnesses.

For secondly and *on the other hand,* and this is decisive here, we hear this witness of the apostles with that transcendental hope in resurrection which we have already discussed. Hence we do not learn something which is totally unexpected and which lies totally outside of the horizon of our experience and our possibilities of verification. Moreover, we hear the message of the resurrection which we believe with God's "grace" and with the interior witness of the experience of the Spirit. This statement is not tainted in the least with the suspicion of mythological theory. It means rather that we experience in faith and in the hope of our own resurrection the courage to stand beyond death, and indeed by gazing upon the risen Jesus who comes before us in the apostolic witness. And in this courage as freely exercised the risen Jesus himself gives witness that he is alive in the successful and inseparable correspondence between transcendental hope in resurrection and the categorical and real presence of such a resurrection. The two reinforce each other mutually in this circle and give witness to us of their truth.

It is not the case, then, that we have no contact at all with the reality to which witness is being given. We ourselves experience the resurrection of Jesus in the "Spirit" because we experience him and his "cause" as living and victorious. This statement does not make us independent of the apostolic witness to the resurrection, nor does it deny what was emphasized at the beginning of this section. For even if and *precisely* if we assume that there is a transcendental hope in resurrection and that this always seeks its categorical tangibility and testimony, this transcendental hope in resurrection can give to its ground and its object their categorical names only by means of the *apostolic* witnesses to *Jesus* as the risen one. And this assumption is offered to anyone who believes in the possibility of *Christian* salvation for *everyone* even if most people have not heard the explicit message of the gospel. The transcendental hope in resurrection can be mediated to itself categorically and in a Christian way only in and through the apostolic witness. But this very witness also includes the fact that there is this spirit-inspired hope in resurrection, and the credibility of the apostolic witnesses is supported by this experience in the Spirit of the invincibility of life, our life and the life of Jesus, just as conversely the transcendental experience becomes fully itself only in and through this witness. All of this can also be clarified in Paul by means of the relationship of *mutual* conditioning between the experience of the Spirit and faith in the resurrection. It could be clarified still further if the original unity and identity of structure between the process of revelation and the process of faith in the revelation could be presented in more detail than is possible here.

e) The Resurrection Experience Of The First Disciples

Presupposing what was said up to this point, we must now analyze the apostolic witness itself to show the credibility of this witness to the "resurrection" of Jesus. We can admit without any qualms that the reports which are presented to us at first glance as historical details of the event of the resurrection or of the appearances cannot be harmonized completely. Hence they are to be explained as secondary literary and dramatic embellishments of the original experience that "Jesus is alive," rather than as descriptions of the experience itself in its real and original nature. So far as the nature of this experience is assessible to us, it is to be explained after the manner of our experience of the powerful Spirit of the living Lord rather than in a way which either likens this experience too closely to mystical visions of an imaginative kind in later times, or understands it as an almost physical sense experience. There is no such sense experience of someone who has really reached fulfillment, even presupposing that he must indeed have freely "manifested" himself. For this manifestation to imply sense experience, everything would have to belong to the realm of normal and profane sense experience.

Beginning with the simple confessional formulas ("he is risen") and continuing on to the texts which dramatize the Easter experience under the most varied theological motifs, an analysis of the resurrection texts shows that they were conscious of the peculiar nature of the Easter experience: it is given from "without," not produced by oneself, and is different from the visionary experiences which were quite familiar. It is related very closely to the crucified Jesus with his quite definite individuality and fate, so that *this* is experienced as valid and redeemed, and not merely an existing person to whom this or that happened earlier. It is given only in faith and yet it grounds and justifies this faith. It is not to be expected indefinitely nor is it able to be reproduced, but is reserved to a definite phase in salvation history. Consequently, the witness necessarily has to be passed on to others, and hence it bestows a unique task on these witnesses. Witness is being given, then, to an experience which is strictly *sui generis* and is different from the experiences of religious enthusiasm or mysticism which can be stimulated and repeated. One can refuse to believe these witnesses. But one cannot do so by pretending that one understands their experience better, or because these witnesses have falsely interpreted a religious phenomenon which is familiar to us elsewhere.

It can be said that by "historical" means we would not reach the resurrection of Jesus, but only the conviction of his disciples that he is alive. If by historically accessible facts is understood something which in itself and in its own existence belongs to the realm of our normal, empirical world of time and space as a phenomenon which occurs *frequently*, then it is obvious that the resurrection of Jesus neither can be nor intends to be a "historical" event. For otherwise it would not be the assumption of the fruit of our ongoing history into its final and definitive state. If someone says that all that is historically tangible is the subjective Easter experience of the disciples, he must not in any case understand by this just any arbitrary "experience," but exactly what the disciples describe, and he must distinguish this from what we are inclined to understand by it. And *then* he must ask us whether we still have a right to refuse to believe the disciples, even if this denial in our concrete situation would be in the concrete a rejection of our own transcendental hope in resurrection.

In abstract, conceptual theory, an affirmation of our hope in resurrection *and* a rejection of the apostolic experience of this resurrection in Jesus is logically conceivable. Consequently, there is disbelief in the resurrection of Jesus which does not entail guilt. Whether *for us today,* in view of a two-thousand-year history of faith and in the face of the testimony of the disciples, this is possible in the case of every individual is a question of decision which is directed to every individual who hears the message of the resurrection of Jesus today. If this message is rejected in such a way that this also denies in unacknowledged despair the transcendental hope in resurrection, whether this is admitted or not, then this rejection of a contingent event, which cannot be deduced a priori and therefore can easily be doubted, becomes a rejection which is an act against one's very own existence, whether one intends it to be or not, and whether one knows it reflexively or not.

This mutual interlocking of our own transcendental and unavoidable hope in resurrection and faith in the resurrection of Jesus should not of course blur the difference which obtains between the resurrection of Jesus and our hoped-for resurrection. According to the New Testament understanding of the resurrection of Jesus, his resurrection is distinguished from ours by the fact that by his resurrection Jesus was made "Lord" and "Messiah." This does not deny that because of God's already realized intention he was this from the beginning of his human existence on, but conversely this reached its historical fulfillment in reality and for us in his resurrection. Independently of the question whether the New Testament statements about the appearances of the risen Jesus can be harmonized, the conviction is common to the whole New Testament that the resurrection is the exaltation of Jesus and his enthronement as judge over the world or as Lord, and to this extent it is distinguished from our hoped-for resurrection. It should be noted in passing that there obtains here a difference similar to the one which we mentioned briefly earlier, namely, the difference between our own being graced with God's self-communication, which must also be asserted of Jesus, and the special relationship between God and Jesus which we call the hypostatic union.

It should be noted, finally, that according to the synoptics Jesus did not teach a belief in the resurrection of everyone as something new which had to be taught by him, but maintained it as something to be taken for granted against the liberal Sadducees. More than one hundred and fifty years before Jesus, during the Maccabeean troubles, this faith had achieved its victory in Israel and it was a general belief of the people at the time of Jesus. In this connection we do not have to pursue the question here to what extent this faith, especially with regard to the possible resurrection of one of the prophets, furnished a quite intelligible horizon of understanding for the disciples of Jesus and their experience of the risen Jesus. Nevertheless, the New Testament's general belief in a future and hoped-for resurrection for everyone seems to us to justify from this perspective too our insistence upon an intrinsic interlocking between a transcendental hope in resurrection for ourselves and faith in the resurrection of Jesus.

f) The Original Theology Of The Resurrection Of Jesus As The Starting Point Of All Christology

Bearing in mind once again the preliminary remarks we made at the beginning of this sixth section of chapter six, we must now articulate the "original" theology of the resurrection, that is, we must answer the question: What is really experienced, witnessed and believed with the resurrection of this Jesus? In doing so a knowledge "in faith" of the "metaphysical" divine sonship of this Jesus may not be already presupposed, so that the resurrection of Jesus would be at most the actual conclusion of his life, and from God's side the extrinsic confirmation of his self-understanding for fundamental theology. And this self-understanding would have already contained more or less explicitly and clearly this metaphysical divine sonship before Easter. We may not proceed in this way here especially because according to the New Testament the experienced resurrection contributed to the *content* of the interpretation of the essence of the person and the work of Jesus, and was not merely the divine confirmation of a knowledge already clearly expressed by Jesus before the resurrection.

THE VINDICATION AND
ACCEPTANCE OF JESUS' CLAIM TO BE THE ABSOLUTE SAVIOUR

This Jesus with his *concrete* claim and his history is experienced in the resurrection experience as of permanent validity and as accepted by God. What real claim inseparable from himself is thereby experienced as valid? The claim which he made during his life. We have established this claim historically perhaps much too minimalistically. But what we reached is enough: the claim that there is present with him a new and unsurpassable closeness of God which on its part will prevail victoriously and is inseparable from him. He calls this closeness the coming and the arrival of God's kingdom, which forces a person to decide explicitly whether or not he accepts this God who has come so close.

By the resurrection, then, Jesus is vindicated as the absolute saviour. We can also say more cautiously at first: as the *final* "prophet." For on the one hand the self-interpretation of Jesus in his message which was vindicated by the resurrection makes him a "prophet," that is, one who brings a word of God to concrete historical existence over and beyond all "eternal truths," and calls one to a decision. But this prophet holds that his word is final and unsurpassable. This stands first of all in contradiction to the self-understanding of every other genuine prophet, a self-understanding either explicitly present or to be assumed with the genuineness of a prophetic call from a God who is free. In his word a genuine prophet must allow God in his unlimited possibilities to be greater, and he speaks his word to a definite situation which presently exists, but then gives way to a new and different situation. He must experience and proclaim his word essentially as a promise reaching out into an open and unlimited horizon. Hence Jesus is a prophet who surpasses and subsumes the essence of a prophet with the claim of his word. We must bear in mind here that his word as God's final word can be understood to be definitive not because God now ceases arbitrarily to say anything further, although he could have said more, and not because he "concludes" revelation, although he could have continued it had he just wanted to. It is the final word of God that is present in Jesus because there is nothing to say beyond it, because God has really and in a strict sense offered *himself* in Jesus.

It is only from this perspective that the religious radicalism of Jesus becomes intelligible: he abolishes religious and moral categories such as those touching family, marriage, nation, the law, the temple, the sabbath and the origins of religious authority, not out of mere fanaticism because of their inadequacies, which is always possible. Rather he is constantly breaking through them and subsuming them because they have now *been broken through* by a new and real immediacy of God coming from God himself. Consequently, they no longer have that precise function of mediating and representing God which they once correctly claimed to have.

Jesus, then, is the historical presence of this final and unsurpassable word of God's self-disclosure: this is his claim and he is vindicated in this claim by the resurrection. He is of eternal validity and he is experienced in this eternal validity. In this sense in any case he is the "absolute saviour."

THE POINT OF DEPARTURE FOR "LATE" NEW TESTAMENT CHRISTOLOGY

It is this about him that late New Testament theology and the Christology of the church want to express. He is *the* Son and *the* Word of God first of all in a sense which is still prior to the notion of a pre-existent Logos and Son, in a sense which can and must be predicated of his *human* reality because this has been assumed by God as *his* expression. This does not subscribe to the adoptionism or double sonship which were rejected in classical Christology. For he is not a "servant" in the ongoing line of prophets with their ever provisional mandate which may never be identified with God himself however much it *comes* from God. Hence he is "Son." He does not bring *a* word from God which can and must be replaced because God in his own self has not yet given himself totally and definitively in it. Hence he is *the* Word of God which is spoken to us in everything which he was and said, and which as this final word was definitively accepted and confirmed in the resurrection.

One might express the uniqueness of the relationship between God and Jesus as he wants. The classical Christology of the church is *one* such way, perhaps the clearest and the easiest to ascertain for the churches in common, and it is also true in what it intends to say and does say. However, and we shall discuss this more extensively later, it is not to be regarded a priori as the only possible way. For on the one hand it does not exhaust the mystery, and hence other statements can be added to it at least by way of supplement, and these are not necessarily merely a development of its formulas. On the other hand, moreover, the dialectic between the individual statements within it can move it from within towards further historical development. Besides this there is the fact that already in the New Testament we find many and perhaps rudimentary Christologies which are not simply and only verbal variations of one and the same basic model, a model in which the faith conviction is brought home that the concrete risen Jesus with his claim is the presence in our midst of the unique and unsurpassable existence of God *himself*. Hence there might be different conceptual models, terminologies and points of departure for expressing the faith experience of the risen Jesus along with his unique claim. The presupposition for all Christologies is always that this uniqueness is preserved and remains clear, and that this unique relationship is understood as a relationship between God and him in his reality and in his real history, and not merely in his spoken "word," because it is in *this* that he was accepted and remains valid.

This gives us a point of departure, and we intend nothing more than this here, for a Christology developed from the perspective of the unity between the historically tangible claim of Jesus and the experience of his resurrection. It is a point of departure for the kind of "ascending Christology" which is *still* tangible in many places in the New Testament. It begins with the historical Jesus not only insofar as it hears a "Son-Logos descending Christology" expressed on his lips, and in his resurrection professes it in faith, but it also has an experience of this redeemed man along with his claim *upon us*, and here it experiences what the classical Christology expresses in a metaphysical and objective way. This point of departure resolves from the outset the dilemma between a "functional" and an "essential" Christology by showing it to be a pseudo-problem. It also opens our ears to a solution to the problem of verification in Christology because it is in fact a unity, and one successfully experienced as such, between a transcendental experience, that is, transcendental Christology and the transcendental hope in resurrection, and the historical experience which corresponds to it.

g) On The Theology Of The Death Of Jesus From The Perspective Of The Resurrection

THE INTERPRETATION OF THE DEATH OF JESUS AS CAUSE OF SALVATION

At least in the "late" New Testament soteriological Christology a redemptive significance is acknowledged for the death of Jesus: it blots out our sinfulness before God and establishes a salvific relationship between God and man. It cannot be said that according to the New Testament as a whole the death of Jesus merely convinces us of a forgiving and salvific will of God which is absolutely independent of this death. The death of Jesus is obviously regarded as a cause of our salvation in a true sense, but in what precise sense? This causality is presented among other ways as that of a sacrifice of his blood which is offered to God, the blood which is poured out for us or for "the many," and so on.

We can say on the one hand that in the New Testament milieu such expressions were a help towards understanding the salvific significance of the death of Jesus, because at that time the idea of propitiating the divinity by means of a sacrifice was a current notion which could be presupposed to be valid. But on the other hand we have to say, first of all, that this notion offers little help to us today towards the understanding we are looking for, and, secondly, that the connection between the idea of the death of Jesus as a sacrifice of propitiation and the basic experience of the pre-resurrection Jesus and of the risen Jesus is not immediately clear.

On the first point we have to say that the general idea of sacrifice in the history of religions cannot easily be shown to be tenable without some verbal subterfuge if we maintain clearly that God's mind cannot be "changed," that in salvation all the initiatives proceed from God himself (and the New Testament is aware of this too), and finally that all real salvation can only be understood as taking place in the exercise of each individual's freedom. If someone objects that this "sacrifice" is to be understood as a free act of obedience on Jesus' part (and this according to the New Testament too since it "desacralizes" his sacrifice this way); that by God's own free initiative through which he makes this act of obedience possible, God gives the world the possibility of making satisfaction to the just holiness of God; and that the grace given in view of Christ is precisely the condition for saving oneself by appropriating God's salvation freely, perhaps this is all correct. But he has not only explained the notion of an expiatory sacrifice; he has also criticized it.

For in this explanation it is precisely a God who loves the sinner originally and without reasons who is the cause of his reconciliation. Hence God is reconciled as one reconciled by himself, and it is as reconciled in this way that he obviously wills on his own initiative one and the same grace which both establishes Christ *and* gives us the possibility of freely turning to God. Then the only question which would arise and which has not yet been answered is how the connection (and there is no doubt that there is one) between the death of Christ as God's grace and our freedom as liberated by grace is to be understood more exactly. For then we can answer more clearly the question about the salvific efficacy of Jesus' death for us.

On the second point we have to say that it is not established historically beyond dispute whether the pre-resurrection Jesus himself already interpreted his death as an expiatory sacrifice, and did this in the context of the servant of God suffering in expiation in Deutero-Isaiah, and of the just man suffering innocently and in expiation in late Jewish theology. Besides, if after some hesitation this question is to be given an affirmative answer, it is still not clear what exactly this is supposed to mean.

Finally, going beyond the two points just mentioned, the question has to be asked whether we can try to acquire from the resurrection of Jesus an adequate understanding of the salvific significance of his death, an understanding which clarifies the meaning as well as the limits of the soteriological statements about the death of Jesus which we find perhaps on the lips of Jesus, and certainly in later New Testament soteriology.

THE FOUNDATION OF
THE SOTERIOLOGICAL INTERPRETATION OF THE DEATH OF JESUS

It may perhaps be presupposed from the mentality of the Old and New Testament scriptures, as well as from man's self-understanding in general, that human history is a *single* history, and that the destiny of one person has significance for others, however the unity of this history and the solidarity of mankind might be explained further and in more detail. If, then, God wills and brings forth a man who in his reality, and this includes his words too, is God's final, irrevocable and unsurpassable word and offer to mankind, and if this is grasped in history itself and not merely in transcendental hope; if this offer is and can be final only if it prevails victoriously, and hence exists as accepted at least and in the first instance in this man; if this acceptance can only take place in and through the single history of the single and entire life of this man, a history which becomes final and definitive through death; and if therefore besides this God's word and offer is complete only if man's acceptance and response to it becomes manifest historically as accepted by God and as in God's presence in what we call "resurrection," *then* we can and must say that this eschatological word and offer of God arises from his own free initiative, has been really actualized in the life of Jesus and is historically present for us, and reaches fulfillment in his free acceptance of his death. This death *as* entered into in free obedience and *as* surrendering life completely to God reaches fulfillment and becomes historically tangible for us only in the resurrection.

The pure initiative of God's salvific will establishes the life of Jesus which reaches fulfillment in his death, and hence this salvific will becomes real and becomes manifest as irrevocable. The life and death of Jesus taken together, then, are the "cause" of God's salvific will (to the extent that these two things are regarded as different) insofar as this salvific will establishes itself really and irrevocably in this life and death, in other words, insofar as the life and death of Jesus, or the death which recapitulates and culminates his life, possess a causality of a quasi-sacramental and real-symbolic nature. In this causality what is signified, in this case God's salvific will, posits the sign, in this case the death of Jesus along with his resurrection, and in and through the sign it causes what is signified.

If the death of Jesus is understood this way, then perhaps it becomes clear that its soteriological significance when correctly understood is already implied in the experience of the resurrection of Jesus, and moreover that the "late" soteriology in the New Testament when correctly understood is a legitimate, but nevertheless somewhat secondary and derivative expression of the salvific significance of the death of Jesus. This is so because it works with concepts which are applied extrinsically as a possible but not absolutely indispensable interpretation of the original experience of this salvific significance, which is simply this: we are saved because this man who is one of us has been saved by God, and God has thereby made his salvific will present in the world historically, really and irrevocably. On this point too there follows for the New Testament and for later theology, as its history shows, the possibility in principle of a variety of legitimate models for soteriology. This is true especially because its presuppositions (for example, the essential unity of history and the solidarity of all mankind) are indeed realized unthematically in the original experience of revelation, but they are not themselves made clearly thematic, and hence they can be interpreted in a variety of ways.

7. The Content, Permanent Validity and Limits of Classical Christology and Soteriology

a) The Content Of Classical Christology And Soteriology

PRELIMINARY REMARKS

The classical Christology and soteriology which was expressed in the great Councils of the early church (Nicaea, Ephesus, Chalcedon) and was handed on in the traditional theology of the schools without very much further inquiry or deeper development will not be repeated here from these sources. That would not be advisable for the purposes of this introduction and, should anyone wish to consult them, the texts are readily available to everyone in the *Enchiridion Symbolorum* of Denziger-Schönmetzer. We can only give a brief summary of this classical Christology here.

It was mentioned earlier that the "late" New Testament Christology, which is a theological reflection upon the original experience of the disciples with the crucified and risen Jesus, is going to be considered here along with the classical Christology of the church, and together they will be measured against the original experience of the risen Jesus. By "late" we mean in relation to the original experience of the risen Jesus. We are not maintaining that this New Testament Christology, which is already found in the earliest letters of Paul, was not written down until later in time than the gospels, which give us accounts of the experiences of the first disciples with the risen Jesus. This is not to maintain, of course, that between the "late" Christology of the New Testament and the classical Christology of the church there exist no differences at all with regard to terminology, horizons of understanding, "metaphysical" presuppositions, and so on. But if we may presuppose here that "functional" Christological statements in the context of salvation history also and inevitably imply ontological statements either implicitly or explicitly, and this simply presupposes that one can think onto-logically and does not read ontic statements about personal and spiritual realities in a false and objectivistic way, then it is quite legitimate here to disregard these indisputable differences between late

New Testament Christology and the classical Christology of the church. This is true especially because if the New Testament statements are taken seriously and are not rendered innocuous (for example, the statement that "the Word became flesh") they express something about Jesus which is not surpassed even by the classical Christology in its metaphysical terminology. At least this is the case if we do not absolutize the classical Christology along with its "metaphysics" in a way which is not required even of someone who recognizes them as the binding norm of his faith. Another reason why nothing more than a summary of the classical Christology need be offered here is the fact that we have already made an attempt towards an essential and descending Christology by way of prelude in the fourth section of this chapter.

THE OFFICIAL CHRISTOLOGY OF THE CHURCH

The official Christology of the church is a straightforward descending Christology which develops the basic assertion: God in his Logos becomes man. This is the basic assertion which is developed and defended by further precisions against misunderstandings which quite clearly were a threat. It is the assertion to which they always returned and from which they always set out as the primary assertion which was clear and taken for granted.

This descending or incarnational Christology presupposes the classical theology of the *Trinity*, although in their historical development the two mutually influenced each other. This trinitarian theology says: there are three "persons" in God who are distinct from one another; one of them, the second person, is the "Logos" from all eternity and independently of the Incarnation of the "Son"; he is born of and expressed by the Father through an eternal "generation;" he is of the same essence as the Father and is distinct from him in a relational difference while sharing in the same divine essence; he proceeds from the Father in the first of the inner-trinitarian processions *(processio)*, and through this generation he possesses the divine essence or the divine "nature" from the Father.

This divine person of the Logos assumes a complete human reality called a human "nature" as his own, namely, that of Jesus, and does this in a "union" which is "hypostatic," that is, it does not consist in a mingling of the "natures," but rather it has to do with the Son's "hypostasis" as such. The Logos joins this human nature with his hypostasis in such a way that this hypostasis is the substantial "bearer" of this "nature," and this human nature belongs inseparably to this hypostasis as the ultimate "subject" of both its being and its expression. Consequently, all of the predicates of this human nature can really and truly be expressed of this hypostasis or person of the Logos as the ultimate subject by which it is borne. This is so precisely because this nature is united with this person and subject "substantially" and is possessed by him, and hence it can and must be predicated of him.

The official teaching of the church does not explain the essence of this substantial union and unity with the divine hypostasis of the Logos any further. It simply clarifies it by saying that it allows and requires as an ontological presupposition that the human be truly and genuinely predicated of the Logos himself. Attempts were made to develop more exact theories of this hypostatic union in the Middle Ages and in baroque theology, but they did not find universal acceptance, nor were they incorporated into the official teaching of the church.

This hypostatic union allows a real difference to exist between the two "natures" of the single divine hypostasis of the Logos. These natures do not merge into a third "nature," but rather they exist "unseparated" from the Logos and "unmixed" between themselves. Hence the real ontic and logical subject does not arise out of the "natures" through their union, but rather is the subject of the Logos which pre-exists prior to the union. This should be noted to counter a "nestorian" understanding of the word "Christ." In accordance with the fact that the natures are unmixed, basically the active influence of the Logos on the human "nature" in Jesus in a physical sense may not be understood in any other way except the way this influence is exercised by God on free creatures elsewhere. This of course is frequently forgotten in a piety and a theology which are tinged with monophysitism. All too often they understand the humanity of Jesus as a thing and as an "instrument" which is moved by the subjectivity of the Logos.

In view of the fact that the natures are unmixed and that the wholeness of the human nature is not diminished, the insight must be preserved in order to counter monothelitism, or it must be acquired again and again in order to counter a piety and a theology which are tinged with monophysitism and in which the genuine subjectivity of the man Jesus even vis-à-vis God is constantly forgotten, the insight, namely, that the human nature of Jesus is a created, conscious and free reality to which there belongs a created "subjectivity" at least in the sense of a created will, a created *energeia*. This created subjectivity is distinct from the subjectivity of the Logos and faces God at a created distance in freedom, in obedience and in prayer, and it is not omniscient.

The whole doctrine of the hypostatic union reaches its goal, and this was also its religious point of departure, in the doctrine of the *communicatio idiomatum* or the interchange of predicates in both an ontic and a logical sense: because one and the same Logos-subject or person or hypostasis possesses and bears both "natures" substantially, there can be predicated of that which is named according to one of the two natures the characteristics of the other nature. Thus, for example, we can say not only that the eternal, divine Son is omniscient, but also that the eternal Son of God died, that Jesus of Nazareth is God, and so on. And conversely: because faith's experience of the unique presence of God in Jesus requires such an interchange of predicates, it justifies the doctrine of the hypostatic union as its indispensable presupposition, and as a defense of the legitimacy of the titles of majesty which are already applied to Jesus in the New Testament.

CLASSICAL SOTERIOLOGY

The classical soteriology is hardly developed beyond the statements of the New Testament, if indeed it really even does justice to them at all. Prescinding from a "doctrine of physical redemption" which is found in the Greek Fathers, and according to which the world appears as saved because it is physically and inseparably united with the Godhead in the humanity of Jesus, and prescinding from a few images of a more visual kind in the Fathers (for example, the ransoming of man by Christ from the initially legitimate power of the devil, or the outwitting of the devil who unlawfully seizes Christ by mistake), in the Middle Ages since the time of Anselm of Canterbury the attempt was made to clarify the biblical notion of redemption by a sacrifice of expiation or by the "blood" of Jesus. The clarification ran as follows: because of the divine and therefore infinite dignity of his person, the obedience of Jesus which was confirmed in the sacrifice of the cross represents infinite satisfaction vis-à-vis the God who was offended by sin, and this sin is measured by the dignity of the God who was offended. Consequently, it satisfies God's "justice" and liberates us from it if and because God accepts this satisfaction of Christ for the human race. Since the Middle Ages this theory of satisfaction has been current (and easily understandable for German ways of thinking). It also appears on the periphery of official church statements, but the extraordinary magisterium of the church did not take a position on it in any detailed way.

b) The Legitimacy Of The Classical Doctrine Of Incarnation

The legitimacy and the permanent validity of the classical Christology lies, first of all negatively, in the fact that when it is presupposed it prevents Jesus unambiguously from being reduced merely to someone in a line of prophets, religious geniuses and reformers, and from being incorporated within the course of an ongoing history of religion; and, positively, it clarifies the fact that in Jesus God has turned to us in such a unique and unsurpassable way that in him he has given himself absolutely. In Jesus God is not represented by something other and different from himself just like every other creature is different from God, so that this mediation would not mediate an immediacy to God in his own self. Anyone who cannot understand what the hypostatic union and the interchange of predicates mean (as we have explained them) in any other concepts except those of this classical theology of Incarnation will judge this classical Christology to be in a direct sense *the only* way of expressing our faith in the true relationship between Jesus and God, and our faith in our relationship to him, and hence he will retain it. However, especially today, he may not overlook what is still to be said about the limits of this classical Christology. Moreover, and this is not as easy a task as many believe in their all too traditionalistic ways of thinking, he has to learn how to express this classical Christology and to explain it especially to those who have reservations about this doctrine and suspect it of being mythological, although they profess in their Christian faith that Jesus is the indispensable and definitive way to God.

Anyone who thinks that he is able to express what is meant in the classical Christology of the Incarnation in another way without doing violence to what is meant, he may express it differently. This presupposes that he respects the official teaching of the church as a critical norm for his own way of expressing it, and that he knows that this teaching has to be an indispensable norm for him when he enters into the public discourse of the church. But neither must he make its significance absolute. His recognition of this does not banish him from the public discourse of the church because the official teaching of the church must also be interpreted and brought into contact with contemporary ways of thinking, and this cannot be done by merely repeating this official teaching.

c) The Limits Of Classical Christology And Soteriology

It does not contradict the character of an absolutely binding doctrine of the church to call attention to the limits which accompany a particular dogmatic statement.

THE PROBLEM OF HORIZONS OF UNDERSTANDING

In earlier times which thought more "mythologically" in their horizon of understanding, a merely descending doctrine of the Incarnation might more easily have been sufficient *by itself* than it is today. In its explicit assertion about Jesus it jumps over the point which gives us access to the ultimate mystery about him which the doctrine of the Incarnation expresses: *from the outset* it is the incarnate Word of God who has come down to us. Consequently, everything is seen and understood as coming *from* above, and not as going *towards* that point. But then it really is no longer so easy to exclude mythological misunderstandings from the correct and orthodox doctrine in our consciousness and in our piety. The humanity of Jesus is thought unreflexively to be the livery which God donned and in which he discloses himself and at the same time hides himself. What is still left and accepted of the humanity understood as the livery and body of God appears as pure accommodation and condescension on God's part for our benefit.

THE PROBLEM OF THE "IS" FORMULAS

When the orthodox descending Christology of the Incarnation says that this Jesus "is" God, this is an abiding truth of the faith *if* the statement is understood correctly. But as the statement reads it can also be understood in a monophysitic sense, and hence in a heretical sense. For such statements are constructed according to the rules for the interchange of predicates and are meant in this sense, and nothing about them indicates explicitly that this copula "is" appears and should be understood in a quite different sense than it is in other familiar statements with apparently the same copula "is." For when we say that Peter is a man, the statement expresses a real identification in the content of the subject and predicate nouns. But the meaning of "is" in statements involving an interchange of predicates in Christology is *not* based on such a real identification. It is based rather on a unique, otherwise unknown and deeply mysterious unity between realities which are really different and which are at an infinite distance from each other. For in and according to the humanity which we see when we say "Jesus," Jesus "is" not God, and in and according to his divinity God "is" not man in the sense of a real identification. The Chalcedonian *adiairetos* (unseparated) which this "is" intends to express (*D.S.* 302) expresses it in such a way that the *asynchytos* (unmixed) of the same formula does not come to expression. Consequently, the statement is always in danger of being understood in a "monophysitic" sense, that is, as a formula which simply identifies the subject and predicate.

These formulas do not intend this, but neither do they prevent it positively, and they are formulas which are thought to be shibboleths of orthodoxy: "Do you believe that Jesus is God, yes or no?" The misunderstandings with which these formulas resonate do not harm the pious in their traditional piety. They think rather that these misunderstandings are the most radical form of orthodox faith. But people today are inclined in many ways to understand these misunderstandings as parts of orthodox faith, and to reject it as mythology. This is only fair under *this* supposition. We should admit this and in pastoral matters take account of the fact that not everyone who has problems with the statement "Jesus is God" must for this reason be heterodox.

Hence as presumed parallels to "is" statements elsewhere in our everyday use of language, the Christological "is" formulas (for example, "the same" person is God and man) are constantly *in danger of being interpreted falsely*, a danger which flows from these parallels. The identity which they suggest but do not really mean is not excluded clearly and early enough by an explanation given sometime later, even prescinding from the fact that the explanation is quickly forgotten. This is not to question the legitimacy and the permanent validity of these Christological "is" statements. But we have to recognize that they are fraught with the danger of a monophysitic and hence a mythological misunderstanding. If, for example, someone says, "I cannot really believe that a man is God and that God has become a man," the first correct and Christian response to such a declaration would not be to say that this is a rejection of a basic Christian dogma. The correct response is rather that the interpretation presumably given to the rejected statement does not correspond to the really Christian sense of the statement.

The real *Incarnation* of the Logos is indeed a mystery which calls for an act of *faith*. But this should not be burdened with a lot of mythological misunderstandings. Although the Christian dogma in itself has nothing to do with the divine man myths of antiquity, we can readily admit that certain formulations of the dogma which are situated within the realm of *this* concrete and historical horizon of understanding (for example, that God "came down," that he "appears," and so on) were more easily taken for granted and accepted and used as a help towards interpretation in earlier times than is possible for us today. *Today too* Christology has an urgent task, a task which is not accomplished by merely repeating literally the ancient formulas and their explanation, something which is usually done anyhow only in learned theological circles. And for a variety of reasons which we are not going to go into here, neither can this task consist in abolishing the ancient formulas. But it is an urgent necessity that we broaden the horizons, the modes of expression and the different aspects for expressing the ancient Christian dogmas.

THE INDETERMINATION OF THE POINT OF UNITY
IN THE HYPOSTATIC UNION

One thing which remains very formal and indetermined in the traditional Christology is the point of unity in the hypostatic union in the sense of the point which forms the unity between person and natures, and which at the same time is the unity which is formed, namely, the "person" of the Logos. Now this point of unity can be called the "hypostasis" or "person" of the Logos. If we employ the hypostasis designation, whereby what is understood by this is the "bearer" of the divine and human reality or "natures" of the concrete, single being who "is" God and man, the assertion that the hypostasis is the bearer and possessor remains rather formal and abstract, or else in the attempt to explain it further it very easily falls back into the more simple and basic statement of Christology. Consequently, nothing more is accomplished than a verbal reassurance against the tendency to explain this basic assertion away rationalistically.

But if we call this point of unity *person*, either we have to state explicitly that this term is to be understood in the sense of the Christological use of "hypostasis," and this is just as easily and just as soon forgotten, or else the term "person" brings with it from its *modern usage* the constant danger that the Christological statements will be misunderstood in the sense of monophysitism or monothelitism. For what is understood by this is a *single* center of activity, namely, the divine center. This would overlook the fact that the man Jesus *in* his human reality exists with a created, active and "existentiell" center of activity vis-à-vis God and in an absolute difference from him. He prays, he is obedient, he comes to be historically, he makes free decisions, and in a process of genuine historical development he also has new experiences which surprise him, and these are clearly in evidence in the New Testament. But to overlook this is basically to have a mythological understanding of the Incarnation, and it makes no difference whether this misunderstanding is rejected as mythology or is "believed in." Finally, there is the further point that it is only with great difficulty or at most only indirectly that either "hypostasis" or "person" as the point of unity brings out in a clear and intelligible way the *salvific* significance of this unity "for us."

INADEQUATE EXPRESSION OF
THE SOTERIOLOGICAL SIGNIFICANCE OF THE CHRIST EVENT

In its explicit formulation the classical Christology of the Incarnation does not give expression in a clear and immediate way to the *soteriolog-*

ical significance of the Christ event. This is especially true of western Christianity's understanding. Perhaps because of western individualism, the idea of an "assumption" of the *whole* human race *in* the individual human reality of Jesus is rather foreign to their way of thinking. Within this horizon of understanding, then, the hypostatic union is the constitution of a person who *performs* redemptive activity, provided that his actions are moral and that his accomplishment is accepted by God as representative for the human race. But he does not mean in his very *being* salvation, redeemer and satisfaction. But from the perspective of scriptural statements and of our own understanding today, it would be desirable to have a formulation of the Christological dogma which indicated and gave immediate expression to the *salvific* event which Jesus Christ himself *is*, and which did this prior to explicit and special soteriological statements. Then the selected formulations could help to avoid more easily a monophysitic and hence a mythological misunderstanding.

8. On the Question of New Approaches to Orthodox Christology

It cannot be our task here to develop a new Christology systematically beyond what has already been given up to now as indications and approaches to such a Christology. All that is possible here is to add a few somewhat disparate and arbitrarily chosen remarks on this question. In new approaches to a contemporary Christology the following *among other things* would have to be taken into account:

1. The approaches to Christology which are found in the Christological conceptions of the New Testament and which are relevant for contemporary theology merit renewed reflection.

2. We would have to aim for a closer unity between *fundamental theology* and *dogmatic theology* in our Christology just as much as we do for fundamental theology and dogmatics in general. In doing so we would have to bring in again and develop the reflections on "transcendental Christology" which were indicated only in a very abstract and formal way in the third section of this chapter, and therefore they should be expanded somewhat at this point.

a) The Need For Closer Unity Between Fundamental Theology And Dogmatic Theology In Christology

PRIORITY OF THE LIVED ACTUALIZATION OF EXISTENCE TO REFLECTION UPON IT

Salvation and faith as a total event of the single, whole person cannot *be constructed* completely by mere reflection after the manner of an individual science. For basically reflection both in the everyday and in the scientific sense cannot recapture completely the unreflexive actualization of existence, and a person never lives merely by reflection alone. Hence this is also true for Christology when it is seen as a central element in Christian salvation and Christian faith. In fundamental theology, then, Christology may not and hence need not proceed as though it had to construct faith in Christ in a purely reflexive and synthetic way and by scientific retort, and this is true both with regard to *fides qua* and *fides quae,* both the act and the content of faith. This does not mean that the only fundamental theology there could be in Christology would be an *apologia ad intra,* that is, a confirmation of faith in Christ *for the believers themselves,* and that there could be no *apologia ad extra,* no way of giving an "account of the faith" before *others.* Perhaps though it does mean that fundamental theology's *demonstratio christiana ad extra* addresses itself to a person whom it presumes to be a person of morally good will, and hence to be existing in the interior grace of God and in Christ, and it *presupposes* that he has already uttered an interior and unreflexive "yes" to Christ. It makes no difference whether he knows this or not, nor whether in its efforts the *demonstratio christiana* reflected explicitly or not on whether its efforts were successful.

It follows from this that in the first place a Christian may and must accept without hesitation and courageously the "Christology" which he is living out in his life: in the faith of the church, in the cult of its risen Lord, in prayer in his name, and by participating in his destiny up to and including dying with him. The profession of faith in Gal. 1:8 ff. is still valid for this global experience, which to be sure cannot be made reflexive completely, but it does give its own witness to itself. And in view of it a Christian even today can still say with John (6:68): "Lord, to whom should we go? Thou hast the words of eternal life." When a person reflects upon the faith which makes him free and is the basis of his life, and which includes everything within a hidden and unfathomable meaning, and the believer does receive all of this from Jesus Christ, this reflection as reflection might in the first instance understand faith in Jesus Christ merely as *one* abstract and conceivable possibility among others for coming to terms with life and death. But neither does reflection as such have to accomplish anything more than this: it grasps *this* possibility as given, as already actualized, and as salvific; it does not see any other and better concrete possibility. This is sufficient in order that, beyond the possibilities of reflection, the believer may allow himself to be grasped by the absolute claim of Jesus. It is *faith*, not reflection, which responds to this claim with an absolute and exclusive "yes."

APPEALS IN A "SEARCHING CHRISTOLOGY"

From what has been said it follows further that, besides what always and hence today too has to be said by way of the traditional grounding of the faith, Christology in fundamental theology *today* can in three ways turn in a kind of "appeal" to this global understanding of existence which is already "Christian" because of antecedent grace. This global understanding cannot be made reflexive complctely, but it can nevertheless be appealed to. This would represent a somewhat more reflexive and more complete working out of the content of one part of "transcendental Christology." These three appeals have in common the supposition that if a person accepts his existence resolutely, he is really already living out in his existence something like a "searching Christology." These appeals do not try to do anything but clarify this anonymous Christology somewhat. The conviction that this "searching Christology" encounters what it is searching for precisely in Jesus of Nazareth, and is not merely "waiting upon someone who is to come," this conviction of course must accompany this appeal to the unreflexive and "searching Christology" which is found in the existence of every person. With respect to this we would simply have to ask where else this searching Christology could find what it is searching for, and what it affirms at least as a hope for the future, and ask whether Jesus and the faith of his community does not justify an act of faith that what is in any case being sought is found in *him*.

THE APPEAL TO AN ABSOLUTE LOVE OF NEIGHBOR

In this appeal what is said in Matt. 25 would havc to be taken seriously and interpreted radically, and indeed from "below," from the concrete love of neighbor, and not merely from "above." If we do not turn the saying of

Jesus that *he himself* is truly loved in every neighbor into an "as if" or merely into a theory of juridical imputation, then, when this saying is read from out of the experience of love itself, it says that an absolute love which gives itself radically and unconditionally to another person affirms Christ implicitly in faith and love. And this is correct. For a merely finite and ever unreliable person cannot by himself justify the sense of the absolute love which is given him, a love in which a person "involves" and risks himself absolutely for the other person. By himself he could only be loved with reservations and in a "love" in which the lover either makes reservations or risks himself absolutely on what is possibly meaningless.

If this dilemma were *only* to be overcome by an appeal to God himself, and hence to God as the guarantee and the limit of the absoluteness of this love, this would perhaps be possible in the abstract and "speculatively" from the perspective of a universal concept of absolute love. But a love whose absoluteness is experienced, even though it becomes fully itself not by virtue of itself, but only by virtue of its radical unity with the love of God through Jesus Christ, this love wants more than just a divine guarantee which remains transcendent to it. It wants a unity between the love of God and love of neighbor in which, even though this might merely be unthematic, love of neighbor is love of God and only in this way is completely absolute.

But this means that it is searching for a God-Man, that is, for someone who as man can be loved with the absoluteness of love for God. But it is not searching for him as an idea, because ideas cannot be loved; but rather as a reality, whether it is already present or is still to come. This reflection presupposes, of course, that the human race forms a unity, and that true love is not individualistic and exclusive, but rather that with all of its necessary concreteness it is always ready to encompass everything. And conversely: love for everything must always become concrete in the love of a concrete individual. Consequently, in the single human race the God-Man makes possible the absoluteness of the love for a concrete individual.

THE APPEAL TO READINESS FOR DEATH

However much radical significance the death of Jesus has for salvation, the average sermon looks too much for a particular, categorical event which takes place on the world's stage alongside many other events. It looks for an event which is different, but does not really give expression to and actualize very much of what belongs to the innermost essence of the world and of man's existence. This is the case because we look too quickly to the external cause and to the violence of this death, and in a theory of satisfaction we estimate its value merely as an external and meritorious cause of redemption.

A theology of death can connect the event of the death of Jesus more closely with the basic constitution of human existence. Death is the one act which pervades the whole of life, and in which man, as a being of freedom, has disposal of himself in his entirety. Indeed he has this in such a way that this disposal is, or should be, the acceptance of being disposed of absolutely in the radical powerlessness which appears and is endured in death. But if this free and ready acceptance of radical powerlessness by a free being who has and wants to have disposal of himself is not to be the acceptance of the absurd, which could with equal "right" be rejected in protest, then in a person who deeply affirms in his history not abstract ideas and norms but present or future reality as the ground of his existence, this acceptance implies the intimation or the expectation or the affirmation of an already present or future and hoped-for death which is of such a nature that it reconciles the permanent dialectic in us between doing and enduring in powerlessness. But this is the case only if this real dialetic is "subsumed" by the fact that it is the very reality of something which is the ultimate ground of this dialectic.

THE APPEAL TO HOPE IN THE FUTURE

Man hopes, and he goes to meet his future both making plans and at the same time opening himself to the incalculable. His journey into the future is the constant effort to lessen the self-alienation which is within him and outside him, and to lessen the distance between what he is and what he should be and wants to be. Is absolute reconciliation, both individual and collective, just the eternally distant and only asymptotically sought-after goal which hovers in the distance, or is it an attainable goal and an *absolute* future which, when it is attained, does not have to abolish the finite and swallow it up into the absoluteness of God? If the absolute future of God really is our future, is this reconciliation the goal in the sense of something which is simply still outstanding, or is it the goal of history in such a way that history already bears within itself the irrevocable promise of this goal, and therefore in such a way that, although it is still in progress, history is now already moving in this sense *within* its goal? A person who really hopes has to hope that in both instances these questions are answered in and through the reality of history by the second alternative. A Christian acquires from this hope an understanding of what faith professes in the Incarnation and in the resurrection of Jesus Christ as the irreversible beginning of the coming of

God as the absolute future of the world and of history.

We can summarize the content of these three appeals of Christology within fundamental theology by saying that man is searching for the absolute saviour, and he affirms at least unthematically his past or future coming in every total act of his existence which is finalized by grace towards the immediacy of God.

b) The Task Of A "Christology From Below"

We have called attention frequently up to now to the necessity of an ascending Christology or a Christology "from below." Contemporary Christology has to devote itself to this task more intensively. Such a Christology could proceed approximately in the following steps.

MAN AS A BEING ORIENTED TOWARDS IMMEDIACY TO GOD

The insight can be developed in "transcendental Christology" that man is a being with a *desiderium naturale in visionem beatificam,* that is, a "natural" desire for the beatific vision of God. It makes no difference in this context to what extent and in what sense this ontological orientation *(desiderium)* towards immediacy to God belongs to man's "nature" in the abstract, or to his historical nature as elevated in grace by the supernatural existential. This latter, however, belongs to his basic ontological constitution. Secondly, since man can experience and actualize his ultimate, essential being only in history, this orientation must come to appearance in history. Moreover, since God's offer can be actualized only in and through a free act of God, if it is to find its irreversible actualization and validity, man must expect and look for this offer within this historical dimension.

THE UNITY BETWEEN
ESCHATOLOGICAL EVENT OF SALVATION AND THE ABSOLUTE SAVIOUR

From this perspective we can come to the idea of an "absolute event of salvation" and of an "absolute saviour," which are two aspects of one and the same event: it is the historical and personal event, and not merely a word which is added to the reality or merely a verbal promise, in which man experiences his essential being in the above sense as really affirmed by God in and through his absolute, irreversible and "eschatological" offer of himself. This touches all of his dimensions because it is only then that salvation is the fulfillment of the whole person. This personal and absolute event of salvation along with the event of the saviour, who *is* salvation and does not merely teach and promise it, must be God's real offer of himself to mankind, an offer which is irreversible and not merely provisional and conditional. This unity between the eschatological event of salvation and the absolute saviour must be historical because nothing "transcendental" as such can be of final validity by itself unless it were already the vision of God, or unless the fulfillment of man's transcendentality could take place without including his history. It must also at the same time be the *free* acceptance of God's offer of himself, and this is effected by the offer. And it also belongs to the absolute event of salvation that it not merely be thought, but that it be done in life and in deed.

This eschatological, salvific event of the absolute saviour may not be understood as "absolute" in its structure in the sense that it is identical with the fulfillment of the human race in the immediacy of the beatific vision. For otherwise history would already be complete. It must be the real irreversibility of the process towards this fulfillment in such a way that the future of each individual is left open, although, because of the new closeness of God's kingdom which comes only with Jesus, each individual stands before an offer of God which transcends an ambivalent situation of freedom on God's part.

Of course we are presupposing here, first of all, that Jesus of Nazareth understood himself as this absolute saviour, and that it became fully manifest in his resurrection that he really is. Jesus of course did not make use of the abstract formulations with which we are trying to sketch and give some brief indication of the notion of an absolute saviour. But he certainly did not understand himself as one of the prophets after whom other revelatory acts of God could take place in an ongoing and completely open history, acts which would surpass the previous ones in a fundamental way and place them in question, and which would therefore open radically new epochs in the history of salvation. Rather the salvation of a person is decided by his relationship to Jesus, and the new and everlasting covenant between God and man is established in his death. Secondly, we are presupposing besides that this self-understanding is not only witnessed to as being credible, but also that Jesus himself reaches the final and definitive moment of his function as mediator of salvation, and hence reaches fulfillment.

THE CONNECTION BETWEEN THIS REFLECTION AND THE CHURCH'S DOCTRINE OF INCARNATION

Now the absolute event of salvation and the absolute mediation of salvation by a man mean exactly the same thing as church doctrine expresses as Incarnation and hypostatic union. This presupposes that the notion of

Incarnation is thought through radically to its logical conclusion, and that the notion of hypostatic union is not misunderstood in a monophysitic and mythological way, and finally that we are clear about the specific nature of a "real" act of revelation by God in the world. This act is never merely of the nature of a thing, but rather it always has an ontological character. This means that it must exist as a created reality of self-presence, of word, and hence of a self-conscious relation to God. God's salvific acts, his "activity" as distinguished from his "metaphysical attributes," are free and exist within a truly infinite realm of possibilities. The history of salvation, therefore, is in itself always open towards the future. Consequently, every event in it is always surpassable and conditional, and exists with the qualification that something new might happen, especially since this history of salvation is also the history of created freedom towards an unplanned future which cannot be calculated unambiguously from what comes earlier. Hence it is all the more true that we cannot determine in advance what is going to result from the interaction of these freedoms. A *mere* "prophet" or a mere religious genius in the sense of a productive model for a particular religious relationship between God and man can never in principle be "the last."

If, nevertheless, God performs his ultimate and unsurpassable salvific act, which is indeed finite because it exists within the realm of other possibilities, but which is still final and definitive, then this act cannot be provisional and cannot in principle belong to a particular epoch in a still ongoing history like other revelatory "words" (the revelatory word itself of course is constituted by both word and deed). Hence neither can this provisional character be removed by the fact that God simply "declares" merely in words that he will "not say anything more" but will be satisfied with this word as final. This is true not only because such a "declaration" would itself exist with the qualifications and with the provisionality of this kind of word, but also because such a declaration would decree that the history of salvation is finished. The declaration would not really bring this history to a genuine conclusion of this history, but at the same time it would merely allow it to continue as the execution of what had happened previously, and hence it would destroy its true historicity.

An absolute and "eschatological" salvific act, therefore, must have a really different relationship to God than God's other salvific activity has in a history of salvation which is still open. Unlike other things which are different from God, it cannot be characterized by the pure difference between creatureliness and God, nor by the difference between a "more circumscribed" reality and a "broader" range of possibilities. It cannot merely be a history which is empowered and directed by God, but is lived out by us alone. In the absolute event of salvation God must live out its history as his own history and retain it permanently as something done in freedom, for otherwise it would remain something inconsequential and provisional for him. Only if this event is his own history, a history which, as lived out in divine and of course also in created freedom, determines him once and for all and hence becomes irrevocable, only then can we speak of an absolute and "eschatological" event of salvation. The offer of himself which becomes manifest in history as irrevocable must be his own reality in its createdness, and not only in its divine origin. And this very own reality of his, which he can no longer undo as something which has been surpassed, must exist on our side as our own real salvation, that is, on this side of the difference between God and creatures. This gives us an initial approach towards a Christology "from below" which is objectively identical with the church's classical Christology "from above," and which at the same time can also clarify the unity between incarnational, essential Christology and soteriological, functional Christology.

ON THE RELATIONSHIP BETWEEN ASCENDING CHRISTOLOGY AND THE QUESTION OF ETERNAL, DIVINE SONSHIP

Let me add an explanatory remark to what has just been said. What was said implies the understanding that, if and to the extent that an ascending Christology reaches the idea of an absolute saviour from both transcendental and historical considerations, this ascending Christology has already reached a Christology of eternal and divine Sonship. This Son-Christology does not signify a new knowledge in addition to it which would supplement and go beyond the Christology of an absolute saviour. We derive this Son-Christology first of all, of course, from the biblical sources, especially from John, and we do not have to maintain that we would *in fact* develop a Christology of the eternal Son of the Father and of the Logos in Jesus exclusively from the abstract concept of an absolute saviour if we had not already found this development in the New Testament. But neither does this mean conversely that, given the prior existence of this New Testament Son and Logos Christology, we could not know that this Christology is already contained in the notion of an absolute saviour. Of course, confirmation of the correctness of our explication must come from the New Testament.

We are not going to explain all of this in detail here and prove that it is legitimate. Let me just call attention to two things briefly. First of all, if we presuppose a correct and also a critical understanding of the classical theology of the Trinity, and if we are clear about the fact that we know anything at all about the "immanent" Trinity only insofar as we experience a trinitarian God in the "economy of salvation," and that the two are identical, then basically it is clear that a knowledge of the eternal Son and Logos is contained and grounded in the fact that we experience the historical self-expression of God in its historical reality, and there we experience it in its eternal possibility. And this is precisely the experience of the absolute and eschatological saviour. It is both legitimate and necessary to understand and to ground the later New Testament Christology in Jesus and from Jesus insofar as it is contained in his proclamation of the eschatological closeness of God's kingdom and in his work. We are not obliged to understand all of the statements of the whole New Testament as equally original in a kind of biblical positivism. But if this is the case, then we can and also have to ask: How does the later New Testament in the Christology of Paul and John know that Jesus is the eternal "Son" and the eternal Logos? Very likely there is only one answer to this question, and it is found by maintaining the thesis that a Son and a Logos Christology are already implied in the notion of an absolute saviour, and that they do not come in addition to the Christology of an absolute saviour.

c) Specific Dogmatic Problems

THE POSSIBILITY OF AN ORTHODOX "CONSCIOUSNESS CHRISTOLOGY"

In a *new* orthodox Christology we may without any qualms reckon with the possibility of a "consciousness Christology" alongside the classical Christology. In Protestant theology at the beginning of this century there was admittedly a consciousness Christology which in fact was heretical. It was a kind of modern edition of the nestorian "trial and probation" Christology. For wherever on the basis of a merely human reality one allows secondary and hence derived contents of a man's consciousness to arise and be combined, for example, an especially intensive trust in God, and holds that these attitudes or contents of consciousness are all that is properly meant in Christology, here lies a rationalistic and hence a heretical Christology. But basically there is absolutely no problem with an *ontological* Christology complementing an *"ontic* Christology," this latter being a Christology which formulates its statements with the help of concepts such as "nature" and "hypostasis" which can be derived from realities from the world of things. An *ontological* Christology is a Christology whose concepts, paradigms of understanding and so on are orientated towards onto-logical realities in the strict sense and towards the original identity in them of being and consciousness. In many respects this Christology could avoid the danger of a monophysitic and mythological misunderstanding from the outset and much earlier than an "ontic Christology."

The presupposition for an "ontological Christology" is the insight which is already found in classical Thomism that in their ultimate meaning being and consciousness are the same thing, that an existent possesses being to the degree that the existent is "present to itself" and "returns" to itself, and thereby is responsible for itself in knowledge and freedom, and precisely in this way becomes open to the whole of reality and is both *intelligens et intellectum: ens et verum convertuntur; in tantum aliquid est ens actu, in quantum est intelligens et intellectum actu,* that is, the degree of the *reditio in seipsum* or the return to self is identical with the degree of *esse actu,* and vice versa.

This presupposition cannot be further justified here at this point. But if it is legitimate, then we can say: an ontic Christological statement must in principle be able to be transposed into an ontological statement. This principle has its "practical" significance, for example, in explaining and grounding the scholastic teaching that Jesus always possessed an immediate vision of God. Much of the Johannine Christology, for example, the "I" sayings, could presumably be made more clearly intelligible both exegetically and objectively from the perspective of a "consciousness Christology." Likewise the connection between "transcendental" and "categorical" Christology could be shown more clearly.

In order to show these connections more precisely we would have to undertake the following analysis: the man Jesus exists in a unity of wills with the Father which permeates his whole reality totally and from the outset, in an "obedience" from out of which he orients his whole human reality; he is someone who continually accepts himself from the Father and who in all of the dimensions of his existence has always given himself over to the Father totally; in this surrender he is able to accomplish due to God what we are not able to accomplish; he is someone whose "basic constitution" as the original unity of being and consciousness is to have his origins in God radically and completely, and to be given over to God radically and completely. If we were to explicate these statements concretely, they would readily be able to be transposed back into the classical ontic Christology, but this of course would have to be shown more exactly. If the presuppositions we mentioned are really understood, these statements would no longer be the expression of a heretical consciousness Christology, but rather a possible ontological Christology. This ontological Christology would always be obliged in the light of ontic Christology to push its own statements to their ultimate and radical meaning, but it could itself legitimately transpose the content of ontic Christology and lead to a better understanding of these ontic statements.

THE PROBLEM OF PRE-EXISTENCE

The new Christology will have to treat the question of the pre-existence of Christ more explicitly and more cautiously than has been the case up to now. On this point let me say the following:

The question of the necessity of the "pre-existence" of Christ for orthodox Christology is being raised again today, and sometimes with doubts about its necessity. This is true at least to the extent that it appears to be a necessary implication of the Christian dogma and intends to be more than a conceptual model. But if Jesus Christ is the absolute and eschatological expression and offer of God's own self, and without this Christology is not Christian, and if along with this he is the free and created acceptance of this offer, an acceptance effected by the offer in a formal predefinition, and it is only then that he can be the absolute event of salvation, then the one who expresses himself and offers himself, namely God, is "pre-existent." Indeed he is so in a radically different way than is the case when God is pre-existent to some other temporal creature which is not his own self-expression.

Exegetes, however, may and should be allowed the freedom to investigate impartially whether exactly what Jesus *himself* means by "Son" of the Father in an absolute sense is simply identical with the God who expresses himself in time, and hence also as pre-existent, or whether it *also* contains an element which is not identical with this God and hence is not "pre-existent." Even the second possibility does not exclude the fact that the self-expressive, divine subject whom the classical terminology calls "Son" as well as Logos is pre-existent. Besides, this question is a problem in the theology of the Trinity rather than in Christology, and is connected with the inevitability and the difficulty of speaking of three "persons" in God. If by three persons, or, more precisely, by the formalities which form the "person" and distinguish the "person," we understand three modes of subsistence in the one God, and the second of these is exactly identical with God's *ability* to express himself in history, which ability precisely as such belongs immanently and essentially to God and is inner-trinitarian, then we can and also have to speak of a pre-existence of the subject who expresses himself in Jesus Christ. Nor does this lead to the difficulties which the questioning and the doubts about the pre-existence today apparently want to avoid.

THE DISCUSSION OF THE DEATH OF GOD

The new orthodox Christology would have to throw light on the grain of truth which is found in the heretical death-of-God theology. It has to do this not in order to promote the superficial fad of a death-of-God theology, but rather in order to reflect objectively in a contemporary Christology upon the death of Jesus not only in its salvific efficacy, but also in itself, especially since this death is not only a biological occurrence, but also a total human and personal occurrence. If someone says that the incarnate Logos "merely" died in his human reality, and implicitly understands this to mean that this death did not touch God, he has only said half of the truth and has left out the really Christian truth. The "immutable God" does not indeed "in himself" have a destiny and hence neither does he have a death. But because of the Incarnation he *himself,* and not just the other, does have a destiny in the other. Like the humanity of Christ, this very death expresses God in the way that *he himself* is and wanted to be in relation to us by a free decision which remains valid forever. This death *of God* in his being and in his becoming in the other of the world obviously must belong then to the law of the history of the new and eternal covenant which we have to live out. We must share the destiny of God in the world. We do this not by declaring with the fad of God-lessness that there is no God, or that we would have nothing to do with him. We do it rather by the fact that our "having" God must pass again and again through an abandonment by God in death, where God alone comes to meet us in a radical way. It passes through this because God surrendered himself in love and as love, and in his death this becomes real and becomes manifest. The death of Jesus belongs to God's self-expression.

9. The Personal Relationship of a Christian to Jesus Christ

THE NEED FOR AN "EXISTENTIELL" CHRISTOLOGY

This topic is not treated in the average dogmatic theology. In a strange way it is left to the teachers of the spiritual life and of Christian mysticism for its only treatment.

But within the framework of our reflections it is important and necessary not only because Christianity in its full and explicit form is not merely an abstract theory, nor a reality to be understood in an objectivistic and ultimately reified way, and then a person would adopt his personal position on it subsequently. In its real and essential being Christianity really understands itself as an existentiell process, and this process is precisely what we are calling a personal relationship to Jesus Christ.

What is to be said about this "existentiell Christology" has to be said and heard with a certain amount of discretion and with some qualifications. There is an implicit and anonymous Christianity. We have had to emphasize very frequently in the course of our reflections that there is and has to be an anonymous and yet real relationship between the individual person and the concrete history of salvation, including Jesus Christ, in someone who has not yet had the whole, concrete, historical, explicit and reflexive experience in word and sacrament of this reality of salvation history. Such a person has this real and existentiell relationship merely implicitly in obedience to his orientation in grace towards the God of absolute, historical presence and self-communication. He exercises this obedience by accepting his own existence without reservation, and indeed precisely in those areas where freedom risks something which cannot be calculated and controlled. Alongside this there is the fullness of Christianity which has become conscious of itself explicitly in faith and in hearing the word of the gospel, in the church's profession of faith, in sacrament, and in living an explicit Christian life which knows that it is related to Jesus of Nazareth.

But the boundary between these two extremes is fluid. This fluid boundary is also found in someone who was baptized as a child and was brought up as an ecclesial Christian in the social sense and continues to live as such. Even for this person there remains the ever unfinished task of slowly incorporating existentielly into the history of his own existence what he knows at first in a more conceptual faith, and what he already is in germ through his supernatural existential, that is, through the self-communication of God which is always offered to him in his freedom, and through the manifestation of this in sacrament, in membership in the church, and in the deliberate practice of church life. A person is always a Christian in order to become one, and this is also true of what we are calling a personal relationship to Jesus Christ in faith, hope and love. Something like this is not simply there or not there. Rather, as an existentiell reality in a Christian it is always present through God's self-communication in the depths of his conscience, through living a sacramental life, through the preaching of the gospel and the deliberate practice of a Christian and ecclesial life, but through all of these things it is always present as something which a person still has to realize and bring to radical actualization in the living out of his whole existence throughout the whole length and breadth and depth of his life.

If, therefore, much of what has to be said about this personal relationship of the individual Christian to Jesus Christ might strike many as demanding too much or as an unreal ideology, as something for which at first glance they do not think that they can find a point of contact in their own individual religious experience, this is not an argument against the truth of what is going to be said. It expresses the real truth and reality of Christian existence, and human experience is nothing else but a challenge to entrust oneself to the development of one's own Christian existence in patience, openness and fidelity, and to do this until slowly, and perhaps painfully and with failures, this life unfolds and develops into the experience of a personal relationship to Jesus Christ. Then this is an experience which captures and confirms in its own right what inevitably can only be said here in pale abstractions, although it is referring to what is most concrete and at the same time most absolute, namely, ourselves in our ever unique relationship to Jesus Christ.

INDIVIDUAL, CONCRETE RELATIONSHIP TO JESUS CHRIST

It is not easy to find a clear approach to what we are talking about here. For we are dealing with the absolute God as he turned to us in the concrete uniqueness of Jesus Christ, so that this God thus really becomes the most concrete absolute. We are dealing with the unique salvation of each individual, who in faith and love is not supposed to entrust a universal human nature which is the same in everybody, or an abstract human existence, to the absolute mystery of the God who communicates himself. Rather each individual is to entrust *himself* in the uniqueness which belongs inalienably and inseparably to him as a historical and free being. But these two things imply basically that there must be a unique and quite personal relationship between Jesus Christ and each individual in his faith, his hope, and his unique love, a relationship which is not exhausted by abstract norms and universal laws. They imply that it is even to be taken for granted that this unique relationship has an individual history in the concreteness of existence which is incalculable and ultimately is not at the individual's disposal, and which indeed is ultimately identical with the destiny and with the deed which is required of every person in his whole life, and for which he is responsible. It can be clarified theologically from two vantage points, both from above and from below, that there can be and is a unique relationship between each individual and Jesus Christ, and that in the individual Christian there must be a quite personal and intimate love for Jesus Christ. Nor is this love merely ideology, nor a vague religious sentiment, nor an analgesic to numb the pain at being frustrated in some other interpersonal relationship.

A THEO-LOGICAL REFLECTION

First of all the vantage point from above: Christian faith professes of Jesus Christ that he is the absolute saviour, the concrete historical mediation of our immediate relationship to the mystery of the God who communicates himself. This faith knows that as the event of absolute unity between God and man, the God-Man does not cease to be with the end of temporal history. Rather, he himself continues to exist and he constitutes an essential element in the eternal fulfillment of the world. This follows from the basic Christian truth about the resurrection of Christ. The human reality of Jesus Christ continues to exist forever as the reality of the eternal Logos himself. But this eternal fulfillment of the *humanity* of Christ beyond time, which as the humanity of the divine Logos enjoys the immediate vision of God, obviously cannot be understood merely as an individual reward and as the fulfillment of the man Jesus in his own human existence all for himself. The "Christ yesterday, today *and forever*" of Hebrews 13:8 must have a soteriological significance for us. The human reality of Christ must always be the abiding mediation of the immediacy of God to us. When we try to ground this personal relationship to Jesus Christ from below, that is, from the specific unity between the love of God and the concrete love of neighbor, we shall understand better that, as the existentielly most real actualization and foundation of the love of neighbor which is our mediation to God, personal love for Jesus Christ can be our permanent mediation to the immediacy of God.

If, then, the humanity of Christ, or better: the man Jesus, has an abiding salvific significance, if this man and his human reality as such is an intrinsic element in the final fulfillment of our own salvation and not only in its temporal history, and if each individual's salvation is unique, then it cannot be denied that a personal relationship to Jesus Christ in personal and intimate love is an essential part of Christian existence. By the fact that a person finds God, that he falls, as it were, into the absolute, infinite and incomprehensible abyss of all being, he himself is not consumed into universality, but rather he becomes for the first time someone absolutely unique. This is so because it is only in this way that he has a unique relationship to God in which this God is *his* God, and not just a universal salvation which is equally valid for all.

We must always bear in mind here that salvation does not mean a reified and objective state of affairs, but rather a personal and ontological reality. Hence salvation and fulfillment take place in the objectively most real reality of the most radical subjectivity. It occurs, then, in the subject's knowing and loving self-surrender into the mystery of God which seems to vanish, but in doing so remains most radically as mystery. This takes place in and through an abiding personal relationship to the God-Man in whom and in whom alone immediacy to God is reached now and forever. This relationship to the man Jesus Christ, however, does not abolish or deny the salvific significance of interpersonal communication with another person, and indeed with all other men.

THE UNITY BETWEEN THE LOVE OF GOD
AND CONCRETE LOVE OF NEIGHBOR

According to the teaching of Christianity about the unity between the love of God and neighbor as an ultimately single and all-encompassing actualiza- tion of existence, an actualization which is borne by God's self-communica- tion and is creative of salvation, love for one's neighbor is not merely a commandment which has to be obeyed if a person wants to exist in a salvific relationship to God. It is rather the actualization of Christian existence in an absolute sense. This presupposes that this love of neighbor has developed into its own full and essential being, and explicitly accepts its ground and its mysterious partner, namely, God himself. For without him, interper- sonal communication in love among men cannot reach its own radical depths and its final and definitive validity.

Now it is certainly undeniable that interpersonal communication in the quite concrete, interpersonal experience in time and space of a quite defi- nite and corporeal Thou who encounters us is of basic and necessary significance for the existence, the development and the maturity of a person's existence, and that it cannot be replaced by anything else. But this love in an immediate and interpersonal encounter wants to be absolutely faithful, and it implies the actualization of a spiritual existence which, at least insofar as it is borne by grace, possesses an absolute depth and an element which is taken up into the "eternal life" between God and man. And ultimately this life always transcends this immediate, corporeal encounter in time and space and understands itself as invincible to death. This presupposes only that in the Christian understanding of existence one understands and dies his death as his fulfillment, and not merely as the conclusion which ends everything.

Such a love, therefore, is not confined within the boundaries of an immediate experience which is simply corporeal. It does not even reach its radical Christian essence and its human fulfillment until it transcends these boundaries in faith and in hope. And for this reason such love for another person, which is the mediation of the love of God and forms an ultimately inseparable unity with it, can be directed to *Jesus*. A person can love him as a true man in the most proper and vital meaning of this word. Indeed because of who the God-Man is, this love is even the absolute instance of a love in which love for a man and love for God find their most radical unity and mediate each other mutually. Jesus is the most concrete absolute, and therefore it is in love for him that love reaches the most absolute concreteness and absence of ambiguity which it seeks by its very nature. For love is not a movement towards an abstract ideal, but towards concrete, individual and irreducible uniqueness, and this very love finds in its Thou the absolute expanse of incomprehensible mystery.

THE RISK OF ENCOUNTER

We have already emphasized that in this context we have to speak very abstractly about something which is the most concrete of all. What has been said can really be understood only by someone who takes the risk and tries to love Jesus in a really personal way by means of the scriptures and the sacraments and the celebration of his death, and by living in the community of his believers. It can be understood only by someone who takes the risk of encountering him personally, and who in doing so receives as a grace the courage no longer to be afraid that he only means the abstract idea of an infinite God when he says the name "Jesus." It can be understood only by someone who experiences how an encounter with the concrete Jesus of the gospels, in all the concreteness and irreducibility of this definite historical figure, does not confine the person who is seeking the incomprehensible infinity of the absolute mystery of God to something concrete which is made an idol either out of love or out of foolishness. He experiences rather that this concrete encounter really opens him to God's infinity. Indeed it does so because every encounter with the concrete man Jesus is an ever unique discipleship. This discipleship is not imitation, but rather an ever unique call from out of one's own concrete life, and into participation in the mystery of the life of Jesus from his birth until his death. This discipleship and participation are at the same time always and everywhere an initiation into his death and his resurrection. Everything finite enters into the infinity of God, and in the immediate experience of this the finite in Jesus and in us does not perish, but rises to its fulfillment.

It is not possible at this point to treat in more detail this discipleship with Jesus and this participation in the mystery of the life of Jesus as we have understood them, and especially participation in his death in an immediate unity between love of God and love for this quite definite man. But what has been said at least calls attention to the fact that Christian life is not merely satisfying universal norms which are proclaimed by the official church. Rather in these norms and beyond them it is the always unique call of God which is mediated in a concrete and loving encounter with Jesus in a mysticism of love. This is always quite unique and it cannot be deduced from anything. Nevertheless, it is practiced within the community of those who believe and love which we call church. For in the church, in its gospel, in the kerygma which is directed beyond all teaching to the unique heart of each individual, in sacrament and in the celebration of the Lord's death, but also in private prayer and in the ultimate decision of one's conscience, Jesus offers himself immediately as the Christ, and in him God offers himself.

This does not deny, of course, but rather implies positively that a person whom Christ has not yet encountered in an explicit, historical witness which comes to him from history can find him nevertheless in his brothers and sisters and in his love for them. Jesus Christ allows himself to be found in them anonymously as it were, for he himself said, "What you did for the least of my brothers, you have done for me" (Matt. 25:40), for him who lives his life in the poor, in the hungry, in those in prison and in those who are dying.

10. Jesus Christ in Non-Christian Religions

What does it mean exactly and concretely to say that Jesus Christ is also present in non-Christian religions? The following reflections want to address this question. The question might have already been considered indirectly and more or less implicitly in previous reflections. But it is perhaps legitimate to raise it again explicitly at the conclusion of this chapter. For in view of the fact that Jesus is limited in time and space, the profession of his universal salvific significance for all times and for all people is always a scandal for non-Christians. In our reflections in this section we really cannot go any further into the more general question about the irreducible relationship of mutual conditioning between man's transcendental essence and his historicity and his history. We have already said something about this in several places.

THE QUESTION WITHIN THE LIMITS OF A DOGMATIC REFLECTION

The first thing to be emphasized is that we are dealing here with an inquiry in dogmatic theology, and not in the history of religion or in the phenomenology of religion. In this question a Christian dogmatic theologian cannot do the work of a historian of religion and his a posteriori investigations because the theologian's own binding sources of faith arose without any immediate contact with the great majority of non-Christian religions. These sources came to be in the Old and New Testament and in the official declarations of the church based upon them. An exception to this lack of contact would be the declaration of the Second Vatican Council on non-Christian religions. For the most part, therefore, these sources have not worked through the material from the history of religion which is germane to our question. Besides this, to the extent that any of these sources deals at all with non-Christian religions from a distance, it does so for understandable reasons rather in order to differentiate itself and defend itself against them, and hence by and large they are not very fruitful for our question. Compared then with the task of a historian of religion, which is to discover Christ a posteriori in non-Christian religions insofar as this is possible, the reflections of a dogmatic theologian to be presented here are a priori. They can only give something like provisional hints to the historian of religion, and perhaps he can then direct and sharpen his search and his inquiry for a task which the dogmatic theologian cannot assume.

The only question here, then, is this: From the perspective of dogmatic principles and considerations prior to an investigation by the history of religion, what seems to have to be postulated in the inquiry and in the presumed result of an investigation into the presence of Christ in non-Christian religions? Such a "presence" of Jesus Christ throughout the whole history of salvation and in relation to all people cannot be denied or overlooked by Christians if they believe in Jesus Christ as the salvation of *all* people, and do not think that the salvation of non-Christians is brought about by God and his mercy independently of Jesus Christ. This presupposes only that these non-Christians are of good will, even when this good will has absolutely nothing to do with Jesus Christ. But if there has to be a presence of Christ throughout the whole history of salvation, it cannot be missing where in the concrete man is religious in his history, namely, in the history of religion. For although salvation takes place and can take place where the salvific act is not made thematic in an explicitly religious way, namely, in every moral decision, still it would make no sense to think that such a salvific act takes place only where it is not objectified and made thematic in an explicitly religious way.

TWO PRESUPPOSITIONS

We shall make two presuppositions in order to answer this question within the limits of dogmatic theology. *First of all,* we shall presuppose a universal and supernatural salvific will of God which is really operative in the world. This implies the possibility of supernatural revelation and faith everywhere, and hence throughout the whole length and breadth of the history of the human race. We treated this in detail in the fifth chapter. This presupposition is also taught explicitly in the Second Vatican Council. The Council indeed is extraordinarily reserved when it comes to the question of *how* such a salvific faith in a real revelation of God in the strict sense can come about outside the realm of the Old and New Testaments. But this does not forbid the theologian to ask the question how such a universal possibility of faith can come about, nor can it really dispense him from raising the question.

We do not have to repeat the answer, or at least one possible answer, to this question here, but rather it may be presupposed, although it is still somewhat like the eleventh chapter of Hebrews and does not clarify the Christological character of this faith which is creative of salvation. Let us just note briefly once again that the elevation of human "transcendentality" in grace along with the supernatural, unreflexive and unobjectified formal object which accompanies it already satisfies the notion of a supernatural revelation and, if it is accepted in freedom, the notion of faith. This is prior to the question of what more precise historical and objectifying mediation the acceptance of this supernatural and revelatory elevation has. If we can presuppose that our question can be answered in the affirmative and has already been clarified to some extent, then we really only have to ask whether and how this salvific revelation and faith can and must also reach *Christ* even outside the realm of explicit Christianity, or whether this is impossible and therefore unnecessary. In this latter case the impossibility of this along with good will would dispense from the necessity that this act of faith which is possible everywhere have a *Christological* character.

But presupposing that an act of faith does take place in one of these two ways, that is, Christologically or non-Christologically, there also remains the question whether non-Christian religions as concrete, historical and social phenomena have a positive significance or not. Depending on the answer to this, then we have to answer the question whether or not Christ is present in non-Christian religions.

In addition to this we are making a *second* presupposition: when a non-Christian attains salvation through faith, hope and love, non-Christian religions cannot be understood in such a way that they do not play a role, or play only a negative role in the attainment of justification and salvation. This proposition is not concerned about making a very definite Christian interpretation and judgment about a concrete non-Christian religion. Nor is there any question of making such a religion equal to Christian faith in its salvific significance, nor of denying its depravity or its provisional character in the history of salvation, nor of denying that such a concrete religion can also have negative effects on the event of salvation in a particular non-Christian.

But presupposing all of this, we still have to say: if a non-Christian religion could not or may not have any positive influence at all on the supernatural event of salvation in an individual person who is a non-Christian, then we would be understanding this event of salvation in this person in a completely ahistorical and asocial way. But this contradicts in a fundamental way the historical and social nature of Christianity itself, that is, its ecclesial nature. In order to bring divine revelation to a non-Christian who is not reached by Christian preaching, there have indeed been suggested private revelations or extraordinary illuminations, especially at the hour of death, and such things as this. But prescinding from the fact that these are arbitrary and improbable postulates, and that it is impossible to see why they may only be allowed to play a role in special and extraordinary cases, such means as this contradict the basic character of Christian revelation as well as man's nature. For even in his most personal history man is still a social being whose innermost decisions are mediated by the concreteness of his social and historical life, and are not acted out in a special realm which is separate.

In addition to this there is the fact that in a theology of salvation history which takes God's universal salvific will seriously, and also takes account of the enormous temporal interval separating "Adam" from the Old Testament revelation of Moses, the whole interval between these two points cannot be understood to have been deprived of divine revelation. It should be noted in passing that Vatican II's constitution *Dei Verbum* (art. 3) passes over this interval a little too quickly. But this revelation would not be simply and absolutely separate from the whole history of concrete religions. For if they are all simply dismissed, then it is impossible to say where God with the history of his salvation and revelation is still to be found in the world. If someone wants to bridge this interval by postulating the transmission of a "primordial revelation," we would have to repeat that, given the enormous duration of the history of the human race, this postulate is very problematic, and especially that in the concrete only the historical and socially constituted religions can be considered to have been the transmitters of a tradition which is supposed to reach the individual. These religions had the possibility and the obligation to awaken and to keep alive man's relationship to the mystery of existence which lays claim upon him, however the individual religions might interpret this primordial mystery of existence and concretize man's relationship to it, and perhaps even do so in a depraved way.

But if at least in this interval we cannot do justice to a universal and operative salvific will of God which is also "infralapsarian," that is, which continues despite "original sin," nor to the universal possibility of salvific revelation and faith which this implies unless pre-Christian religions have a positive salvific function, then there is no reason why we would have to, or even could, deny a priori and in principle at least a partial positive function to non-Christian religions for people who have not yet been reached by the Christian message in a way which would constitute an immediate obligation for them. We do not have to discuss here the concrete way in which a non-Christian religion can have a positive function in making possible real revelation and faith.

CHRIST AND NON-CHRISTIAN RELIGIONS

With these two presuppositions we turn now to our real question: How can Jesus Christ be understood to be present and operative in non-Christian religions from the perspective of Christian dogmatic theology, and hence prior to an a posteriori investigation of this question and an a posteriori description. In our discussion, and this has to be admitted openly and honestly at the beginning, the answer will focus in the first instance and immediately on the question: How is Jesus Christ present and operative in the faith of the individual non-Christian? Referring again to our introductory remarks, we cannot go beyond that here, however regrettable this might seem, that is, we cannot go into the question of non-Christian religions as social and institutional realities. What can possibly be said about the presence of Christ in non-Christian religions beyond his presence in the salvific faith of the non-Christian is a question for theologians doing the history of religion in an a posteriori way.

THE PRESENCE OF CHRIST IN THE HOLY SPIRIT

With the presuppositions and within the limits set above, Christ is present and operative in non-Christian believers and hence in non-Christian religions in and through his *Spirit*. This proposition is to be taken for granted in dogmatic theology. If there can be a faith which is creative of salvation among non-Christians, and if it may be hoped that in fact it is found on a large scale, then it is to be taken for granted that this faith is made possible and is based upon the supernatural grace of the Spirit. And this is the Spirit who proceeds from the Father and the Son, so that as the Spirit of the eternal Logos he can and must be called at least in this sense the Spirit of Christ, the divine Word who has become man.

But this self-evident dogmatic statement does not really exhaust the meaning nor ground the legitimacy of the proposition just formulated. For the precise question is whether the Holy Spirit's supernatural grace of faith and justification as it is at work in the non-baptized can be called the Spirit of *Jesus* Christ, and if so, what exactly this means. Now the Catholic dogmatic theology of the schools will without doubt give an affirmative answer to this question, and will try to clarify it with the explanation that this Spirit who makes faith possible and who justifies is given in all times and places *intuitu meritorum Christi*, that is, in view of the merits of Christ. Consequently, it can correctly be called the Spirit of *Jesus* Christ. This explanation is certainly justified and will also be deemed intelligible at least to some extent, and hence it can serve as the point of departure for our further reflections.

But this explanation certainly does not answer all of the questions which can be raised here. First of all, this statement does not make as clear and intelligible as might appear at first glance the connection between the grace of the Spirit which is given in all times and places and the historical event of the cross at a particular point in time and space. We could ask whether the connection between these two realities exists only in the knowledge and will of the God who transcends salvation history, so that there exists no real connection *between* these two realities *themselves*. Can the event of the cross be understood to "influence" God either "physically" or "morally" so that, on the basis of this influence which comes from the world to him, as it were, and which is known antecedently, God already pours out the grace of the Spirit upon the world? But if we cannot say this in the proper sense because of God's sovereign immutability, because he cannot be influenced or moved, then what does it mean to say that he gives his Spirit because of the merits of Jesus Christ, who is the moral and meritorious cause of this Spirit?

If someone says that the questionable statement does not connect the suffering of Jesus with God as the reason which moves God, but rather connects it with the grace of the Spirit, just as we have to say of the prayer of petition, for example, that it is not the cause of God's decision to hear the prayer of petition but the moral cause of the reality which is given by God in hearing it (and this because God freely connects the two), then the question is what this could possibly mean, especially since this inner-worldly, moral cause which is not supposed to "influence" God himself comes much later in time than its effect. We could also point out that presumably in the example of the prayer of petition it would not occur to anyone to go to God with a prayer for a reality which had already taken place in the world earlier, although this would also have to make sense if the popular interpretation of the *intuitu meritorum* makes sense.

In addition to these difficulties there is the fact that we can and also have to understand God's free salvific will as the a priori cause of the Incarnation and of the cross of Christ, a cause which is not conditional upon anything outside God. Consequently, from this vantage point too it is not easy to see how the cross of Christ can be the cause of God's salvific will for other people if God's salvific will is antecedent to the cross of Christ as its cause, and is not its effect. Moreover, this salvific will cannot be understood in any other way except as related to all people because a salvific will related only to Christ would make no sense to begin with. It would also contradict the fact that Jesus Christ is intended from the outset by God's salvific will as the redeemer of the world.

We get out of these and similar, unmentioned difficulties only by saying that the Incarnation and the cross are, in scholastic terminology, the "final cause" of the universal self-communication of God to the world which we call the Holy Spirit, a self-communication given with God's salvific will which has no cause outside God. This is to regard Incarnation and cross as a cause *in this sense* of the universal communication of the Holy Spirit in the world, as was said in the sixth section of this chapter. Insofar as this Spirit is always and everywhere the entelechy of the history of revelation

and salvation to begin with, and insofar as its communication and acceptance by their very nature never take place in mere abstract transcendentality, but take place rather in an historical mediation, this communication
is oriented to begin with towards a historical event in which this communication and its acceptance become irreversible despite the fact that they are
free, and also become historically tangible in this eschatological triumph.
But this takes place in what we call the Incarnation, cross and resurrection
of the divine Word.

Insofar as the universal efficacy of the Spirit is always oriented towards
the high point of its historical mediation, in other words, insofar as the
event of Christ is the final cause of the communication of the Spirit to the
world, it can truly be said that this Spirit is everywhere and from the outset
the Spirit of *Jesus* Christ, the Logos of God who became man. The Spirit
who has been communicated to the world has himself, and not only in the
intention of God which transcends the world and would be extrinsic to him,
an intrinsic relation to Jesus Christ. The latter is the "cause" of the former,
although at the same time the opposite relation is equally true, as is always
the case between an efficient cause and a final cause. Between them there
is both unity and difference, and a relationship of mutual conditioning.
Insofar as the efficient cause of the Incarnation and of the cross, namely,
the Spirit, bears his goal within himself as an intrinsic entelechy, and
insofar as he realizes his own essence as communicated to the world only
in the Incarnation and the cross, he is the Spirit of Jesus Christ to begin
with. Insofar as this Spirit always and everywhere brings justifying faith,
this faith is always and everywhere and from the outset a faith which comes
to be in the Spirit of Jesus Christ. In this Spirit of his he is present and
operative in all faith.

THE SEARCHING "MEMORY" OF ALL FAITH
IS DIRECTED TOWARDS THE ABSOLUTE SAVIOUR

Jesus Christ is always and everywhere present in justifying faith because this
faith is always and everywhere the searching memory of the absolute saviour. By definition the absolute saviour is the God-Man who reaches fulfillment through death and resurrection. We are not going to explain all of
the elements in this proposition in detail because that would have to take
us too far afield at this point. Hence in particular we are not going to show
further that the historical saviour, who makes God's offer to the world
irreversible and makes it manifest in its irreversibility, is necessarily the
incarnate Logos of God who reaches fulfillment in his earthly reality

through death and resurrection. Nor are we going to show the exact connection between our first proposition and this second one. The two of course are closely connected with each other, but we are not going to go into this in any further detail here.

In view of the subject matter of our reflections, it is important only that we clarify somewhat what is meant by the proposition that the searching memory of all faith is directed towards the absolute saviour wherever this faith exists. We are not going to discuss here the question to what extent the goal of this searching memory has to be explicit here or can just be implicit. This question has to be nuanced, of course, depending on whether we are talking about an individual or a collective consciousness and faith. When we speak of memory, this notion seems from the outset to contradict the characteristic which we are attributing to this memory by saying that it is a searching memory. In the popular understanding of the term "memory," it always seems to be related only to something which is already found in the past. It does not seem to be related to something which is still outstanding either in general or for oneself, still has to be found, and hence still has to be searched for. But if we recall Plato's teaching about *anamnesis* or Augustine's teaching about *memoria*, which we cannot go into here, we see immediately that the matter is not that simple.

Ultimately the whole problematic of the relationship between transcendentality and history points to this, as well as the problematic of the relationship between the a priori and the a posteriori in knowledge. We can find and retain something which encounters man in history only if there is present in the finding and retaining subjectivity of man an a priori principle of expectation, of searching, of hoping. But following a tradition which runs throughout the whole western history of man's spirit, we can call this a priori principle "memory." In doing so memory may not be understood merely as a faculty for receiving everything and anything, simply as an empty space into which contingent history arbitrarily and unselectively brings in everything which might ever have happened in this history. Memory itself has a priori structures which indeed do not simply anticipate what is free and unexpected in history. But they alone make it possible to perceive something in this very history and to distinguish it and locate it in a definite place. Memory is the a priori possibility for historical experience precisely as historical, as distinguished from the a priori conditions of possibility for the a posteriori knowledge of things in the natural sciences.

We can only give here these brief indications of what this theory of memory is about. The main point is the proposition that memory is also, and indeed especially, the anticipation of the absolute saviour which searches and watches in history. It is a formal anticipation, and therefore it does not anticipate the concreteness of history, but rather it endures history and keeps its experience open to it. As spirit and as freedom, man always experiences in his transcendentality his orientation towards the incomprehensible mystery which we call God. Although it is not something owed to him, he experiences within himself the hope that this orientation is so radical that it will find its fulfillment in the immediate self-communication of God. It is an orientation which is borne, liberated and made radical by supernatural grace.

But since man's transcendentality as radicalized by grace is always reflexive at least in an initial way and is either accepted or rejected in freedom, this transcendentality is mediated by the historical experience in whose contents man becomes aware of his own transcendentality. To be sure, this historical experience as man's mediation to his own gratuitously elevated transcendentality can have the most varied contents. It does not necessarily and always and everywhere have to have a religious theme, presupposing only that it mediates a person to himself as freely disposing of himself in his single totality. But as history, which is not merely an amorphous mass of things which are juxtaposed in time or space, this experience has a structure in which its individual elements each have a different place in time and space, and do not all possess the same significance. The searching anticipation which characterizes this structure belongs to the very essence of this memory. Insofar as history is a history of freedom, and insofar as freedom is not the capacity to be always able to do something different arbitrarily, but is rather the capacity to make a decision of final and definitive validity, there belong to the structure of history, as this structure is anticipated and expected by memory, those decisions through which the course of history moves either partially or completely from the open multiplicity of indifferent possibilities to something final and definitive which has been done in freedom.

Now if we presuppose that within a still ongoing history something which has to be accomplished in history, and which is final and definitive for history as a whole, can become historically manifest and tangible, and that something like this does not have to be simply identical with the consummation of history as a whole, then we can say that the memory which belongs to man's gratuitously elevated transcendentality searches in hope and in anticipation for that event in history in which a free decision about the salvific outcome of history is made and becomes tangible. Indeed it is made by God's freedom and man's freedom together, and it is made for the single history of the human race as a whole. But this event which memory expects and for which it is searching is what we are calling the absolute saviour. The absolute saviour is what memory anticipates, and this anticipation is present in all faith.

THE QUESTION ABOUT THE CONCRETE HISTORY OF RELIGION

It is of course a further question, and one which ultimately can be answered only in an a posteriori way by the history of religion, if we ask whether and to what extent, and how explicitly or implicitly this anticipation of the absolute saviour by faith's memory is demonstrable in mythology or in history. As we have already said, at this point the dogmatic theologian has to hand the question over to the historian of religion and to his Christian interpretation of the history of religion. From the perspective of dogmatic theology it seems to be an ultimately secondary question whether the searching expectation of a saviour in myths is objectified or is projected onto historical figures in whom is recognized the character of saviour, either in a merely provisional sense or in a final and definitive sense. In the light of his own presuppositions the dogmatic theologian can only say that we should look to the history of religion in a precise and positive way to see whether and how such saviour figures are to be found in it. He can say that from the perspective of dogmatic theology there is no reason to exclude such discoveries a priori, nor to judge them in a minimalistic way to be merely a negative contrast to faith in Jesus as the eschatological and unsurpassable saviour. Saviour figures in the history of religion can readily be regarded as an indication of the fact that mankind, moved always and everywhere by grace, anticipates and looks for that event in which its absolute hope becomes irreversible in history, and becomes manifest in its irreversibility.

·VII·

Christianity as Church

1. Introduction

THE NECESSARY INSTITUTIONAL MEDIATION OF RELIGION
AND ITS SPECIAL NATURE IN CHRISTIANITY

In the period before the resurrection Jesus Christ knew himself to be the "absolute mediator of salvation," the inauguration of God's kingdom, and the eschatological climax of salvation history. The historical continuation of Christ in and through the community of those who believe in him, and who recognize him explicitly as the mediator of salvation in a profession of faith, is what we call church. And if the period before Christ was already encompassed by God's salvific will and by his self-communication, and hence if it was a history of hope, although it was hope in a future which was open and ambivalent from the perspective of man's freedom and mankind's freedom, then the period after Christ is all the more encompassed by and bears the stamp of an explicit profession and knowledge of the fact that this Jesus Christ is the salvation of the world, and that in him God has offered himself to the world *irrevocably*. Consequently, hope does indeed still remain because, in spite of the closeness of God's kingdom which has come in Christ, man does not lose the responsibility of his own freedom. This hope however has acquired a quite different and "eschatological" character in view of God's irreversible offer of himself to the world. But if the period after Christ is also the "Christian age" on the level of an explicit profession of faith, and in the dimension in which the irreversibility of God's salvific self-expression becomes historically and institutionally tangible, then it is the period of the church.

Looked at from the perspective of the Christian understanding of existence, what we are calling church, that is, the institutional constitution of the religion of the absolute mediator of salvation, is obviously not accidental to man's essence as a being orientated towards God. If man is a being of interpersonal communication not just on the periphery, but rather if this characteristic co-determines the whole breadth and depth of his existence,

322

and if salvation touches the whole person and places him as a whole and with all of the dimensions of his existence in relationship to God, and hence if religion does not just concern some particular sector of human existence, but concerns the whole of human existence in its relationship to the all-encompassing God by whom all things are borne and towards whom all things are directed, then this implies that the reality of interpersonal relationship belongs to the religion of Christianity. But by man's very nature such interpersonal relationships may not be seen merely as a matter of the feelings or of a purely personal and spiritual relationship between two persons, but rather they must also be interpersonal relationships which are concretized in society. If salvation history as the history of God's transcendental self-communication to man is a history which can be experienced in time and space, then it follows from this perspective too that in the Christian understanding religion is necessarily ecclesial religion.

In addition to this there is the characteristic which stems from our own particular epoch and which characterizes us for today and for tomorrow. From the eighteenth century until the first half of the twentieth century it might perhaps have looked as though a person could appropriate his religion in a private kind of interiority. People tried to situate religion someplace where they might escape the rigors of their concrete historical and social nature. But if today we are moving more and more towards the unity of a single history of the world and towards the development of the human community into a closer social network, and if we see that a person cannot discover his personhood and his uniqueness by looking for them as something absolutely contrary to his social nature, but can only discover them *within* his social nature and in function of this social nature; and if there is a relationship of mutual conditioning between love of God and love of neighbor, and hence if love for one's neighbor is not merely a secondary moral consequence of a proper relationship to God; and if, beyond this, love of neighbor cannot merely mean a private relationship to another individual, but also means something social and political, and implies responsibility for social and political structures within which love for one's neighbor can or cannot be practiced, then it also follows from all of this that basically it would be a late bourgeois conception to think that religion has nothing essential to do with society and with church. We are aware today in a quite new and inescapable way that man is a social being, a being who can exist only within such intercommunication with others throughout all of the dimension of human existence. And from this perspective we acquire a new understanding of Christian religion as an ecclesial religion.

THE DOCTRINE OF THE CHURCH
IS NOT THE CENTRAL TRUTH OF CHRISTIANITY

But on the other hand we also have to see just as clearly that the doctrine of the church and of its social constitution is not the core of the ultimate truth of Christianity. There continues to exist right up to our own times an ecclesial consciousness of a militant kind which is a reaction to the individualism of the nineteenth century, a militant ecclesiality which is tempted to make ecclesiality the most specific and central thing about Christianity in an indiscriminate way. For example, among the members of l'Action française at the beginning of the twentieth century there was a slogan to the effect that one is indeed a Catholic, but not a Christian by a long shot. If the point of the slogan was that militant ecclesiality is the specific distinction of Roman Catholicism, and that Christian realities like the Sermon on the Mount, love and freedom of the spirit are highly suspect, this brings out with the utmost clarity the danger which can be associated with our traditional church consciousness.

Vatican II says in its Decree on Ecumenism *Unitatis redintegratio,* (art. 11) that there is an ordered structure or a "hierarchy of truths" in Catholic doctrine. If we reflect upon this, surely ecclesiology and the ecclesial consciousness even of an orthodox and unambiguously Catholic Christian are not the basis and the foundation of his Christianity. Jesus Christ, faith and love, entrusting oneself to the darkness of existence and into the incomprehensibility of God in trust and in the company of Jesus Christ, the crucified and risen one, these are the central realities for a Christian. If he could not attain them, if he could not really realize them in the innermost depths of his existence, then basically his ecclesiality and his feeling of belonging to the concrete church would only be an empty illusion and a deceptive facade.

THE DIFFICULT QUESTION ABOUT THE TRUE CHURCH

It is well known from the theology of the various Christian denominations, and it can be clearly seen in the history of dogma, that the question of the church, the question about the church which was really intended and founded by Christ is one of the most difficult questions and one of the most disputed questions in ecumenical theology. With this question in our discussion of the church we arrive at a point which cannot be ignored, the point when we have to say *which* church we mean, and when we have to say why we believe that our concrete church is *the* church of Jesus Christ. But this question is extraordinarily difficult both from a scriptural and a historical point of view. It is out of the question that we could answer here in an exact, historical way all of the historical questions connected with the origin of the church, with the development of the church's constitution, and with evaluating the different divisions which are found in the history of the church.

It is to be taken for granted that a great deal of what we have to say about the essence of the church in a formal way will be found by many non-Catholic Christians to belong to their own understanding of the church as well. But there are also both formal and material statements about the church which Catholic theology declares to be applicable only to its own church, but which nevertheless it declares to belong to the essence of the church intended by Christ. Ecumenical theology necessarily has to evaluate these statements and the actual state of affairs. In principle this evaluation could consist in a direct investigation into the material content of the issue in question. It would then have to be shown by an exact exegetical inquiry, for example, what Matthew 16 really says about the Petrine office, and hence to what extent the historical Jesus wanted to found a permanent institution in his community of faith, and why an episcopacy with apostolic succession really belongs to the institutional elements of the church which Christ intended definitively. It would have to be shown how this Petrine office continued to develop in the church, that it has remained faithful to its original essence, and that the later interpretation of both the essence and the scope of this office corresponds to its original beginnings, even though it has developed in the history of the church and in the history of dogma. Frequently such development does not allow the identity of the original church and the contemporary church to be recognized all that easily.

But here on our first level of reflection there can be no question of undertaking a direct investigation into the material content of all of the institutional elements of the Roman Catholic Church. We shall try rather to suggest an indirect approach which is appropriate on a first level of reflection and for an introduction to the idea of Christianity in its totality. This approach will consist more in the reflection of a Catholic Christian upon his membership in the Roman Catholic church. From out of his religious situation he will answer to some extent the question why a Catholic Christian believes and is convinced that he really encounters Jesus Christ in his church, and that he has no reason to abandon or to cast doubt upon the membership in his church which has been handed down to him as his own existentiell situation.

2. The Church as Founded by Jesus Christ

THE QUESTION

Without forgetting the methodological principles just mentioned or allowing them to recede into the background, in this section we want to say a few things very briefly about why and to what extent the church was founded by the historical and risen Jesus. Church is meant here in a sense prior to its differentiation into the different Christian churches and denominations. We want to examine at least briefly the connection between the church and Jesus Christ. In the course of the nineteenth and twentieth centuries the context of this question has undergone very frequent and very quick changes. Among the serious theologians of all of the Christian denominations today, hardly anyone any more advocates the opinion that the church is merely a spiritual community in an abstract sense, a community of those who believe in the message of Jesus, a message which itself is not a message of Jesus about the church. Otherwise, of course, the ecumenical question basically could not even arise, that is, the question about the necessity of striving for the unity of the church or of the churches among all Christians today. And otherwise of course we would have to say that Christianity exists wherever there is faith in the forgiving message of Jesus Christ which offers us God himself, and nothing else is needed. To this extent there is a new consensus today that arguing from Christ himself there is or there must be a church in the sense of a real historical entity.

This of course does not make the really controversial questions in theology disappear. For the question whether the historical Jesus himself intended and founded a visible, structured and universal church still remains, and has even become more acute. Moreover, it is even a question whether according to the eschatological message which he directed to Israel he *could* have founded such a church as a permanent entity at all. If it is asserted of him that he only perceived himself as the final prophet, as the final warning before the inbreaking of God's kingdom here and now in his own time, before God's coming in justice and in grace (or, better, through grace), and hence if he based his whole message on an absolute and imminent expectation in a *temporal* sense, and if he had absolutely no knowledge of a period which could be described as a temporal interval, then of course there would be no possibility to begin with of a church being founded within the horizon of Jesus' proclamation.

But in the ecclesiology of all the Christian denominations today it is more or less universally recognized that something like the constitution of the church is found soon after Easter. But there are very different opinions about the original Christian self-understanding at the time, about its unity, and about what from an empirical point of view was a very hesitant entrance of the church into the pagan world. Because this touches the ecumenical questions in ecclesiology directly, the sharpest divergences of opinion have to do with the concrete constitution of the church, and to what extent it can be traced back to Jesus: the primacy of Peter, the place of the twelve, and the question of apostolic succession in the sense of whether the college of the twelve and the Petrine office continue on in the college of bishops and in the Roman papacy as the handing on of an office which Christ founded, or whether this appeal to a community which was structured by Jesus himself is illegitimate.

These differences of opinion are also more complicated in non-Catholic theology insofar as some dispute whether in New Testament times there existed a *common* understanding of the church at all within the post-resurrection communities which called themselves Christian. Some are of the opinion that in New Testament times different conceptions of the church and different types of church structure already existed side by side. Hence the claim that a particular community is *the* church intended by Christ and that it alone is *iuris divini* would contradict the historical evidence.

PRESUPPOSITIONS FOR THE "FOUNDING OF THE CHURCH" BY JESUS

Now if we look first of all to the presuppositions which we have to make in order that something like the founding of a church is even conceivable within the horizon of the historical Jesus, we have to say in the first place: Jesus did not proclaim universal religious ideas, perhaps in an especially original and appealing way, but ideas nevertheless which basically and in themselves were conceivable and attainable in all times and places. Rather he delivered an eschatological message to Israel. He proclaimed a historical event which was present then and there through him and only because he was present. He says that here and now the *basileia*, the kingdom of God, has come in him and in his person in a quite new and radically demanding way. There obviously belongs to this kingdom a people of God and a people of salvation who form the kingdom, for this kingdom is an event which God's salvific will brings about precisely by the fact that he gathers a people of believers. And we see accordingly that Jesus gathered into his following people who were awaiting salvation, for they were the lost sheep of the house of Israel who were without their true shepherd.

But contrary to the other religious groups at the time (for example, the Pharisees and the Essenes) Jesus offers salvation to everyone, even to sinners, provided that they accept the gospel and the good news of the inauguration of God's kingdom and satisfy its moral demands. It is important to emphasize this because it follows from this that Jesus did not really want to found a special group or a kind of religious order within the Jewish synagogue, nor to gather a holy remnant. He really meant *everybody*, he wanted to call everybody. But this creates the situation in which either the Israel to which he first directed his message would be converted as a whole, as a religious institution, into the community which follows Christ and the community which represents the kingdom, or Jesus must found this community of those who believe in him and follow him not within Israel, but outside it. The rejection of Jesus' message by the majority of the Jewish people, therefore, leads to the question how God will realize his plan of salvation in spite of the disbelief of the Jews.

We must see clearly here that even empirically Jesus realizes the necessity of his death and also reveals it to his disciples, at least insofar as he is convinced that his proclamation of the victorious closeness of God's kingdom will not be disavowed by his death, but rather that it will be fulfilled definitively precisely through his death. His death of atonement becomes the foundation of a new and divinely bestowed order of grace, the foundation of a new covenant. Jesus sees a period of time elapsing between his death and the coming of the fullness of the kingdom of God. It is not only a period of waiting, but also a period for gathering and preparing the people of God who have been formed on this new foundation. Someone can deny that these presuppositions are found in Jesus only if he denies that Jesus had a clear intention and acted reasonably up to and including his death. A new people of God exists through him. He gathers it together, and hence he must come to terms with the question what has to happen to this following which had gathered around him if the people of Israel reject the offer to enter into this new people of God and to be its basis.

THE THESIS AND ITS PROBLEM

Jesus "founded" his church. This is the common conviction of the Christian churches as long as we prescind from the question what "founding" means, and which of the explanations of this term which are given in the theologies of the Christian churches is the correct one. Wherever ecclesial

Christianity is found, it is convinced that it has its origins in Christ. It is convinced that it does not establish a relation to Jesus autonomously and by itself, but rather that this relation has its origins in and is established by the crucified and risen Jesus himself, that this is an act of Jesus and not primarily an act of the church itself. If this is correct, then this constitutes both the basic meaning and the legitimacy of the proposition that the church was founded by Jesus. But this still leaves many questions obscure and open in the basic thesis which we formulated, and the meaning of "founded" is itself still obscure.

The relevant questions here are familiar enough. Once again: Given his imminent expectation, could Jesus think in terms of a "period of the church"? Could he see and intend explicitly that his narrow circle of disciples, the twelve, would ever continue with essentially the same function in what we see in the church later as bishops and as the college of bishops? From a historical point of view can one seriously hold the opinion that Jesus himself already foresaw the definite juridical organization of a definite community which accepts and professes his message about the closeness of God's kingdom and about himself, or even foresaw the totality of such communities? From a historical point of view can we think that he himself intended the privileged position which he conferred upon Cephas within the circle of the twelve to be a permanent institution for all future times?

THE ATTEMPT TO RESPOND: THE PRINCIPLES INVOLVED

Prescinding from a great deal which is to be said positively later with historical probability about the founding of the church by Jesus, if one is not inclined to answer these and similar questions with an apodictic affirmative, especially when one sees how much the church was in the process of becoming, how fluid things were after Easter and in the whole apostolic period, and how obscure the social contours of the communities and of the whole church remain for us, then perhaps what is recommended first of all at this point is an indirect method for answering the question to what extent we can in any case speak of Jesus "founding" the church. This is recommended even though it gives us at first a minimalistic answer. We would say, therefore:

First, the church was founded in the first place by the fact that Jesus is the person whom the believers professed to be the absolute saviour and to be God's historically irreversible and historically tangible offer of himself, and by the fact that he would not be who he is if the offer of himself which

God made in him did not continue to remain present in the world in an historically tangible profession of faith in Jesus. This is true *because of the very nature* of God's offer. Abiding faith in Jesus is an intrinsic and constitutive element in God's offer of himself which has become irreversible in Jesus. In this sense, as we said earlier, Jesus is necessarily risen in the faith of his disciples for all times, and we mean this in a positive sense, not in an exclusive sense. Insofar as this faith has its origins in Jesus Christ, the church as the community of these believers has its origins in Jesus. Faith and hence the church may not be regarded simply as the absolutely new and autonomous response of men to the crucified and risen Jesus.

Secondly, this faith may not be regarded as something which happens in the private interiority of an individual. In this case it could never be the continuation of God's offer of himself in Jesus. Rather it must be public, it must be a profession, it must be the faith of a community. Hence the church has its origins in Jesus because faith as a public and communal profession has its origins in him.

Thirdly, the faith which in this sense forms community must have a *history,* and hence so must the church itself, because there is a *history* of salvation. For faith in Jesus in a later generation is always co-conditioned by the tradition of the previous generation, and does not always arise absolutely new by a kind of primordial generation. But this historicity of both faith and the church, a historicity which includes both change and ongoing identity because both of these belong to genuine history, this historicity includes the following: every later epoch in such a history continues to have its origins in the previous epoch, even when it diverges from its previous epoch. But this means that the historical ambivalence or the range of possibilities for historical decisions in an earlier epoch does not simply have to pass on to the later epoch. If continuity and identity are to be maintained within an entity which exists historically, then it is inevitable that in an earlier phase of this historical entity free decisions are made which form an irreversible norm for future epochs. Whether or not this is the case in a particular instance, and hence whether such decisions can be revised by new decisions, depends on the one hand on the depth and the absoluteness of the decision in the earlier epoch, and it depends on the other hand on the fidelity which a later epoch has to the decision of an earlier epoch in order to preserve the identity of the historical.

In any case, if we understand historical change and historical identity in their unity, and if we take the one-directional nature of history seriously, which means that history loses earlier possibilities because of free decisions, then we see that, in the process in which the church comes to be as a free and historical entity, it neither possesses nor has to possess every possibility which was present earlier in the church as the possibility for a decision, or at least was present according to a historical and perhaps even questionable judgment from a contemporary point of view. In order that a historical decision in one epoch be binding for later epochs for the sake of preserving historical continuity, all that can be seriously required is that this decision lay *within* the genuine possibilities of the church's origins and does not contradict these origins. But it cannot be required that this decision was the only possible one and was offered as the only possible one by these historical origins. Although it is not a necessary decision from the viewpoint of its origin, a genuine decision which is binding on the future history of a historical entity which preserves its continuity throughout change c： ｜ certainly be regarded as justified by its origin, as being derived from th ： origin, and as "founded" by this origin.

APPLICATION TO THE PROBLEM OF CONTINUITY BETWEEN JESUS AND THE CHURCH

Presupposing the principles just indicated for an entity which exists historically and freely, and which changes but at the same time preserves its identity, and presupposing that the community of those who believe in Jesus is such an historical entity which grows to maturity in freedom, then these consequences follow:

First, this community has its origins in Jesus and in this sense was founded by Jesus even if in the course of its development and through historical decisions this community adopts structures which are selected from a broad range of genuine possibilities which are possible in themselves and in the abstract, but structures which are nevertheless irreversible and binding on future epochs. From this perspective such structures (for example, a monarchial and episcopal constitution and a permanent Petrine office) can be understood as having their origins in Jesus and as *iuris divini*, at least if they are found in the apostolic period. For during this period the public history of revelation was not yet closed, as, for example, the formation of the normative scriptures of the New Testament shows. These structures can be understood this way even if they cannot be traced back to a specific, unambiguous and historically identifiable saying of Jesus which founds them. This presupposes only that it can be shown that these decisions or these acts of the church which give it its constitution lie within the genuine possibilities which are given through Jesus and through faith in him. Presupposing this, such acts can also be irreversible and binding on later generations, and in this sense *iuris divini*.

Secondly, from this perspective and in accordance with our method which is by hypothesis minimalistic, it is not basically and absolutely necessary that we would have to trace back to an explicit saying of Jesus the more concrete structures of the constitution of the (Catholic) church which the church now declares are always obligatory for it. We would not have to do this in order to understand the church as so constituted to have its origins in Jesus and to be founded by him.

It is on these presuppositions and only on them that we are to understand what is still to be said positively about individual elements in the relationship between the historical Jesus and the earlier and later church in its concrete structures. Without emphasizing it explicitly every time, we can admit without hesitation the historical problems connected with this relationship. If what has been said up to now is correct, it is ultimately unimportant whether this or that element of the church as it is being formed in apostolic times can be traced more or less directly back to the historical Jesus, or whether it is to be understood as a historical but still irreversible decision of the church which lies within the genuine possibilities of the original church. If a church exists which was brought about by the power of the Spirit and by the power of faith in the risen Jesus, and hence if it has its origins in Jesus and was "founded" by him, then not only can we and must we grant her merely the possibility of free and accidental changes depending on the concrete situation in which she finds herself, and no one denies this. We also have to grant the legitimacy of a process of becoming in the church from out of her origins into her full *essence*.

THE ACTS OF JESUS WHICH FOUNDED THE CHURCH

In the following two sections we shall have to summarize some exegetical findings. Since a discussion of the state of exegetical research is neither possible nor sensible for our purposes, let me refer you here to some summary works, especially Rudolf Schnackenburg's article, *"Kirche I,"* in *Lexicon für Theologie und Kirche* VI, pp. 167–172, and his book, *The Church in the New Testament*. His findings will not be established in detail here and hence should be accepted by everyone "at their own risk."

Many of the words and deeds of Jesus have the character of intending to found a church, but have this of course in varying degrees depending on their place in salvation history. We shall explain this thesis in what follows.

First of all, it cannot be doubted that Jesus gathered disciples around himself in order to assemble the people of God around him, and in the first instance this people was Israel. In doing so the formation of the circle of the twelve was of a significance which can hardly be doubted historically. Jesus revealed thereby his claim upon the whole of Israel. Hence even historically it is false to think that Jesus did indeed gather some kind of a circle around himself, but he understood this only as a kind of religious order within Israel, and he did not make any claim upon the whole people. For precisely by their number the twelve were to represent symbolically the whole of Israel, the eschatological Israel which Jesus had in mind. Therefore they were sent out by Jesus to preach, and they participated in the healing power of Jesus which was a sign for him that the eschatological kingdom as a present and pressing reality was operative here and now in him.

That the intent of this inquiry to discern acts of Jesus which "founded a church" is legitimate is shown by the fact that the community of disciples stays intact after the rejection of Jesus by the majority of the Jewish people. The recognition of their election by God, the introduction to the mystery of his suffering, and the instructions about coming persecutions, these among other things show that Jesus retained the idea of a community of salvation which gathered around him, and which basically summons everyone to *metanoia,* to conversion and to faith. It is from this perspective that we would have to explain the Last Supper with the institution of the Eucharist as something directed towards the new order of salvation, the new covenant. Likewise the word to Simon (Luke 22:31 f.) shows that the community of disciples is to continue to stay together. There also belongs in this context the promise of an eschatological fulfillment in God's kingdom of what was being done here sacramentally (Luke 22:16, 20, 30a).

Finally, we have to refer to what A. Vögtle calls the "ecclesiological mandate in the sayings of the risen Jesus" because they definitively bestow the powers of Jesus upon the disciples for the continuation of his work in the world (cf. Matt. 28, and so on).

Now the direct intention of Jesus to found a church is expressed in Matt. 16:18 f. First of all, it can be said with certainty that these words to Simon as the rock of the church, as the possessor of the keys in the church of Jesus, as someone endowed with the power to bind and to loose, these words really belong in the ancient gospel of the church. Their authenticity is enforced by the Semitic rhythm and character of the language, by parallels from Qumran, but especially by the Cephas tradition so closely connected with this text. The origins of the Cephas tradition in which this word becomes his own proper name is hardly to be explained otherwise. Simon is called Cephas or Peter everywhere in the early community. And really this change of names can hardly be explained as the reason for the name which Simon had in the early community in any other way except as having its origins in the Cephas saying of Jesus in Matt. 16:18.

A valid rejection of the authenticity of these words would perhaps be possible only if it could be proven that such a saying is impossible to begin with on the lips of Jesus. But this is not the case, for it cannot be maintained that Jesus' imminent expectation and the proclamation that the coming kingdom is already inaugurated in Jesus allow absolutely no room for thoughts of a church within the horizon, the mentality, the theology and the self-interpretation of Jesus. However, we do not of course have to break our heads over the question how far ahead the historical Jesus must have thought explicitly, and how concretely he must have thought when he conceived of a somewhat institutionalized community of those who believed in him and in his message, and who expected the final and definitive coming of God's kingdom as something which could no longer be delayed. It would not really be intelligible why and how the early community itself in Jerusalem accomplished something in their creative theology which we may not believe Jesus himself to have been capable of. We can leave to the exegetes the question where the saying of Jesus in Matt. 16:18 is to be located historically in the life of the pre-resurrection Jesus, since ultimately this is not of decisive importance for our reflections. Even if one thinks that Matthew situates it at a point in the course of the life of Jesus which could not have been its original place historically, ultimately nothing follows from this for our question. A comparison with the text in Luke 22:31 f., a text which is not suspect, shows that at least immediately before his passion the pre-resurrection Jesus could have made such a statement.

The meaning of the statement is: Jesus wants to found his community of salvation on Simon and on his person as on a rock, and against the Pharisees he assures his *ecclesia* of its survival against the powers of death, or the "gates of hell." By receiving the keys, which designate the administrator of the house, not the porter, Peter is given power to grant admission to the future kingdom. This becomes even clearer when compared with the text directed against the "scribes and Pharisees" in Matt. 23:13. This fundamental power of Peter as the rock in the new house of God, which as the church of Jesus is differentiated explicitly from Israel as the previous people of God, is explained in more detail by the image of binding and loosing. In the first instance it makes no difference to us at this point what exactly this power to bind and to loose means within the individual community and within the whole church. It is also given to the twelve or the apostles in Matt. 18.

In accordance with our intention to give a historically indirect and immediately existentiell argument, it is enough for us to establish that Jesus evidently willed a church as his own church, and that he gives it a certain basic constitution insofar as he constitutes Simon as the rock and the possessor of the keys and endows him with the power to bind and to loose. By doing so he really gives it a basic constitution, although it has not yet developed very far. This fundamental "Petrine" position which is acknowledged for Peter (Matt. 16:18) is confirmed as a position of preeminence in the circle of the brothers by Luke 22:31 f., and in John 21:15 ff. his power to lead the flock of Christ is expressed in a saying of the post-resurrection Jesus. The rest of the twelve also receive the power to bind and to loose. In this context it is of no immediate importance for us to ask how the twelve's power to bind and to loose is related to the power to bind and to loose which is found in the post-apostolic community. Finally, we have to refer to John 20:22, where in a text which we are not going to examine any further a power is promised to the Apostles by the risen Jesus which is conceived analogously to the power to bind and to loose.

We certainly may also say conversely that beyond these basic provisions Jesus left everything else to the Spirit who was promised, and to the history of the church which was guided by the Spirit, and especially of course to the history of the original church. He did this insofar as this fundamental beginning was concretized and consolidated in the early apostolic history of the first generation, and this fundamental beginning remains basically normative for the following ages of the church. If, finally, the question arises whether and to what extent Jesus himself could have thought of the organization of his community around Cephas as valid for all ages, ages which he could not have foreseen concretely, for this question we simply have to refer, or so it seems, to what we have already said above about the process of becoming in the essence of a historical entity.

3. The Church in the New Testament

ON THE SELF-UNDERSTANDING OF THE ORIGINAL COMMUNITY

If what has been said so far will have to be enough to show the legitimacy of saying that Jesus himself founded the early church, we must now say something very briefly about the self-understanding of the church as it is witnessed to in the New Testament. In doing so we shall not go any further into the question with what right this self-understanding of the apostolic church can appeal to Jesus himself.

The first name which the Christians applied to themselves as those who believed in Jesus as their risen Lord and Saviour was probably "the saints" (Acts 9:13, 32, 41; 26:10), and perhaps also the "community of God," this latter taking over the Old Testament characterization of Israel. Indeed this designation "community of God" or "church of God" was applied first to individual Jewish Christian communities and then also to Pauline communities, and then finally to the whole church (Acts 20:28; 1 Tim. 3:15; cf. the introductions to Paul's letters in general). In the beginning the original community in Jerusalem was bound closely to the civil and religious community of Israel. But it did not understand itself as a special group within Israel, but rather as the community which was assembled by Jesus, its Messiah, and called by him to summon all of Israel to faith in Jesus and to conversion (Acts 2:36, etc.). It already had its own cult, and finally, after some opposition, it followed the call of God to extend its mission to the pagan world. With the coming of the Spirit on Pentecost this community experienced itself as the eschatological community of salvation which was obligated to holiness of life, even when it tried to fulfill this obligation within the framework of the Jewish law. This picture is nuanced a great deal through more recent exegetical research. But this research naturally has a very strong hypothetical and heuristic character, so that we can leave it out of consideration in our reflections since it cannot alter the basic lines decisively or with the necessary degree of certainty.

ON THE THEOLOGY OF THE CHURCH IN LUKE AND MATTHEW

We have a real *theology* of the church in Luke and Matthew, and all the more so and quite explicitly in Paul. If we look for Luke's special contribution to the theology of the church in the foundations and development of his Gospel and of Acts, which are to be seen as interrelated since they belong together, we would have to see it in the fact that he situated the "period of the church" and its missionary task explicitly between the "ascension" of Jesus and the Parousia. This is not to say that this idea of the church only arose because of the experience that those who believed in Jesus did not simply and merely have to await the imminent arrival and manifestation of God's kingdom which Jesus had promised. But in his theology of the church Luke undoubtedly developed more clearly the idea that there really was a period of the church between the ascension of Jesus and his return. Consequently, Luke's theology of salvation history recognizes three periods: the period of Israel (cf. Luke 16:16), the period of Jesus as the "center of time," and the period of the church. This latter extends until the full manifestation of the final and definitive eschaton which has come about in the center of time or in the period of Jesus. It follows as a result of this salvation-history perspective that the church turns first to Israel, the former people of God, and then only because of the disbelief of the Jews does it take up its mission to the pagans definitively. The church moves from Jerusalem out into the whole world, but in doing so it retains its continuity with the old Israel in salvation history in spite of the radical caesura which is created by Jesus and by the disbelief of his people which he encountered.

Matthew is also concerned about the position of Israel and the interpretation of it in salvation history. It is said of the Jewish people: "the kingdom of God will be taken from you and given to a people which will bring forth its fruit" (Matt. 21:43). This people is the true Israel which is made up of Jews and pagans who believe in Jesus. The Gospel of Matthew takes pains to show the essence and the structure of this people. Hence it becomes the real "ecclesial Gospel" (Schnackenburg). It is within this context that the individual elements have to be seen: the law of Christ is proclaimed for this new people of God and for this new covenant in the Sermon on the Mount. The universality of the church becomes manifest (cf. Matt. 8:10 ff.; 28:18 ff.: Jesus' command to go forth), and its constitution, its leadership and the discipline of the communities are also clarified. This Gospel is conscious of evildoers in the community, and of the presence and support of the Lord for his community. Of course all of this is still within a very small and modest framework—think, for example, of the community rules in Matt. 18. Communities are presupposed here which can no longer exist today from a sociological point of view. But basically this does not change the fact that there is already a "theology of the church" in Matthew's Gospel. The call of Jesus and its salvific significance does not merely address the individual in the interiority of his conscience, but rather it really builds church communities around Jesus with his "laws," which break out of and transcend the law of the Old Testament, with a cult and its anamnesis of the salvific death of Jesus, and also with a leadership which is in the hands of Simon Peter and the twelve.

ON THE PAULINE THEOLOGY OF THE CHURCH

Paul's letters develop a theology of the church in the proper sense which cannot be surpassed even in the contemporary theology of the church. For us it is of relatively little importance to know to what extent and in what sense Paul reflected upon the social constitution of the church. He is a genuine apostle who speaks with the authority of one sent by the exalted Lord. He certainly perceives himself as a church authority. Consequently, prescinding from the Pastoral Epistles, the question of a church constitution for later times when this direct apostolic mission is no longer present does not have to be a very real question for him. But Paul still knows that he has to be in agreement with Peter and the original Jerusalem community. He preaches a doctrine which he has received from the tradition in a genuine process of *paradosis*. Hence he is not merely a Christian charismatic follower of someone who has risen from the dead, but rather on the whole he is an apostle who is functioning within a church, and for this reason he always feels himself responsible to the Jerusalem community. Even when he disagrees with Simon to his face, he knows that he has obligations to him, and hence basically he respects the church in its totality with its antecedent structures, structures which are binding on him even though he was added to the list of apostles.

We can sketch the basic lines of his theology of the church briefly as follows. The church is made up of Jews *and* pagans, and in the possibly deutero-Pauline letter to the Ephesians the union of the two is the "mystery of Christ" in an absolute sense (cf. Eph. 3:4, 6). But the unfinished role of Israel in salvation history is also recognized (cf. Rom. 9–11). This new community of the church is founded sacramentally on baptism and the Eucharist. The mystical body of Christ lives by that body which is received at the Lord's Supper. We also find without doubt a consciousness of the total church in Paul. To be sure the individual communities are also called church or *ecclesia*, and the presence of Christ becomes manifest in them as the final and eschatological salvation. To this extent there is no doubt that for Paul the individual communities are not merely a kind of administrative district within a large organization which alone may be called church. But despite this, a consciousness of the total church is found clearly in Paul. And if the church is in Ephesus or in Colossae, still when this expression is correctly interpreted it means once again that the whole community gathered in faith around Jesus through baptism and in the Lord's supper throughout the whole world is the church, and this church becomes manifest in its fullest actuality here in these individual local communities.

The church is also for Paul a cosmic reality and a heavenly presence, and this becomes especially clear in the ecclesiology of Ephesians. The penetrating idea of the body of Christ was developed first and with special clarity by Paul. But it would also be false to want to reduce Paul's ecclesiology exclusively and in a one-dimensional way to this concept of the church. For Paul had at his disposal a much richer and more comprehensive symbolism: the symbol of the plant, the building, the temple, the new Jerusalem, and the bride or the spouse of Christ. The eschatological understanding of the church also comes to expression in Paul.

Leaving open the question of the authorship of the Pastoral Epistles, in any case we do have in them a self-understanding of the church in the apostolic period. The church is described in these letters as the well-ordered house of God and therefore as the pillar and foundation of truth. They contain very clear instructions about offices, ordination, catechetical instruction and the purity of doctrine. We find here without doubt an image of the church which bears a strong institutional stamp, but it does not by any means for this reason contradict the eschatological image of the church. Rather, beginnings which are certainly found in the main Pauline corpus are developed further for more advanced situations.

OTHER NEW TESTAMENT ECCLESIOLOGIES

The main text for our question in the First Epistle of Peter (1 Pet. 2:4–10) fuses a variety of ideas, images and Old Testament themes into a theological synthesis: Christ as the cornerstone, the church as the spiritual house erected in the Holy Spirit, the holy priesthood of all Christians offering spiritual sacrifice in this temple (and this priesthood is a royal priesthood), a new people of God made up of Jews and pagans. This letter also reflects upon the dispersion and persecution of the church, and on the strength it receives from its brotherhood in hope. So much for a brief look at some of the basic ideas in the First Epistle of Peter.

A different kind of synthesis of ecclesiology is found in the Epistle to the Hebrews. It takes up the Old Testament Exodus motif, the motif of the "pilgrim people of God" (E. Käsemann; cf. Heb. 3:7 to 4:11). In another theological reflection which likewise takes up Old Testament themes, it relates the promise of a heavenly vocation, entrance into God's sabbath rest, and hence the participation in the joys of heaven which is due to the fact that the high priest of this pilgrim people of God, namely, Christ, has already entered into heaven (Heb 13:14)—all of this it relates to their eschatological expectation. Hence there is a kind of interpenetration of promise and fulfillment: the church belongs to the heavenly Jerusalem and to the festival assembly at God's throne, while at the same time it is involved in the earthly struggle of suffering and trial.

Looking to the Gospel and the Epistles of John, in contrast to the letters of Paul the church is never really mentioned there explicitly by the name "church." But the church is nevertheless present everywhere in them: there are sacraments in this pneumatic Gospel, and in them and through the Spirit who comes from the Lord this exalted Lord carries out his salvific work and only in this way does he really bring it to completion. The gaze of the earthly Jesus is constantly directed to the future in which, after he has been lifted up, he will "draw all things to himself" (John 12:32), and will continue his mission. This is the future in which the gathering together of the scattered children of God will bring about one flock, and in which he will be united with his own like a vine which gives its living power to the branches. The witness of the church to Christ in the Holy Spirit, the Paraclete, will transform the world.

In the Apocalypse or the secret revelation, which intends to give the present church the power of faith and of life, the persecuted church is reminded of its dignity as the eschatological Israel which is protected by God's seal (cf. Rev. 7). Perhaps the heavenly woman who is the adversary of the satanic dragon (Rev. 12) is also to be interpreted ecclesiologically. In union with the flock of the redeemed in heaven, from which union it draws power and the assurance of victory, the church as the bride of the lamb awaits its wedding feast (Rev. 19:7). Hence the church in its consummation enters into the new Jerusalem, into the eschatological kingdom of God.

UNITY AND VARIETY IN THE NEW TESTAMENT IMAGE OF THE CHURCH

We see just from this brief sketch that the New Testament image of the church has very many levels. We find a church which is already institutional. It has bishops, deacons and presbyters, and is organized—particular offices and powers have a definite rank and place in the church. The individual communities are somehow connected organizationally. On the other hand we also have a theology of the church which looks especially to the interior reality of the church in grace and in faith, for example, when it is seen as the pilgrim people of God, as the community of those who are gathered around Christ as witnesses, as the body of Christ into which an individual is incorporated by baptism, the body of Christ which is quickened and constituted ever anew by the celebration of the Lord's Supper. In spite of the many images in these developing views, ultimately there does exist a deeper unity in the idea of the church in the New Testament.

Contrary to older opinions in New Testament research, it can no longer be held that Paul's concept of the church is incompatible with that of the original community. Nor can we or must we maintain any irreconcilable differences between the original Jewish Christian community, the Jewish Hellenistic communities, and Hellenistic Christianity (and besides, this latter is not so neatly distinguished in research any more), nor between Paul and the so-called early Catholicism which becomes clear in Luke and in the Pastoral Epistles.

Ultimately the same basic convictions and the same basic theological structures are found everywhere. There is the one church which was founded by Christ and was won by Christ and is united with Christ. It is at the same time a visible and an invisible church, it has an earthly and a heavenly mode of existence, and it possesses both an exterior form and an interior, Spirit-filled and mysterious essence. We do not have to maintain that the same image of the church prevailed everywhere on the level of existentiell and directly religious understanding. In that period, when the church perceived itself in radical opposition to the whole pagan and Hellenistic milieu, and when the profession of faith in Christ and baptism were the central events in the life of a Christian, it is to be taken for granted that many other sociological aspects of the church were still in flux. They did not have to enter into reflexive consciousness as much as they did in later times when the social presuppositions of a church of the masses would have to bring about these shifts in emphasis.

In addition to this there is the fact that from the perspective of a Catholic understanding of the church we have to take into account that the legal structure or the constitution of the church during the apostolic period until the end of the first century was of such a nature that it was not until the end of the apostolic period, and hence not until the beginning of the second Christian century or even later (consider, for example, the formation of the canon of the New Testament), that we find everything which we correctly regard today as the divine constitution of the church. Just as every Christian, even when he is inquiring about the canon, regards Holy Scripture as a whole as the document of Christian faith which is normative for him, and does this even though different aspects of theology are found within the New Testament scriptures, and even though a theological development is in evidence there, so too it is altogether compatible with the Catholic ecclesiological concept of a constitution which was given to the church in its basic lines by divine right to observe a development within the apostolic period. It is a development in which not all of the elements which were present originally necessarily develop to maturity. If, then, we see perhaps a more "democratic" constitution in a Hellenistic community, this does not yet mean that the episcopal structure of the individual churches which we find at the end of the first century is a false development, nor even that it is just an arbitrary development, and that in addition to it we have completely different possibilities for structuring the church today.

4. Fundamentals of the Ecclesial Nature of Christianity

CHRISTIANITY IS NECESSARILY CHURCH

The church is more than a social organization for religious purposes, even if these purposes would be Christian and would bear the stamp of Christianity. Wherever there are human beings there is "church" in the sense of a religious organization. Wherever any religious attitudes and any religious practices at all are found, even among those who protest against church, they form a community from the viewpoint of the sociology of religion and constitute something like a "church" in this very broad and provisional sense even if they call themselves a "free religion." When we say that Christianity must be constituted as church, we mean that this ecclesial community belongs to the religious existence of man as such, quite independently of the question how it must be constituted more precisely in the concrete. It is part of man's question about salvation and it is fundamentally co-constitutive of his relationship to God. It is in this sense that we are maintaining that church has something to do with the essence of Christianity, and that it is not merely an organization for the practice of religion, which in its real meaning would also be conceivable independently of such a religious organization.

When we say that church exists only when the question of religious organization itself is part of the real essence of what is Christian and what is religious, and hence when it acquires salvific significance itself, this does not mean that anyone who does not belong to such an ecclesially constituted Christianity loses his salvation, nor that he cannot have the ultimate and decisive relationship to God which is grounded in the grace of Christ. But the fact that God's salvific work is offered in principle to all people, and that in principle it effects the salvation of every person if it is accepted in obedience to one's moral conscience, this does not exclude the fact that the full and historically actualized Christianity of God's self-communication is an ecclesial Christianity.

The question about the church is not merely a question of human expediency, but rather it is a question of faith in the proper sense. By the very nature of Christianity, church must be understood in such a way that it springs from the very essence of Christianity as the supernatural self-communication of God to mankind which has become manifest in history and has found its final and definitive historical climax in Jesus Christ. Church is a part of Christianity as the very event of salvation. We cannot exclude communal and social intercommunication from man's essence even when he is considered as the religious subject of a relationship to God. If basically God is not a particular reality alongside all other possibilities, but rather is the origin and the absolute goal of the single and total person, then the whole person including his social and interpersonal dimension is related to this God. By the very nature of man and by the very nature of God, and by the very nature of the relationship between man and God when God is understood correctly, the social dimension cannot be excluded from the essence of religion. It belongs to it because man in all of his dimensions is related to the one God who saves the whole person. Otherwise religion would become merely a private affair of man and would cease to be religion.

THE AUTONOMOUS CHARACTER OF
THE CLAIM OF JESUS CHRIST'S MESSAGE

If religion is not a projection of existence which proceeds from man, but rather signifies a call of God, a call of the living God, and if, without prejudice to the divinity of God, this call of a free and personal God cannot be merely a transcendental affair of the innermost conscience of a person but rather comes in history, then there belongs to the essence of such a religion which has been implanted by God in history what we can call the element of the authoritative. Religion as the religion of God and not of human discovery, and religion which is really a historical reality must confront man in such a way that this religion does not become something real in human life only when man has projected and structured it in accordance with his own mentality. The simple question for the religious person is whether there is within the realm of his experience and his history a reality which he sees to be established independently of himself, and which he can allow to triumph as a power which is not at his disposal, but rather which disposes of him. If religion were basically nothing but what each individual perceives as the representation and interpretation of his own feeling about existence and his own interpretation of existence, then this religion would lack its essential ground and an essential characteristic.

Of course religion in order to be religion and Christianity in order to be Christianity must be taken up and transposed and realized subjectively. It is really present only where a personal decision in faith, hope and love is present. And of course the objective and the authoritative and the institutional can never take the place of the personal dimension in Christianity. But a genuine subjectivity which sees itself situated in God's presence, and therefore knows to begin with that it has to allow itself to be at the disposal of something objective which it has not established, this subjectivity understands what church is within the realm of the religious: it understands, namely, that here is something which obliges me, and which forms a point around which I can orientate myself, but which is not present only when I begin to be religious with my own subjectivity. By its very nature, the subjectivity of man, which no one can replace and for which no one can shirk responsibility, requires that it encounter an objectivity which is the norm for this subjectivity.

Within the potential of being a subject as something freely and personally granted, this objectivity must be able to appear as a norm for this subjectivity. As something which is able to act authoritatively, this objectivity must be the religion of God and not only an explication of my own feeling about existence. Christianity is the religion of a demanding God who summons my subjectivity out of itself only if it confronts me in a church which is authoritative. Otherwise the concrete person, who is not only transcendentality, but a concrete person with body and soul, with historical conditioning and with a subjective subjectivity, remains abandoned to his own poverty and problems and to the possibility of perverting and misinterpreting the religious. If Christ is not only an idea, but a concrete person, if salvation in Christ takes place not only through the communication of an ideology which basically could also be reached independently of Jesus and his proclamation, and if salvation depends on the concrete event of his cross, death and resurrection, then this salvation cannot only be found in and based upon a subjective interiority. The concreteness of Jesus Christ as something which challenges me must confront me in what we call the church. It is a church which I do not form and which is not constituted only through my wishes and religious needs, but rather it is a church which confronts me in a mission, a mandate and a proclamation which really make the reality of salvation present for me.

THE NECESSARY HISTORICAL AND SOCIAL MEDIATION OF SALVATION

We can express the whole problem of the church in a very simple question: Is man religious merely through his transcendental relation, however this is to be interpreted more exactly, or does this indubitable and fundamental relation of God to man and man to God in what we call Spirit and grace have itself a tangible and concrete history? Basically and ultimately there are only two possibilities in all of the forms and mixed forms of religion. Either history is itself of salvific significance, or salvation takes place only in a subjective and ultimately transcendental interiority, so that the rest of human life does not really have anything to do with it. If the first solution is the only really and genuinely human solution, then the church itself belongs in the salvation history of God's grace not only as some useful religious organization, but rather as the categorical concreteness and the mediation of salvation and grace, and only this makes church really church.

The time is past when a person could believe that the most specific thing about his existence, namely, the human and the really personal, could exist and be lived in an intimacy which has nothing to do with the hard reality of man's everyday life, with the society of men in its concrete intercommunication, and with wide-ranging socialization. The illusion does indeed still exist that men can organize themselves in a reasonable and social way, and beyond this views about the world can be kept out of these social arrangements. But it will become clearer and clearer that even the most secular society which is maintained by the use of force cannot do without an "ideological" foundation and world-view, and that it will produce them and defend them. This does not mean that the ideology of a future and highly organized society either has to be identical with Christianity or must necessarily be anti-Christian. But the development towards which we are moving shows that such a close relation and connection exists between the social dimension of man and the human dimension of man, including his world-view and interpretation of existence, that these two things cannot simply be separated in a society which is neutral about world-views. This shows, then, that man is also a social being in his world-view. If Christianity says conversely that man as Christian is also an ecclesial being in his ultimate relationship to God, this is not an ancient and long obsolete opinion, but rather something which is going to become very clear to people in our age in the years ahead.

In pointing out that by the very nature of man as an existent who actualizes his transcendentality in history, and because of the autonomous character of the claim of Christ's message, a Christian has to be an ecclesial

Christian, we may not of course obscure the obvious fact that the free acceptance of the church and its authority is itself once again an act of freedom and decision for which every Christian including a Catholic Christian has to take responsibility in the loneliness of his own conscience. Nor can he depend on the authority of the church as such at *this* point in the history of his freedom. Moreover, the fact that the authority of the church does become effective for an individual Christian always remains based upon this "lonely" decision. There is no essential difference on this point between a Catholic Christian and an Evangelical Christian* who recognizes any authoritative instance at all, for example, Holy Scripture, as coming "from without" and hence as binding.

5. An Indirect Method for Showing the Legitimacy of the Catholic Church as the Church of Christ

The normal method of fundamental theology, and one which is entirely justified in its understanding of methodology, usually aims at furnishing a direct historical proof for the fact that in the concrete the Roman Catholic church is the church of Christ, that it was willed by him as it actually exists in its own understanding of itself and of its essential constitution, and that it comes from Jesus Christ in historical continuity. We do not think that this approach is impossible in principle. But it is without doubt extraordinarily difficult for a concrete Christian today who is separated from Jesus Christ by an interval of two thousand years. In other words, it would involve so many difficult historical questions and proofs that in view of the knowledge which is really possible and at the command of a "normal" Catholic, it is not a *practically* feasible way to satisfy the demands of conscience and truth.

We shall try, therefore, to suggest an indirect way, indirect in relation to historical proofs for the identity of the church now with the church of Jesus Christ. From another point of view this indirect way is the more direct way because it proceeds more immediately from our own concrete and lived Christianity. With this purpose in mind we must *first of all* consider some formal principles connected with this method. Then, in a

* Here and elsewhere the term "Evangelical" refers to the Lutheran church in Germany. —Trans.

second reflection we have to apply these principles to the concrete question of the church, and ask what follows from them for the process of self-reflection which shows the legitimacy of our *Catholic* Christianity.

ON THE NECESSITY OF CHURCH

As we have already said, Christianity is essentially ecclesial, and not just in a secondary way or from the viewpoint of the social or pedagogical aspects of religion. The church as such belongs to Christianity, at least when Christianity really becomes conscious of itself and when it intends to maintain the continuity of a real history of salvation and has to prolong this continuity. Church is more than merely a practical and humanely unavoidable organization for fulfilling and satisfying religious needs. Christianity as the event of salvation, as God's act upon us and as man's response to God's ultimate self-communication, is ecclesial. We tried to show this from man's ultimate salvific situation and from the fact that Christianity claims the whole person for the salvation of the whole person. For man is essentially a being of intercommunication and community, and therefore he is also a historical and social being. We also tried to acquire a further understanding of this by saying that no matter how this works out more exactly in the concrete, a Christian has to anticipate an authoritative church. He has to anticipate a church which is more than his own social organization if and to the extent that Christianity is essentially more than an affair of his own subjective and pious dispositions and his own religious consciousness, and is more than the objectification of this. From this perspective church means the church which makes a claim upon me, the church which is the concreteness of God's demands upon me. Basically this concreteness is to be expected precisely if Christianity is not a religion which I create, but rather is the event of salvation which God bestows upon me by his own incalculable initiative. And if this salvific event as an act of God is not merely to come to me in the ultimate depths of conscience, but rather in the concreteness of my existence, then the concreteness of this God, who makes demands upon me and who is not my discovery or my creation, is Jesus Christ and his concrete church which makes demands upon me in the same way.

The same thing also follows from the fact that, insofar as Christianity is the personal self-communication of the mystery of God, it comes to us in such a way that there is a real history of God's self-communication to us. God's supernatural and transcendental self-communication is necessarily mediated historically. If, then, there is a history of salvation, and indeed one which ultimately has unfolded to its absolute and irreversible climax in the history of Jesus, the crucified and risen one, then the concreteness of salvation history as the concrete mediation of my supernatural and transcendental relationship to God in grace must continue to exist, and this means that church has to exist.

THE CHURCH OF JESUS CHRIST MUST BE ONE CHURCH

The second principle which we have to mention is the insight that this church of Jesus Christ has to be *one* church. If and insofar as church is not something which pious and Christ-inspired Christians form as a society for the further development of their own religious subjectivity, but rather is the coming of salvation history in Jesus Christ, then it is clear that church cannot be constituted by the fact that arbitrary groups of Christians form pious religious communities. A church which truly is a church and wants to remain one comes from Christ, and comes to me with its demanding claim that it is the representation of Christ in the ongoing history of salvation which bears the stamp of Christ.

It is in fact the case that in the New Testament the unity of the church is required and is presupposed in Paul as well as in John. Of course the relationship of the individual communities of Christians in particular places, in their celebration of the Lord's Supper and in their proclamation of his message, is not simply that of an administrative district within the church in the sense of the whole church. It is to be taken for granted that the relationship between the local church and the universal church is to be understood differently than in the case of a state or some other secular society. It is certainly true that according to the witness of the New Testament there was the church in Ephesus, in Colossae, and so on. And it is certain that church, not in the sense of a local community but in the real theological sense, takes place wherever the Lord's Supper is celebrated, wherever there is baptism, and wherever the word of Christ which demands faith is proclaimed in the Spirit of Christ. But this does not exclude, but rather includes the fact that there is *one* church.

First of all, Paul's basic conviction is that the church of Christ, the community of those who believe in him, the body of Christ and the people of God become manifest in a local community precisely because the individual local communities are not simply realities existing for themselves which then combine into a larger organization afterwards for some ideological reasons or other. Rather, all of this becomes manifest because the single reality which is the church actualizes itself and becomes manifest as church precisely in these individual communities. Therefore if they are truly churches in the full sense, they are united to begin with. One and the same people of God filled with the Spirit of God becomes manifest in every local community.

Then it is also obvious that this unity which reaches into the deepest levels of their reality must also become manifest on the social level. The individual communities cannot simply perceive themselves as founded by God vertically, and then discover afterwards that the event of grace in this community of faith also exists elsewhere. These different communities came from Jerusalem through the preaching of the apostles who were carrying out the mission of Jesus, and in the apostolic period they knew that they were connected on the social level as well. An apostle felt that he was the authoritative leader of a community even when he was not present. The communities exchanged letters. They knew that ultimately they were built upon Peter as the rock of the church. At this point we do not have to go into the question how the social structure of the church must be understood more exactly, what belongs to it necessarily, and what can perhaps be a historically conditioned and contingent realization of this unity. In any case it is clear from the New Testament and from the essence of the church that there can be only *one* church.

Today it is a conviction common to all Christians that there has to be one church, and that the question whether there is one church or any number of Christian religious communities is not for Christians to decide as they will. This of course does not settle the question about what this unity has to consist in, and what social realities have to exist in order that there be such unity. Nor does this settle the question where we find such a church which traces itself back to Christ legitimately. Nor is there as yet a consensus on the question whether the various ecclesial communities which exist are not already united with one another as a single church on a deeper level. Looking at Christianity as a whole, today there is a conviction which is experienced as an element of Christian faith, a conviction that there has to be *one* church, and moreover that in the concrete situation of Christianity as a whole today the unity which Christ willed and which follows necessarily from the essence of the church is not yet realized sufficiently. There are separations and divisions, there are differences in their professions of faith, and there is no communion in the Lord's Supper. None of this should exist, because it is incompatible with the essence of the church. There has to be *one* church, and this and only this really does justice to the essence of Christianity.

LEGITIMATE CONFIDENCE IN ONE'S OWN ECCLESIAL COMMUNITY

Now an individual Christian by all means has the right to presume that his own historical and ecclesial existence is to be recognized in the first instance as a legitimate existence. It is the existence which forms the horizon of his thought, and to which he holds fast until the opposite is proven. Man is a spiritually free and historical being who has to begin to take responsibility for his existence. But first of all he is someone who relies confidently on the situation in which he finds himself. He is of course a reflexive being and a critical being, a being who raises questions. He is a being who questions and examines the historical situation in which he finds himself, and in certain circumstances he overcomes it and goes beyond it. This is also true for an existentiell revolution in which he breaks out of the situation of his existence in which he finds himself and perhaps changes it radically. It is a very different question how deep this kind of a revolutionary change can really go in the final analysis. Even on the level of the free and personal existence for which he is therefore responsible, no one simply begins at the absolute zero point and projects the totality of his existence in an absolutely new way.

In the first instance, therefore, every Christian has the right to accept as something whose legitimacy is presumed the Christian and ecclesial situation which was bestowed on him in history and which he has appropriated. This is undoubtedly a proposition which is hardly reflected upon and is not expressed explicitly in the usual abstract and theoretical fundamental theology in the Catholic church. But this basic and general fundamental theology does not deny in itself and in the abstract the fact that we are bound to a particular situation, nor does it deny that we are justified in presuming the legitimacy of our historically conditioned situation.

This is true of course not just for Catholic Christians, but for everybody. Obviously we recognize that, for example, an Evangelical Christian or an Orthodox Christian or a member of some sect will have an antecedent trust in the meaning of his existence, and will accept the situation which has been given to him and in which he finds himself. He will think from out of this situation and rightly so. No Christian has the task and the obligation because he is a Christian to step out of the historical situation of his existence, and to want to ground the concreteness of his existence exclusively by means of reflection. Such a thing is impossible a priori both for human knowledge and for the actualization of human existence, and hence it cannot be required here. This of course does not deny a person's obligation to reflect responsibly upon his own situation, to place it in question in a certain sense, and perhaps in certain circumstances, because of his existentiell experience of life and his reflection upon it, even to alter very radically the situation in which he finds himself.

But a person begins first of all with the fact that he trusts his parents, that he accepts the culture which has been handed down as meaningful, and that in the first instance he also presumes the legitimacy of the values which have been handed down. This does not mean that he affirms them absolutely, but he does recognize them as meaningful and trustworthy, and as a real and genuine basis for existence. In addition to this there is the fact that, no matter what denomination he belongs to, a Christian within his particular denomination of Christianity has experiences of Christian existence, of grace, of the salvific character of his existence, and of an ultimate consolation in existence, experiences which he perceives quite correctly as coming from his own concrete Christianity. For it is not the case that within the innermost sanctum of his subjective consciousness and conscience a concrete Christian experiences something of God's grace, of his forgiveness, and of the meaningfulness of his existence, and then declares that this experience is completely independent of the concrete Christian church in which he finds himself. No, this interior experience of Christianity comes to him from the community, from the preaching of the word, and from the reception of the sacraments, and it makes no difference in what Christian community he has this experience. And because of this he has the right to presume that the Christian denomination which has been given to him historically is legitimate at least for him.

If we grant this without hesitation, there is no doubt that it makes things more difficult for Catholic fundamental theology as an apologetic for the Roman Catholic church which is also intended for other Christians. If, nevertheless, Catholic theology makes the claim that the Roman Catholic church is the church of Christ, then it must not only try to prove in a theoretical way and with historical arguments why the legitimate succession of the church of Christ is found in Roman Catholic Christianity. Rather an apologetic must also come to terms with the fact of this real and genuine Christian experience which comes from other ecclesial denominations. It is only when it also does this that it can claim to be a real apologetic for the Catholic church. If we take this position as our point of departure, then it is to be taken for granted that, although it is perhaps open to criticism for its interpretation and might need such criticism, every genuine experience of Christianity may and must be regarded as an experience of the power of our existence which is really grounded in the mystery of God.

Now with regard to the concrete institution in which we find ourselves and which in the first instance we presume to be legitimate, we have to say, *first of all*, that this institution may certainly not contradict the basic substance of Christianity, that basic substance of Christianity which we grasp in our personal experience as well as in our theoretical reflection upon it; and, *secondly*, that it obviously must be required of this institution that it stand in the closest possible historical continuity and proximity to the original Christianity in its ecclesial constitution. A person will expect an answer to these questions from his church because these other ecclesial communities are found within the realm of his existence. In view of these other communities he will ask his church whether it exists in the closest possible approximation to the church of Christ, whether the genuine substance of Christianity has really been preserved along with such a historical, institutional and social approximation, and whether it is really church in the sense which we discussed at the beginning.

The presumption of a trusting reliance on the Christian and ecclesial existence in which a person finds himself is something which we may presuppose here in our reflections. While a theoretical, rigorously scientific and reflexive fundamental theology puts this presumption in parentheses, no matter in what confessional theology and denomination it is being done, here we are presupposing this presumption explicitly and reflexively, and precisely as a given for our reflection upon our understanding of the church. By calculating it explicitly into our considerations, we acquire a method for our reflections upon an intellectually honest justification of our membership in a concrete church. It is a method which legitimately spares us in our concrete situation many historical inquiries, proofs and investigations. This does not make these investigations of theoretical and reflexive fundamental theology superfluous. Rather it simply acknowledges the plain fact that such a reflection upon the grounds of a person's Christian and ecclesial existence can never be complete in the concrete situation of any person, and that it does not have to make the claim that it is.

THE CRITERION OF CONTINUITY WITH THE ORIGIN
AS A DEFENSE AGAINST ECCLESIOLOGICAL RELATIVISM

Given this presupposition, the method which we are suggesting here means that we can rely upon the concrete Christian church which has come down to us and in which we find ourselves *if* it has the closest possible historical approximation to the original Christian church of Jesus Christ. The closer the concrete historical connection is between our Christianity and the original Christian church, the greater is the prospect and the presumption that the Christian church which has come down to us is the church of Christ.

There are those among Evangelical as well as Catholic Christians today who presuppose that the ecclesial communities, churches and confessional denominations which in fact exist are to be regarded as more or less equally legitimate. Consequently, the question to which church a specific Christian wants to belong is more a question merely of historical accident and individual taste. For us, however, this kind of ecclesiological relativism is out of the question. Among other reasons, this is so because this ecclesial relativism was also completely foreign to the early churches of the Reformation period, and hence to the evangelical understanding of the church among the reformers of the sixteenth century. They held the dogmatic opinion and view that the concrete church of Jesus Christ had to exist in their own time. As distinguished from and in rejection of other such communities, this church alone could make the claim to be the church of Jesus Christ. In the sixteenth century too, of course, there was no agreement about what criteria were to be established for making this claim. But the lack of agreement about where the true church of Jesus Christ was to be found in the concrete did not prevent them from having the basic conviction at that time that this concrete church of Jesus Christ had to exist, that in any case there should be no divisions, and that it could be established where the true church of Christ is. If the Augsburg Confession establishes as the only valid criteria for this the legitimate preaching of the gospel, the legitimate authority for this preaching, and the correct administration of the sacraments of baptism and the Lord's Supper, this difference in the criteria to be established and applied to the church does not alter the fact that in the concrete, for example, the reformers were convinced in an absolute decision of faith that especially in its Pope and his claims the Roman church was an anti-Christian phenomenon and was the church of the anti-Christ.

If, then, there are very many Christians today who basically regard the different ecclesial communities as equally legitimate churches, this relativistic opinion in ecclesiology presupposes either that the church of Jesus Christ as he willed it does not exist at all, or that in spite of the divisions among Christians it exists to such an extent that it does not really have to be brought about. Basically, then, all ecumenical efforts and endeavors for a single church would be superfluous to begin with, or ecumenical endeavors only strive for an additional unity which ultimately would have nothing to do with the essential unity of the church which already exists.

If we do not take this ecclesiological relativism as our point of departure, and if we look for this concrete church in concrete reality, then we can propose the first norm, namely, that we most likely find the church of Jesus Christ where a church has the closest and most simple and most tangible continuity with original Christianity and with the church of original Christianity. If we really believe in the Incarnation and in the historical nature of Christianity and its grace, it is necessarily out of the question that we would have the church ever being constituted anew. Every real Lutheran or every reformed Christian will lay claim to the church before the Reformation as his church. He neither can nor wants to make the claim that the church was not founded until the Reformation. He will say that this earlier ecclesial community which we call church suffered from many depravities and obscured the gospel message. But if he maintains at all that the church is an article of his own apostolic profession of faith, he cannot maintain that the church absolutely did not exist, nor in fact does he maintain this.

He lays claim to the church before the Reformation as his church, as the church which comes down to him with historical and ecclesial legitimacy, and which finds its legitimate continuation in the churches of the Reformation. Hence we can propose in a formal way as the first principle that an ecclesial institution can be regarded as an institution to which we can entrust ourselves as the church of Christ if and to the extent that it has the most concrete historical continuity possible with the church of original Christianity. We cannot simply leap over the ages in between and reject them as anti-Christian, anti-church, and anti-Christ. For otherwise we would have done away with this incarnational, historical and corporeal continuity, and hence also with a corporeal and ecclesial reality which is independent of us.

THE CRITERION OF PRESERVING THE BASIC SUBSTANCE OF CHRISTIANITY

The second principle in our indirect method of justifying our faith in a concrete church is that the basic substance of Christianity may not be fundamentally denied in this concrete church, that substance which we ourselves have experienced in our own religious existence as an experience of grace. If we were to take as our point of departure abstract ecclesiological principles and proceed after the manner of a theoretical fundamental theology, we could omit this second principle about finding in its purity the real and basic substance of Christianity in the concrete church. For one is trying to prove in such an ecclesiology that the preservation of this basic substance in the church in question is guaranteed by the structures and characteristics of this church. But here we are certainly justified in saying conversely: because as a concrete Christian in my concrete experience of faith I know in a certain way what Christianity is, and because I am convinced that the true church of Jesus Christ exists only where there is found the pneumatic reality of Christianity which I have already experienced by the power of the Spirit, for these reasons I can regard a Christian church and community as the real church of Jesus only if and to the extent that it does not contradict the basic substance of Christianity which I have already experienced in my own existence.

And to this extent the Reformation principle of the Augsburg Confession, namely, that the true church can exist only where the gospel is preached in its purity, is in itself and in a formal sense perfectly correct: an ecclesial community which authoritatively and in its own essence and dogmatic self-understanding denies or disputes or abolishes a basic and essential structure of Christianity cannot be the true church of Christ. And to this extent I can certainly also appeal to the witness of the Spirit, who bears witness to the reality of Christianity for me in a personal and existentiell way in my concrete life. Of course this does indeed leave open the question where and how I can find the church of Jesus Christ *if* a difference which divides the church cannot be settled in favor of one side or the other by this interior witness. The question also remains open whether I am always and everywhere so certain about this experience of the living Christianity of Jesus Christ that I can construct a criterion to distinguish the churches by means of it. But with regard to a concrete existentiell situation which cannot be made completely reflexive, this available subjective and pneumatic criterion has its legitimate place and its validity.

THE CRITERION OF OBJECTIVE AUTHORITY

The third principle is this: the religious community of church must obviously exist as a reality which is independent of my subjectivity. We are taking for granted that even the most objective reality which I am looking for, however distinct it is from my subjectivity, is always found and mediated only in and through the existentiell decision of my own conscience. But this does not alter the postulate that, if the church is to exist at all, Christian religiosity is not yet religion unless it includes the concrete and social reality of a church which is independent of me. Within this circle of subjectivity and objectivity there must be a concrete distinction between this subjectivity of mine and objectivity, even though this objective reality which can be a norm for me and is not simply at the disposal of my subjectivity can only confront me within my subjectivity. If basically subjectivity and conscience and our own responsibility neither does nor can exclude an objective reality as something which is normative, then this is also true in our case. Without prejudice to the ultimacy of conscience and the free decision of conscience, we can say without hesitation: if church is to belong to and to be a part of Christianity as a constitutive element of this incarnational Christianity, then church really has to be church, that is, a reality which is not simply dependent on my preferences. It is of course another question how this church does become church. It is conceivable that an Evangelical Christian and theologian would readily affirm this third formal principle, but would consider this objectivity of the church to be present in the objectivity of the written word of God, that is, in the New Testament alone.

THE SPECIAL APPLICATION OF THESE CRITERIA IN OUR SITUATION

Let us try now to apply these formal principles of an indirect justification to our own Catholic Christianity. In doing this, of course, it is inevitable that our reflections will touch upon ecumenical questions at least indirectly. Even today we still have to ask: Where is the church of Jesus Christ for my conscience? And the plain fact that an answer to this question contradicts the answer of another Christian is neither an argument nor a justification for omitting this question, nor for simply tabling it as unanswerable. Obviously every Christian will admit that this question is very difficult to answer. And he may make this admission without qualms because the hierarchy of Christian truths, which is recognized in the Decree on Ecumenism (*Unitatis redintegratio*, art. 11), and which says that Christian truths do not all have the same existentiell and salvific significance, this hierarchy allows for the fact that perhaps finding Jesus Christ and his liberating gospel is easier than answering the difficult question: In what concrete community do we find the true church of Jesus Christ with its basic substance and with lawful and historical legitimacy?

There is no doubt that we Christians today readily admit as a requirement of our Christian faith, and not only as a pacifist concession, that other Christians live in the grace of God, that they are filled with the Holy Spirit, are justified, are children of God and are united with Jesus Christ, and that in the ecclesial and social dimension too they are united in very many respects with all other Christians and with all other denominations. Without doubt, then, much more and much more fundamental things unite Christians of the different churches than separate them.

In this situation we can say first of all that for a Catholic in the West who lives in his Catholic church and has had there the experience of Christianity, it is perhaps only the profession of the Reformation Christianity of the sixteenth century and the Christianity which has come down from it that is really an existentiell question. He does not simply place himself at the point of absolute zero or at a standpoint outside all concrete historical existence, but rather he asks: Do I in my faith have the right before conscience to be Catholic and to continue to belong to the Catholic church? In this situation it is only the Evangelical church or churches which can seriously be a question for those of us in the West, and can be be a threat to our presumption. For Evangelical Christianity really belongs to our own inescapable historical existence and it is a concrete question for us.

THE HISTORICAL CONTINUITY OF THE CATHOLIC CHURCH

If with these presuppositions we now ask as Catholics why with these presuppositions and by this method we find the church of Christ in the Catholic church, we can answer: because according to the very simple evidence it possesses in the concrete a closer, more evident and less encumbered historical continuity with the church of the past going all the way back to apostolic times.

This statement does not deny, of course, that as this church has come down to us from apostolic times through the first fifteen centuries it has gone through extraordinarily great changes, amplifications and developments in its consciousness of the faith and in its concrete structure and constitution. But from the viewpoint of our method it is neither necessary nor practically feasible to establish this continuity and the legitimacy of this continuity by a reflexive historical investigation. This is not impossible a priori and in principle, and it is the task of a theoretical fundamental theology working with historical methods, but in the concrete it is out of the question for us.

Nevertheless we can say, however, that the historical continuity between the post-tridentine and post-Reformation church and the ancient church is greater, more evident and less ambiguous in the Catholic church than in the other ecclesial communities, including those of Evangelical Christianity. The Catholic church is a church in which there is a Petrine office and an episcopacy which have an evident historical connection with the church going all the way back to apostolic times. Perhaps, for example, the Petrine office might also have gone through an extraordinarily great development in juridical explicitness and clarity when we compare the beginnings at the end of the first century or in scripture with the papacy of the Middle Ages. Nevertheless, it cannot be denied that there was a Roman episcopacy and a certain authority in this Roman episcopacy in the church before the Reformation, and that there is therefore a closer, more immediate and more self-evident continuity between post-Reformation Catholic Christianity and the ancient church. For Evangelical Christianity to prove its own historical and theological continuity with the ancient church, it must declare a great deal in this earlier, pre-Reformation church to be either superfluous or even un-Christian and anti-Christian. We can say that at least with regard to the episcopal constitution of the church, with regard to the normal and evident transmission of this episcopacy, and with regard to the Petrine office the more self-evident, more unbroken and more directly transmitted continuity exists between the ancient church and the church of post-tridentine Catholicism. Something similar can also be said for many other things, for example, with regard to law and with regard to sacramental practice.

It is also unambiguous from an historical point of view that the original Evangelical Christianity of the Reformation period in the first instance regarded a church with bishops and Pope as in itself the legitimate church of tradition, and this is very clear in the Augsburg Confession. It withdrew from it only because Evangelical Christianity was convinced that in an unambiguous and unacceptable way this concrete church did not preserve, or did not preserve with sufficient clarity, true Christianity, namely, the church's doctrine that we are saved by grace alone. In this case, then, but only under this presupposition, it can of course regard the elements of church which it acknowledged in the ancient church, namely, baptism, the preaching of the gospel, the Lord's Supper, and so on, as what alone was essentially constitutive of church in earlier times too. Basically it does not have to be denied by a Catholic Christian either that there were massive tendencies in the church of the late Middle Ages, in its life, its practice and its mentality, which contradict the real and basic concern of Evangelical Christianity, and which provoked strong opposition against a further development of the concrete church as was offered by the situation of the times. But a Catholic Christian cannot see that the church of the Middle Ages or the tridentine or post-tridentine Catholic church taught in an authoritative and absolutely binding way that something belonged to its own definitive self-understanding which was so contrary to the real and basic concerns of the reformers that a Christian would therefore simply be forced to leave the Catholic church.

THE CRITERION OF PRESERVING THE BASIC SUBSTANCE IN THE LIGHT OF REFORMATION CONTROVERSIES

Let us consider from this perspective the three famous "only's": only by grace, only by faith, and only scripture. They represent the core of the original Reformation Christianity, and they give the reason why an Evangelical Christian declares both then and now that according to his conscience he cannot belong to the Catholic church, even though he does not deny that in itself the clearer and more self-evident historical continuity would speak in favor of the Catholic church.

SOLA GRATIA: BY GRACE ALONE

With regard first of all to *sola gratia*, our concern here of course is not to investigate every interpretation of grace which is found in Evangelical theology and in the Evangelical understanding of the term. For even within Evangelical Christianity there is no consensus on the more specific interpretation of this basic Evangelical axiom, and hence such an interpretation purely as such can neither form a church nor divide a church. But if we say that "by grace alone" means that a person really finds his salvation through the free and absolutely sovereign grace of God, and hence that in this sense there can be no synergistic cooperation between God and man in the sense that a person could himself contribute something to his salvation which is not given to him by God's free grace, then this is not only a doctrine which can be presented and taught as undisputed within Catholic doctrine, but it is also a doctrine which belongs absolutely to the Catholic doctrine of the relationship between God and man.

The Council of Trent teaches, of course, that a person is free in the process of attaining his salvation. But a human freedom, a human capacity, or a human power which could contribute something of its own and something positive to salvation all by itself and by its own autonomy and power, so that Christian salvation would not be totally a pure gift of God which God bestows upon man in a love which cannot be coerced, this conception is not found in the official and binding doctrine of the Catholic church. Perhaps it might be found here and there in popular Catholicism, but then it contradicts the official teaching of the church. Nothing which contributes to man's salvation can be anything else but the pure and free grace of God, and this grace gives not only the capacity or the possibility of salvation, but also the actualization of salvation. If the Council of Trent emphasizes that man exercises his freedom in the history of salvation, this conception is not denied in Evangelical theology by an opposite and "official" view which is constitutive of the Evangelical church.

But it is Catholic doctrine that in spite of this freedom, only a freedom which is empowered by God both in its potentiality and in its actuality, only a freedom which has been set free by God for salvation, for love and for obedience to God, only this freedom is salvific freedom. This very doctrine was defined explicitly in the Council of Trent, perhaps against some nominalistic distortions in the late Middle Ages. Pelagianism or a real semi-pelagianism, or a popular notion of synergistic cooperation which apportions salvation in two parts between God's grace and man's freedom, none of these is found in official Catholic doctrine. Wherever a person attains his salvation in freedom, he will attribute to God both the capacity for and the act of his freedom in praise and in thanks, for it is an act which God has given him in a grace for which there are no reasons.

We can and must, therefore, hold the doctrine "by grace alone" with an ardour which is both Christian and Catholic. And much of what provoked the protest of Evangelical Christianity at the time of the Reformation, for example, the doctrine of freedom, the doctrine of merit, and the doctrine of so-called infused grace, could perhaps at the time, and certainly can now, be recognized as a mutual misunderstanding and can be laid to rest. Freedom does not abolish the absolute gratuity of salvation, and the doctrine of grace intends to say nothing else but that by an act of God, by a free act of God which cannot be coerced, a person really and truly is changed interiorly from being a sinner to being justified. He is a justified person who can never judge about this justification because it is constantly threatened, and because it is a hidden reality in him. To this extent even as justified he cannot assume an autonomous position in relation to God.

SOLA FIDE: BY FAITH ALONE

The doctrine of *sola fide*, that is, the doctrine that a person is justified by faith alone, is nothing else but the other and subjective side of the *sola gratia* doctrine. Because salvation is a free gift of the grace of God which has no reasons and which cannot be coerced, the act in which this salvation is accepted must itself be an act which God bestows upon this freedom. In this sense it is not an autonomous merit which a person brings to God by his own capacity in order to be able to coerce his grace, his love and his gift of salvation. In this sense the act of response to God's grace which alone gives salvation is not a work, but rather, in Pauline terms, it is faith. The Catholic doctrine is that this faith is not merely a dogmatic theory, that this faith must be based interiorly on a hope in the pure grace of God, and that this faith must be interiorly illuminated and fulfilled by what Holy Scripture calls love, calls justifying and sanctifying love. Basically an Evangelical Christian cannot raise any objections against this. The fact that the somewhat schematic scholastic distinction in the Middle Ages between faith, hope and love can in certain circumstances obscure the totality of the single and basic act of justification which God's grace bestows upon man freely and as freedom, and the fact that that this whole scheme needs to be interpreted cautiously, do not change anything in a correct Catholic and Pauline understanding of the *sola fide*.

SOLA SCRIPTURA: SCRIPTURE ALONE

The third *sola* which Reformation Christianity proposed as a basic characteristic and a basic axiom of faith, and hence also of their understanding of the church, is "scripture alone." It is here that we can establish more easily a really objective and not just terminological difference in the content of doctrine between Evangelical and Catholic Christianity. For Catholic doctrine emphasizes the necessity and the validity both of tradition as well as of the Catholic teaching office.

First of all, as a result of the modern and quite legitimate historical study of the Bible and exegesis which arose precisely within Evangelical Christianity, an Evangelical Christian today will grant that scripture is a product of the church in a very essential way. Indeed it is something very heterogeneous, and it is only with rather great difficulty that it can be brought under an intrinsic canon. Looked at from a historical point of view, scripture is the writing down of the history of the faith of the original community. From this perspective it is to be taken for granted that in the first instance scripture is based upon and arose from the concrete, living preaching of the living church. And to this extent scripture is already the result of tradition. As a legitimate succession of witnesses, who do not appoint themselves, but rather who must prove their legitimacy through their origin in legitimate witnesses going all the way back to the great witnesses to Jesus Christ, the concept of tradition is a notion which was taken for granted by everyone in the earliest church.

There is such a thing as an authoritative mission, a giving witness to faith in Jesus Christ, and scripture itself represents the result and the consequence of this living tradition. Tradition is at once a transmitted succession both of witnesses and of what is being witnessed to. Scripture, then, presents itself as something which appears only in connection with the living and authoritative mission of the church and with the testimony of the church which is grounded in the Spirit. From this perspective, however much scripture has a normative character for the later church, it will manifest nevertheless an ecclesial character. It exists because the church exists. It is not just something which forms church. And this church is a living church teaching authoritatively in tradition, and hence it has scripture. This also follows from the fact that basically, without such an intrinsic connection between tradition and scripture, the canon of scripture as formative of church cannot really be determined. The authoritative significance of scripture for the church could not be shown and made legitimate.

Someone can say, of course, that the power of scripture to convince conscience comes from itself insofar as it is understood not as a dead letter, but rather as an event of the Spirit himself. Even if we grant this, and even if ultimately as Catholics we can grant this without hesitation, there still remains the question how and to what extent and in what way this interior and pneumatic power of scripture can seriously be formative of church, and can also divide the church. And at this point the principle of scripture alone breaks down. Ultimately the axiom of scripture alone is self-contradictory, at least when it is understood indiscriminately. This is shown by the fact that the old Reformation doctrine of scripture alone, which was necessarily and intrinsically connected with the notion of a *verbal* inspiration of scripture, is untenable from a historical point of view, nor is it taught any longer in contemporary Evangelical theology.

For only when scripture is understood as the one and only product which comes immediately from God independently of any historical and very differentiated process of becoming can I ascribe to scripture an authority which makes it completely independent of the living testimony of the church. But basically one cannot abandon the principle of an absolute, verbal inspiration of scripture, as in fact has happened, and still maintain the principle of scripture alone in the sense which it had at the time of the Reformation. One cannot do this without contradicting oneself, or without simply making the single principle of faith not scripture alone but rather man's ultimate, inescapable and existentiell experience of the Spirit. But then we do not really have a scripture any more which is found in scripture, in concrete books. Rather we have a principle which is ultimately formative of scripture, and which is at most inspired by scripture. Then the church would be more like something which is constituted subsequently by Christians, but it would not be something which is a really binding authority for individual Christians.

In any case scripture is a literary concretization of the living testimony of the church. The church and its proclamation existed before scripture and scripture is based upon them. For historical reasons this cannot be denied. Scripture is always a reality which is formed in a church, in a church which is already formed and which already appears with authority. It is formed as a reflection of its living proclamation. Nor can this relationship be changed by the fact that the church gives witness to scripture as something inspired and authoritative, and hence it is accepted by Catholics too as a *norma non normata* for the *future* church. The Catholic understanding of scripture in no way denies that, although scripture is based upon the church and is witnessed to by the church, as the written word of God scripture is and remains the concrete norm for the post-apostolic church in its future understanding of the faith. It is taken for granted by the Catholic understanding of faith and of the church, and by the Catholic interpretation of what we Catholics call the teaching office, that scripture as such and as written is a real norm for the post-apostolic church. The church does not receive any new revelation over and beyond this scripture, nor over and beyond the apostolic preaching of the original church. Rather the church's understanding of the faith and its teaching office have no other task except to remain within the ultimate and eschatological revelation which has been handed down.

The Catholic church is convinced, however, that there is a real development of the single deposit of faith whose substance is immutable. Scripture is not simply something which expresses the dogma of the church with an invariability which is set down in writing. Rather this constant itself continues to have an historical nature because it had a history during the apostolic period and during the period when the canon was formed, and it is impossible to see why this history should suddenly and absolutely cease to exist. Not only is there scripture and a variable, temporally conditioned theology, but there is also an understanding of the *faith* which comes down from the apostolic tradition and has a genuine history. It is only in this genuine and developing history that it is something really dialogical in relation to each era's changing understanding of existence, and hence that it can make Christ himself present in every age.

A great deal in exegesis and in biblical theology will in fact remain open and be left to human theology, but basically the Catholic church maintains that the community of believers can give at least a basic interpretation of scripture which is binding on individual Christians. It does this in its common profession of faith and with the help of the organs which form the common consciousness of those who profess the same faith. Otherwise, of course, the church basically ceases to exist as a reality which is independent of one's own subjectivity and private theology. Then we would be left to some extent to our own subjectivity and to our own interpretation of scripture. If an Evangelical Christian could counter by saying that in fact the Spirit of God will prevent religious subjectivity from robbing scripture and the letter of scripture of its authority, we would have to say according to the Catholic understanding of the church and of faith that we believe that the word of God and scripture are capable of exercising such a power to form faith. But for us Catholics the precise question is *how* this takes place in the concrete, and how in the concrete this power of God in the church and in the witness of scripture can be understood. This does not dethrone scripture. It does not cease to be the *norma non normata* for the church and also for its teaching office. We did not discover the Bible somewhere by our own curiosity, but rather, as something which awakens faith and brings faith and communicates the Spirit, it comes to us only in the preaching of the concrete church. And this says to us: here is the word of God, a word which it gives witness to in such a way that according to the Catholic understanding of the faith too it can manifest itself by its own power.

If we suppose that scripture itself exists within the church which gives witness to scripture, then we can say that everything which belongs to the original apostolic kerygma has been written down in scripture, and that there is no tradition alongside it or beyond it. In this sense, then, we can readily hold the principle of "scripture alone." For Catholic Christians too, tradition and the teaching office's understanding have their material source and their *norma non normata* only in Holy Scripture. Even if we would want to assume with many theologians at least since Trent that there is a tradition which mediates a definite content of faith from apostolic times which is not found in scripture (this is not a binding doctrine of the Catholic teaching office, and can be denied), then the fact still remains that this tradition would once again have its norm in scripture. No Catholic theologian can deny or doubt that alongside the really living tradition of divine revelation there is already found in the earliest period human theology, human theories, and historically and temporally conditioned theological notions which did not last. Hence if someone asks what content in the concrete tradition is really divine revelation, and what content is human theory or the positive and mutable law of the church, ultimately the teaching office can give a decisive answer to this question. But basically only scripture can be the norm for this teaching office, for it does not receive any new revelations.

Scripture offers divine revelation in human concepts and human statements, and in an understanding which changes in history. But at the same time it receives for Christian faith as Catholics understand it the guarantee that the human form of divine revelation does not alter or corrupt this revelation. To this extent, according to the Catholic understanding of scripture, the Holy Scripture of the Old Testament and all the more so of the New Testament is once again a norm such as nothing else in the church is. However, faith's living understanding of scripture, and scripture's transposition into faith's really pneumatic experience of the reality which scripture means are processes whose place scripture itself cannot take, and the process of faith's living understanding of scripture has itself an ecclesial structure. It is not simply and merely an affair of the individual's religious subjectivity. Rather it is more originally an affair of the church as such, an affair of the single community of believers within which the individual Christian acquires his concrete understanding of the faith. This community of faith is not only the sum of individual religious subjectivities, but rather it really has a structure, a hierarchical constitution, and an authoritative leadership through which the church's single understanding of the faith receives its unambiguous meaning and its binding character.

In order to be Catholic, then, the *sola scriptura* does not have to be denied; this is, rather, a principle which not only can but also must be recognized by Catholic dogmatic theology.

THE THREE REFORMATION "ONLYS" AND CATHOLICISM: THE RESULT

For a Catholic understanding of the faith there is no reason why the basic concern of Evangelical Christianity as it comes to expression in the three "onlys" should have no place in the Catholic church. Accepted as basic and ultimate formulas of Christianity, they do not have to lead a person out of the Catholic church. Where of course other and more fundamental dogmas of the Catholic church are denied, a consensus could no longer be arrived at. But these theologies, for example, the theology of demythologizing, or a theology which denies the divinity of Jesus Christ or the Trinity, are not formative of church from an Evangelical point of view. For the reformers of the sixteenth century did not deny the traditional doctrines of God, of

Christ, of the one divine person in Christ, and of the two natures. Rather they presupposed them as something to be taken for granted, although here and there in Luther and in Calvin, because of their basic and ultimate theological stance, dogmas coming from the whole Christian tradition were modified somewhat in their interpretation as far as emphases and perspectives go.

THE POSITIVE SIGNIFICANCE OF EVANGELICAL CHRISTIANITY FOR THE CATHOLIC CHURCH

If a Catholic understanding of the church cannot simply recognize in non-Roman churches the *same* salvific and theological quality with regard to the question about the church of Jesus Christ, this in no way denies a positive significance in Evangelical Christianity for Evangelical Christians and also for the Catholic church. According to the Catholic conviction too, scripture exists as an authority within Evangelical Christianity. There is valid baptism, and there is a great deal else even in the social and ecclesial dimension which is a historical concreteness of Christianity which is willed positively by God. The Catholic understanding of faith and of the church in no way denies that within Evangelical Christianity there is grace and justification and the Holy Spirit, and hence there exists that reality as the event and the power of God's grace for which everything institutional, all words and sacraments, everything juridical and organizational, and all the techniques of administration are only the preparation and the historical manifestation, and except for this they are nothing. Consequently, there is a unity in very many elements which are formative and constitutive of church in the tangible and categorical dimension of salvation history, and beyond this and all the more so there is a unity in the pneumatic dimension. And with respect to both dimensions, of course, Evangelical Christianity as it touches individual Evangelical Christians has a positive and spiritual function.

In spite of all the questions and in spite of the guilt which is to be presumed on *both* sides, Evangelical Christianity also has a positive function for the Catholic church. Let us say that by the will of Christ the Catholic church is the church which professes in principle to preserve everything Christian, professes to know Christianity not only in an ultimate reduction to the basic and ultimate knowledge, and professes to live not only in the basic and ultimate event of justifying grace. Rather it wants to be the church which develops these ultimate and most fundamental things abundantly throughout the whole length and breadth of the historical and the social dimension and on the level of reflection, and does so without fearing that this development by means of the ultimate power of its origins has to be a defection from these origins. Then in relation to this Catholic church Evangelical theology, Evangelical Christianity and also the Evangelical churches can have a positive function for the Catholic church in their reduction to the ultimate, to what is most specific, to the animating power, and to that which gives Christianity its ultimate meaning. They can call the attention of the Catholic church again and again to the fact that grace alone and faith alone really are what saves, and that with all of our maneuvering through the history of dogma and the teaching office, we Catholic Christians must find our way back to the sources again and again, back to the primary origins of Holy Scripture and all the more so of the Holy Spirit. By God's grace he forms the innermost center of our existence and is at work there.

In his understanding of the church the Catholic Christian will say in the abstract, of course, that this would have to be possible for the Catholic church as founded by Christ even if there were no Evangelical Christianity. But a Catholic Christian can readily acknowledge that the concrete activity of God and of his Christ on his Catholic church is to a large extent mediated and carried out in the concrete by what in fact and in its historical concreteness comes as the goad of the Reformation, as a corrective influence, and as a warning from Evangelical Christianity to Catholic Christianity. In the Catholic understanding of the church it has to be readily admitted that the Catholic church in modern times owes a great deal to the existence of Evangelical Christianity. From a *historical* point of view the concrete reality of Catholic Christianity cannot even be imagined outside an historical situation to whose powerful historical moments Evangelical Christianity did not also belong.

THE FUNDAMENTAL UNITY OF CHRISTIANITY
AND THE QUESTION ABOUT THE "MEANING" OF THE DIVISION

It is taken for granted in Catholic dogmatic theology that there is a "hierarchy of truths." It is therefore also taken for granted that beyond the divisions in Christianity not only is there a unity among Christians and among the Christian churches insofar as they have a great deal in common even in the social and ecclesial dimension, but that there is also a unity even beyond this. In and through our profession of faith in the God of Jesus Christ the redeemer, in his grace, in his word, and in the eschatological salvation which is given through Christ, we are united in the hierarchy of truths in a unity which is deeper than the unity which is hindered by the controversial theological questions which divide the churches. If we make distinctions within this hierarchy of truths and within their religious and existentiell importance, then from this perspective, too, it is to be taken for granted that Christians are united in a more radical sense than they are divided, although they are divided in a true and important sense. We cannot dismiss in a so-called fundamentalism all of the controversial points which divide Christianity as mere theological squabbles. But as Christians we can and must say that what unites us in our profession of faith is more fundamental, more decisive and more significant for salvation than what divides us.

From this perspective we can presumably reach some insight into the question why then God in his salvific providence allows this division in Christianity. This question is more difficult to answer today than it was at the time of the Reformation. At that time it was presupposed by both sides in practice and in the concrete, although perhaps not in their sublimest theories, that this division implied guilt, and indeed each side presumed that the guilt was on the other side. Today we admit that the historically identifiable reasons and guilt for the division of the church lie on both sides. Beyond saying this it is impossible for Christians and even for historians to measure more exactly the guilt which is to be apportioned to the two sides. A judgment in this sense is forbidden to Christians because this judgment is left only to the judgment of God. Both sides, then, mutually have to presume the good faith of the other side. In a human judgment and also in an optimism about salvation which is completely justified, and which indeed is required of Christians as the virtue of hope, we can even say that on all sides in Christianity at least the majority of Christians really exist in an interior, positive and guiltless relationship to their church and to the other churches.

But if we presuppose this, then in a theologically radical way the question about the division is a question of theodicy, a question which has to be placed to *God.* The moment a definite historical fact stems immediately from man's guilt, there is indeed still the question how God could permit this guilt, how the holy and just and infinitely loving God could permit and create a world in which such guilt exists. But where we cannot assume such guilt, or at least do not have to assume it, the theodicy problem becomes more acute. For historical facts which do not stem from guilt are to be placed "on God's account" in a much more immediate and intensive sense than those facts which stem from a real, subjective and serious guilt on man's part. And to this extent, at least presupposing that people today are by and large innocent with respect to the divisions in Christianity, we have to ask and demand much more intensively that these facts have and must have a positive meaning in God's salvific providence than we would if these facts were just the objectification of an abysmal guilt on man's part.

If, then, we pose the question about the salvific and providential meaning of the division differently, then presumably we can say that Christians perceive and experience the really radical and fundamental truths and realities of Christian faith and of Christian existence more clearly than perhaps would be the case if everyone were in the same social and ecclesial situation, and if they all naturally and obviously belonged to one and the same church. The radical question about what Christianity really is, and the constantly critical attitude towards the Christianity which they themselves embody remain present in this division. We cannot say, of course, that this process of salvation may dispense Christians from devoting all of their powers towards striving for the unity of the church, nor from feeling responsible for this unity. But as long as we are separated, as long as in God's dispensation people's consciences are convinced that their churches have to be separated, we can certainly ask about a positive salvific meaning in this situation and say that we have to make the best of it.

This means that we have to force each other mutually to be and to become as Christian as possible, and to understand what is really radical about the Christian message a little better. Even in its divisions Christianity exists today in a historical, social, cultural and spiritual situation which obliges all of these separated Christians to ask themselves how they can do justice to the future which is pressing upon us. And where the theologies of the different churches are making an effort really to answer the questions which a non-Christian age is posing to Christianity, there will there be the best chance that this new theology being done by people who belong to different churches will slowly develop a theological unity from out of the questions which are being proposed to all of them in common. This unity will then move beyond many of the controversial theological problems which at the moment are insoluble, and will render them to a certain extent otiose.

6. Scripture as the Church's Book

This is perhaps the appropriate place in our reflections, or at least it is a possible and legitimate place, to discuss at least the fundamentals about Holy Scripture, both in the Old and the New Testaments. For if we regard scripture as the church's book to begin with, this gives us perhaps the best access to an understanding of what the official doctrine of the church itself says about its holy book. This will avoid the danger of "mythologizing" the nature and the task of scripture.

SOME REFERENCES TO EARLIER DISCUSSIONS

We have already discussed scripture under different headings quite frequently elsewhere either implicitly or in passing. For the basic and ultimate theological problem with regard to the essential nature of scripture is a question whose content runs through all of our reflections: the problem of the unity between transcendental and historical revelation. The history through which grace is mediated to man, and hence the history through which God's turning to man in *revelation* is mediated to him, is not indeed always and in the first instance a word, and consequently it is not a scriptural word. It is rather salvation history as a whole, and, as we have already said, this does not have to be made thematic always and everywhere in an explicitly religious way. However, it is when this history is made thematic in an explicitly religious way that it reaches its real goal and its climax, and hence becomes the history of salvation and revelation in the usual sense.

If, then, scripture is understood as one of the ways, although a preeminent way, in which God's revelatory self-communication to man becomes explicit and thematic in history, then it is clear that everything which we said especially in the fifth and sixth chapters about the relationship between transcendental revelation and history already pertains to the real and basic problem about scripture. It really is also clear immediately that scripture can be understood as the word of God as distinguished from a word *about* God only if it is understood in connection with what is called grace, God's self-communication, the Spirit, gratuitous transcendental revelation and faith. We are not, of course, going to go into this problem all over again at this point. It should just be mentioned that we have already said some very essential things about scripture earlier without mentioning it by name.

Moreover, we have already discussed the prophets and their function, for example, a function by which, under the dynamism of grace and God's special providence, universal revelation and the universal history of revelation becomes concrete in an authentic and pure way in the special history of the Old and New Testaments. We spoke further about the relationship of the Old and New Testaments to each other, and in doing so we took the history of the old covenant and its holy book together. Finally, in the sixth chapter we evaluated the New Testament from the viewpoint of fundamental theology to the extent that this was possible within the scope of these lectures. We did this in answering the question who Jesus of Nazareth is, and what he means to us. Also, we have already discussed Evangelical Christianity's axiom "scripture alone." Hence we have already discussed scripture in these and similar contexts.

THE CHURCH'S BOOK

Nevertheless, we are going to say something about scripture in a more explicit way at least briefly. We regard it as the church's book, the book in which the church of the beginning always remains tangible as a norm for us in the concrete. Indeed it is norm which is already distinguished from those things which are found in the original church but which cannot have a normative character for our faith and for the life of the later church. If the church in every age remains bound to its origins in its faith and in its life; if the church as the community of faith in the crucified and risen Jesus is itself to be in its faith and in its life the eschatological and irreversible sign of God's definitive turning to the world in Jesus Christ, a sign without which Jesus Christ himself would not signify God's irreversible coming into the world and would not be the absolute saviour; and if this church of the beginning objectifies itself in scriptural documents at least in fact, and also does so necessarily given the historical and cultural presuppositions in which the church came to be, then in all of this together we have a point of departure for understanding the essence of scripture.

It is also a point of departure from whose perspective we can arrive at an adequate and at the same time a critical understanding of what is really meant by the inspiration of scripture and by a binding canon of scripture. Since scripture is something derivative, it must be understood from the essential nature of the church, which is the eschatological and irreversible permanence of Jesus Christ in history. It is to be understood from this perspective as something normative in the church. (We have already mentioned in the fifth chapter the most important points about how from this perspective the Old Testament can be understood not merely as a collection of documents about the history of Israel which are of interest for the history of religion, but rather can be understood as a part of what is normative for Christian faith.)

THE APOSTOLIC AGE

Scripture, we are saying, is the objectification of the church of the apostolic age which is normative for us. We have already said in another context that for a variety of reasons we may not understand the duration of this apostolic age in too limited a way. Hence we may not consider it in too primitive a fashion as ending with the death of the "twelve" as *the* "apostles" and with the death of Paul without getting into superfluous theological difficulties. We cannot of course simply deduce the exact temporal duration of the apostolic age from theological principles. But there are no special objective difficulties in saying that, according to the self-understanding of the ancient church, the age ended with the writing of the final books of the New Testament, and hence around the first decades of the second century. This obviously involves a bit of a circle: the apostolic church is supposed to be normative, and hence the apostolic age is the criterion for what can be valid as scripture. And, conversely, we are defining what can be valid as the apostolic age from the duration of the history of the canon. But by the very nature of the case this circle belongs to the essence of a historical reality which itself determines the scope of its "beginning" to some extent. Consequently, from the mass of things which are found in this initial period it knows essentially what should have a normative character for it in the future, but it does not know this with a clarity which can any longer be made completely rational.

Given these presuppositions which we have done no more than indicate, we can say then: the church of the apostolic age objectifies itself in scripture. Therefore this scripture has the character and the characteristics which belong to this church in its relationship to future ages of the church. What this means more precisely will follow as we now try in the coming sections to say something about the canon and the formation of the canon, and about the inspiration and the inerrancy of scripture. We shall do this more from the perspective of the traditional data of the church's official doctrine and the theology of the schools.

THE FORMATION OF THE CANON

It is not possible here to trace the history of our knowledge of the scope of the canon. That is a task for the introductory course in the biblical sciences which we cannot assume here. The difficulty in this undertaking for the dogmatic and systematic theologian was just indicated: the canonicity and the inspiration of the individual parts of what is in fact the New and the Old Testament should not be constituted by being recognized by the church, a notion which the First Vatican Council rejected (cf. *D.S.* 3006); but the scope of the canon and hence the inspired character of the individual books in the strict and theological sense is only known to us in fact through the teaching of the church. But as we can see from the history of the canon, this teaching of the church cannot be grounded by saying that by means of an oral tradition which goes back to the explicit testimony of the first recipients of revelation (that is, the apostles until the death of the last apostle) the church has acquired through explicit testimony a knowledge of what is inspired and what is not inspired in the scriptural deposit of the apostolic age, and consequently has acquired a knowledge of what belongs in the canon of Holy Scripture. We shall indeed have to agree with the First Vatican Council that inspiration and canonicity cannot be constituted by means of a recognition of definite books on the part of the later church, by means of a recognition which comes to these books from outside as it were, and which dictates to them from outside a higher value than they have by themselves.

But if we understand the origin of these writings themselves as a moment within the formation of the original church as something which is normative for future ages, as a moment in the process in which the essence of the church in the theological sense comes to be, as a moment in the constitution of this essence which can certainly have a *temporal* duration, then to derive the essence of scripture from the essence of the church does not fall under the censure of the First Vatican Council. During the apostolic age the real theological essence of the church is constituted in a historical process in which the church comes to the fullness of this essence and to the possession of this essence in faith. This self-constitution of the essence of the church until it reaches its full historical existence (and it is not until then that it can fully be the norm for the future church) implies written objectifications. Therefore this process is *also,* but not exclusively, the process of the formation of the canon: the church objectifies its faith and its life in written documents, and it recognizes these objectifications as so pure and so successful that they are able to hand on the apostolic church as a norm for future ages. From this perspective there is no insuperable difficulty with the fact that the formation of these writings and the knowledge that they are representative as objectifications of the apostolic church do not simply coincide in time, and that the formation of the canon was not finished until the post-apostolic age. In this understanding the canonicity of scripture is established by God insofar as he constitutes the church through the cross and the resurrection as an irreversible event of salvation, and the pure objectifications of its beginning are constitutive for this church.

THE INSPIRATION OF SCRIPTURE

From this perspective, or so it seems to us, we can also clarify what is called "inspiration" in the church's doctrine on scripture. In the documents of the church it is said again and again that God is the *auctor* (author) of the Old and New Testaments as scripture. The school theology, which is at work in the encyclicals of Leo XIII and up to those of Pius XII, tried time and time again to clarify by means of psychological theories how God himself is the *literary* author or the writer of Holy Scripture. And it tried to formulate and to clarify the doctrine of inspiration in such a way that it becomes clear that God is the literary author of scripture. This, however, did not deny (and the Second Vatican Council affirmed it explicitly) that this understanding of God's authorship and of inspiration may not reduce the human authors of these writings merely to God's secretaries, but rather it grants them the character of a genuine literary authorship of their own.

This interpretation of the inspired nature of scripture which we have done no more than sketch can of course be understood in such a way that even today one does not necessarily have to accuse it of being mythological. We would have to recall in this connection what we said in the fifth chapter about the unity between transcendental revelation and its historical objectification in word and in writing, and about the knowledge of the success of these objectifications. In any case it cannot be denied in the Catholic church that God is the author of the Old and New Testaments. But he does not therefore have to be understood as the literary author of these writings. He can be understood in a variety of other ways as the author of scripture, and indeed in such a way that in union with grace and the light of faith scripture can truly be called the word of God. This is true especially because, as we said elsewhere, even if a word *about* God is caused by God, it would not by this very fact be a word *of God* in which God offers himself. It would not be such a word *of God* if this word did not take place as an objectification of God's self-expression which is effected by God and is borne by grace, and which comes to us without being reduced to our level because the process of hearing it is borne by God's Spirit.

If the church was founded by God himself through his Spirit and in Jesus Christ, if the *original* church as the norm for the future church is the object of God's activity in a qualitatively unique way which is different from his preservation of the church in the course of history, and if scripture is a constitutive element of this original church as the norm for future ages, then this already means quite adequately and in both a positive and an exclusive sense that God is the author of scripture and that he inspired it.

Nor at *this* point can some special psychological theory of inspiration be appealed to for help. Rather we can simply take cognizance of the actual origins of scripture which follow for the impartial observer from the very different characteristics of the individual books of scripture. The human authors of Holy Scripture work exactly like other human authors, nor do they have to know anything about their being inspired in reflexive knowledge. If God wills the original church as an indefectible sign of salvation for all ages, and wills it with an absolute, formally pre-defining and eschatological will within salvation history, and hence if he wills with this quite definite will everything which is constitutive for this church, and this includes in certain circumstances scripture in a preeminent way, then he is the inspirer and the author of scripture, although the inspiration of scripture is "only" a moment within God's primordial authorship of the church.

THE INERRANCY OF SCRIPTURE

From the doctrine that Holy Scripture is inspired theology and the official doctrine of the church derive the thesis that scripture is inerrant. We can certainly say with the Second Vatican Council (*Dei Verbum*, art. 11): "Therefore, since everything asserted by the inspired authors or sacred writers must be considered to be asserted by the Holy Spirit, we must profess of the books of scripture that they teach with certainty, with fidelity and without error the truth which God wanted recorded in the sacred writings for the sake of our salvation." But if because of the very nature of scripture as the message of salvation we acknowledge the inerrancy of scripture first of all in this global sense, we are still far from having solved all of the problems and settled all of the difficulties about the meaning and the limits of this statement which can be raised because of the actual state of the scriptural texts. The inerrancy of scripture was certainly understood earlier in too narrow a sense, especially when inspiration was interpreted in the sense of verbal inspiration, and the sacred writers were only regarded as God's secretaries and not as independent and also historically conditioned literary authors. That difficulties still exist here in the understanding and in the exact interpretation of the church's doctrine on the inerrancy of scripture is shown even by the history of the conciliar text just cited. It follows from this history that the Council evidently wanted to leave open the question whether the phrase about the truth which God wanted to have recorded *for the sake of our salvation* is supposed to restrict or to explicate the meaning of the sentence.

We cannot of course treat and answer all of these questions and difficulties in detail here, especially since we cannot go into individual scriptural texts which raise special difficulties with regard to their "truth." We shall have to leave them to the introductory disciplines and to exegesis. Nor can we go into the question here whether in the papal encyclicals of the last century and up to Pius XII the doctrine on the inerrancy of scripture was not understood here and there in a too narrow and materialistic sense. It is also obvious that much of what was said elsewhere in this book, for example, about the inerrancy of Christ and the inerrancy of real dogmas in the teaching of the church, can have its corresponding validity in this question too.

We only want to say here very briefly: scripture in its unity and totality is the objectification of God's irreversible and victorious offer of salvation to the world in Jesus Christ, and therefore in its unity and totality it cannot lead one away from God's truth in some binding way. We must read every individual text within the context of this single whole in order to understand its true meaning correctly. Only *then* can it be understood in its real meaning, and only then can it really be grasped as "true." The very different literary genre of the individual books must be seen more clearly than before and be evaluated in establishing the real meaning of individual statements. (For example, in the New Testament stories it is not impossible in certain circumstances that we find forms of midrash and that they were originally intended to be such, so that according to scripture's own meaning the "historical" truth of a story can be relativized without any qualms.) Scriptural statements were expressed within historically and culturally conditioned conceptual horizons, and this must be taken into account if the question of what is "really" being said in a particular text is to be answered correctly. In certain circumstances it can be completely legitimate to distinguish between the "correctness" and the "truth" of a statement. Nor may we overlook the question whether the really binding meaning of a scriptural statement does not change if a particular book has its origins outside the canon as the work of some individual, and then is taken into the totality of the canonical scriptures.

Just as by the very nature of the case there is an analogy of faith which is a hermeneutical principle for the correct interpretation of individual statements in the official teaching of the church, so that the individual statement can only be understood correctly within the unity of the church's total consciousness of the faith, so too and in an analogous sense, or as a particular instance of this principle, there is also an *analogia scripturae* or an analogy of scripture which is a hermeneutical principle for interpreting individual texts of scripture. If there is a "hierarchy of truths," that is, if a particular statement does not always have the same objective and existentiell weight which another statement has, then this has to be taken into account in interpreting individual scriptural statements. This does not mean that the statement which is "less important" in relation to another statement has to be qualified as incorrect or as false.

If we grant the validity of and apply these and similar principles, which follow from the very nature of the case and from the nature of human speech and are not the principles of a cheap "arrangement" or a cowardly attempt to cover up difficulties, then we certainly do not inevitably have to get into the difficulty of having to hold that particular statements of scripture are "true" in the meaning which is really intended and is intended in a binding way, although a sober and honest exegesis might declare that they are incorrect and erroneous in the sense of a negation of the "truth."

SCRIPTURE AND TEACHING OFFICE

With regard to the relationship between scripture and the church's teaching office, the most important points will be covered in the next section which treats the church's teaching office. Insofar as the church's teaching office in later ages continues to be bound permanently to the original church's consciousness of the faith which is the constitutive beginning of the church as a whole, and insofar as this consciousness has been objectified in an authentic and pure way in Holy Scripture, the teaching office does not stand above scripture. Rather it only has the task of giving witness to the truth of scripture, of maintaining this truth in a vital way, and of always interpreting it anew in historically changing horizons of understanding as the one truth which always remains the same.

SCRIPTURE AND TRADITION

If everything which has been said so far is understood correctly (and would be developed more clearly), then there also follows the correct understanding of the relationship between scripture and tradition. Scripture itself is the concrete process and the objectification of the original church's consciousness of the faith, and by means of it this consciousness of the faith is "transmitted" to later ages of the church. The formation of the canon is a process whose legitimacy cannot be established by scripture alone, but rather it is itself a fundamental moment in the tradition. Conversely, the Second Vatican Council refused to make tradition a second source for us today which exists by itself alongside scripture, a source which testifies to individual, material contents of faith which have no foundation at all in scripture. However much the more precise relationship between scripture and tradition still needs a great deal of further theological clarification, it is perhaps obvious from what has already been said earlier that the "scripture alone" of the Reformation is no longer a doctrine which distinguishes and separates the churches. For Evangelical theology too recognizes that scripture is the objectification of the original church's living consciousness of the faith, and is so in the midst of a very clear pluralism in the original church's preaching and in the theologies which are found there. This pluralism can ultimately be held together in unity only by the church's single and living consciousness of the faith.

With regard to Holy Scripture in the life of the church and in the life of the individual Christian, we may refer to the sixth chapter of the Second Vatican Council's Constitution on Revelation, *Dei Verbum,* and recommend this chapter for serious spiritual reading.

7. On the Church's Teaching Office

THE PROBLEM OF THE UNIQUENESS OF AN "ECCLESIAL TEACHING OFFICE"

If we want to understand the real meaning of an ecclesial teaching office in the Catholic understanding of the church, we have to ask first of all the basic theological question *why* according to the Catholic understanding there is something like an authoritative teaching office in the church. Given certain presuppositions, this teaching office even has an absolute and ultimately binding authority vis-à-vis the conscience of an individual Catholic Christian, although in order to be effective in the concrete for an individual person it has to be accepted by the conscience of this individual in a free decision.

We have to reflect first of all on the fact that in spite of God's salvific providence in the Old Testament, in spite of a true and positive history of salvation and revelation there, and in spite of an official "ecclesial body" which was willed by God, nevertheless before the church of Christ this absolute authority of a teaching office did not exist. The Old Testament knew of no absolute and formal teaching authority which was recognized as such. Its "official" representatives themselves could fall away from God, his revelation and his grace. Christianity professes this insofar as it knows on the one hand that it has its origins in the Old Testament, and recognizes on the other hand a radical caesura in the history of salvation insofar as the official Old Testament did not recognize Jesus Christ, but rather rejected him.

This shows at least that even in Catholic dogmatic ecclesiology we cannot be satisfied with saying that God endowed the authorities of the church of Jesus Christ, namely, the whole episcopate with Peter and his successors as its head, with formal authority of a fundamental kind. In itself this is correct, of course, but it does not give the real, intrinsic reason for this teaching authority from the innermost essence of the church. Consequently, it always runs the risk of being misunderstood in a formalistic way because this conception of such a radical authorization merely by being formally established by God's will no longer seems probable to people today.

THE CHRISTOLOGICAL REASON FOR THE TEACHING OFFICE

Therefore we must recognize a really Christological reason for this teaching authority of the church and formulate it. And this consists ultimately in the fact that Jesus Christ himself is the absolute, irreversible and invincible climax of salvation history. The fundamental self-communication of God upon which the whole history of man's salvation is based has reached such a historical tangibility in Jesus Christ that as a result in this eschatological phase the victory of God's self-communication as truth, as grace and as holiness is irreversible, and indeed even in the dimension of its historical manifestation. Jesus Christ is the fact which makes it manifest that God's self-communication is present in the world as the truth of ultimate love, that God's loving truth and his true love are not only offered to man and his history, but also that they have really triumphed in this history and can no longer be abolished by man's rejection. Jesus Christ is the word in whom the dialogue between God and the freedom of creatures and the drama which was still open until Christ reach their ultimate decision. God expresses his truth and his love and really brings them to victory. He does not eliminate man's freedom, but he encompasses it in the sovereign power of his grace in such a way that man's freedom as a whole really accepts this truth and preserves it, although this tells us nothing about the individual and his individual destiny.

THE CHURCH AND PERSEVERANCE IN THE TRUTH

Now the church of Christ is the ongoing presence and the historical tangibility of this ultimate and victorious word of God in Jesus Christ. If

Christ is really to found the eschatological age, the church must participate in the specific characteristic which comes from the fact that God's offer of himself as truth and as love was *victorious*, that is, ultimately the church as a whole can no longer lose this truth and this love. This is true not because man's freedom or his history have been abolished, but rather because in his powerful word in Jesus Christ God has already encompassed every conceivable rejection, and has really redeemed man's freedom and his history into God's life, into his truth and into his love.

It is precisely the Evangelical Christian, who understands Christianity as God's mighty deed upon man, who basically must say that the church of Jesus Christ as a whole can no longer lose truth and grace, can no longer lose God's love and his salvation. This is true not because we men could not continually pervert the truth, nor because we are not liars, who of ourselves would be more pleased with our own human shortsightedness than with the light of God's strong and hard and incomprehensible truth. Rather it is true because in his grace God has also triumphed in Jesus Christ over our human dishonesty, and because he will maintain this victory of Christ as an eschatological act of salvation until God's truth will shine upon men from face to face.

Consequently, the controversial theological question between the Evangelical and Catholic understanding of the church cannot really be whether or not the church of Jesus Christ can lose the truth, but rather it can ultimately only be the question *how* in the concrete God triumphs in the church in his victorious presence and in his communication of the truth. But if in the light of the New Testament and because of the whole history of the church's self-understanding we profess that this church has a hierarchical structure, and that there is an authority in it which teaches by the mandate of Christ and by his authority, then a Catholic Christian cannot allow himself to get into the dilemma of either losing this truth and this reality, or of rejecting the structure of the church in its concrete hierarchical constitution. If there is in the church a teaching authority which speaks in the name of Christ and not merely from its own religious subjectivity, and which is sent by Christ to speak just as he was sent by the Father, and if there is teaching which is binding, then a Catholic Christian regards it as an impossible dilemma that he would have to choose between losing the truth of Christ and such a radical disobedience to the authority of the church that the concrete authority of the church would be denied or rejected. If because the church is the church of Jesus Christ, and therefore is the church of absolute and eschatological salvation, it does not lose the truth of Christ on a decisive point, and if this church is at the same time a church with the power of a mandate and with an authoritative right to teach, and this according to the testimony of the New Testament and according to the practice of the apostles, including Paul, then the dilemma we mentioned cannot exist in this eschatological situation.

TEACHING AUTHORITY
ACCORDING TO THE CATHOLIC UNDERSTANDING OF THE CHURCH

From this perspective, the perspective of this eschatological situation which is the situation of Christ himself, the Catholic understanding of the church says that when the church in its teaching authority, that is, in the whole episcopate along with the Pope, or in the personal head of this whole episcopate, really confronts man in its teaching with an *ultimate* demand in the name of Christ, God's grace and power prevent this teaching authority from losing the truth of Christ. We emphasized earlier that this teaching authority of the Pope, and of the whole episcopate with the Pope, is not an authority through which we receive new revelation from God. It is rather an authority which mediates authoritatively the single understanding of the faith of the church as the church of Jesus Christ to the individual and to his conscience, and does this in a way which is binding on the whole church and can be effective in the whole church. This teaching authority simply interprets, develops and actualizes in ever new historical concretions the message of Christ, but it does not really increase it and it does not receive any new revelations. It is only as it were the concrete organ and the embodiment of the historical tangibility of the whole church's understanding of the faith, and this understanding is ultimately mediated to it by the Spirit of Jesus Christ and through the victory of his grace.

This ultimate and fundamental conception, of course, still leaves a great deal to be said about the practice of a Catholic Christian. As is the case with every authority, the function of the ecclesial teaching office in the church of Christ has many levels which correspond to the various concrete faith situations. The teaching office speaks with all of its authority only in relatively rare instances. Usually its declarations, teaching, interpretations, instructions, warnings, and so on, are provisional and limited exercises of the real authority which is present in the total consciousness of the faith of the church as an eschatological reality. And correspondingly, of course, the Catholic Christian's obligation in conscience to this church authority varies a great deal depending on the level of the authority exercised. We cannot develop in detail here the casuistry of these various levels and the conduct of the Catholic Christian in relation to this teaching office. To do so we would have to go into numerous questions, including the question of the development of dogma and the question of the concrete institutions and authorities in which the church's teaching authority is exercised. We would have to go into the question of how the particular degree of authority in the exercise of this office, and hence of the whole church's consciousness of the faith, is recognized and evaluated, and what possibilities for criticism and protest against lesser declarations of the teaching authority are granted to a Catholic Christian, and indeed in certain circumstances *must* be exercised by him. There is something like a teaching authority of the church within Evangelical Christianity too. In certain circumstances there are also disciplinary proceedings in matters of doctrine. In other words, a church cannot be a church if it would never have the courage to declare something anathema, if it could tolerate absolutely everything and anything as an equally justified opinion among Christians. The only difference from Catholic Christianity, then, lies in the fact that an absolute and *ultimately* binding declaration of the church's teaching office is rejected within the Evangelical church.

THE "HIERARCHY OF TRUTHS" AND ITS SUBJECTIVE APPROPRIATION

We may not understand the individual statements of the church's teaching in an isolated way to begin with. They are intelligible for faith only when a person enters into the totality of these revealed truths in faith. As we mentioned before, Vatican II's Decree on Ecumenism (*Unitatis redintegratio*, art. 11) refers to the "hierarchy of truths." Although all these truths are revealed, they have a quite different relationship to the real core of faith. Consequently, objectively as well as subjectively it belongs to the essence of the individual truth that it be grasped within the totality. Faith is not the process of taking a position on or of accepting or of realizing existentially a sum of individual propositions. Rather its focus is always on the single totality of truth, and therefore it can understand the individual truth only within the total act of faith. For as a personal relationship to God revealing himself, faith grasps and affirms the individual propositions within the act of a personal relationship to the living God who communicates himself. In the faith of a Catholic Christian, then, there is indeed a sum of articulated, individual propositions which are materially distinct from one another, and these are the church's dogmas. But this sum can be known and appropriated only in an act which does not attain to human propositions of faith, but rather attains to immediacy to God. We can exercise this act only in this sum and in this unity because the living God who reveals himself is a *single* God, even in his relationship to me. The objective sum of these propositions is intrinsically interconnected and has a quite definite structure, and basically the act of faith as the subjective act of an individual is a single and individual act.

From this perspective, if a Catholic Christian has really understood the church's teaching office, and the essential nature of eschatological truth and reality and of the God who reveals himself personally, he cannot confront a choice among the individual, revealed propositions of the church's faith which have been taught authoritatively as dogmas in the sense that he accepts some as true or as probable or as appropriate for him, and rejects others. But although Catholic faith is always an entrance into the one church's understanding of the faith as something formed authoritatively, and is not a subjective and arbitrary selection of opinions which are personally agreeable, there is nevertheless a subjective appropriation of the hierarchy of truths which have different relationships to the core and to the substance of Christian faith. Indeed this difference is far more possible within the subjective actualization of faith. A Catholic Christian always lives by the single understanding of the faith of the community of those who believe in Jesus Christ, and he finds this understanding in his ecclesial community.

But this does not necessarily mean, however, that he is required to assimilate the faith in all of the differentiated nuances which it has objectively and has acquired in history. An individual Christian need not be concerned with all of that, but can live in the implicit faith of the church even when he is Catholic and accepts the authority of the church absolutely. Not every Christian has to be interested in everything in the same way in his existentiell faith. He leaves to the church's consciousness of the faith certain questions and even settled issues in the church's understanding of the faith which neither do nor can touch him very closely in his concrete, existentiell situation. We even have to say that many times it would be better if Christians knew less about certain details of the Catholic catechism, but had really grasped the ultimate and decisive questions in a genuine and profound way, questions like God, Jesus Christ, his grace, sin, love, the unity between the love of God and neighbor, and prayer. If they were to do this, then they may live calmly with a bit of ignorance about certain catechism questions which they do not doubt. A Christian lives in the church's total consciousness of the faith because his own consciousness of the faith depends on it not only on the level of external, formal teaching authority, but also in the interior reality of the very thing which is believed in, and which as believed in is found in the church, namely, in God's grace.

THE QUESTION OF THE POST-TRIDENTINE DEVELOPMENT OF DOGMA

There are Evangelical theologians who maintain that it is conceivable that the separated western churches could reach agreement on the dogmatic teachings which were held in common in the pre-Reformation church. But they are of the opinion that in its post-tridentine dogmas of the primacy and the teaching authority of the Pope, of the Immaculate Conception of the Blessed Virgin Mary, and of the Assumption of the Blessed Virgin into heaven, the Roman Catholic church has declared dogmas to be binding which non-Catholic Christians have to reject in principle. The Catholic church has to be accused of creating new and insuperable obstacles to church unity, obstacles which were not present before the parting of the ways in the sixteenth century. Now there is no doubt that we have to admit that before the Reformation these dogmas did not exist in the Catholic church to the same degree of theological reflection, and were not binding in the same reflexive and explicit way. Dogmas have been added, then, which an Evangelical Christian would have to accept as Catholic doctrines of faith if he wanted to become a Catholic, doctrines which go beyond an agreement about the disputed questions at the time of the Reformation.

THE PRIMACY AND TEACHING AUTHORITY OF THE BISHOP OF ROME

With regard first of all to the claim to primacy by the bishop of Rome or the Pope, and, under certain conditions, his infallible teaching authority, we have to say that only those prerogatives are ascribed to the Pope as the visible head of the church which belong unambiguously to the church as such according to the Catholic and the pre-Reformation understanding of the faith. For the pre-Reformation church there could be no doubt that in a council the church as such can speak with an ultimate and irreversible authority which is the binding norm for the conscience of Christians. The ancient councils were regarded in this way as the definitive and irreformable teaching of the church, although this teaching could develop in the future, and they were regarded as a binding norm for the conscience of the faithful. Consequently, the only question with regard to the teaching authority of the Pope is whether this authority which was present in the church according to the pre-Reformation understanding of the faith can also belong to the Pope as such. When we say the Pope "as such," this does not mean of course the Pope as a private person. It means rather the Pope insofar as he is the highest authority in the hierarchical church, and insofar as he acts in this capacity. It means that the Pope is infallible only in a situation where he appeals to his highest authority in a question of interpretation concerning the revelation which is in scripture and hence also in tradition, and makes a final decision by virture of his position in the church.

To this extent, therefore, the dogma of the First Vatican Council means nothing else but that a proposition is asserted of the Pope which was always present in the Catholic understanding of the faith as asserted of the church and of ecumenical councils. It has to be said on this point that the theological difficulty in ascribing such a function to a definite individual person in the church is no greater than when it is ascribed to councils or the whole episcopate, presupposing that the Pope is always regarded as acting as the head of the church and as the person who represents the whole college of bishops. To introduce democratic considerations at this point is out of place for the church and for the issue in question. With regard to this ultimate decision in questions of faith which are supposed to touch the ultimate and innermost conscience of a person, a large number of bishops quite certainly does not represent and does not guarantee more truth and more infallibility than an individual person does. This only presupposes that the whole episcopate in a council or the Pope as a so-called individual person are always seen only as the concreteness of the concrete church. This church is preserved in its eschatological reality and truth not by the capacity or the intelligence or the theological education of men, but by the Spirit of Christ. Looking at the question from this perspective, we may say that ultimately a personal head of the church's synodal and collegial representation is more natural and sensible from a human point of view too.

From a human point of view, of course, it is always a great risk for the Pope to have this kind of authority, situated at the cutting edge, as it were, between human fallibility, finiteness and historicity on the one hand, and on the other hand the power of the Spirit of Christ who preserves the church in its truth, in and in spite of its humanity. But this is also true of the church as a whole. For the sum of all men does not make man and humanity less human than the individual already is. For we are not dealing here with a collective discovery of the truth, where basically and by the very nature of the case more people really do have a greater chance to discover the truth than an individual has. But we are dealing here with the gift of the Spirit to the church. Just as with regard to the truth of faith as a matter for the free decision of a person, ultimately the Spirit does not necessarily have to address the individual and his conscience, although this would be within the totality of the church, so that the faith which is heard and accepted in faith is the ground of a faith which can be taught and preached authoritatively, so too the basic idea which is behind the teaching primacy of the Roman Pope, namely, that such a teaching authority cannot be separated from a concrete person, is an idea which shows the intrinsic theological justification of the primacy in an adequate way.

In accordance with the indirect method which we are following, we are not concerned in this question with deriving the infallible teaching authority of the Pope from Matt. 16:18 by means of the direct approach of biblical theology. We are concerned here with the question whether the Catholic church necessarily erred when through its whole episcopate in the First Vatican Council it declared that this primacy and power of the Pope belongs to its own understanding of the faith, and whether it must have violated the innermost essence of Christianity, so that a Christian would have to leave the Catholic church in the name of Christianity. If there is and can be such an ultimately binding teaching authority in the church, then there is no theological reason to protest in the name of Christianity against a personal possessor of this power.

This also follows from the observation that Luther, and all the more so modern Evangelical theology, do not really deny just to the Pope the possibility of such an absolute obligation of conscience in matters of faith, but they also deny it to a council or to any other tangible authority in the church which is capable of acting. But in reality this changes the difference between the various Christian churches of the present from a difference which arises only with the First Vatican Council to a difference which has to be dated back to a time far beyond the time of the Reformation. For the fact that an authority like that of scripture itself must be acknowledged for the first ecumenical councils considered *formally,* and that to contradict what they say would simply abolish the church and Christianity, this was already clear in those ages of the church and its consciousness of the faith when neither the division between the Reformation churches and the Catholic church nor the division between eastern and western Christianity existed.

If the church is one, and if in spite of the multiplicity of local churches with their bishops this unity is a single unity, and as such and for this reason it has and must have a head who is capable of action, then no basic protest in the name of Christianity can be possible against the primatial power of the Pope in the proper sense as distinguished from the teaching authority of the Pope. This is not yet a cogent deduction of a personal head with the power of primacy and the power of leadership in the church. But it maintains that it does not really contradict the essence of Christianity as a Christianity which exists in the form of a concrete universal church.

THE "NEW" MARIAN DOGMAS

It is also the case with the "new" Marian dogmas that they have to be seen within the context of the total understanding of Christian faith. They can be understood correctly only if a person really believes in what we call the Incarnation of the eternal Logos himself in our flesh, and counts this as part of Christianity's very existence. From this perspective it has to be said immediately and according to the witness of scripture that Mary is not simply and only an individual episode in a biography of Jesus which has no theological interest, but rather that she is someone who has an explicit historical role in the history of salvation. When we read Matthew, Luke and John, and when we pray the Apostles' Creed in which we profess the birth of Jesus, the divine Logos, from the Virgin Mary, they say in however simple a form that Mary was not only the mother of Jesus in a biological sense. Rather Mary is seen as someone who assumes a quite definite and indeed unique function in this official and public history of salvation. Mary has a place in the apostolic profession of faith, and Luther himself did not really deny her this place, although he believed he saw at the time in the Marian cult of the late Middle Ages tendencies which threatened or denied the *sola gratia* principle.

The dogma says nothing else but that Mary is someone who has been redeemed radically. From this perspective the basic conception is really to be taken for granted that, as someone who accepted in faith the salvation of the world in her personal motherhood and not just in her biological motherhood, Mary is also the highest and the most radical instance of the realization of salvation, of the fruit of salvation, and of the reception of salvation. For fifteen hundred years this was really taken for granted in both eastern and western Christianity, although not always in this explicit and reflexive way. And from this perspective it is relatively easy to understand what "immaculate conception" and "assumption into heaven" mean without them becoming dogmas which would have to be arrived at by speculation from out of and in addition to the real and ultimate substance of Christianity. Take the case of an Evangelical Christian today who says that he sees a great problem with original sin itself if today more than ever, and quite biblically at that, we understand Adam's sin to have been transcended and encompassed by God's salvific will and by the redemption of Christ.

Consequently, we have to say that we are always sanctified and redeemed insofar as we have our origins in Christ, just as we are sinners without the Spirit insofar as we regard ourselves as having our origins in Adam. From this perspective there really is no special difficulty with the statement that the mother of the son was conceived and willed from the beginning by God's absolute salvific will as someone who was to receive salvation in faith and love.

The Assumption of the Blessed Virgin, body and soul, into heaven says nothing else about Mary but what we also profess about ourselves in an article of faith in the Apostles' Creed: the resurrection of the flesh and eternal life. We are going to say a few things about how the resurrection of the flesh in general is to be explained in a more exact theological way when we come to eschatology. But in any case it is at least a possible opinion in Evangelical theology that the fulfillment of the single and whole person does not necessarily take place on a temporal axis which is our own, but rather that it takes place for a person with his death and in his own eschatology. If, then, as Catholics we assert that Mary has reached fulfill-ment because of her quite special place in the history of salvation and because we profess that she is the most radically successful instance of redemption, then at least from a theological point of view it is impossible to see why this dogma has to contradict the basic substance of Christianity.

Further theological reflection is possible about whether and why it was opportune for Pius XII to define this dogma, and on this point a Catholic is quite certainly not obliged by the dogma to hold one particular opinion. But in any case we see that nothing is said here which would basically contradict the real substance of the faith. For we profess about Mary the very thing which we profess as our hope for all of us. The Assumption is nothing else but the fulfillment of God's salvific act on a person, on this person, the fulfillment of God's salvific act and of his grace alone, and we hope this for ourselves too. Its basic substance, then, and its objective meaning are things which are completely taken for granted by all Chris-tians.

On our first level of reflection we cannot go explicitly into the further question of how the Marian dogmas are contained at least implicitly in the apostolic tradition, although there is certainly no explicit testimony in scripture, nor are they found in the explicit tradition of the first centuries. Nor can we go into the question of how this theological process of a development in the basic knowledge about the Blessed Virgin's place in the history of salvation proceeded more precisely.

8. The Christian in the Life of the Church

ON THE ECCLESIAL NATURE OF A CHRISTIAN

There has to be a church in the Christian understanding of faith and of human existence. Christianity is not the ideological creation of a religious enthusiasm, nor of the religious experience of an individual. It comes to the individual rather by the same route from which he receives the rest of his life, including his intellectual and spiritual life: it comes from history. No one develops and unfolds from out of the purely formal and antecedent structure of his essence. Rather he receives the concreteness of his life from a community of persons, from intercommunication, from an objective spirit, from a history, from a people and from a family, and he develops it only within this community, and this includes what is most personal and most proper to himself. This is also true for salvation and for the Christian religion, and for the Christianity of an individual.

Obviously a Christian is a Christian in the innermost depths of his divinized essence. Nor would he ever be or ever become a Christian if he were not to live from out of the innermost center of his essence as divinized by grace. But the very thing which he is in his innermost depths and in the origins of his most individual existence, and is by the grace of God whose domain he cannot leave, this very thing comes from the concrete history of salvation to meet him in the concrete as his very own: it comes in the profession of faith of Christians, in the cult of Christians, in the community life of Christians, in a word, it comes in the church. An absolutely individual Christianity in the most personal experience of grace and ecclesial Christianity are no more radically opposed than are body and soul, than are man's transcendental essence and his historical constitution, or than are individuality and intercommunication. The two condition each other mutually. The very thing which we are from God is mediated in the concreteness of history by what we call church. And it is only in and through this mediation that it becomes our own reality and our own salvation in full measure. For this reason church exists and has to exist. It is simply taken for granted by Christians of every denomination, and is taken for granted as something which is a necessary dimension of their Christian existence.

Moreover, therefore, a Christian can and may see this church very soberly as the church of his everyday Christian life. There is, of course, a hymnic enthusiasm about the church, and this is already found in the theology of the New Testament (cf. Ephesians, for example). But however true what is experienced and expressed there might be, a Christian is truly not obliged to have any illusions about the sober, everyday reality of the church, nor to overlook it. Just as love for one's father, one's mother, one's concrete historical situation, and for the mission and the historical task of one's own people can be binding, indeed has to be binding, with an absolutely sober and objective honesty which sees the finiteness and the problems of one's own family, which recognizes the horrors in the history of one's own people, and which recognizes the problems with the spirit, the objective spirit, of the West, so too we can and we must profess our faith in the holy, Catholic church along with the Apostles' Creed. For this very reason we are obliged to see the church in its concreteness, in its finiteness, with the burdens of its history, and with all its negligences and perhaps even false developments, and *in this way* to accept this concrete church without reservations as the realm of our own Christian existence: with humility, with courage and sobriety, with a real love for this church and a willingness to work for her, and even with a readiness to share her burdens in ourselves and in our lives, and not to add the weakness of our own witness to the burdens of this church.

For ultimately it is true, and this is an element in the new experience and understanding of the church in the Catholic church of the Second Vatican Council: we ourselves are the church, we poor, primitive, cowardly people, and together we represent the church. If we look at the church from outside, as it were, then we have not grasped that we are the church, and basically it is only our own inadequacies which are looking at us from the church. Not only does a Christian not have a right to idealize his church in a false way. He is also obliged by his faith to recognize the church of God and the assembly of Jesus Christ in this concrete church with its inadequacies, with its historical dangers, with its historical refusals, and with its false historical developments. For the victory of God's grace on us men who together are the church is won right here in the form of this servant and under the cross of its Lord, and under the ongoing shadow of the powers of darkness. It is won inside it and not outside. This church always continues to be a living church not only because there really takes place within it faith, hope and love, not only because the Lord's Supper is celebrated and his death is proclaimed, but also because the real thing which constitutes the church does become manifest again and again in a way which is sufficient for anyone who looks at the church with an open heart and with the eyes of faith.

ON LAW AND ORDER IN THE CHURCH

As a community, as the body of Christ, as the assembly of the faithful, and as the representation of Christ, of his word and of his grace, the church necessarily has an hierarchical structure. Without a holy law, without a division of labor, functions and hence also of rights among different individuals, without this kind of a differentiation of functions in the community the church would cease being the people of God, the house of God, the body of Christ and the community of the faithful. It would become a disjointed conglomerate of religious individualists. There has to be in the church a holy order, a holy law, and hence also a power which may and must be exercised juridically by one person in relation to others. And to this extent there exists over and beyond the power which all have to give witness to the truth a power to lead and to govern in the church, both in the individual local churches and in the universal church. Every religious community which calls itself Christian has adopted at least in the long run a church order and a church law. No matter how the binding power of this law is interpreted theologically more precisely and exactly, there is the universal conviction that an individual Christian has a real obligation in conscience to church authority and to the necessary claim which it has by the very nature of the case.

Obviously there is an essential difference between a divine law, or the claims of God and Christ on the conscience of the individual, and the claims which the church makes on the conscience of the Catholic Christian on the basis of its power to govern. Divine law and church law are not the same thing. A human authority speaks in the latter, although one which is legitimate by God's will. It speaks in laws, in regulated customs, and in the common life of the church. Although all of this lays claims upon the consciences of individuals, it is basically mutable, as distinguished from divine law, and in the first instance it is also subject to the criticism and to the desires for change on the part of the faithful. The church can only proclaim a divine law which comes from man's essence or from the intrinsic essence of the historical salvation which has been constituted in Christ. To the extent that it is possible, the church can make an effort to see that this divine law is really obeyed. But she herself stands under this law and she cannot change it. She can explain it, but she is not the lord of this law.

But many laws, for example, the law that particular days of fast and abstinence be observed, and many things in church law which affect the life of the individual in very practical ways are church laws, and the relationship of the Catholic Christian to these church laws is an essentially different relationship than he has to really divine norms and laws. The immediate origin, the mutability or the immutability, and the religious and existentiell significance of these two kinds of laws are all essentially different. If church laws are also laws which are addressed to the conscience of a Catholic Christian, still his relationship to them remains much looser and much freer than is the case when a person confronts the real will of God himself, although perhaps he confronts it on the lips of the church.

It cannot be our task here to draw the boundary between these two kinds of laws in all of the particulars and concrete questions which are involved. But to take a concrete example, basically the law about mass on Sunday cannot be traced back to the Sinai law about keeping the sabbath holy and cannot represent a direct divine law. It is a completely different question to what extent something is hidden behind such a law which goes beyond a church law, and this with regard to the spirit which is realized concretely in the law (for example, with regard to the relationship to the Last Supper of Christ which is required of Christians). A great deal which concerns church laws and regulations for marriage is likewise church law and not divine law. It is altogether fitting and proper even for Catholic Christians who are not theologians or priests to know something about drawing the boundary in these matters which touch their lives, and to be able to apply this distinction in their concrete lives. There is much more room for interpretation by the individual in church laws which are not immediately divine laws. The individual person can recognize that in certain circumstances he is not bound in conscience by a particular church law or a particular church regulation. In these cases love, for example, and not only the pressure of circumstances, can excuse us from a church law, prescinding altogether from the fact that there is also of course the possibility of an explicit church dispensation by a church authority.

LEVELS OF RELATIVITY IN THE LAW

A discrepancy can occur between the level of what is regulated and can be regulated by the church on the one hand, and the real realm of the individual Christian's conscience on the other, a discrepancy which cannot be resolved by further norms with material content. We must call attention to the fact that we are not dealing here with the teaching authority of the church, but rather with practical norms of the church, with church laws and rules and regulations which in principle, of course, address the conscience of the individual Catholic Christian with a demand for loyal obedience, and have the right to do so. But the more complicated human life becomes, and the more differentiated individual persons in the church become and have the right to become, the more frequently can there be an instance of the discrepancy which we are referring to here between the level of what is regulated and can be regulated by the church and the concrete situation of an individual Christian. Today's educated Christian must know that something like this really exists.

There is a real relativity in the church with regard to its *law*. This relativity in the church's law has very variable degrees and modulations, depending, for example, on whether we are dealing with the sacraments and their necessity and obligation, or with the non-sacramental law of the church, and depending on whether we are dealing with divine law or human law in the church, with statutory law or customary law, with rigid laws or flexible laws, and with perfect laws or imperfect laws. When we speak here of a relativity in the law, this relativity of the law is related to the law as such, that is, the law insofar as it is really dealing with norms for the church's social order, and hence not with moral norms insofar as these signify a divine law either of revelation or of nature, and express a state of affairs which is established immediately by God alone and is in itself of real and immediate salvific significance. Indeed legal norms themselves can include a genuinely moral demand and hence a demand of salvific significance. And when and to the extent that this is the case, there can be no question of relativity here. But the law contains this kind of a moral demand in the proper sense only when and to the extent that it serves the social order, in our case that of the church. But this social order does not touch all of the dimensions of human existence, nor, insofar as it can be contained in universal material norms, is it always and in every case of such a nature that it would be or would have to be self-evident that it did not conflict with a person's other dimensions, realities, rights and freedoms.

Let us illustrate this by a few concrete questions: Is there, for example, no possibility for a baptized, Catholic Christian to marry if no priest and no witnesses to the marriage are available for a longer period of time? In itself church law ordains that witnesses are required for the validity of a marriage even when no priest is available. Does this hold always and in every conceivable case? Another example: Does someone who cannot prove the nullity of a previous marriage in a church court really no longer have a right to marry? What can someone do who was ordained a priest and cannot prove that the conditions of canon 214 in the code of canon law really apply in his case, conditions which would free him from all priestly obligations if it could be proved that they were present? Could a refugee priest living among refugees, and this of course is an extreme case, not ordain another to the priesthood even if there was an urgent need for it, and presumably no bishop would be available for a longer period who could do the ordaining? Are there not situations behind the various iron curtains which permit an action, and even require it, which is not foreseen either materially or formally in the church's law? Is it certain that the formal and material norms of the universal law as the product of human reflection cover in advance every conceivable human situation in such an adequate way that a particular action either can be justified before the forum of the church as having taken place according to these norms, or, because it contradicts the letter of the law, it is by this very fact immoral, and can be declared by the church to be such?

There are perhaps very many cases which we can think of in a particular context and which can be handled by appealing to excusing causes or to legal equity or to other formal norms for applying the letter of the church's law. We admit this, and it is to be taken for granted that something like this should always be attempted. But at least in some cases where such an attempt is possible and perhaps even obligatory, the interpretation and the application of these formal principles will only be possible by means of an interpretation of these formal principles, an interpretation which, although it is perhaps objectively correct, is not approved at least positively by church authority as the representative and the guardian of the universal material and formal norms of the law. Nor presumably can it be approved positively and officially in many cases because the situation can consist precisely in the fact that such an official interpretation is not possible in the concrete. By the very nature of human knowledge no interpretation can cover all of the cases which are to be interpreted. Rather it essentially and inevitably only creates new problems, especially since the conceivable approval of a particular, individual action by the church would not be infallible. Ultimately the person would be left to his own decision and his own responsibility. Because the decision of a church authority would once again be a decision about principles, the concrete problem in this particular case would not be covered completely any more than it was by the other principles which have already been made reflexive.

The relativity of the law which we are driving at here is not a "situation law" as it could be suspiciously called by analogy with the situation ethics which has been rejected by the church. The relativity of the law which we are talking about is not this because if it were, then the same accusation could be made against *epikeia* and also against the force of custom in relation to the law, and both of these are accepted. Both of them go counter to the letter of the law, and they are what they are supposed to be only so long as the lawgiver is not asked and explicit permission is not given. For such a permission would make such things as excusing causes, *epikeia* and the force of custom a new law, or would at least make them a real dispensation by the lawgiver.

We may also call attention to the following situation in dogmatics which is not usually seen from this perspective: sacraments can be subsumed under the sacral law of the church even though they are of "divine" law and do not just belong to the positive law of the church. The doctrine about the obligatory nature of particular sacraments and even their necessity as a means of salvation points in the same direction as we are moving here. A person is bound here by a definite norm for his activity, an activity which has a social dimension. Nevertheless, dogmatic theology declares that the really decisive effect of these sacraments can also be acquired without them, although the sacraments do not for this reason cease being obligatory. An example of this would be the grace of justification. The Council of Trent declares explicitly with regard to spiritual communion, for example, that by means of it the *res sacramenti* or the real and ultimate reality of the sacrament of the Eucharist is present, and can be present even when the sacrament itself is missing (cf. *D.S.* 1648). This shows in any case that the sacramental law of the church foregoes basically and explicitly making the claim to be valid always and everywhere in such a way that the reality which the sacrament is really all about would be present only when the sacrament itself is present and celebrated.

If in spite of the necessity and obligation of at least some sacraments there is this relativity in the sacraments and in sacramental law, then all the more so can we say in general: the relativity of church law in general is the same as is taught explicitly with regard to the necessity and the obligatory nature of the sacraments. If someone objects to this that a law would lose all of its normative power and validity if in a certain sense it is merely granted relative validity, this is not correct. All inner-worldly and materially binding authority, whether it be the infallible teaching authority of the church, the church's pastoral authority, or a law, must necessarily first be recognized as valid by the moral conscience of the individual in order to be able to be really effective. And in the moral decision which recognizes these very authorities prior to their binding power these authorities are not the norm of conscience, for it is conscience which has to recognize them. It cannot be said, then, that all obedience to inner-worldly authority has to have as its norm this authority itself in order that it be able to be effective. Moreover, it is not contradictory to be obedient to an authority and at the same time to presuppose that it is relative, and that in certain circumstances its claim is not binding or is erroneous. It is quite possible, for example, that in individual instances church authorities command something which is sinful and which the conscience of the individual has to reject. The inner assent which an ecclesial teaching authority can and must require can in certain circumstances be refused. There does exist authority which is real and yet relative, and there does exist the possibility that it will be obeyed even when its relativity is recognized. And this can also be said about law in the church.

A relativity which entrusts the law to a conscience which basically is ready for obedience is not a situation ethic. It only means that the individual must examine himself before his own conscience, and must take a critical attitude towards himself by taking into account the possibility and even the danger that in a moral or legal libertarianism he is placing himself unjustly above the legitimate claim of church authority. Finally, the relativity of the law which we mean here follows simply from the ontological fact that the concrete instance, which is always more than a mere instance, can never be covered completely by universal laws which are formulated in human concepts, and that the concrete situation, which is relevant with all of its elements for the question of the applicability of universal principles, can never be made reflexive completely. And, besides this, the traditional teaching has always said the same thing by granting that in very many concrete cases in moral matters, and especially in legal matters, we cannot strive for theoretical certitude in the realm of the concrete, but only for a greater or lesser degree of probability.

If someone were to blame this fact on man's ignorance, we would have to say that the limitations of our knowledge cannot necessarily and always be eliminated even by all the intelligence of the church in many cases, and indeed in extremely important cases. If this consideration is correct, then it can happen that a conscience which is ready to be obedient to the law, and which has also submitted this basic readiness to proof in the concrete life of this Christian in the church, that this conscience gets into a situation in which it cannot expect a real solution of the question by church authority as the solicitor of the law. Rather a decision against the letter of the law can be made, or even has to be made. If there are such instances, then by the very nature of the case the one who makes the decision cannot expect his decision to be approved explicitly by the official church in the public forum of the church, nor to be accepted as legitimate by the official church. Anyone who demands this would either be denying the authority of office and the basic legitimacy of universal laws themselves, or he would be demanding of the church that his concrete reality, which cannot be made completely reflexive and reduced to universals, be elevated to a universal law. For example, if a person believes that in very definite circumstances a baptized person is married in the eyes of God even though there were no witnesses, he may not demand that this fact also be recognized by the church before he establishes it by satisfying the universal legal norms in the public forum.

In this respect the usual Christian in the Catholic church often does an injustice to the church. In certain circumstances he correctly claims a freedom with regard to a particular positive law of the church, and does this because in his concrete situation he has considered the matter before God and thinks that he is not really morally bound by the universal law of the church, and perhaps he cannot consider himself bound by it. If he is convinced of this, he can be completely justified, but he cannot demand at the same time that the church explicitly approve this concrete, individual decision by its own verdict. Canon law in the Middle Ages always saw that there can be such cases insofar as it readily took account of the fact, for example, that someone can be punished for his decision by an excommunication, but despite the excommunication he has to abide by the decision of his conscience—but, of course, in the external forum he also has to accept and bear certain consequences of this excommunication without rebelling against the church and its authority and its universal norms. In secular matters too there are situations which cannot be settled completely and in which a social authority may secure recognition for its view of things even by force, and perhaps even has to. But nevertheless this same authority presupposes that basically it has to leave room for the free moral decision of the subjects, and that in concrete, individual cases the subject is objectively justified in going against the civil authority.

The difference between universal norms and concrete, individual cases, and between the letter of the law and a concrete decision which perhaps violates the letter in order to be faithful and obedient to the real spirit of all the laws in the church, is to be ascribed on both sides, that of the church and that of the individual, to the pilgrim state both of the individual and of the church. It has to be accepted as a characteristic of this pilgrim state, and this conflict cannot be "resolved" by basically eliminating one side or the other. But this would happen either if individuals adopt a "situation law," and this is something quite different from the relativity of the law which we mean, or if church law is absolutized.

The very concrete and practical significance of this reflection lies in the fact that the imposition of laws in the church is a real self-actualization of the church as a society and as a pneumatic community only if the law is maintained with a humility and a spirit of service which knows that law in God's church can provide space for his life and his grace, and even provide their presence. But nevertheless and for this reason it may not simply be identified with God and his Spirit and with what is supposed to be mediated by this law. Obviously this opinion and this evaluation of church law, and hence also of obedience in the church, implies some risk for the church's law and for the obedience of the Catholic Christian. But this risk cannot be avoided by simply absolutizing church law in a false way, and by declaring that a discrepancy between a moral "ought" or something morally allowed on the one hand, and on the other hand the prescriptions of the positive law of the church is impossible a priori and in principle. If a person uses all of these reflections only to place himself above all church regulations in a moral and legal libertarianism, basically he cannot be helped. He has applied a correct principle falsely, and has done so by his own fault, and he has to take responsibility for this before his own conscience and before God.

THE CHURCH AS THE PLACE FOR LOVE OF GOD AND OF NEIGHBOR

When a Christian understands the church as the historical tangibility of the presence of God in his self-communication, he experiences the church as the place for the love of both God and neighbor. Both "loves" are experienced in human life when they are taken seriously as a given, as something which a person cannot simply produce by himself. They are something in which and in which alone a person discovers himself and his true essence, but which nevertheless are always a gift from another. And insofar as the church is the concreteness of Christ in relation to us, and insofar as Jesus Christ is really the absolute, irrevocable and victorious offer of God as the absolute mystery who gives himself to us in love, the church is the tangible place where we have the assurance and the historical promise that God loves us.

If a person really grasps that this self-disclosure of the absolute and incomprehensible mystery which is not at our disposal and which we call God is the most wonderful and the most unexpected of all things, and is something without which ultimately we could not live, he most certainly will want to experience God's loving self-offer in the mystery of his own existence not only in what we call grace or the experience of grace in the ultimate depths of his conscience. Rather as a historical, corporeal and concrete person he hopes and expects that something of this will become manifest in his existence as a tangible pledge, as a sacrament in the deepest and broadest sense. And where Christ becomes manifest as this corporeal and incarnate offer, namely, in the church with all of its historical conditioning and its provisionality, in baptism and in the Lord's Supper, there a Christian experiences that God loves him, provided that he understands this form of faith.

And this is also the case with regard to love among men. Basically all merely human love is something without which a person cannot live, but at the same time it is again and again an attempt which reaches a dead end and, from a human point of view, comes to naught. It is an attempt which only temporarily removes the separation and the chasm which divides people, and which by itself does not have and cannot have a final guarantee and an ultimate hope that it will find ultimate success. Of course this ultimate success of interpersonal love always remains something which we hope for in our existence and which we risk in hope. It is something which cannot simply be possessed as something tangible and taken for granted. It is something which in this hope and only in it is the single and total act of our lives. But in this way an ultimate success is promised to this love in hope.

Although it can be grasped only in faith and hope, this ultimate success is pledged and is sacramentally present in the church because interpersonal love can find ultimate success only if it takes place within the realm of God. In this realm something different is affirmed as different and is kept together in unity by the one God who affirms creatively. Because in the church, and especially in the Lord's Supper, this divine realm of interpersonal love becomes manifest as a possibility and as a promise of the triumph of this love, for this reason a Christian can persevere in Jesus Christ with patience and confidence and courage in the apparent collapse and disappointment and provisionality of all love, the love without which he cannot live. The ultimate triumph of interpersonal love is promised in the love offered to us in him, it is already given in hope, and is present in the church. The church of course would have to be or has to be actualized in the concrete local church, and in concrete interpersonal relations between believing and hoping Christians, and this includes the concreteness of everyday life. We neither can nor must go any further into the question here how this takes place more precisely, and to what extent the church often does not appear very credible precisely in this respect.

THE UNIQUENESS OF THE CHRISTIAN OFFER OF MEANING
IN A PLURALISTIC SOCIETY

We live in a secular world. There are in this secular world not only different functions in the material and biological spheres and in the social sphere in the narrower sense. There is also a pluralism in man's intellectual and spiritual endeavors, in his ideologies, in his conceptions of things, in his concrete life-styles, in his cultures and in his political parties. From this perspective it could seem as though, insofar as the church also has a social constitution, it is merely one of the different groups with a particular view of the world, and that it exists in direct competition with other and similar organizations with their view of the world.

There can be no doubt that this is the case on the level of empirical social realities, and that it is also experienced in this way by us Christians and has to be accepted. But if a Christian understands himself correctly, and understands divine life, divine grace, and hence the genuine reality of the church, in the final analysis the church transcends this pluralistic life with its competing groups. This is true for two reasons. First of all, it is true because basically the church does not represent an ideology in which a definite human reality within the realm of human existence is absolutized. The most real thing about the church itself is precisely the liberation of man and of human existence into the absolute realm of the mystery of God himself. For in his faith in Jesus Christ, the crucified one, a Christian really knows that in and through death, and hence in and through an ultimate solitude and differentiation from every possible human dimension of competition, he also dies into and lives into the incomprehensible and infinite fullness of the holy God. In him alone everything really becomes one and no longer enters into mutual competition. However much a Christian and the church make individual statements, however much there is an ecclesial institution, and however much there are concrete sacraments, basically nevertheless a Christian and the church do not say something which others are against. Rather they express their faith that the ineffable One who has no limits is not only an absolute distance, but rather is a blessed closeness which loves and communicates itself. And by the very nature of what this means, the "yes" or the "no" of genuine competition cannot oppose the real essence of Christian existence, nor therefore of the church.

In addition to this there is the fact that a Christian does not understand non-Christians as those who in living out their existence simply say and live the exact opposite. He recognizes every person in the ultimate depths of his conscience, of his person and of his existence as someone to whom the infinite, nameless and indefinable God, who is the true content of every spiritual life, has offered himself as salvation to the freedom of this person. And a Christian also knows in his hope that this offer of the absolutely incomprehensible, nameless and infinite God to man's freedom can be accepted in man's concrete and unthematic actualization of existence as his justification and his salvation even when in his historical conditioning this person interprets his existence without fault in a different way or in a non-Christian way, perhaps even in an atheistic way.

For wherever a person accepts his existence ultimately and uncondition-ally, and in an ultimate trust that it can be accepted, and wherever a person allows himself to fall into the abyss of the mystery of his existence with ultimate resolve and ultimate trust, he is accepting God. He is accepting not a mere God of nature, nor the mere nature of spirit, but rather he is accepting the God who gives himself in all of his incomprehensibility in the center and in the depths of his existence. And for this reason a Chris-tian stands beyond all of the pluralistic confusion and hopes that in this beyond an ultimate "yes" is hidden in everyone who is of good will, a "yes" which cannot once again succumb to opposing opinions. And to this extent he sees the church as a circle of believers who on the level of explicit reflection and of the official church really and ultimately profess only one thing in faith, hope and love, namely, that the absolute and living God is victorious in his self-giving love throughout the whole length and breadth of his creation.

·VIII·

Remarks on Christian Life

1. General Characteristics of Christian Life

THE FREEDOM OF CHRISTIANS

The basic and ultimate thrust of Christian life consists not so much in the fact that a Christian is a special instance of mankind in general, but rather in the fact that a Christian is simply man as he is. But he is a person who accepts without reservations the whole of concrete human life with all of its adventures, its absurdities, and its incomprehensibilities. A real non-Christian, on the other hand, a person who could not even be called an "anonymous Christian" in the *ultimate* depths of the way he lives out human existence, is characterized precisely by the fact that he does not muster this unconditional acceptance of human existence. In the concrete a Christian is a person who is distinguished in a great variety of ways from a non-Christian: he is baptized, he receives sacraments, he belongs to a very definite organization, he receives norms from this organization, he has to acquiesce calmly in a certain life-style with the same kind of patience with which he confronts the uncontrollable givens in other areas of his life, and so on. But these are not the ultimate and real thing about a Christian and his life. The really ultimate thing is that he accepts himself just as he is, and does this without making anything an idol, without leaving anything out, and without closing himself to the totality of what in the ultimate depths of reality is inescapably imposed upon man as his task.

From this perspective we could characterize Christian life precisely as a life of freedom. For freedom is ultimately an openness to everything, to everything without exception: openness to absolute truth, to absolute love, and to the absolute infinity of human life in its immediacy to the very reality which we call God. In Pauline theology, too, freedom is a word which should characterize Christian existence, for Paul declares that through Christ we are made free for freedom. Ultimately this freedom is not the absence of forces which determine our existence. We can strive for

402

this kind of freedom to a certain extent; this is also possible and it is a real task in human life. But for us who were born without being asked, who will die without being asked, and who have received a quite definite realm of existence without being asked, a realm which ultimately cannot be exchanged, there is no immediate freedom in the sense of an absence of any and every force which co-determines our existence. But a Christian believes that there is a path to freedom which lies in going through this imprisonment. We do not seize it by force, but rather it is given to us by God insofar as he gives himself to us throughout all of the imprisonments of our existence.

THE REALISM OF CHRISTIANS

The life of a Christian is characterized by a "pessimistic" realism and by the renunciation of any kind of ideology in the name of Christianity. Judging by the average brand of catechism-style theology one could think that Christianity begins for the first time when a person respects certain norms, be they moral norms or cultural norms or ecclesiastical norms. But this is not the case. The real and total and comprehensive task of a Christian as a Christian is to be a human being, a human being of course whose depths are divine. These depths are inescapably present in his existence and open it outwards. And to this extent Christian life is the acceptance of human existence as such, as opposed to a final protest against it. But this means that a Christian sees reality as it is. Christianity does not oblige him to see the reality of the world of his experience and the reality of his historical experience of life in an optimistic light. On the contrary, it obliges him to see this existence as dark and bitter and hard, and as an unfathomable and radical risk.

A Christian is a person who believes that in the very brief course of his existence he really makes an ultimate and radical and irreversible decision in a matter which really concerns his ultimate and radical happiness, or his permanent and eternal loss. If he ventures to have this vision, if he maintains and wants to maintain this view of the radical risk involved in reality, he will to be sure have hope, and he will leap beyond himself to the promise of the living God that *He* will triumph over the risks of human existence with His powerful love. But one has to see and recognize that life is threatened radically in order to grasp what God is and wants to be for us. It is only then that one can believe and hope and grasp God's promises in the good news of Jesus Christ.

Moreover, this "pessimistic" Christian realism will see that human existence really and radically and inescapably has to pass through death. Presupposing that a Christian faces death, every struggle for existence and every inner-worldly hope in the future is legitimate—indeed it is imposed upon him. But he is a Christian only if he believes that everything positive and beautiful and everything which blossoms has to pass through what we call death. Christianity is the religion which recognizes a man who was nailed to a cross and on it died a violent death as a sign of victory and as a realistic expression of human life, and it has made this its own sign. Someone could say, of course, that we Christians must always point to the risen One as the expression and the sum of what we believe. In fact, however, Christianity has placed the cross on the altar, has hung it on the walls of Christian homes, and has planted it on Christian graves. Why? Evidently it is supposed to remind us that we may not be dishonest and try to suppress the hardness and darkness and death in our existence, and that as Christians we evidently do not have a right not to want to have anything to do with this aspect of life until we have no choice. At that point death comes to us, but we have not gone to death. But death is the only passage to the life which really does not die any more and which does not experience death at its innermost core.

Among the central mysteries of Christian and church life we proclaim in the Lord's Supper the death of the Lord until he comes again. We Christians, then, are really the only people who can forego an "opiate" in our existence or an analgesic for our lives. Christianity forbids us to reach for an analgesic in such a way that we are no longer willing to drink the chalice of the death of this existence with Jesus Christ. And to this extent there is no doubt that in living out its Christian existence Christianity is required to say in an absolute and sober realism: yes, this existence is incomprehensible, for it passes through something incomprehensible in which all of our comprehending is taken from us. It passes through death. And it is only when this is not only said in pious platitudes, but rather is accepted in the hardness of real life—for we do not die at the end, but we die throughout the whole of life, and, as Seneca knew, our death begins at our birth—and it is only when we live out this pessimistic realism and renounce every ideology which absolutizes a particular sector of human existence and makes it an idol, it is only then that it is possible for us to allow God to give us the hope which really makes us free.

THE HOPE OF CHRISTIANS

This "pessimistic realism" which belongs to the essence of Christianity, although it is not the whole of its essence, is possible only if a Christian is a person of hope, the hope which makes us free. A person is free for this kind of pessimistic realism only if he is a Christian, that is, if he professes that the absolute and infinite future is his own future. It is a future which he cannot win for himself all by himself and by his own power, but rather it is a future which gives itself again and again in free grace by its own power. Hence a Christian is a person who is always under attack and can always be disputed. For what he hopes for he cannot present in advance, and what a person can simply enjoy here and now is not his ultimate and decisive hope. Hence he will always be regarded as a utopian by the absolute pessimists, and also by those who believe that they are able to be absolute optimists within their experience of existence. He will be regarded as a utopian who hopes for the infinite and therefore confronts the finite calmly. He is not a person who grasps for something tangible so that he can enjoy it until death comes, nor is he a person who takes the darkness of the world so seriously that he can no longer venture to believe in the eternal light beyond it.

But it is this very hope and it alone which makes a person free. It also makes him free of course for a positive view of all the immediately tangible, inner-worldly values of the spirit, of love, of life, of joy, of success and of work. For the meaning of human existence obviously cannot lie in seeing these values positively only by suppressing their limits and their finiteness and their disappointment. Of course the Christian experience of existence is also historical. Christians too know joy at one moment and tears at another. They experience the grandeur and the vitality of human life, and at another moment they taste death, transitoriness and disappointment. But to be able to open oneself to the reality of life freely and unsystematically, and to do this without absolutizing either earthly life or death, this can be done only by someone who believes and hopes that the totality of the life which we can experience is encompassed by the holy mystery of eternal love.

CHRISTIANS AND THE PLURALISM OF HUMAN EXISTENCE

Another thing which characterizes the life of Christians is a ready acceptance of the pluralism of human existence. Someone could think that a Christian is a person who wants to construct everything from God, and to construct everything from the perspective of a religious meaning which permeates life directly. This is true, of course, insofar as a person knows that everything earthly, his existence in spirit and in nature, in life and in death, everything is encompassed by the incomprehensible One whom we call God, and whom we profess as the Father of eternal love, the Father of our

Lord Jesus Christ. But all of this is encompassed precisely by *God,* and hence by someone who is incomprehensible and who ultimately cannot be situated in the calculus of one's own life at a definite and definable point which would be calculable. And to this extent a Christian can calmly confront the pluralism of his life, of his world of persons and his world of things, and of human society. He is a person who longs for God, prays to him, tries to love him, and tries to orientate his life towards God.

But along with this ultimate religious task he finds himself entrusted with and burdened by a pluralistic world, the world of his occupation, of art, of science, of politics, of the biological sphere, and so on. And a Christian cannot integrate all of these pluralistic elements of his existence into an intelligible system under his mastery and control. There is a genuine pluralism in reality. This pluralism in a nature which has been differentiated by God is not merely an empty appearance behind which the reality of the one and absolute God exists in such a way that basically everything is either an empty illusion or the one and absolute God himself. If a Christian really professes that God can be and is God so very much that he can establish in reality something which is really different from himself in its absolute and incalculable plurality, then a Christian can and must open himself in real trust and without reservations to this pluralism in human existence. The church, of course, will preach continually to man and will admonish him and exhort him so that he does not overlook the single and ultimate and absolute meaning of his life. But this very meaning which is found in the event of God's absolute self-communication to man takes place in and is mediated by a real, genuine, unqualified and trusting self-abandonment to this pluralism in human existence.

A person is tempted time and time again to construct the whole of his existence on a definite, inner-worldly value which he can experience and perhaps which he can even create, and to want to integrate everything else into it. The point is not whether this value is truth, or God's power, or love, or art or something else. Because the point of absolute unity in a Christian's existence lies beyond the realm of his immediately tangible reality, and because it is precisely in this way that it becomes the innermost part of his existence, a Christian has the right and the obligation to give himself in trust and without reservations to the pluralism of his existence. He experiences both love and death, both success and disappointment. And through and in everything he can find in trust the very God who willed this incalculable pluralism in his world. He willed this so that precisely by going through this pluralism man would have an intimation that all of this is encompassed by the eternal mystery. A Christian, then, is distinguished from someone who really is not a Christian either reflexively or anonymously by the fact that he does not turn his existence into a system, but rather allows himself without hesitation to be led through the multiplicity of reality, a reality which is also dark and obscure and incomprehensible.

THE RESPONSIBILITY OF CHRISTIANS

The crucial struggle involved in moral striving is not of course denied or trivialized by the fact that a person really becomes a Christian by accepting himself as the person he really is, and does not erect a system in protest, a system with whose help he protests against what he is: a creature who in darkness is oriented towards light, and who is life in the midst of death. Nor is this struggle denied or trivialized by the fact that he becomes a person for the first time by accepting himself as a person in order to be a Christian. According to the popular notion of Christian existence a Christian is someone who has to observe many moral norms and codes which have all the weight of a demand which comes from the absolute God himself. And man really is a being who is characterized by guilt and by the possibility of being lost absolutely. It follows from this that he is a being who is characterized by moral struggle, a being with moral demands and with moral responsibility. But if he really accepts himself without reservations as he experiences himself, he has already accepted himself as a free being with moral responsibility. For quite independently of whether moral imperatives coming from without are presented to him and imposed upon him, he does experience himself as a being in whom there is a difference between what he is and what he should be. The difference between what we simply in fact are and what we should be is primarily an experience which grounds our existence as moral beings.

Now the Christian message correctly presents man with a very detailed catalogue of moral obligations right from the New Testament, and not just with the ten commandments, and it tells him rather exactly what he should be and what he is forbidden to be or to do. But however much we respect and have to respect the sum of these objective norms, and however much this multiplicity of moral norms arises from man's pluralistic essence and its many dimensions, we can nevertheless take a perspective here which approaches the matter from the opposite direction: we can say that every person always finds himself in his experience face to face with the *difference* just mentioned. And this difference obliges a person to accept *it*. To accept and to endure with patience and with trust in an ever greater God and his grace the difference between what we are and what we should be is itself a positive task for Christians. A correct acceptance indeed always includes an attempt to overcome this difference in an upward direction, and hence it includes a "no" to something and a "yes" to something else and better. For this difference is always found as something concrete, not as something abstract. And here we have a concrete morality of a very definite and material kind, although perhaps it is definite only for this individual, and nevertheless we have a situation in which we are dealing with an absolute decision for or against God.

From this perspective a Christian can see and affirm without hesitation the real meaning of the distinction which Christian and Catholic moral theology has basically always seen and maintained, the distinction between an obligation which exists objectively, and an obligation which is present subjectively here and now, and which a concrete person sees and either rejects and becomes guilty, or accepts in an act which is conducive to salvation. The objective norm which Christianity preaches, but preaches, however, in a form which to some extent is historically conditioned, is the sum of what a person basically should become and can become if he is open to God and gives himself over to the movement of his existence with trust and courage. In certain circumstances this kind of objective and as it were total morality can be for a concrete person here and now only the asymptotic goal towards which he is striving of his moral movement. But as a Christian he has to grant that basically there is always this difference in his existence here and now, a difference which he has to overcome in an upward direction. It is the difference between the inertia of his spirit and his egoism on the one hand, and the light of truth, of love, of fidelity and of selflessness on the other. It can be a matter of very small differences, and the material reality in which this difference becomes concrete can be very insignificant. Ultimately this is not the point. But in the concrete moral situation a person is always being asked whether or not he wants to be open to the innermost openness of his existence towards God.

If with regard to a particular, material moral norm a person has the impression that basically world history and nature are more horrible and more indifferent about such inner-worldly and interpersonal values than an individual person can ever be in his own freedom, this is not in itself a false judgment. For Catholic moral theology will always maintain that in the first instance very many individual moral norms which are binding on Christians reflect structures which belong to concrete reality which is different from God. Social justice and certain norms of sexual morality are in the first instance descriptions of the structures of created realities, of finite, conditioned and contingent realities, and they are descriptions which have been transposed into normative language. From this perspective a person's impression that it cannot be all that absolute and indisputable with regard to this or that question is not a false impression. And if from this point of view a person would have the impression that God could not have resolved to maintain the structures of a finite and created reality more absolutely than the realities themselves are, neither is this a false impression.

But if someone thinks that these inner-worldly structures and the norms which are derived from them can simply be disdained, and that basically this material morality of inner-worldly moderation can be disdained without coming into conflict with the absolute God himself, this is a deception and an error which would manifest the evil of the human heart. For in any case a person is asked whether he loves God more than some concrete, inner-worldly value. And he is always asked whether in fact he really wants to overcome or to lessen in an upward direction the difference which belongs to his essence between what he is and what he can be and should be. He is always asked whether he ultimately wants to absolutize a particular inner-worldly value in a godless ideology and make an idol of it, so much so that he makes it his absolute (perhaps not in the theory of his moral views, but in practice), and he is asked whether or not he wants to construct his whole existence upon this finite and yet absolute point.

If we reflect with precision upon what is called "sin" in current Christian practice, and if we reflect upon the really serious possibility of the case in which a concrete person can become subjectively guilty with regard to a particular objective norm, and if we analyze exactly what happens in this case, then basically it is always the process in which a person makes an earthly value absolute, whether it be the happiness of his existence, his success, his consolation or his peace, and therefore can no longer see another value. In spite of the mere finiteness of these values in their competition among themselves, we are dealing here with an a-theistic person who closes himself in practice, not in theory, with a person who does not believe that the infinite fullness of all values dwells in unity beyond this immediately tangible reality, and that this fullness offers himself to him in his self-communication through grace as the fullness and as the ultimate meaning of his existence. Basically he does not believe in God if he maintains a particular inner-worldly value to the radical detriment of another value, even though both are finite, and makes this the absolute norm of his existence. And to this extent materially determined morality also has a transcendent or a religious dimension, although not always in the same way in every concrete case.

It is certainly possible that a person does not see the relevance of his concrete moral decision for his relationship to God, and therefore, in the terminology of Catholic moral theology, he has not sinned subjectively, although objectively a definite norm has been violated here, a norm which points to the goal and ideal which at least has to be striven for asymptotically. But basically the religious significance of striving upwards in moral matters, and the mediation of our relationship to God by the realm of concrete, inner-worldly morality cannot be denied. The prophetic piety of the Old Testament inculcated this time and time again. And if we are aware of the unity between the love of God and neighbor in the gospel and perhaps experience it today in a new and more urgent way in our own times, this really says the same thing, presupposing only that we do not understand love for neighbor as some kind of an impulse or a feeling. It presupposes rather that we know that it can demand our decision, our responsibility, and also our renunciation and our self-denial if it wants to be real love for the free person of our neighbor in his immediacy to God. If, according to the gospel, love for our neighbor can be understood as the absolute sum of all moral obligations, and if at the same time it is something which basically always transcends an ethic of laws about objectively calculable good works, and if love for God and neighbor can only be exercised in one and the same love for our fellow man, then this also implies the intrinsic unity between morality and religion.

A Christian person who experiences the struggle of moral striving as an inescapable datum of his own existence always knows, of course, that although basically he neither can nor wants to deny his responsibility for this striving, he is always one who fails, one who always falls short of his task, his responsibility and his real possibilities. Hence he is always a person who recognizes that he is encompassed by God's love, and at the same time he is a sinner in some sense and to some incalculable degree. And to this extent he is a person who is still being led through the history of his existence. He is always moving beyond his refusals and pressing forward to what lies ahead. In the incomprehensibility of his own dark and obscure freedom he knows that he is always encompassed by God's grace, and he knows that he must always take refuge in this grace of God. He is always a person who does not add up his account before God, but rather he leaves to God and to his grace all of his accounts, and all of the moral struggles and moral trials which were imposed upon him and which of course he cannot ultimately "judge." As a Christian, then, he is always *simul justus et peccator,* always both justified and a sinner at the same time. He believes and he hopes that he is made holy by God's Holy Spirit, and, as the Council of Carthage at the time of Augustine said (cf. *D.S.* 229), he prays not only in humility but also in all truth: "Forgive us our guilt."

2. The Sacramental Life

The lengthy treatise on the Christian doctrine of the sacraments can only be considered here in a few brief remarks which cannot really do justice to the importance of this topic. On the other hand, however, given the nature of the subject matter it makes a great deal of sense to take up the treatise on the church's sacraments in this chapter where we are discussing Christian life. For from a methodological point of view it is highly questionable to consider the seven sacraments in isolation. For then the specific nature of the individual sacraments is not brought out clearly enough, nor is their relationship to the church and to concrete Christian life brought out clearly enough.

THE CHURCH AS BASIC SACRAMENT AND THE SEVEN SACRAMENTS

This becomes immediately clear if we recall what we said in general about the nature of salvation history. For the official history of salvation is nothing else but the process in which there becomes explicit and historically tangible the history of salvation and grace which pervades all of man's dimensions and extends throughout the whole of his history. The history of salvation and grace has its roots in the essence of man which has been divinized by God's self-communication. We are not people who have nothing to do with God, who do not receive grace and in whom the event of God's self-communication does not take place until we receive the sacraments. Wherever a person accepts his life and opens himself to God's incomprehensibility and lets himself fall into it, and hence wherever he appropriates his supernatural transcendentality in interpersonal communication, in love, in fidelity, and in a task which opens him even to the inner-worldly future of man and of the human race, there is taking place the history of the salvation and the revelation of the very God who communicates himself to man, and whose communication is mediated by the whole length and breadth and depth of human life.

What we call church and what we call the explicit and official history of salvation, and hence also what we call the sacraments, are only especially prominent, historically manifest and clearly tangible events in a history of salvation which is identical with the life of man as a whole. As the universal and collective history of the salvation of all mankind, this salvation history has entered into its final, eschatological and irreversible phase through Jesus Christ. Through Jesus Christ the drama and the dialogue between God and his world has entered into a phase which already implies God's irreversible triumph, and which also makes this victory in the crucified and risen Jesus Christ historically tangible. The all-encompassing word of God has been proclaimed in such a way that its victory and God's "yes" can no longer be undone by man's "no."

This also becomes effective in the *individual* history of the salvation of an individual. And wherever the finality and the invincibility of God's offer of himself becomes manifest in the concrete in the life of an individual through the church which is the basic sacrament of salvation, we call this a Christian sacrament. As the ongoing presence of Jesus Christ in time and space, as the fruit of salvation which can no longer perish, and as the means of salvation by which God offers his salvation to an individual in a tangible way and in the historical and social dimension, the church is the basic sacrament. This means that the church is a *sign* of salvation, and is not simply salvation itself. But insofar as the church is the continuation of God's self-offer in Jesus Christ in whom he has the final, victorious and salvific word in the dialogue between God and the world, the church is an *efficacious* sign. And to this extent the church is what is called *opus operatum* as applied to the individual sacraments. In Jesus Christ and in his presence, that is, in the church, God offers himself to man in such a way that by God's act of grace this offer continues to be definitively bound up with the acceptance of this offer by the history of the world's freedom. From this perspective the church is the sign and the historical manifestation of the victorious success of God's self-communication. It is not just the sign of an offer which is still open, the sign merely of God's question to his creatures, a question about which we would not know how it will be answered by the world. It is rather the sign of a question which itself, looked at from the totality of human history, effects and brings with it a positive answer without prejudice to man's freedom. And to this extent the church is a sign, but it is the sign of an *efficacious* and successful grace for the world, and it is the basic sacrament in this radical sense.

Now when as this basic sacrament, and as God's victorious offer of himself to the world and to individuals, the church addresses itself to and involves itself totally in existentielly decisive situations in human life, then we have what we call in Christian terminology the sacraments in the usual sense of the term or the seven sacraments. As defined by the Council of Florence and especially by the Council of Trent (cf. *D.S.* 1310 and 1601), Catholic dogmatic theology recognizes and enumerates seven of these sacraments.

INSTITUTION BY JESUS CHRIST

If we see the sacraments from the perspective of the very essence of the church, and recall what we said earlier about the possibility of a process of becoming in the essential law of the church; if, moreover, we take into account the fact that today, in contrast to the time of the Reformation, even baptism cannot be traced back very easily to a verbal institution by the historical Jesus, and that therefore, at least prescinding from the institution of the Lord's Supper, the same problem exists for all of the sacraments with regard to their "institution" by Jesus (and this includes the sacraments which are recognized in non-Catholic churches), then we can say that the origin or the institution of the sacraments has to be understood, and also *can* be understood, in a way which is analogous to the institution of the church itself by Jesus. The sacramentality of the church's basic activity is implied by the very essence of the church as the irreversible presence of God's salvific offer in Christ. This sacramentality is interpreted by the church in the seven sacraments, just as the church developed its own essence in its constitution. From this perspective an individual Christian can accept without hesitation and live out this seven-fold sacramental order as it in fact exists.

"OPUS OPERATUM"—"OPUS OPERANTIS"

In his own individual history of salvation, the history which he can survey, an individual is free and he has no *certain* knowledge of a victorious conclusion to his *own* history of God's grace. If we can put it this way, the individual is still running "out in the open" towards the mystery of God's election. As an individual he cannot apply to himself with theoretical certainty what we said about the basic eschatological situation of the history of the salvation of the world as a whole, the history which has been founded in Christ, although he grasps this basic eschatological situation in the firm *hope* that it is also true for him. He is still on his way to meet God's history, and he does not know reflexively how God will judge the secret depths of his own freedom. In our Christian faith and in the collective hope which this implies, we can and indeed we have to say that the world as a whole is redeemed, that the drama of salvation history as a whole will reach a positive conclusion, and that God has already overcome the world's sinful rejection through Jesus Christ, the crucified and risen one. And to this extent of course the individual sacrament encounters the individual person with this eschatological finality and certainty.

Because God has offered himself unambiguously to the world in history, and because Christ with his life, his death and his resurrection is promised to the individual as his own destiny, God's offer of his grace to us has an absolute unconditionality and certainty which is effected by the word of God itself. To this extent we say that a sacrament is an *opus operatum:* as the unambiguous and efficacious word of God it causes of itself. But insofar as this sacrament is offered to a person in his individual and still open salvation history, *he* cannot say with absolute, theoretical certainty that he accepts with the same absolute certainty the word and the offer which comes to him from God with absolute certainty. But as the Council of Trent says (cf. *D.S.* 1541), not only is he given the power of a "most firm hope," but he is also obliged to have it, for the grace of God which comes to him in the sacraments has already mysteriously outstripped the possibility in him of a rejection of this grace. Prescinding here from sacraments which are administered to those who have not come of age, as the irrevocable and absolute word of the offer of God's grace the *opus operatum* encounters the still open word of an individual who responds with a "yes" or a "no," and this is the *opus operantis.* And insofar as the *opus operatum* of the sacraments encounters the *opus operantis* of the believer or the person who accepts God's act, it is clear that sacraments are only efficacious in faith, hope and love. Hence they have nothing to do with magic rites. They are not magic because they do not coerce God, and because they are God's free act upon us. Moreover, they have nothing to do with magic because they are efficacious only to the extent that they encounter man's openness and freedom. If a person responds to God's offer with an acceptance, he has to profess, of course, that this acceptance of his also takes place by the power of God's grace.

This statement does not deny that in individual instances of personally unenlightened people a concrete Christian can misunderstand the sacraments in a magical way and also does in fact misunderstand them. Such a person misunderstands them if he thinks that the sacraments do not address the freedom of his faith and his love, or if he thinks that they exist in order to relieve him of his ultimate and personal decision in faith, hope and love. Sacraments are nothing else but God's efficacious word to man, the word in which God offers himself to man and thereby liberates man's freedom to accept God's self-communication by his own act.

THE SACRAMENTS OF INITIATION

To make sense, the individual sacraments have to be considered on the one hand from the perspective of the church as the basic sacrament, and on the other hand they have to be incorporated into the history of an individual life. Here they become manifest as the sacramental manifestation of the Christian life of grace in the *existentielly fundamental moments* of human life. Hence there is first of all a complex of sacraments of initiation: baptism and confirmation.

In *baptism* a person becomes a Christian and a member of the church. It is the first sacrament of the forgiveness of sins, of the communication of the glory of God's grace and of God's nature, and of the reception of the interior and permanent capacity to believe, to hope and to love God and man. But this interior, permanent and individual reception of grace by a person who was a sinner and becomes justified takes place in baptism by the fact that by this initiation rite he is received into the socially and hierarchically constituted people of God, into the community of those who believe and profess God's salvation in Christ. In baptism God gives a person grace for his own individual salvation by making him a member of the *church*. Membership in the church and belonging to the church is the first and most immediate effect of this sacrament of initiation which every Christian receives, and which for every Christian is the foundation of his Christian existence in any and every aspect which this life possesses, and this includes hierarchical, sacramental and supreme powers. For no other sacrament can be validly received by the unbaptized, nor can they possess any juridical power in the church.

A person receives grace for his own salvation in baptism insofar as he becomes a member of the church in baptism. But this statement may not be made innocuous by being taken to mean that the church membership which is conferred in baptism exists only in order that the other and remaining elements of his individual justification and sanctification can be bestowed upon the baptized, and for no other purpose. That this is completely false is shown just by the fact that in emergency cases this merely individual justification and sanctification can be acquired by means of faith and love alone and without the sacrament, and that this situation certainly occurs for many unbaptized people. Prior to this individual salvific effect, therefore, baptism must have a positive content and significance for the individual which have to be more than this individual salvific effect. Membership in the church is not only a means for the purpose of attaining individual salvation, but rather it receives its own meaning from baptism. This meaning follows from the meaning and the function of the church as such.

The meaning and the purpose of the church is not merely and exclusively to make it possible and to make it easier for the sum of many individuals to find their individual salvation. For it could indeed be regarded as useful and important for this purpose, but not as unconditionally necessary; this purpose is often achieved without any tangible intervention of the church, however much this salvation is oriented towards the church by God's command and by his obligatory will that the sacrament be received. But in the concrete there is one thing which is not possible without the church: that the grace of God in Christ be present in the world as an event, as an ongoing event with historical tangibility and with incarnational corporeality. Anyone who receives grace in baptism by being incorporated into the church as the historical and social corporeality of the grace of Christ in the world necessarily receives along with the grace of the church a share in, and the mandate and capacity for participating in, this function of the church to be the historical tangibility of God's grace in the world. He receives the mandate really to appropriate this function by a personal decision and to exercise it throughout his entire life. He is appointed by baptism to be a messenger of the word, a witness to the truth, and a representative of the grace of Christ in the world.

But how then can a difference be established between *baptism* and *confirmation?* First of all, in spite of the legitimate separation of baptism and confirmation which was sanctioned by the Council of Trent (cf. *D.S.* 1601 and 1628), the tradition of the church testifies that these two sacraments belong together as the single Christian initiation. In them the church offers Christ and initiates a person into Christ in a historical way and not just in the depths of existence. Indeed it does this in a final and definitive way so that, by the very nature of this first and definitive initiation into human and Christian existence, these two sacraments cannot be repeated. Both sacraments, then, belong together in the single Christian initiation: they are distinguished to some extent inasmuch as a more negative and a more positive aspect can be distinguished in a process which, although it is extended in time, is ultimately one.

In *baptism* a person dies into the death of Christ in a sacramental, social and tangible way in time and space. He is incorporated into the church with an appeal to and in the name of the trinitarian God: in the name of the Father who calls, and of the Son who is the word of the Father to mankind, and of the Holy Spirit in whom this offer of the Father in the Son really comes to man to sanctify and to redeem. *Confirmation* is the positive aspect of one and the same process, and it also emphasizes the social and functional aspect of the baptized insofar as he is empowered by the communication of the Holy Spirit. It is the sacrament of giving witness to the faith, of charismatic fullness, of the mission of one sealed with the Spirit to give witness to the world so that it will become subject to the Lordship of God. It is the sacrament of being strengthened in the faith against the powers and forces of this world, the powers of untruth and of disbelief, and of the demonic *hybris* to want to redeem oneself. The grace of confirmation, then, is in a correct sense the grace of the church for its mission to the world and for proclaiming the world's transfiguration. God and his call and the distribution of the charisms of the Spirit decide which functions of this grace are shared more directly by an individual as his special mission. These charisms are nothing else but more pronounced directions in the unfolding of one and the same Spirit whom all received in confirmation.

THE SACRAMENTS OF STATES IN LIFE

We distinguish moreover the two sacraments which confer a state in life because these are without doubt decisive existentiell moments in human life. We are making this distinction not in the sense that by their very nature these sacraments would have to found *different states,* so that basically they could not be given to the same person. But when a person accepts an ultimate, basic and all-encompassing function in a human or in a Christian community, there is no doubt that something quite decisive takes place existentielly, and also therefore in an individual history of salvation. The sacramental visibility of the fact that in the acceptance of a decisive function in his own individual history a person is also called by God in a decisive way with regard to the history of his *salvation* lies in the sacraments of *orders* and *matrimony.*

If we want to reflect upon the ecclesiological aspect of the sacrament of orders or of the various levels of ordination as a salvific event for the individual, we can take as our starting point the basic principle that a sacrament is present when the church involves itself absolutely and exercises one of its basic acts, an act in which it actualizes its essence fully as the primordial sacrament of grace, and actualizes it upon an individual in a situation which is decisive for his salvation. It is easy to see that the really basic offices in the church are essentially constitutive of the church. For the church is itself only if it possesses and hands on the mandates which have come down to it from Christ, and also the powers which are connected with these mandates and serve them. But why is this basic act of the church in which it hands on its offices, and in which it goes on constituting itself, an act which is also directed towards the sanctification of the person who receives the office, and hence can also be called a sacrament?

To answer this question we have to begin with the essence of the church. It follows from this essence that it is not a matter of indifference for the meaning and the essence of office in the church whether or not this office is exercised and administered in a holy way. The office does indeed retain its validity and the officeholder retains his power even if as an individual he is a sinner and also administers his office in a sinful way. This was already clearly formulated in the ancient church in its struggle against Donatism. But this possible separation of power in office from holiness in office in an individual case does not adequately describe the relationship between office and grace. For there obtains here a relationship similar to the one which obtains in the question whether individual persons who remain members of the church can be and remain sinners without detriment to the holiness of the church. For in spite of the possibility that individual persons in the church are sinners, and in spite of the fact that in general, therefore, it remains uncertain until the death of the individual and it remains hidden until God's judgment in which members of the church of a particular age the church realizes its own holiness, nevertheless there is operative in the church by formal predefinition God's will that there be efficacious grace which infallibly makes members of the church holy and preserves them in grace, so that the church never ceases to be holy.

Now if the church is to be the holy church indefectibly, and is to remain the presence and the manifestation of the eschatologically victorious grace of Christ, then there also has to be the very same will of God with regard to office in the church. An office which is absolutely unholy throughout the whole of its exercise is incompatible with a holy church. For if we were to assume that office *as a whole* could accomplish its task in an unholy way, then the holiness of the members of the church could not be essentially dependent on the exercise of office, which in fact it is, nor could office continue to be what it is: an office for the sake of man's holiness. It is not the efficaciousness of a sacrament when it is administered which is dependent on the holiness of the minister, but rather, looked at as a whole and in the long run, it is the existence and continuation of sacraments in the church which has this dependence. If, then, God wills the existence of sacraments in the church as a whole absolutely, he must also will the holiness of the hierarchy as a whole absolutely. For otherwise he would not be willing the foundation upon which the actual existence of the administration of the sacraments is based.

We turn now to the second of the "sacraments of states in life." Two baptized persons are united in *matrimony*. This is something which happens *in* the church. Because of the sign character of married love and because of what it points to, marriage is never merely "a secular thing." For it is an event of the grace and the love which unites God and man. When a marriage takes place in the church, therefore, it is a moment in the self-actualization of the church as such. It is a moment which is performed by two baptized Christians who were empowered by baptism for active participation in the church's self-actualization. As baptized persons, then, they do precisely what is specific to the church: they manifest clearly the sign of love in which there becomes manifest *that* love which unites God and man. But a sacrament is present when an *essential* self-actualization of the church becomes effective in a concrete and decisive situation in some person's life.

We are used to saying from the catechism that marriage is an image of the unity between Christ and the church, and is therefore a sacrament. If we read the text in Ephesians (5:22–33) which is the basis of this formula, perhaps we first get the impression that the decisive point in the similarity between Christ and the church on the one hand and marriage on the other lies in the fact that the man represents Christ and the woman represents the church. The unity of the marriage as such would then be a relatively secondary reflection of the unity between Christ and the church, for the marriage partners would be considered separately and with different roles. But maybe we have to say that in Ephesians itself this way of looking at it is secondary, that it is conditioned perhaps by the paranetic context, and that it is also colored by the historical and social situation. In this case we would have to focus on the central assertion of the text (5:29–33) in which the unity of the love itself in *one* flesh and in one body constitutes the parallel between Christ-church and marriage. If we presuppose this here, then we only have to clarify where Christ fits into the basic conception of this reflection.

First of all, it is clear in Ephesians, as in the second chapter of Genesis, that the order of creation is seen as incorporated into the order of grace and redemption, so that from the beginning on, and hence from the marriage of Adam on, the former would have significance for the latter. In our terminology, which of course arrives at this assertion from other theological starting points, this means that all human moral behavior, and hence its presuppositions too, are always and everywhere based upon and encompassed by God's communication of grace to creatures. "Covenant" is the all-encompassing goal towards which creation, as the establishment of the condition of possibility or the establishment of a possible covenant partner, is oriented and by which it is encompassed. This implies that objectively all human moral activity has a hidden relation to Christ, in whose being and action this communication of grace finds its eschatological culmination and manifestation. Because he is its goal, he is the ground of the whole dynamism of human history in grace towards immediacy to God.

Hence whenever there is a unity in love between two persons, a love which is not merely a pragmatic unity for earthly goals, but rather which unites the persons themselves in their final and definitive validity, this is the effect and the manifestation of the grace which forms the most real unity among persons. But conversely, too, this very same grace as a unifying force between God and man becomes manifest in the unity between Christ and the church. Indeed it is a manifestation which, because it is the absolute and eschatological goal, is the ground of all other grace and its unifying function in the world. There exists, therefore, not only an extrinsic similarity between the unity in the love of two persons and the unity between Christ and the church, but there also exists a relationship of conditioning between these two unities: the former exists *because* the latter exists. Their mutual relationship of similarity is not something subsequent to the two unities, but rather it is a genuine relationship of participation because of the causal origins of the marriage unity in the unity between Christ and the church.

Marriage, then, opens out into the mystery of God in a much more radical sense than we could have suspected just from the unconditional nature of human love. Everything is indeed still hidden under the veil of faith and hope, and perhaps all of this has not yet unfolded from out of the secret depths of our existence into our everyday life. Nor is there any question that this truth does not come about without man and his freedom and his interior assent. Hence there is no doubt that those who are united in married love experience this reality to the same degree that they open their hearts to it in faith and love. Perhaps it has become clear that this theology of marriage may not be understood in an introverted and "privatized" sense, but rather that genuine Christian marriage in every age is a real representation of the unifying love of God in Christ for mankind. The church becomes present in marriage: marriage is really the smallest community of the redeemed and the sanctified. Its unity can be built on the same basis on which the unity of the church is founded, and hence it is truly the smallest individual church. If we were able to reflect upon these things in all of their significance and to live them, then we could come back to our pressing "marriage questions" and the endless discussion of them with a bit more confidence and courage and in truly Christian freedom.

PENANCE AND THE ANOINTING OF THE SICK

If the new life which becomes concrete in quite definite basic functions is always the threatened life of a sinner, and if to this extent and in this respect God's word of forgiveness has to be offered to people time and time again, then we have the sacrament of *penance*. And we also have the complement to this sacrament in the situation in which the threatened nature of our salvation as well as our sinfulness in grace becomes most manifest: the sacrament of the *anointing of the sick*.

In this chapter and in earlier chapters we have looked at man as a being who possesses responsibility in freedom. We have discussed personal guilt and the fact that man is entangled in the guilt of his social world of other persons. We cannot repeat or develop any of this here. But if we have really understood what guilt means as a possibility or as a terrible reality in our lives, and if we have experienced how hopeless real guilt before God is just from our own human perspective, then we long to hear the word of forgiveness from God. This word is never experienced as something to be taken for granted, but rather as a miracle of his grace and of his love. Forgiveness is the greatest and the most incomprehensible miracle of God's love because God communicates himself in it, and does this to a person who in something which only appears to be a mere banality of everyday life has managed to do the monstrous thing of saying "no" to God.

God's word of forgiveness is not only the consequence, but is also and ultimately the presupposition of the conversion in which a guilty person turns to God and surrenders himself in faith, trust and contrition, and it can be heard in the depths of conscience. For as the ground upon which conversion is based, this word of forgiveness dwells within the trusting and loving return of a person to God, the return in which this person repents and does homage to the merciful love of God. Throughout the length and breadth of the history of the human race this quiet word of forgiveness often has to be enough by itself.

But what usually occurs in such a hidden and inarticulated way in the history of human conscience, namely, the grace of God which offers everyone salvation and forgiveness, has its own history in time and space. And God's word of forgiveness to mankind which becomes concrete in time and space has found its climax and its ultimate historical irrevocability in Jesus Christ, the crucified and risen one. He entered into solidarity with sinners in love, and he accepted God's word of forgiveness for us in the final act of his faith, hope and love and in the midst of the darkness of his death, the death in which he experienced the darkness of our guilt. This word of God's forgiveness in Jesus Christ, in whom the unconditional nature of this word has also become historically irrevocable, remains present in the community of those who believe in this forgiveness, in the church. The church is the basic sacrament of this word of God's forgiveness.

This single word of forgiveness which the church is, and which remains a living presence of power and efficaciousness in the church, is articulated in a variety of ways which correspond to man's nature. It is present in the preaching of the church as a basic message to everyone: "I believe in . . . the forgiveness of sins," says the Apostles' Creed. In a fundamental way which remains normative for the whole history of the individual person, the church's word of forgiveness is addressed to this person by the church in the sacrament of baptism. This word of forgiveness continues to live and to be efficacious in the prayer of the church. In this prayer the church asks with confidence again and again for God's mercy for itself, the church of sinners, and for every individual. Hence it accompanies the ever new and ever to be deepened conversion of each person which does not reach its fulfillment and its definitive victory until death. This word of forgiveness, which always builds upon the word which was spoken in baptism, is addressed again to the individual by the church in a special way if and when this person, who also remains a sinner after baptism and can fall into new and serious sin, repents and confesses his serious guilt or the poverty of his life to the church in its representative, or if in certain circumstances he brings them before God and his Christ in the common confession of a community. When this word of God's forgiveness is addressed to an individual baptized person upon the confession of his guilt by a representative of the church who has been expressly designated for this, we call this event of God's word of forgiveness the reception of the sacrament of penance.

Insofar as this efficacious word of forgiveness is addressed precisely to an already baptized member of the church upon his confession of sin, it has a definite characteristic: by his serious or "small" sins the baptized Christian as a member of the church has also placed himself in contradiction to the essence of the holy community to which he belongs, that is, to the church whose existence and life is supposed to be a sign of the fact that God's grace as love for God and man is victorious in the world. Hence by its word of forgiveness the church also forgives the injustice which a person's sin does to the church. Indeed we may say that by the word of God's forgiveness which is entrusted to it the church forgives sin *by* forgiving a person the injustice done to itself, just as it communicates the Holy Spirit of the church to a person in baptism *by* incorporating him into itself as the body of Christ. Because the church's word of forgiveness is addressed to an individual's concrete situation of guilt as the word of Christ and with an ultimate and essential involvement of the church, and because it is not merely a word about God's forgiveness, but rather is the *event* of this forgiveness, this word really is a sacrament.

The situation of *sickness* also belongs to the decisive situations of a person's life which are part of the history of his *salvation,* situations which at first might appear very secular. They are situations which force him to a decision about how he freely wants to understand the totality and the real meaning of his life, whether as absurdity, or as the dark mystery in which incomprehensible love draws close to him. When we speak of sickness in this context, we mean those serious illnesses which are the harbingers signaling the approach of death, even if there can be hope of recovery. They make very obvious the intrinsically threatened nature of man's life and his deterioration into death, and both of these push a person back into the most inexorable loneliness where he has to come to terms with himself and with God all by himself. As we have already mentioned frequently, the responsibility of every person for himself, for his freedom, for his own unfathomable self which he cannot make completely reflexive—all of this belongs to man's very essence, and it may not be taken from him. But this is one side of human existence. In his abiding loneliness a person is not alone. God is with him. But there also surrounds him the holy community of believers, of those who love and pray, of those who in life try to exercise the obedience of death, and who in life try to gaze upon *the* dying one in faith. And because this holy community which is called the church always lives from out of the death of its Lord, the dying who always die alone are not abandoned by their brothers and sisters.

We cannot develop any further here the salvation history and ecclesiological dimensions of this, but if we accept this experience of faith in all of its depths, then we ourselves want the community of those who have willingly surrendered in faith to this mystery with Jesus, the man who was completely obedient, we want this community or the church to appear visibly at the sickbed. We want this so that the mysterious course of divine life might not only circulate freely within us, but also so that it might become incarnate in the tangibility of our lives, and hence so that grace might become more deeply imbedded in us through its very manifestation, and might permeate our life and our death more fully with its salvific power.

This word, which brings hidden grace to a corporeal and quite incarnational manifestation, is spoken by the church through its designated representative. It allows not only grace and the interior acceptance of it which takes place in the one who receives the word, but also the grace of the *holy* church which is filled with God's Spirit to become a tangible "event." In this word grace becomes manifest and takes place *by* becoming corporeal. In this sense the manifestation is the cause of grace, and of course the converse is also true: the unity between what manifests itself and its manifestation is ultimately irresolvable. If this word of grace, which in certain circumstances becomes clearer and more tangible through further gestures such as anointing and the laying on of hands, is addressed to a definite person in a decisive situation of his life by the church in an ultimate involvement of its own essence—which as a whole and as the "primordial sacrament" is the historical presence of God's grace—and hence if the church knows that here it is creatively speaking the efficacious word of God's grace, then it is saying and doing something which we call a sacrament: it is speaking the irrevocable word of God's grace by God's mandate. This word does not only speak "about" grace, but rather it allows this grace to become event. One of the seven sacramental words of this kind which the church recognizes is the prayer of faith over and the anointing of a sick person whose sickness is a situation of grace and of salvation in an urgent way. Therefore this sickness calls out for this word of the church which makes grace corporeal and efficacious. In this word the hidden grace of the church and of its member's critical situation is expressed tangibly at least as an offer, and it works its salvific effect. To this extent it is only received by a person who believes and who is longing for forgiveness.

THE EUCHARIST

The sacrament of the Eucharist should not simply be counted among the seven sacraments. However much it involves the individual and brings him time and time again into the community with Christ, it is nevertheless the sacrament of the church as such in a very radical sense. It is precisely the institution of the Lord's Supper which is of decisive importance for the founding of the church and for the self-understanding of Jesus as the mediator of salvation.

Because of the importance and the special nature of the Eucharist within the framework of the sacraments we feel the need to mention here a few things from biblical theology. However, we can only give a brief sketch of this material. The reality which is designated by the term "Eucharist" has its foundation in the Last Supper of Jesus (cf. especially Luke 22:14–23 and 1 Cor. 11:23–26). There, according to his own words, Jesus gives his "body" and his "blood" to be eaten and drunk under the appearance of receiving bread and wine. The content and meaning of this action follow from the situation and from the concepts which are employed. The idea of death is of decisive importance: Jesus accepts his fate consciously and connects it with the central content of his preaching. Moreover, Jesus understands this meal in an eschatological way as an anticipation of the joy of the final and definitive banquet. Finally, at this meal with Jesus the idea of community is constitutive, that is, the union of Jesus with his friends and the foundation of the community of these friends among themselves.

From the concepts which are employed there results the following: according to the Semitic usage "body" designates the corporeal tangibility of the person of Jesus; in addition to the word over the bread Jesus is said to be the servant of God in an absolute sense (cf. Isaiah 53:4–12). but the blood is clarified more precisely as being poured out in order to establish the new covenant with God (cf. Isa. 42:6, 49:8). This characterizes Jesus as dying a bloody death. The gifts, therefore, are identical with Jesus, the servant of God who accepts a violent death in free obedience, and thereby establishes the new covenant. The identity between the Eucharistic food of the church and the body and blood of Jesus is defined quite exactly in the First Epistle to the Corinthians: it is the body which was offered by Jesus at the Last Supper. It is the crucified body of Jesus, and hence in eating it the death of Jesus is proclaimed as salvific and is made efficacious. It is the flesh and blood of the exalted one, and by eating it an individual is incorporated into the community of the one pneumatic body of Jesus Christ. The permanence of this food in the church and as *the* food of the church follows from the command to remember him which is connected immediately with the words of institution: "Do this in memory of me." In the mandate to continue to do "this" there is an assurance that the total reality of Christ is always present and efficacious wherever the Lord's Supper is celebrated legitimately by the disciples of Jesus.

At the same time the bloody sacrifice of Jesus Christ on the cross becomes present in the repetition of the Lord's Supper which Jesus himself wanted, because it is the flesh and blood of the *suffering* and *dying* servant of God *as* sacrificed and poured out for "many" which become present, and according to the institution of Jesus himself it is only as such that they can become present; and also because this presence of the one sacrifice of Jesus Christ is found in a liturgical, sacrificial action of the church. The Eucharistic celebration of the church, therefore, is always a real meal insofar as the body and blood of Jesus Christ are really present there as food, and at the same time it is a real sacrifice insofar as the *one* sacrifice of Jesus continues to be efficacious *in* history, and continues to be made efficacious in the celebration of the Eucharist by the liturgical act of representation in a church which is essentially historical. Hence these two realities in the one celebration of the Eucharist cannot be completely separated in theological reflection. Moreover, the incarnation, resurrection and exaltation of Jesus also become present.

In the context of our reflections we do not have to present the historical development of the Eucharist in dogma and theology, for example, with regard to the questions about real presence and transubstantiation.

In the celebration and reception of the Eucharist the church and the individual believer really give "thanks," which is what "Eucharist" means, and they do this in the fullest possible and specifically "ecclesial" way which is only possible for the church of Jesus Christ. But at the same time this is imposed upon the church as a basic law: by really "having" Jesus Christ himself in her midst and by really accepting him as food—although she does this in the courageous reality of faith—the church "says," that is, she realizes and actualizes her thankful response to God's offer of grace, namely his self-communication. Hence this self-communication is the most intense self-communication because it is "formulated" in flesh and blood by the life of Jesus which has always been loved and has been definitively accepted. The "effect" of the Eucharist, then, is not only to be understood as an individual effect which takes place in the individual, the effect through which the individual receives his personal participation in the life of Jesus Christ, and also receives the grace to live out this participation in a "Christian life" in the strictest sense, that is, the very life of Jesus Christ in love, obedience and gratitude to the Father, a life which represents forgiveness and patience. But this effect is also and especially a social and ecclesiological effect: in the Eucharist the gratuitous and irrevocable salvific will of God for all men becomes present, tangible and visible *in* this world insofar as through the Eucharist the tangible and visible community of believers is fashioned into *that* sign which does not only point to some possible grace and salvific will of God, but rather *is* the tangibility and the permanence of this grace and this salvation. It is obvious, therefore, that, insofar as the Eucharist is the sacrament of the most radical and most real presence of the Lord in this celebration in the form of a meal, the Eucharist is also the fullest actualization of the essence of the church. For the church neither is nor wants to be anything else but the presence of Christ in time and space. And insofar as everyone participates in the same meal of Christ, who is the giver and the gift at the same time, the Eucharist is also the sign, the manifestation and the most real actualization of the church insofar as the church is and makes manifest the ultimate unity of all men in the Spirit, a unity which has been founded by God in grace.

COMMON ASPECTS OF THE SACRAMENTS

It should have become clear by now that the individual sacraments do have common aspects. There is present in all of the sacraments the efficacious word of God and, when they are not only received validly but also fruitfully, as theology says, there is also present man's response, and indeed not only in the depths of his free and graced being, but also in his historical and social dimension. Hence a sacrament is a tangible word and a tangible response. It comes from God and from man. And since, however much man is a being of word and of language, he is also a being of gesture, of symbol and of action, the sacraments, which ultimately can be brought under the common definition of an *efficacious word of God,* also contain in themselves forms other than words in various ways and in various intensities. These forms are cultic rites: being baptized with water, eating, anointing and the laying on of hands. But according to the Catholic understanding these elements do not belong necessarily to the essence of the sacrament; this is seen in the fact that in matrimony as a sacrament and in the church's word of reconciliation to a sinner the efficacious word of Christ is present basically only in a human word. To this extent it is theologically legitimate to understand the sacraments as the most radical and most intensive instance of God's word as a word of the church when this word represents an absolute involvement of the church and is what is called *opus operatum.*

It is to be taken for granted that the whole dialectic between a person as an individual and as a member of the church is also found in the sacraments. All of the sacraments have a quite specific ecclesiological meaning, and they always relate a person to the church. The sacraments are not only something which is administered by the church, but they are also and really the self-actualization of the church, and indeed both in the one who administers the sacrament and in the one who receives it. And at the same time they represent the most individual, historical and salvific results for the individual in his individual history of salvation, although they take place in the church. This also includes the Eucharist, which is received by the individual.

A sacrament is a dialogue and a partnership between God and man in the sense in which such a relationship has to be understood when the partners are so radically different as is the case between the absolute God and his creatures. This partnership is nevertheless a genuine partnership, for God's absolute power establishes creatures in their own reality and freedom, and this same God empowers man by grace to give an answer which is worthy of him.

Obviously we also have in the sacraments the dialectical unity, relationship and non-identity between the individual person as an individual and as a member of the community. It is precisely in a sacramental word, where the church addresses God's word to an individual in his quite concrete salvific situation, that the individual precisely as individual is addressed by the word of God in a way which is not found in the general word of preaching even in a really existentiell sermon. On the other hand this individual precisely as individual is called through the sacraments by the church, which makes demands upon a person as a person of the church and as a member of the community. For the church does not merely give and administer the sacraments, but rather in giving and administering them it also actualizes its own essence as the ongoing presence of eschatologically victorious grace. And for this reason every sacrament has its own quite special ecclesiological and ecclesial aspect. Every sacrament is really an event in the relationship between the individual and the church, and the individual receives a quite definite place in the church and a quite definite function in the church. He is incorporated into the church by baptism; he is reconciled again with the church's community of grace by the sacrament of penance; or as a member of the holy people of God and of the altar community of Christ he concelebrates the deepest mystery of the church in the Eucharist. In this mystery the church really exists in the fullest sense, exists as the presence of its dying, crucified and risen Lord, so that Christ himself is present in the midst of the altar community.

Moreover, as St. Thomas Aquinas has made very clear (cf. *S. Th.* III, q. 60, a. 4 corp.), the sacraments are always at the same time *signa rememorativa, demonstrativa* and *prognostica* of salvation, that is, they always point, each in its own way, to the historical salvific event of Christ, to the event of his death and his resurrection. As *signa rememorativa* they are an anamnesis of the historical, salvific event of God's historical offer of himself to mankind in Jesus Christ, and in this event to every individual. They are *signa demonstrativa,* that is, a word which really effects what it expresses: the self-communication of the Holy Spirit in grace. And they are *signa prognostica,* that is, they point in advance to the fulfillment of God's offer of himself in eternal life. They are events, therefore, which really and intrinsically unite past, present and future in a mysterious way which corresponds to the essence of man and to the essence of God and his self-communication to the world, and they give expression here and now to each of these essential moments of man in its own way.

OFFICIAL-ECCLESIAL SALVIFIC ACT AND EXISTENTIELL SALVIFIC ACT

The sacraments or the *opus operatum* are not distinguished from the *opus operantis,* that is, from the personal, free, moral and religious act of the recipient by the fact that grace takes place in the *opus operatum* of the sacraments, but this would not be the case in the recipient's *opus operantis.* When a person's free act is not sinful, it too is an event of grace in the present order of salvation under God's absolute salvific will to communicate his own self. When a person believes, when he hopes, when he loves, when he turns to God, when he turns away from his sin, when he acquires an inner and positive relationship to his death, when he opens himself in eternal love to another person in an ultimate way, when any of these things happen salvation takes place, there is a dialogical relationship to God in grace, and there is an event of salvation and an event in a person's real and most intimate history of salvation. *Opus operantis* and *opus operatum,* therefore, are not distinguished as an act of God upon man in grace and a merely free human act. Rather they are distinguished as the official and explicit history of man's salvation becoming manifest in an ecclesial way in the sacraments, and a merely existentiell salvific act of man in God's grace.

Just as we distinguished earlier between an anonymous and universal history of salvation which is coexistent with the history of man's spirit, and the official and explicit history of man's salvation, the same thing is true in an analogous way of the relationship between *opus operatum* and *opus operantis.* Both belong to the history of God and his grace and to the history of man's salvation. They are only distinguished in the same way as elsewhere in human history explicit and social acts which are also juridically present in the social sphere are distinguished from acts which take place in the realm of one's own personal and intimate self, a realm which is not immediately explicit in the social dimension. In both instances a person is always both an ever unique individual and a member of a community of persons united in intercommunication. But a person is not always and in every instance a member of society as such in every one of his acts in an explicit, official and juridically constituted way. And in an analogous way everything in human life is indeed the history of salvation, but not everything is for this reason sacramental in this narrower and stricter sense. In both, nevertheless, a person lives out the one relationship between himself as a free person and the eternal and holy God, the God who gives himself as man's own in eternal and incalculable love.

REDUCTIO IN MYSTERIUM

If we have understood these remarks on the Christian life correctly, then it is clear, as the sacraments show, that a Christian does indeed live a tangible and ecclesial life, but that the ultimately Christian thing about this life is identical with the mystery of human existence. And hence we can readily say that the ultimate and most specific thing about Christian existence consists in the fact that a Christian allows himself to fall into the mystery which we call God; that he is convinced in faith and in hope that in falling into the incomprehensible and nameless mystery of God he is really falling into a blessed and forgiving mystery which divinizes us; and that he also knows this on the level of reflexive consciousness and of his explicit faith, and he hopes for it explicitly, and does not just live it out in the anonymity of his actual existence. And to this extent to be a Christian is simply to be a human being, and one who also knows that this life which he is living, and which he is consciously living, can also be lived even by a person who is not a Christian explicitly and does not know in a reflexive way that he is a Christian.

· IX ·

Eschatology

1. Presuppositions for Understanding Eschatology

This ninth chapter deals with Christian eschatology, or the doctrine about the last things. It is the doctrine about man insofar as he is a being who is open to the absolute future of God himself. We are going to see that this Christian eschatology is nothing else but a repetition of everything we have said so far about man insofar as he is a free and created spirit who has been given God's self-communication in grace. Eschatology is not really an addition, but rather it gives expression once again to man as Christianity understands him: as a being who ex-ists from out of his present "now" towards his future. Man can say what he is only by saying what he wants and what he can become. And as a creature, basically he can say what he wants in his freedom only by saying what he freely hopes will be given to him and will be accepted by his freedom. Because of man's very nature, therefore, Christian anthropology is Christian futurology and Christian eschatology.

ON THE HERMENEUTICS OF ESCHATOLOGICAL STATEMENTS

There follows from this a few hermeneutical principles for understanding Christian eschatology correctly. In view of the mode in which eschatological statements are made in the Old and New Testaments, a Christian is always tempted to read and to interpret the eschatological statements of Christianity as anticipatory, eyewitness accounts of a future which is still outstanding. This gets him almost inevitably into problems and difficulties with regard to the credibility of eschatological statements as he understands them, difficulties which objectively are quite avoidable. The Old and New Testaments as well as the doctrine of the church do say a great deal about the future, about what is one day going to be, about death, about purgatory, about heaven, about hell, about the return of Christ, about a new heaven and a new earth, about the last days, and about the signs by which the

431

coming and the return of Christ can be recognized. Christian eschatology speaks about man's future by making statements about the futurity and the future of man in all of his dimensions.

Because Christian eschatology makes statements about the future of the single and total person as he actually is, there is necessarily an eschatology which makes assertions about man insofar as he is a free person, insofar as he is a concrete, corporeal being in time and space, and insofar as he is an ever unique individual who cannot be deduced. And there is an eschatology which makes assertions about the same person insofar as he is a member of a community and an individual within a collective history. This is a collective eschatology which makes assertions about the future of mankind and of the world insofar as this world is understood by Christianity to begin with as the milieu and environment of transcendental spirit. This spirit's milieu and environment coincides with reality as such.

Now if we want to read the eschatological statements of the New Testament correctly, because of the very nature of man they are necessarily conclusions from the experience of the Christian *present.* What we know about Christian eschatology is what we know about man's present situation in the history of salvation. We do not project something from the future into the present, but rather in man's experience of himself and of God in grace and in Christ we project our Christian present into its future. For man cannot understand his present in any other way except as the beginning and the coming to be of a future and as the dynamism towards it. Man understands his present only insofar as he understands it as the approach towards and the opening up of a future. Hence he has to develop a futurology and an eschatology, but he knows about these last things by means of an aetiological anticipation of what he knows here and now about himself and about his salvific present.

It is perhaps from this perspective that we can best see the difference between real eschatology and apocalyptic as a particular kind of theological utopia. Eschatological statements and apocalyptic statements are not necessarily different in the means they employ to represent the future. When Jesus Christ says that we shall sit at table in the kingdom of God, the same images can also appear in a much cruder form in an apocalyptic which believes that to some extent it already knows by means of eyewitness reports what is going to happen in the future. We cannot go any further here into the difficult conceptual and objective difference between eschatology and apocalyptic, except to say that apocalyptic can be understood as a mode of expression through which man really takes the concreteness of his eschatological future seriously, and does not forget the fact that his final and definitive future really arises out of his present life, both individual and social, and that this future is the final and definitive validity of his free actions. These actions, of course, are of a more radical nature because of God's self-communication. But eschatology is man's view from the perspective of his experience of salvation, the experience which he now has in grace and in Christ. It is a view of how the future has to be if the present as the beginning of the future is what man knows it to be in his Christian anthropology. Because man always has to speak in images and likenesses and also may do so without any qualms, and because he has to admit that people in earlier ages expressed their eschatology in the images and perceptual materials which were at hand in their spiritual, historical and social situation, we cannot expect that there has to be a very sharp difference in their modes of expression between apocalyptic and the eschatology which Christianity really means.

But if we understand this basic hermeneutical principle correctly, that is, if we understand that eschatological statements are a transposition into the future of something which a Christian person experiences in grace as his present, then we have a practical principle, and one which is very important for faith today, for distinguishing between the conceptual mode and the real content of an eschatological statement. When we read in Paul that Christ will come again amidst the trumpets of the archangels, or when in the synoptic apocalypse we read that people will be gathered together by the angels and divided into two groups, the good and the evil, the sheep and the goats, or when the later tradition situated this event in the valley of Josaphat, it is obvious that these are images which intend to say something very essential and very real. But they intend to say just what can be said by Christian anthropology about the last things, and nothing else. And we can say at least in principle: whatever we cannot arrive at in this way about the last things belongs to the mode of representation in eschatological statements and to the realm of images, and not to the content.

Of course we have to be a bit cautious in applying such a principle, because it could be that basically something really could be arrived at from the starting point of eschatology. Then it would belong to the content of the statement, even though because of his own inability an individual theologian and Christian is not able to discover this particular implication about the last things in his own Christian anthropology today. But taking this into account and therefore applying this hermeneutical principle with caution, we can say that we know no more about the last things than we know about people who have been redeemed, who have been taken up by Christ, and who exist in God's grace.

THE PRESUPPOSITION FOR A UNIFIED ESCHATOLOGY

But we have to consider here what the basic knowledge is which Christian anthropology has about man. If we maintain, for example, that man is not a spirit who has wound up in a body and in history and in time and space because of some kind of strange misadventure, but rather that he really is a corporeal person with an absolute and ultimately irresolvable unity of matter and spirit, then when this anthropology is applied to "futurology" it must necessarily say something about the salvation of the single and total person. Christian anthropology would be incomplete and even false if it wanted to understand the individual's final state merely as the salvation of an abstract human soul, and if it wanted to ascribe immortality only to this soul and to make its destiny independent of the transformation of the world and of the resurrection of the flesh, that is, independent of the salvation of the single person. From the viewpoint of a correct Christian anthropology, then, it is clear to begin with that Christian eschatology cannot understand man's salvation in the rationalistic way of the Enlightenment merely as the immortality of the soul, although there are some very considerable undercurrents of this kind in Christian theology.

THE HIDDENNESS OF THE LAST THINGS

In everything which man is and lives he passes through the zero point of death, and for Christian anthropology the God who alone is supposed to be man's absolute future remains the incomprehensible mystery to be worshipped in silence. This is also true for an eschatology which is not apocalyptic. Consequently, as Christians we do not have to act as though we knew all about ourselves in heaven. Perhaps Christian hope speaks many times in the emphatic way of an initiate, of someone who knows his way around better in eternity with God than in the dark dungeon of the present. But in reality this absolute fulfillment remains a mystery which we have to worship in silence by moving beyond all images into the ineffable.

2. The One Eschatology as Individual Eschatology

THE DEFINITIVE VALIDITY OF FREE HUMAN ACTIONS

It is also clear from this hermeneutical point of departure that we Christians see man as a free being who can decide against God forever. Hence we also have to extend into the future what we experience in the present as our capacity to be free, and, recalling what was said in the third chapter, we have to say something about the possibility that man's freedom might suffer absolute loss in its final and definitive state, that is, the possibility of "hell." But eschatological statements about the meaning of "heaven," which is the final and definitive state of happiness and fulfillment for a person who enjoys God's self-communication in grace, and statements about "hell" are not parallel statements. For since we are living in the eschaton of Jesus Christ, the God-Man who was crucified for us and who has risen for us and who remains forever, we know in our Christian faith and in our unshakable hope that, in spite of the drama and the ambiguity of the freedom of individual persons, the history of salvation as a whole will reach a positive conclusion for the human race through God's own powerful grace. But we neither can nor must say anything about the end of an individual who suffers final loss except that a person who is still living in history and who is just now exercising his freedom must reckon with this possibility seriously. He may not abolish indiscriminately the ambiguity of his own individual history of salvation by anticipation and by holding a positive, theoretical doctrine about an apocatastasis, that is, the salvation of absolutely everybody. But, from the perspective of Christian anthropology and eschatology, and in a serious and cautious interpretation of scripture and its eschatological statements, we are not obliged to declare that we know with certainty that in fact the history of salvation is going to end for certain people in absolute loss. As Christians, then, we do not have to regard statements about heaven and hell as parallel statements of Christian eschatology.

When we consider that as spirit and as corporeal being, as *both* a transcendental being bounding on the absolute *and* as a being in time and space, man is an absolute unity which cannot simply be split up into body and soul, and when we consider that we know spirit only as corporeal and historical spirit, and that we experience and know our corporeality as the corporeality of a spiritual and free being, then it is also clear that eschatological statements about the fulfillment of the soul and the fulfillment of the body are not of such a nature that they could be completely separated from each other and assigned to different realities. From the perspective of this methodology and hermeneutics of eschatological statements, therefore, it is ultimately superfluous to ask what a person does while his body is in the grave and his soul is already with God. We cannot subsume these two dialectical statements into a higher synthesis. In eschatology we always have to speak both collectively and individually, both spiritually and corporeally, just as we have to in anthropology. This duality cannot be subsumed and transcended, but neither can this duality be understood as indiscriminate statements about quite different realities. The single, concrete person reaches fulfillment when he is fulfilled in God as a concrete spirit and as a corporeal person. This can be expressed as the finality of his personal history and as the finality of his corporeal and collective reality as a concrete person, that is, it can be expressed as the beatitude of the soul and as the resurrection of the flesh. Both statements always refer ultimately to the single and total person. The two statements cannot be added to each other nor be assigned to different realities, nor can the two statements be transcended and subsumed into a higher statement.

DEATH AND ETERNITY

When the doctrine of the Catholic church and its theology consider man's *death*, they proceed from a twofold viewpoint in which *both* philosophy *and* revelation are interwoven.

In addition to difficulty which this causes there is another. In this doctrine about the reality of man which is not abolished in death, but rather is transposed into another mode of existence, it is also necessary to avoid clearly and from the very beginning the impression that we are dealing with a linear continuation of man's empirical temporality beyond death. This way of conceiving of it could be a harmless and maybe even useful conceptual model for clarifying what is really meant. But for people today it creates more problems than it solves, and it tempts them to reject not only the conceptual model which they can no longer assimilate, but also to reject its real meaning as something which is unintelligible and incredible.

Hence if we have to speak in Christian eschatology of the dead who are still alive, we have to say first of all what this means, or, better, what it does not mean. It does not mean that things continue on after death as though, as Feuerbach put it, we only change horses and then ride on—that is, as though the dispersion and the empty, indetermined and ever determinable openness characteristic of temporal existence continued on. No, in this respect death marks an end for the whole person. If we simply have time continue beyond a person's death, and have the "soul" survive in this time, so that new time comes to be instead of time being subsumed into its final and definitive validity, then we get into insuperable difficulties today both in understanding what the Christian doctrine really means and also in living it existentielly.

But if a person thinks conversely that with death everything is over because human time does not really continue on, and because time which had a beginning also has to have an end, and finally because a time which spins on into infinity in its empty course towards something ever new which constantly annuls what went before is really unintelligible, and indeed would be more terrible than hell, this person is caught in the conceptual model of our empirical temporality just as much as is the person who has the soul continue on.

In reality eternity comes to be in time as time's own mature fruit, an eternity which does not really continue on beyond experienced time. Rather eternity subsumes time by being liberated from the time which came to be temporarily so that freedom and something of final and definitive validity can be achieved. Eternity is not an infinitely long mode of pure time, but rather it is a mode of the spiritual freedom which has been exercised in time, and therefore it can be understood only from a correct understanding of spiritual freedom. A time which does not exist as the seedbed of spirit and of freedom does not offer us any eternity. But because it is from time that we have to infer the time-conquering final and definitive validity of man's existence which has been actualized in spirit and in freedom, and because in our conception of it we almost unwillingly have to think of it as an endless continuation of time, naturally we get into difficulties. We have to learn to think without images and to demythologize in a very correct and basically harmless sense and say: the achieved final validity of human existence which has grown to maturity in freedom comes to be *through* death, not *after* it. What has come to be is the liberated, final validity of something which was once temporal, and which came to be in spirit and in freedom, and which therefore formed time in order to be, and not really in order to continue on in time. For otherwise it would exist precisely in a mode which would not be final and definitive, but rather it would have before it an open future of a temporal nature in which everything could once again go on becoming different indefinitely.

But how do we know that this comes to be from out of the transitoriness of time, the time which we are and of which we have bitter experiences?

At this point in our discussion there enters into the dogmatic and theological Christian doctrine on death the combination of revelation and our own human knowledge and experience which has always been our point of departure. In order to have someone who is at all open to the message of the gospel, and in order to be able to reach people at all with the real point of the Christian promise, God's revelation in word summons us to a clearer and more resolute realization of the self-understanding of man which is to be found almost everywhere in the history of the human race where people believe that the dead survive in some form.

But from our own perspective today can we still appropriate this conviction about the survival of personal existence despite biological death (and in the first instance it makes no difference here at this point what we might call this conviction, whether metaphysical knowledge or a religious conviction or an ethical postulate)? We can if our spirits are awake and our hearts are humble and wise, and if we get used to seeing what the superficial or the impatient are prevented from seeing. First of all: Why are all those who love with great hearts humble and reverent as though they had been blinded by the splendor of an inexhaustible and indestructible mystery which they glimpse in the depths of the great moments of their love? Why is any kind of radical moral cynicism impossible for a person who he has ever discovered his real self? Would not cynicism about this real self have to be what is really and truly incorruptible if this real self simply fell into an empty nothingness? Why does ultimate fidelity not capitulate in the face of death? Why is real moral goodness not afraid of the apparently hopeless futility of all striving? Why does moral experience distinguish clearly between goods which are beautiful only because they pass away, and the good in an absolute sense, something for which it would be foolish to be afraid of getting too much of, and therefore foolish to wish that this good were transitory? Is this not the great wisdom which we long for and venerate, and is it not the quiet splendor of the untroubled peace which can only reign in a person who has nothing more to fear? Does not the person who looks ahead to his end with real calm show that he is more than time, more than a time which would have to be afraid of its end if it were only time, for empty nothingness cannot produce anything? And conversely, is not what is really deathly and painful about death the fact that in its obscure and invincible ambiguity it seems to take away the very thing which has ripened in us into an experience of immortality?

It is only because we have already become immortal in our lives that death and its threatening and impenetrable appearance of annihilation is so deathly for us. An animal dies a less "deathly" death than we do. These and similar experiences would be impossible if the reality which is being lived out here in its own being and its own meaning were something which of itself did not want to exist any more when it dies. Behind all questions of this kind, of course, personal attitudes and decisions and objective metaphysical insights are necessarily closely interwoven. In these questions, therefore, it is always best to appeal right away to those spiritual experiences in which both things are simultaneously at work: the metaphysical insight, which however does not teach in a theoretical and neutral way but rather is acquired by a person in his own real and unique existence, and the radical hope which is given by God through what we call grace, the radical hope to exist and not to perish. These experiences take place in moral decisions in which a subject affirms himself in his unity and affirms his final and definitive validity. In these decisions a subject is immediately present who both in his essence and in his action is incommensurable with transitory time. Of course a person must have made such a decision in all its purity and intensity in order to be able in subsequent thematic and theoretical reflection and articulation to grasp what comes to be in these decisions: something of a validity which exists beyond time and is no longer temporal. Perhaps there are people who have never done this or have never done it with enough spiritual alertness, and who therefore cannot participate in this discussion. But wherever a free and lonely act of decision has taken place in absolute obedience to a higher law, or in a radical affirmation of love for another person, something eternal has taken place, and man is experienced immediately as transcending the indifference of time in its mere temporal duration.

It really does not make any intelligible sense to cast doubts upon this original and immediate presence of the eternal in the absolute value of a moral decision, and to say that a person only thinks that this is the case. Just as it makes little intelligible sense to doubt the absolute validity of the principle of noncontradiction as though it were merely a subjective opinion (since of course in doubting its validity this validity is once again affirmed as the ground of the possibility of doubting), so too the very same thing holds for a moral decision. If in a free moral decision a subject doubts or denies the absoluteness of the moral law or the value of the human person, in the absoluteness of this negative *decision,* for which the subject cannot shirk responsibility, there takes place once again an affirmation of what the decision denies. Freedom is always absolute, and is an affirmation which is conscious of itself and wants to be valid forever in its truth. The "valid now and forever" which it expresses is spiritual reality. It is not merely a questionable idea about a reality which has been assumed and thought up, but rather it is that reality against which everything else has to be measured.

To put this more concretely and at the same time in more scriptural categories: if someone who has to live out his moral existence before God and God's absolute claim could take flight into the radical emptiness of what merely has been, and could disappear in this nothingness, then basically he would be able to escape from this God and the absolute claim of his will. Hence he would be able to escape from the very thing which becomes present in a moral decision as unconditional and inescapable. The nothingness of what merely has been would be the stronghold of absolute arbitrariness vis-à-vis God.

But what is affirmed in a moral decision is precisely that this radical and empty arbitrariness no more exists than does the possibility of denying a radical difference between good and evil in an act of decision. The absolute distinction in this difference would be abolished if it were only to be understood as existing precisely now but not afterwards. In an act of free and absolute obedience and in an act of radical love this act is willed as something which is set over against a merely passing moment, and this truth which survives time can be doubted outside the act, but not within the act itself. But if it were really nothing more than time which melts away, then this fact would not even be intelligible as an illusion or as fantasy, for even this imagined illusion needs a basis on which to exist. But there could be no appearance of eternity if there were no eternity at all, if time did not live by eternity and not vice versa. No, wherever a person exists in self-presence and in this self-possession risks himself in freedom, he is not actualizing a moment in a series of mere nothings. Rather he is gathering time into a validity which is ultimately incommensurable with the merely external experience of time. This validity cannot be really and genuinely and originally understood after the conceptual model of a continuation, and much less is it swallowed up by the cessation of what is merely temporal in us. But it is only the revelation in word which tells man in a reflexive and objective way what his essence means in the concrete. It alone brings him to a reflexive and courageously objectified experience of his possible eternity by revealing the fully real eternity.

The gospel message about fulfillment contains many elements. Eternity as the fruit of time is an entrance into God's presence either in an absolute decision of love for him, love for his immediacy and closeness face to face, or in the finality of closing oneself against him in the consuming darkness of eternal godlessness. Revelation presupposes God's power to enable every person, no matter what his everyday earthly life looks like, to have enough spiritual and personal eternity in his everyday life so that the possibility for eternity which is found in a spiritual substance is in fact actualized as eternal life. Scripture does not know of any human life which is so common-place that it is not valuable enough to become eternal, and this is its high optimism. Nothing is too much for scripture. Since every person is known by God by name, and since every person exists in time in the presence of the God who is judgment and salvation, every person is a person of eternity, and not just the noble spirits of history. Moreover, it becomes clear in Johannine theology that eternity is seen as existing within time, and that therefore eternity comes to be from out of time, and is not just a reward which is given after time and added to it.

Scripture describes the content of the blessed life of the dead in a thousand images: as rest and peace, as a banquet and as glory, as being at home in the Father's house, as the kingdom of God's eternal Lordship, as the community of all who have reached blessed fulfillment, as the inheritance of God's glory, as a day which will never end, and as satisfaction without boredom. Throughout all of the words of scripture we always surmise one and the same thing: God is absolute mystery. And therefore fulfillment and absolute closeness to God himself is also an ineffable mystery which we go to meet and which the dead who die in the Lord find, as the Apocalypse says. It is the mystery of ineffable happiness. It is no wonder, then, that our ears do not hear the pure silence of this happiness. According to the revelation of scripture, this eternity brings the temporality of the single and total person into its final and definitive validity, so that it can also be called the resurrection of the flesh. But this scriptural doctrine is not merely said in words, but rather it becomes tangible in faith as a reality which is already dawning in the resurrection of the crucified.

ON THE DOCTRINE ABOUT A "PLACE OF PURIFICATION"

There is still another difference between the Catholic articulation of the faith about the dead and that of most Evangelical Christians: on the one hand Catholic doctrine maintains strongly in its teaching about so-called "purgatory" that through death the basic disposition of a person, which has come about through the exercise of his freedom, acquires a final and definitive validity; but on the other hand, because of the many levels in man, and consequently because of the unequal phases in the process of becoming in which he reaches fulfillment in all of his dimensions, it seems to teach that there is a process of maturation "after" death for the whole person. It is a process in which his basic decision permeates the whole length and breadth of his reality. It does not seem to think that this permeation of the whole concrete, corporeal existence of a person by his basic decision necessarily comes with death as such. We are saying "seems" because the question to what extent these different phases which follow from man's multiple structure can somehow fit into *temporal* categories, so that we can still speak of a process of becoming "after" death, is a question which we do not have to settle here. Nor is it settled in the really dogmatically defined doctrine of purgatory, which is something different from a "purifying *fire.*" This inequality of phases, which follows from man's multiple structure, also occurs between an ultimate and basic decision in the core of a person and the complete integration of the total reality of the subject into this basic decision; between the fulfillment of an individual person in death and the total fulfillment of the world; and between the final and definitive validity of a person which comes with death and the total permeation and manifestation of this fulfillment in the glorification of the body which, at least in a certain sense, does not come with death as such.

If, then, we can hardly deny an interval in a person's destiny between death and the corporeal fulfillment of this person as a whole, then neither can anything decisive be said against the notion of a personal maturation in this interval, the maturation which is called a "purifying fire," or perhaps better a "state of purification" or a "place of purification." But in Catholic theology the question is not yet settled with regard to the sense in which and the degree to which temporal categories can still be applied here, whether it is an unavoidable conceptual model, or whether it belongs to the real content of the doctrine. An orthodox Catholic Christian may also have some reservations about the usual and traditional conceptual model. We should simply be warned not to extend the difficulties about the *mode of expression* to the dogma itself which has to be maintained. A great deal of work still has to be done here, and many of the difficulties against the doctrine about this interval and about purgatory could certainly be cleared up. Let me just call attention to the question whether in the Catholic notion of an "interval," which seems so obsolete at first, there could not be a starting point for coming to terms in a better and more positive way with the doctrine of the "transmutation of souls" or of "reincarnation," which is so widespread in eastern cultures and is regarded there as something to be taken for granted. This is a possibility, at least on the presupposition that this reincarnation is not understood as a fate for man which will never end and will continue on forever in time.

ON THE NECESSARY PLURALISM OF STATEMENTS ABOUT FULFILLMENT

We have to recall our hermeneutical principles time and time again, because we necessarily have to make a multiplicity of statements which always refer to one and the same person. Hence we also have a multiplicity of eschatological statements about the fulfillment of one and the same person. They always refer to the same person, and they cannot be constructed into a plastic conceptual model of the whole in such a way that this one conceptual model would really be able to incorporate into itself all of these different, multiple, unavoidable and true statements, and would be able to reconcile them with one another positively. In our eschatological statements about man, about the immortality of the soul, about the resurrection of the flesh, about an interval, and about the relationship between individual eschatology and universal, collective eschatology, we always have to bear in mind the pluralism of statements about the fulfillment of one and the same person, a pluralism which necessarily follows from the pluralism of our anthropological statements. It is not surprising if these different statements cannot be synthesized into a neat conceptual model. We also see this in the straightforward way in which the Old Testament and especially the New Testament handle these statements about man's fulfillment.

THE POSSIBILITY OF ETERNAL LOSS

With regard to the doctrine of hell, we have already tried in a variety of contexts to explain man as a being who has the possibility of incurring guilt. We said that man is a being who in the course of his still ongoing history has to reckon absolutely and up to the very end with the possibility of reaching his end in an absolute rejection of God, and hence in the opposite of salvation. As someone who is still in the course of his individual and still open history of salvation, and who is still exercising his freedom in the openness of two radically different possibilities, a person cannot say that absolute loss as the conclusion and outcome of his free guilt is not a possibility with which he has to reckon. But he does not need to know anything more than this about hell. In any case he may interpret the eschatological statements in the New Testament in the light of our hermeneutical principle, and hence he may distinguish between the content of a statement and its mode of expression, between the nonperceptual content which is really meant and its conceptual model. Consequently, even in the statements of Jesus about the last judgment and its outcome, and also in his statements about Judas, for example, he may read nothing else in this but that a person has to reckon with the possibility of eternal loss.

But it follows from this that the statement which asserts of man a blessed fulfillment in the risen Jesus Christ for those whom the Catholic church venerates as saints is not a statement which is parallel to a statement about hell. In our profession of faith in eternal life in the Apostles' Creed we profess that the world and the human race as a whole will find a blessed and positive fulfillment in Jesus Christ by the power of God's grace. In the doctrine of hell we maintain the possibility of eternal loss for every individual, for each one of us, because otherwise the seriousness of free history would be abolished. But in Christianity this open possibility is not necessarily the doctrine of two parallel ways which lie before a person who stands at the crossroads. Rather the existence of the possibility that freedom will end in eternal loss stands alongside the doctrine that the world and the history of the world as a whole will *in fact* enter into eternal life with God.

3. The One Eschatology as Collective Eschatology

THE ANTHROPOLOGICAL NECESSITY OF COLLECTIVE STATEMENTS

Man as a corporeal, historical reality and man as a transcendental, personal spirit; man as an individual and man as a member of the human race, as a member of a collective reality; man as spiritual person and man as a reality to whom there necessarily belongs a world as the milieu and environment in which he actualizes his existence: all of these phrases in their plurality are the presuppositions for eschatological statements. They retain this plurality, nor can this plurality be transcended in eschatology. Therefore there is necessarily an *individual* and a *collective* eschatology, not as statements about two disparate realities, but rather as statements about each concrete person himself. But the fulfillment of this concrete person cannot be expressed in any other way except by his being regarded *both* as an element in a human collectivity and in the world *and also* as an ever unique and incalculable person who cannot be reduced to the world and to society.

Because individual eschatology cannot be separated from man as a corporeal, historical being and as a member of a collectivity and of the world, however many distinct phases there might be, Christian eschatology cannot understand eschatology in such a way that the world and its history simply continue on indefinitely, and only the individual as individual, as a personal existence, is liberated from this ever ongoing history, and hence reaches his own fulfillment as understood in this individualistic way. The eschatology of the concrete, individual person can be complete only if we also develop a collective eschatology. And from this perspective, that is, ultimately from the perspective of the final and definitive validity of personal history which at the same time is always and inseparably a part of the collective history of the world, Christian eschatology says that as a whole the history of the world, the history of spirit, and the history of salvation and its opposite is a one-directional history moving towards its final and definitive validity, and hence that it is not a history continuing on into infinity.

THE CULMINATION OF THE HISTORY OF MANKIND
IN GOD'S FULL SELF-COMMUNICATION

With regard to the question about the end of this history, we have to repeat the reservation here that we may not allow the spiritual and collective history of the world to come to an end within a world-time which continues on. Purely a priori that would not be inconceivable in itself. The following is not very probable for anyone thinking in categories of development, given the unimaginable size of the cosmos, but if someone presupposes that spiritual, corporeal and free beings who work out their destiny before God exist only on our earth, and if he imagines that this total and collective history of the human race will come to an end through some cosmic or historical catastrophe for the human race, for example, by an atom bomb or by the biological extinction of the race, then of course he could readily conceive of the continuation of the world and its physical history. But this conception does not really take seriously the fact that, in spite of all the legitimate natural sciences, we know matter only as the seedbed of spirit and of subjectivity and of freedom, even though we have to assume that temporally this preparation ground lasted a very long time before free subjects existed.

Without a very clear view of the history of the material cosmos, the dogma itself says first of all that the history of the human race as a whole is moving in its history towards a fulfillment of the human race which will end history. Taking a hypothesis about which ultimately we have no exact knowledge, if we presuppose that in the dynamism of God himself matter has transcended itself into subjectivity, unlimited transcendentality and freedom in other places in the cosmos besides on our earth, and if we assume that in fact this transcendentality in other places is also borne by God's self-communication in grace, for grace is the reason for creation, then we could move towards the idea that the material cosmos as a whole, whose meaning and goal is the fulfillment of freedom, will one day be

subsumed into the fullness of God's self-communication to this material
and spiritual cosmos, and that this will happen through many histories of
freedom which do not only take place on our earth.

If we keep in mind our hermeneutical principles, there is little chance
of our being able to make an unambiguous statement about the more exact
relationship between the fulfillment of an individual person through death,
a fulfillment which is going on now continually, and the fulfillment of the
human race and with it the fulfillment of the world, the world which has
no other meaning to begin with except to be the realm of spiritual and
personal history. But it also follows from the same principles that we cannot
forego a collective eschatology of the human race and of the world in favor
of a purely existential interpretation of the individual eschatology of each
individual. The fulfillment of the whole history of the human race is being
accomplished in these individuals. After individuals have played their role
here, they do not depart from a drama which as a whole continues on
endlessly, a drama which continues to give spiritual individuals the possibility of performing their act on a stage which has been erected permanently.
The *whole* is a drama, and the stage itself is also part of it. It is a dialogue
between spiritual and divinized creatures and God, a dialogue and a drama
which has already reached its irreversible climax in Christ. The world, then,
is not merely a stopping-off place which is always there and which gives an
individual the opportunity to make further progress in the course of his own
individual history.

INNER-WORLDLY UTOPIA AND CHRISTIAN ESCHATOLOGY

When we discuss this collective eschatology, it could legitimately be asked
(and we would have to treat the question) what the more exact relationship
is between Christianity's expectation of the kingdom of God in which a
Christian awaits the absolute future which is God himself, and the inner-
worldly task of individuals, of peoples, of nations, of historical epochs, and
finally of the human race in the totality of its futurology and ideology about
the future. The absolute future of man and of man's history is God himself
as the origin of its dynamism and as its goal, God himself, who is not just
the mythological cipher for a future which is eternally outstanding, a future
which man creates from out of his own emptiness in order to let it fall back
again into the nothingness from out of which it arises. But nevertheless
as the event of God's *self*-communication, this inner-worldly history means
everything for man even with regard to his salvation. For it is within this
history and not alongside it that there takes place the event of God's

self-communication to creatures and the history of the free acceptance of this infinite God. God is the absolute mystery who communicates himself to man, and does not just make a created and finite future possible for him.

Ultimately, then, there exists between this inner-worldly utopia (taking "utopia" in this context in a very positive sense) and Christian eschatology the same relationship of unity and difference which, for example, a Christian sees in the light of the New Testament with regard to the unity and difference between love for God and love for neighbor. For if it is understood correctly, every such inner-worldly act is love for neighbor becoming concrete, and because our responsibility to love our neighbor is absolute, it too is something for which we are absolutely responsible, and it is of eternal significance and validity. And this love for neighbor is the concrete way in which we love God, although with regard to the term of the love it is not simply identical with love for God. And to this extent we can say as Christians: by the very fact that a person performs his inner-worldly task out of love for others, there takes place for him the miracle of the love and of the self-communication in which God gives himself to man. There is, therefore, between inner-worldly utopia and eschatology the same unity and difference which is found in the ultimate and basic axiom of Christology: in Christology man and God are not the same, but neither are they ever separate.

Epilogue:
Brief Creedal Statements

After we have spent so many pages trying to reflect upon and to grasp an "idea" of Christianity, the result for many readers might well be that the clarity of the "idea" has been obscured rather than clarified by the scope of the material, by the length of many of the presentations, by individual difficulties in the development of the thought, and sometimes more by the pregnant insight for which we were striving. In conclusion, therefore, we want to try again and in another way to bring the whole of Christianity into view.

THE NEED FOR BRIEF CREEDAL STATEMENTS OF CHRISTIAN FAITH

For some years now there has been a discussion in Catholic theology about the need today for brief and new basic creeds in which the Christian profession of faith is expressed in a way which corresponds to our present cultural situation.

Attention has been called to the fact that the Apostles' Creed had this kind of a function, especially as a baptismal profession in adult baptisms, and in fact these very brief formulations of the faith are already found in the New Testament. It has been emphasized that, even presupposing basic and extensive religious instructions, this kind of a creedal statement is necessary today for retaining what has been learned in instructions for catechumens, and also for seeing a clear structure in the "hierarchy of truths" (*Unitatis redintegratio*, art. 11). Without this kind of a creed the fullness of Christian faith very quickly becomes amorphous, or a believer very easily places too much value in his religious practice on things which are only secondary. It has been said, and rightly so, that a Christian lay person, who does not have to be an expert in theology but does nevertheless have to take responsibility for his faith in his non-Christian milieu, must have at his disposal this kind of a brief formulation of his profession of faith which is orientated towards the essentials of this faith.

This also brings out another aspect of the question: the effective mission of the church in the face of modern disbelief likewise requires a testimony to the Christian message in which this message really becomes intelligible for people today. This too presupposes a separation of what is essential from everything which is of secondary importance. For otherwise a modern "pagan" cannot distinguish the essence of Christianity from the often not very inviting and even repelling appearance and image of the church which he gets from sermons, religious practices, social relationships, and so on. Then he transfers his partially justified resistance against Christians onto Christianity itself. Hence the Christian message has to exist in such a way that it can offer a clear critique of Christians and of concrete Christianity itself. This message has to be able to express the essentials *briefly* for busy people today, and to express it again and again. This kind of a repetition is not boring if it really focuses on what is decisive and what is essential. A person will not experience this as an "ideology" which is just imposed on him from without, and which changes nothing about the "facts" of his life, but rather he will experience it as the reality of his very own life as he has experienced it and as he has suffered it.

In all of these reflections, of course, we are proceeding from the presupposition that however ancient and venerable the Apostles' Creed is, however important is the fact that it is used in all of the Christian churches, and however much it will always be a permanent and binding norm of faith, nevertheless it cannot simply perform the function of a basic summary of the faith today in an adequate way because it does not appeal directly enough to our contemporary intellectual and spiritual situation. This is shown especially by the fact that in it the existence of a God who transcends the world, or at least the meaning of the word "God," is presupposed or can be presupposed as something to be taken for granted. This is obviously impossible in an age of anti-metaphysical pragmatism and of worldwide atheism. It is for these reasons that the desire for a new creedal statement or for new creedal statements is being expressed.

THE MULTIPLICITY OF POSSIBLE CREEDAL STATEMENTS

Can we reckon with the possibility that a single basic creed can be formulated at least for the whole of Catholic Christianity, and perhaps even one which would have an official doctrinal character like the Apostles' Creed, and hence could replace this creed in religious practice and in the liturgy? Or is something like this no longer conceivable to begin with? I think that we have to answer this question with the second and negative alternative.

There will no longer be any single and universal basic creed of the Christian faith which will be prescribed as authoritative and binding for the whole church. In this sense the Apostles' Creed will not have any successor and hence it will survive.

In order to show the impossibility of a single, new, basic and universal creedal statement we may perhaps call attention first of all to the fact that attempts to create a common and universally valid world catechism and to introduce it officially have collapsed, and have met with the unambiguous resistance of both preachers and catechists. This is true despite the fact that there was once an official tridentine catechism, although in spite of its advantages it never managed to become a textbook for practical use. It is also true despite the fact that under Pius XI Gasparri made an attempt to create this kind of a new world catechism. In view of these attempts it has been pointed out again and again, and rightly so, that because of the very different mentalities of the listeners, the concrete situation in which the faith is preached among individual peoples and in different cultures and social milieus is too heterogeneous to allow the same monotone and uniform catechism to be taught everywhere in these different situations. But the same thing is true then of these basic creedal statements because of their brevity.

In spite of its brevity this kind of basic creed should be as immediately intelligible as possible to the listeners without a great deal of commentary, and should be able to "reach" them. But given the extremely great differences in people's horizons of understanding, it is quite impossible that a basic creed with the characteristics we have indicated would be the same everywhere in the world. Great differences are already manifest among the basic creedal statements which are found in the New Testament. Just think of the different titles of exaltation in which the reality of Jesus and his salvific significance for us are expressed.

In addition to this thesis that *different* basic creeds are necessary in the church because of the various situations in which the gospel has to be preached, other considerations have to be taken into account today. Our reflections so far would have required that these basic creeds should have been reformulated the moment that Christianity left the homogeneous world of Hellenistic, Roman and western culture. Hence the brief creedal statements of the faith which were appropriate for the western situation should not merely have been "exported." The fact that they were can very likely be explained completely only by taking into account the strange feeling of superiority which characterized European colonialism and imperialism. Now the moment that this theological European imperialism no longer possessed its obviousness and its power, and the moment that the once homogeneous West itself disintegrated into a very deep spiritual and cultural pluralism, it became clear first of all that, in spite of one and the same church and one and the same profession of faith in this church, we can no longer count on one and the same homogeneous theology today.

In theology too, which is a systematic reflection upon Christian faith in the light of the total situation and of man's total self-understanding, there is necessarily emerging today a pluralism of theologies. They do not indeed have to contradict one another, and ultimately they may not contradict one another in the strict sense, but in the concrete they can no longer be integrated completely into a single theology by an individual or by individual groups. The pluralism which is found in the worldwide church and which is recognized as legitimate, a pluralism of equally legitimate situations for theological reflection which are no longer dominated by a European mentality, this pluralism is forcing us into a pluralism of theologies which can no longer be integrated. Now it is true indeed that a profession of faith and theology are two quite different things, they always have been, and they will remain all the more so in the future. But there is, nevertheless, no profession of faith which can be formulated in absolute independence of any theology. Even formulas of faith bear the mark of a particular theology, so much so that different theologies can already be observed in the New Testament in spite of its unity as revelation. Hence if there are different theologies today which cannot be integrated, it is not to be expected that one and the same basic creed could prevail for everyone in the church.

Perhaps the Second Vatican Council already gives some indication of this. It was able to produce commonly accepted doctrinal texts in a somewhat eclectic mixture of the traditional neo-scholastic theology of the nineteenth and early twentieth centuries and modern theological tendencies. In view of today's intellectual and spiritual pluralism this was by no means to be taken for granted, and hence it is a noteworthy phenomenon from the standpoint of the politics of this intellectual and spiritual situation. But the Second Vatican Council did not attempt any new and official doctrinal definitions. This is very likely the case not just because of a more sympathetic and more understanding toleration of "heretics." It is very likely also due to the perception that a longer doctrinal text which makes a positive statement in a homogeneous theological language which would be equally intelligible to everyone can no longer be so readily expected today. However, the exercise of the power to make definitive doctrinal decisions is not therefore a thing of the past, but rather it can continue to exist in the form of negative anathemas, and even in earlier times this was the predominant mode of these official doctrinal definitions.

We can say, therefore, that we may try to formulate many of these basic creedal statements of the faith. They can vary not only according to the differences of the nations, of the cultural and historical areas, and of the world religions which co-determine a particular situation. They can also vary according to the social level, the age, and so on, of those to whom the basic creedal statement is directed.

These different basic creeds will vary especially according to what knowledge can be presupposed, and what new and unknown matter they will contain. For the differences in the situations of the listeners to which the various creeds have to be adapted are especially important when it comes to the question of what the listeners in a particular situation take for granted, and hence what can be used as a presupposition and as a point of departure for understanding the *new* matter. If, then, a basic creed appears more or less unintelligible in a milieu other than the one for which it has been formulated, this circumstance does not speak against the creed, but on the contrary it speaks for it.

REQUIREMENTS FOR A BASIC CREEDAL STATEMENT

Among the fundamental questions which have to be asked about basic creedal statements belongs of course the question what really has to be expressed in this kind of a creed and what can be left out. It is perhaps clear that these basic creeds may not be brief summaries of systematic or dogmatic theology. It cannot express at the same time everything which makes up the church's consciousness of the faith. None of the earlier creeds before Trent expressed everything which belongs to Christian faith. The Second Vatican Council's teaching about the "hierarchy of truths" says that not everything which is true must for this reason be equally significant. A basic creed would only have to contain what is of fundamental importance and what provides a basic starting point for reaching the whole of the faith. If in addition to this we consider that we can legitimately distinguish between an objective hierarchy of truths and an existentiell and situational hierarchy of truths, and that a basic creed which is only intended to be one among many may place the emphasis on expressing an approach to and a point of departure for the whole content of faith which are correct and effective from an existentiell and situational point of view, then it becomes clear that these basic creeds can also vary a great deal in their content. It also becomes clear that this content should consist primarily and especially in what constitutes for the listeners in question an initial and hopefully successful point of departure for reaching an understanding of the whole of Christian faith.

A further question would be what the scope of a basic creed should be in a purely quantitative sense. On this point very considerable differences are conceivable, beginning with a basic creed in a few phrases, as in the Apostles' Creed, and extending to a creed which runs for several pages. The three brief creedal statements to be offered in what follows will aim for extreme brevity. But presumably the various possible basic or brief creedal statements of Christian faith do not have to be equal in this respect.

We must mention one further question about these basic creeds in general. For this kind of a creed really to be a Christian profession of faith, it has to give expression to our faith in the historical Jesus as our Lord and as the absolute saviour, and it has to be related to this historical facticity. There is indeed something like an anonymous Christianity in which grace, the forgiveness of sin, justification and salvation take place without the person in question being related explicitly in his objectified consciousness to the historical event of Jesus of Nazareth. Moreover, a great deal can be said about the most central reality of Christian faith without this being seen in an immediate connection with Jesus Christ. This is true especially because not every explicit relationship to the historical Jesus is already a relationship of faith, and hence the specific theological nature of this relationship itself has to be explained. In certain circumstances it can be explained in the light of other fundamental faith statements which in the first instance and *quoad nos* can be made without being explicitly related to Jesus Christ. An example of this would be the first article of the Apostles' Creed. But it is to be taken for granted that even a merely *basic creedal statement* of explicit Christian faith has to express explicitly the relationship of the other elements expressed to Christ, or the relationship of Jesus to these other elements, and hence it has to have an explicit Christological structure in its profession. To this extent the second of the following three brief creedal statements has to be read very carefully lest this Christological implication be overlooked.

In order to make what has been said so far a bit more concrete and to give some examples of it, we shall present three brief theological creeds and explain one possible way of understanding them. It can perhaps be better clarified at the end why there are precisely three brief creedal statements, and so we shall leave this question open for the moment.

Because of their brevity these three creeds are formulated very "abstractly." They will try to express briefly the innermost essence of the collective or individual history of salvation which Christianity is and will always remain. The abstract formulation which this implies is certainly not appropriate for everyone. It is to be taken for granted, then, that these brief creedal statements do not of themselves make any claim to be binding for everyone, and that they were formulated from out of a western milieu and are directed to a European situation.

A Brief Theological Creed

The incomprehensible term of human transcendence, which takes place in man's existentiell and original being and not only in theoretical or merely conceptual reflection, is called God, and he communicates himself in forgiving love to man both existentielly and historically as man's own fulfillment. The eschatological climax of God's historical self-communication, in which this self-communication becomes manifest as irreversible and victorious, is called Jesus Christ. [The German text is on page 460.]

EXPLANATORY REMARKS

We shall offer a few reflections by way of commentary on this first brief creed, which we are calling a "theological" creed. It contains three fundamental statements. The first has to do with what we mean by *God.* It tries to suggest an understanding of God both in his essence and in his existence by characterizing God as the *term* of human transcendence, and hence precisely as a mystery which remains incomprehensible.

This emphasizes that the experience of God which is implicit in the experience of transcendence is not found in the first instance and originally in theoretical reflection, but rather takes place basically and originally in our everyday acts of knowledge and freedom. On the one hand, therefore, this experience of God is inescapable, and on the other hand it can take place in a very anonymous and preconceptual way. A person should be challenged to discover this universally present experience of God reflexively and to objectify it conceptually. This first theological creed, then, must not only say *that* God exists, a God about whom it is clear *what* he is, as Thomas Aquinas thought. The creedal statement intends rather to indicate how we reach an understanding of *what* God really means.

The second statement in this theological creed explains that God as understood in this way is not merely man's eternally asymptotic goal, but rather—and this is the first decisively Christian statement—he gives himself in his own reality in *self-communication* to man as man's own fulfillment. Indeed he does this on the presupposition that man is a sinner, and hence in forgiving love. It says that this self-communication takes place both existentielly and historically at the same time. This expresses two elements in their relationship of mutual conditioning: it expresses what is called in the usual theological terminology the grace of justification at least as an offer and this is the existentiell self-communication of God in the "Holy Spirit"; and it also expresses what is called the history of salvation and revelation. The latter is nothing else but the historical self-mediation and the historical and historically ongoing objectification of God's self-communication in grace which has been permanently imbedded in the ground of history at least as an offer. This statement about God's twofold self-communication to the world, that is, about the two "missions" in the economy of salvation, the existentiell mission of the "Spirit" and the historical mission of the "Logos" or the "Son," this statement, along with the fact that the original, incomprehensible and abiding mystery of God as "Father" has already been mentioned, gives us first of all the Trinity in the economy of salvation. And it also gives us the immanent Trinity, because if there were no immanent Trinity the former would not really be God's *self*-communication.

The third basic statement says that this historical self-communication of God, which makes the existentiell self-communication in grace objective historically and is its self-mediation, has its eschatological and victorious climax in *Jesus of Nazareth*. For when God's historical self-communication reaches the climax in which it is not merely present as directed and offered to man's individual and collective freedom, but also has been accepted irreversibly, victoriously and definitively in the human race as a whole (without this marking the absolute end of the history of salvation), then we have precisely what is called in the church's dogma the God-Man or the hypostatic union, and this includes the death and the resurrection of the God-Man. Hence the third statement in this creed professes that the eschatological climax of God's historical self-communication to the world has already taken place in the concrete in the historical person of Jesus of Nazareth. Since this eschatological event cannot be understood without understanding along with it its historical continuation in the still ongoing history of salvation, this creed also contains an adequate starting point for a theology of the *church*. For in its deepest essence the church can only be understood as the abiding sacrament of God's salvific act in Christ for the world.

A Brief Anthropological Creed

A person really discovers his true self in a genuine act of self-realization only if he risks himself radically for another. If he does this, he grasps unthematically or explicitly what we mean by God as the horizon, the guarantor and the radical depths of this love, the God who in his existentiell and historical self-communication made himself the realm within which such love is possible. This love is meant in both an interpersonal and a social sense, and in the radical unity of both of these elements it is the ground and the essence of the church. [The German text is on page 460.]

EXPLANATORY REMARKS

Perhaps we can distinguish three statements here too. The first says that in the existentiell self-transcendence which takes place in the act of *loving one's neighbor* a person has an *experience of God* at least implicitly. This first statement is only a further specification of the first part of the theological creed. It makes concrete what was said in the first statement of the first creed, namely, that the basic and original actualization of human transcendence does not take place in theoretical reflection, but rather in the concrete and practical knowledge and freedom of "everyday life," and this is what is meant by interpersonal relationships. The first statement of this second creed is also established theologically by the truth about the unity between love of God and love of neighbor. This presupposes that this truth is not reduced to the platitude that a person cannot please God if he disobeys his commandment to love his neighbor.

The second statement in this creed says that it is precisely through his *self-communication* that God creates the *possibility for the interpersonal love* which in the concrete is possible for us and is our task. In other words, then, this second statement says that when interpersonal love really reaches its own deepest essence, it is borne by the supernatural, infused and justifying grace of the Holy Spirit. If we understand God's self-communication in the more exact sense in which it was nuanced in the first creedal statement—that is, in the unity, the difference and the relationship of mutual conditioning between God's existentiell self-communication in grace and God's historical self-communication with its climax in the Incarnation of the divine Logos—then the statement that by his self-communication God made himself the realm within which such radical interpersonal love is possible also contains everything which was said in the first creed and its explanation about God's self-communication as the very essence of Christian faith. If a person reflects upon Matthew 25, he certainly does not have to deny a priori that the entire salvific relationship between man and God and between man and Christ is already found implicitly in a radical love for one's neighbor which has been realized in practice. If someone should miss in the second statement of this anthropological creed a more explicit expression of the relationship which a person and his love for neighbor has to Jesus Christ, then we could say explicitly: *The self-communication of God to man by which man's love for neighbor is borne has its eschatological, victorious and historical climax in Jesus Christ, and therefore he is loved at least anonymously in every other person.*

The third statement of this second creed says that this love in which God is loved in our neighbor and our neighbor is loved in God has itself two dimensions: an *existentiell* dimension of *intimacy,* and an *historical* and *social* dimension. These two dimensions correspond to the two aspects of God's self-communication. When this love reaches its high point, and indeed in the unity of both of these aspects, then we have in fact what we call *church.* For what characterizes the church as distinguished from other social groups consists precisely in the eschatologically inseparable unity (not identity) between Spirit, truth and love on the one hand, and on the other hand the historical and institutional manifestation of this communication of the Spirit as truth and as love.

A Brief Future-Oriented Creed

Christianity is the religion which keeps open the question about the absolute future which wills to give itself in its own reality by self-communication, and which has established this will as eschatologically irreversible in Jesus Christ, and this future is called God. [The German text is on page 460.]

EXPLANATORY REMARKS

This shortest of the creedal statements transposes the statement about man's *transcendentality* in the first creed by interpreting this transcendentality as an *orientation towards the future,* as man's futurity. A transcendentality which is absolutely unlimited implies by this very fact the question about an absolute future as distinguished from an indefinite series of finite and partial futures. The creedal statement says of this future that it is not merely the asymptotic goal of history which keeps this history in motion but is never reached in its own reality. Rather, this future wills to give itself through its own self-communication. It says of this self-communication of the absolute future, which is still in the process of historical realization, what was already said of God's self-communication in the first creedal statement, namely, that this self-communication which is always "existentiell" also has a *historical aspect,* and that in this aspect it has reached an *eschatological irreversibility in Jesus Christ.*

We do not have to show again in detail that the basic starting point of a divine self-communication to the world which has become eschatologically irreversible in Jesus Christ already contains implicitly what the doctrine of the Trinity and Christology say more explicitly. Nor do we have to show again in detail that in the experience of our orientation towards an absolute future, a future which wills to give itself immediately in its own reality, God is experienced, and indeed the God of the supernatural order of grace. Hence he is experienced as mystery in an absolute sense.

Insofar as Christianity is the worship of the one true God as opposed to all the idols which absolutize finite powers and dimensions of man, it is the religion which keeps man open for the absolute future. And insofar as this future is and remains an absolute mystery even when this self-communication reaches fulfillment, Christianity is the religion which keeps open the *question* about the absolute future.

REFLECTIONS OF THE TRINITARIAN FAITH

These three brief creeds to be sure are intended first of all as possible creeds alongside which there can also be other such creeds, and this is still true even when such creedal statements are conceived on a quite definite level of conceptual abstractness. Perhaps, nevertheless, it is not merely empty theological speculation to try to understand these three creeds in their juxtaposition and in their interrelationships as reflections and consequences of Christian belief in the Trinity, or to interpret them as the three approaches and ways which human experience has for reaching an understanding of the Trinity in the economy of salvation first of all, and then from this an understanding of the immanent Trinity.

The first creedal statement speaks of God as the incomprehensible term of human transcendence. When we consider that this signifies the *prin-*

cipium inprincipiatum of all conceivable reality who is absolutely without origin, then this incomprehensible and unoriginated term of human transcendence really signifies the "Father" of the Christian doctrine of the Trinity. If in the second creedal statement the God who in the man Jesus Christ made himself the realm within which there can be radical interpersonal love is the real point of this creed, then this signifies the incarnate God or the "Son." But the absolute future of man, who is God and who communicates himself in his free Lordship over history, is in a special way the "Spirit" of God because he can be characterized as love and as freedom and as ever new and surprising.

Of course this triad of brief creedal statements which we presented would have to be thought out more precisely and more clearly in relation to their trinitarian background, and this is not possible here. But in any case we can say that if, on the one hand, a brief creedal statement should express the basic substance of the reality of Christian faith in such a way that the most intelligible approach possible is opened to this reality from out of man's existentiell experience, and if, on the other hand, this basic substance can certainly be found in God's turning to the world as Trinity in the economy of salvation, then one cannot dismiss out of hand the idea that there would have to be three basic types of these brief creedal statements corresponding to the dogma of the Trinity. This does not exclude the fact that each of these basic types can be very variable both because of further differentiations and emphases in its content, and also because it takes into account the differences among those for whom the basic creedal statement is intended.

EINE THEOLOGISCHE KURZFORMEL

Das unumfassbare Woraufhin der menschlichen Transzendenz, die existenziell und ursprünglich—nicht nur theoretisch oder bloss begrifflich—vollzogen wird, heisst Gott und teilt sich selbst existenziell und geschichtlich dem Menschen als dessen eigene Vollendung in vergebender Liebe mit. Der eschatologische Höhepunkt der geschichtlichen Selbstimitteilung Gottes, in dem diese Selbstmitteilung als irreversible siegreich offenbar wird, heisst Jesus Christus.

EIN ANTHROPOLOGISCHE KURZFORMEL

Der Mensch kommt nur wirklich in echtem Selbstvollzug zu sich, wenn er sich radikal an den anderen wegwagt. Tut er dies, ergreift er (unthematisch oder explizit) das, was mit Gott als Horizont, Garant und Radikalität solcher Liebe gemeint ist, der sich in Selbstmitteilung (existenziell und geschichtlich) zum Raum der Möglichkeit solcher Liebe macht. Diese Liebe ist intim und gesellschaftlich gemeint und ist in der radikalen Einheit dieser beiden Momente Grund und Wesen der Kirche.

EINE FUTUROLOGISCHE KURZFORMEL

Das Christentum ist die Offenhaltung der Frage nach der absoluten Zukunft, die sich als solche selbst in Selbstmitteilung geben will, diesen ihren Willen in Jesus Christus eschatologisch irreversibel festgemacht hat und Gott heisst.

Detailed Table
of Contents

461